# DEFYING CORPORATIONS, DEFINING DEMOCRACY

## A BOOK OF HISTORY & STRATEGY

". . . no culture can be realistically and effectively analyzed by those who elect to leave its central idols untouched; and, if fundamental change is required, it does no good simply to landscape the ground on which these idols stand."

Robert Staughton Lynd
*Knowledge For What?* (1939)

# DEFYING CORPORATIONS, DEFINING DEMOCRACY
## A BOOK OF HISTORY & STRATEGY

*Edited by Dean Ritz*

POCLAD

PROGRAM ON CORPORATIONS,
LAW & DEMOCRACY

THE APEX PRESS, NEW YORK

The Program on Corporations, Law & Democracy (POCLAD) was created in 1995 to instigate conversations and actions that contest the authority of corporations to define our culture, govern our nation, and plunder the Earth. Seeking to strengthen institutions that disperse, rather than concentrate, wealth and power, we work to fulfill the democratic ideals of the Declaration of Independence and the American Revolution.

*Defining Corporations, Defining Democracy* assembles writings by POCLAD authors which represent our collective journey.

Engage us. P.O. Box 246, South Yarmouth, MA 02664
people@poclad.org    www.poclad.org    (508) 398-1145

Published by The Apex Press for the Program on Corporations, Law & Democracy (POCLAD). The Apex Press, an imprint of the Council on International and Public Affairs, is located at 777 United Nations Plaza, Suite 3C, New York, NY 10017. Its publications office may be reached at (800) 316-2739 or (914) 271-6500, P.O. Box 337, Croton-on-Hudson, NY 10520. www.cipa-apex.org.

Book design by Kyla D. Schwaberow. Cover illustration by Adam Wolpert.
Interior linoleum prints by Bev Glueckert.

First published 2001

Library of Congress Cataloging-in-Publication Data
Defying corporations, defining democracy : a book of history & strategy / edited by Dean Ritz.
    p. cm.

    Included bibliographical references.
    ISBN 1-891843-11-7 — ISBN 1-891843-10-9 (pbk. : alk. paper)
      1. Business and politics—United States. 2. Corporations—United States—Political activity.
    3. Democracy—United States. I. Ritz, Dean, 1963-

    JK467 .D45 2001
    322'.3'0973—dc21
2001040044

Printed in the United States of America by Thomson-Shore, Inc., an employee owned company, with soy inks on recycled paper.

# Acknowledgements

The 12 of us are grateful to editor Dean Ritz for a job well done. His creative intelligence, enthusiasm, and attention to detail—along with the good humor which has characterized his relations with the motley POCLAD—are much appreciated.

Our thanks to Judi Rizzi for her meticulous accounting and her profound patience with POCLADer's endless, last minute requests; to Teena Di Nota for securing permissions to reprint many of these articles; to David Dembo for relentlessly tracking down old and obscure references; and to Lynn Hiller for ably managing our information systems.

Richard Grossman & Ward Morehouse
for the Program on Corporations, Law & Democracy

My thanks to all the authors for their time and support over the year it took to put this book together, in particular Greg Coleridge, Mike Ferner, Peter Kellman, Ward Morehouse, Jane Anne Morris, and Mary Zepernick. Extra thanks to Richard Grossman who acted as an on-call tour guide on the journey creating this book; without him I'm sure I'd be wandering in some metaphorical ditch somewhere.

Thanks to George Cheney, Paula Goldberg, and Jeff Berner who provided comments on earlier drafts, some of which found their way into various articles' notes; to Adam Wolpert, Bev Glueckert and Kyla D. Schwaberow for making this a beautiful book to the eyes; to Richard Bernstein for his legal review; to William Meyers for producing the indexes; to Erik Barret-Hakanson for scanning the interior linoleum prints; to Paul Cienfuegos who introduced me to POCLAD; and finally, my gratitude to Kenya Hart who encouraged me in this work and is a model for how good work gets done.

Dean Ritz, *editor*

# Table of Contents

# II. RECOVERING HISTORY

# III. CONQUERING FIBS

# IV. OUT ON OUR OWN

# V. RIGHT SIDE UP

# VI. QUESTIONS, QUESTIONS

# VII.  BREAK THE RULES

# VIII. POINT OF DEPARTURE

# APPENDICES

# PREFACE

Section 1. Popular sovereignty. All political power is vested in and derived from the people. All government of right originates with the people, is founded upon their will only, and is instituted solely for the good of the whole.

Section 2. Self-government. The people have the exclusive right of governing themselves as a free, sovereign, and independent state. They may alter or abolish the constitution and form of government whenever they deem it necessary.

The above defining language is from the constitution of the state of Montana, where I live. It's exhilarating language, if you believe it to be true. It's the language of sovereignty, of self-governance. It states ideals which people fought to advance, gave their lives to protect. It makes one think that anything is possible if only "We the People" decide to put ourselves to the task. Well, why not?

Several years ago I encountered this "why not?" At that time I was immersed in my career, working for large corporations, advising them on licensing technology (their "intellectual property"), negotiating on their behalf (their "intangible property"), and developing strategies to maximize future profits (their "imaginary property"). I was enmeshed in the protection and extension of the power of corporations. I just didn't know it.

I came to know it when I was introduced to the work of the Program on Corporations, Law & Democracy (POCLAD), including many of the articles contained in this collection. In these articles I came upon questions, ideas, histories. I was provoked to learn more, to observe more closely, to identify the assumptions behind the nature of my work and of my world view. Going through such a process one can't help but be transformed. Some of my values were reinforced, others refined. And then others were completely rejected, with new ones defined to take their place.

This book, *Defying Corporations, Defining Democracy*, is a challenge to imagine and then define a future, rather than take the one which has been imagined for us ... by slave owners, by the Pennsylvania Railroad corporation, by ExxonMobil corporation, Disney corporation, Dow Chemical corporation, and Microsoft corporation. It is a book dedicated to the ideals of self-governance, of universal human rights, and respect for the Earth's natural systems of which people are only a part.

*Defying Corporations, Defining Democracy* brings together a dozen authors' unique experiences and perspectives from decades of civic activism. POCLAD's journey—its research, analysis, arguments, thoughts, provocations, and actions—is instructive and genuinely inspiring. This journey reflects the work of small groups everywhere, of peoples' struggles in their communities to understand what is going on, who rules their communities, and how self-governance may be practiced.

When one reads the language of the Montana constitution, similar in its aspirations to many states' constitutions, two points are clear. The first is that it describes an unrealized ideal. The second is that such an ideal is worth working for. As you may know from reading the history of people's popular movements, each generation must engage in this process of examination, imagination, and of definition; that self-governance and sovereignty will remain a myth if people are unable to define their institutions of government. Today, we live with this myth.

Corporations today act in the capacity of governments. Energy corporations determine our nation's energy policies. Automobile corporations determine our nation's transportation policies. Military manufacturing corporations determine our nation's defense policies. Corporate polluters and resource extraction corporations define our environmental policies. Transnational corporations determine our trading policies. And the wealthiest among us—with their wealth deeply rooted in corporations—determine our tax policies.

Corporations are armed with "free speech," "managerial prerogative," "due process," "equal protection," the Commerce clause, the Contracts clause, and all the lawyers, lobbyists, and "buy partisan" support that wealth can buy. With all this at their disposal corporate leaders increasingly define our culture, our schools, our elections, and the operations of our government itself.

"Defying Corporations" is one part of the equation for achieving self-governance; that is, challenging the legitimacy of corporations to act in the capacity of governments. "Defining Democracy" is another part of the equation: What do we mean by "democracy?" What kind of democracy do we have? What form of government is appropriate to our needs today, and with respect to the future? Answering these questions and working towards alternatives is hard work. Is it worth doing? Why, of course!

Finally, we must free our minds to think beyond the institutions and futures imagined for us. The work of POCLAD changed what I see, know, think, and now do. It has given me new sources of personal energy, optimism and aspirations. It is my hope that your engagement with the ideas in this book will bring similar good fortune to you.

Dean Ritz

# NOTES TO THE READER

This book is divided into eight sections. Ideally each section would be read in one sitting with the introductory text in mind, and the articles of greater interest reread at a later time.

## CITATIONS

Detailed bibliographic information for authors or works mentioned in these articles can be found in "Works Cited," and complete citations for legal cases can be found in the "Index of Cases." I did seek complete citations of sources where possible; unfortunately, there are some exceptions.

Within these articles are references to authors, titles of works, and court cases. If these are not detailed in the endnotes accompanying an article look in the section titled "Works Cited" or the "Index of Cases" for details. References in the endnotes are provided as "author-date" citations: *author's last name* and *year of publication*. This is sufficient for locating the work in "Works Cited."

## SPECIAL PHRASES

"We the People" is capitalized to maintain the connection to that phrase's mythic quality in American history and culture. It is quoted when it is an explicit quotation from the preamble of the federal Constitution, or when its use without quotes might appear awkward to the reader.

Nearly all references to the United States of America are noted as "U.S.". The exception is any reference to the historical period prior to the Constitutional Convention of 1787. References to "American revolutionaries," for example, refer to that earlier period. In general, "America" and "Americas" refers to North and South America collectively. "American" refers to residents of the United States.

## EDITING FOR STYLE

Normalization of language is difficult when piecing together more than 70 articles from a dozen authors. As editor I minimized my attempts to make uniform the style of writing, though I did strive for clarity and flow within each article. I preserved variations of capitalization such as "earth" and "Earth", "Native people" and "native people", and "Nature" and "nature" to reflect the author's feeling towards these words. You will also see creative adaptation of words: "provokers", "red herringed", "collective marrows" and "unconsciouses".

Usually, an editor minimizes changes to previously published work. With POCLAD's approval I assumed more freedom. My task, then, in addition to selecting and sequencing the articles, was to make small changes which befitted the preservation of these articles within the covers of a durable book. I hope this has been accomplished to the readers' and authors' satisfaction. ■

# INTRODUCTION

## ENGAGE US

We invite you to engage us in this idea: giant corporations govern. In the Constitution of the United States, they are delegated no authority to make our laws and define our culture. Corporations have no constitutions, no bills of rights. So when corporations govern, democracy flies out the door.

This may be a depressing idea but it is not a new idea or a complicated one. President Franklin D. Roosevelt, among many others, spelled it out:

> The liberty of a democracy is not safe if
> the people tolerate the growth of private
> power to a point where it becomes
> stronger than their democratic State itself.
> That, in its essence, is Fascism—owner-
> ship of government by an individual, by a
> group, or any controlling private power.

There is something else: when people live within a culture of privatized power, common sense scrambles out the window. People cease to trust their eyes and ears, to rely upon their own experiences. Their minds become colonized.

How else to explain that our justice system treats corporate assaults upon life and democracy—such as pouring millions of tons of poisons into air, water and food, denying Bill of Rights protections to employees—as legal. Or that The New York Times Corporation really ran this headline in April 1998: "Times have changed . . . Corporations champion free expression."

To understand the illegitimate authority by which corporations govern, people need to talk about it. To challenge this authority effectively, activist groups need to debate different perspectives, goals and strategies from those we're used to. For the past few years, the Program on Corporations, Law & Democracy (POCLAD) has been provoking such debates.

## VALIANT ORGANIZING, EARLY MORNING DOUBTS

Let's start with what we and you have learned. Thousands of groups know how to: stop an incinerator, organize a union, block a timber harvest sale, decrease a toxic emission, orchestrate a referendum or initiative, enact new permitting and disclosure regulations. People spend years getting regulatory agencies to lessen a single corporate harm.

But sometimes, in the darkness before dawn, have you wondered why—despite all this good activist work—corporate assaults against life and democracy keep increasing? After a century of local, state and federal regulatory laws—pure food, labor, stock exchange, clean water, clean air, public health—why do people in community after community have to struggle for years to get the right to know which corporate chemicals are killing their families? To bring a wrongful damage suit against a corporation? To save a forest? To get a fair collective bargaining election? To get back pay or their own pension money?

We all know stories about small, low-budget groups stopping global corporations from:

siting a deadly factory, clear-cutting a forest, ramrodding through a new law, busting a union, using deceptive advertising, carrying propaganda into a school. This is vital: valiant and persistent organizing has enabled people to stand up to raw power and violence. It has bettered the daily lives of millions, instilled confidence and self-respect, transformed whole communities, taught democracy.

But when the joy of victory fades, imperial corporations remain. Slowed down in one place, they pop up in another. They are in everybody's yards front and back, in little leagues and scouting, in town halls, state houses and Congress.

They keep blocking sane, logical transitions in food, energy, transportation, health care, finance, forestry and manufacturing. They keep funding think tanks and university corporations to frame public debate. They keep buying obedience and defining family values. Their leaders still walk off with big money and top community honors.

Unimaginable billions of tax deductible corporate dollars still gurgle through corporate public relations, advertising and law firms. Radio, television, magazine, and movie corporations keep selling their relentless message: "Corporations: efficient; good. Government: wasteful; bad."

Giant corporations bully and browbeat. They denounce people like you and us as Luddites, Commies, tree-huggers and '60s leftovers. They homogenize people into consumers. They turn life into corporate theme parks.

They also manipulate our government. It's nothing personal, of course. It's just that when they turn our own government against us—bureaucracies and courts and police and military paid with our money—they make us into the king's subjects all over again.

But the United States got rid of the king a long time ago. We are supposed to be self-governing people. You know, "We the People."

## POCLAD EVOLVES

During the early 1990s some of us began to research and write about corporate, legal and movement history. We started convening "Rethinking the Corporation, Rethinking Democracy" meetings. In 1995 we formed POCLAD.

Among other things, we realized that in our prior work we had limited our goals and generally restricted our efforts to regulatory and administrative arenas. This was also true for many people's organizations. Yet corporations never limited their designs and actions to anything.

A century ago corporate strategists began to dream up regulatory laws and agencies to replace the chartering processes, general incorporation laws and state constitutions which people had used to define corporations as subordinate. They transformed once potent public cultures of trespass, nuisance, liberty and personal property rights into bastions of private corporate power.

Perhaps you remember thinking this about your past campaigns: If only we had gotten a thousand more letters in the mail; more experts at the hearings; better press coverage; more people at the demonstration...

We remember. But now we see that even with these "if onlys," corporations would still be in charge. This is because the political and legal culture has been diverting activists from political arenas where people can define issues and make the rules; where whether we win or lose, it is clear that the struggle is about who is in charge—corporations or people.

So today, POCLAD is exploring different organizing arenas and reaching for strategies that take into account long-term corporate influences over culture, law, and even activist organizing.

We have intensified our examination of the great colonizer of the twentieth century—the large business corporation. We've tracked its development from a subordinate legal entity created to serve the public good into a fantastic shield for property and wealth. We've helped people see how corporations got courts and legislatures to deny the rights of people and nature via doctrines and laws asserting that the corporation is a legal "person," has property rights in decision-making, is forever.

Our inquiries keep leading us to the activists in every generation who perfected organizations to advocate human rights over property rights, to repel their era's aggressions against democracy. These were people who understood that they could never practice self-governance and enjoy political liberty if they let legislatures, courts and culture define corporations as beyond the authority of the sovereign people.

## RELATIONSHIPS, QUESTIONS

POCLAD's exchanges with activists started with a focus on corporations. Discussion quickly expanded to include governance and democracy, unleashing a torrent of questions:

What should be the legal, political and cultural relationships between people and corporate bodies? Who decides? How were a minority of natural persons in the original thirteen states able to define the majority of human beings as non-persons? To define Africans as property, Native peoples as invisible? Given that Native peoples, women, African Americans, immigrants, debtors, people without property, gays and lesbians are still organizing for justice and equality, how did corporations become superduper legal persons a century ago?

Should people dismantle giant corporations? Transform them? Should a business corporation be regarded as a citizen? As private? Should it have free speech? Are there constitutional rights differences between the NAACP and the U.S. Chamber of Commerce? Between the Sierra Club and the Chemical Manufacturers Association or the Tobacco Institute? Why does the General Motors Corporation have more rights than the United Auto Workers Union?

What is property? Who decides if it's public or private? How did other generations decide? How did corporate leaders get their decisions on investment, production and jobs to be regarded as private?

How much legal and moral liability should shareholders bear beyond their own investments and consciences?

What roles did railroad, banking, mining and other corporations play in the federal government's abandonment of freed women and men of the South? In the writing of the Southern states' apartheid constitutions? In the exploitation of Native peoples? Of immigrants from Asia and the global South?

Who were the Knights of Labor? What did they have to say about railroad, banking, grain and telegraph corporations? About the control of knowledge? Who were the Populists? Why did they risk their farms and jobs to stop the corporation from becoming the dominant institution in the land? What happened to them? Who were the Progressives? Why did they concede that giant corporations were inevitable, and settle for making them a little less dominant?

Why didn't anti-trust laws and all that trust busting of Theodore Roosevelt and Woodrow Wilson fix everything? Did anti-trust fix anything?

Why were regulatory and administrative

agencies like the Interstate Commerce Commission, the Food and Drug Administration, the Securities and Exchange Commission, the National Labor Relations Board, the Environmental Protection Agency, the Occupational Safety and Health Administration, created? Who wanted them? Why? Was there anyone who wanted something else?

What *is* this country's plan of government? How is each generation supposed to discover it? To live it? Why didn't Tom Paine encourage people in Colonial times to search for a more socially responsible king? Do famous phrases like "We the People" and "consent of the governed" mean anything?

Why do environmental laws regulate environmentalists? Why do labor laws regulate unions?

## THE TIME IS RIPE

Millions of people have organized courageously against corporate assaults—of the legal and culturally accepted kind and of the illegal and culturally rejected variety. This is as it should be, as Eugene Debs has noted: "If it were not for resistance to degrading conditions, the tendency of our whole civilization would be downward; after a while we would reach the point where there would be no resistance, and slavery would come."

Thousands of activist groups are flourishing. People from all walks of life have taught themselves to demystify complex issues and their special languages: chemistry, biology, physics, nuclear energy and weaponry, genetic engineering, global finance and trade, civil rights and human rights law, regulatory and administrative law.

After two centuries of struggle, the formerly dissed and disenfranchised have gained the legal status of persons. In recent years, many have invested time and energy exploring identity politics. This means that even as "corporate persons" cast grotesque shadows across a disfigured cultural landscape, there is finally a multitude of human persons who can envision ripening into a self-governing people.

It is now possible to direct organizing struggles beyond lessening the impacts of endless corporate assaults. Isn't it time? Today's giant corporations are not fundamentally different from what they were in the seventeenth century when King James of England chartered the Plymouth Company "for the planting, ruling and governing of New England in America."

We believe that community, labor, environmental justice and other organizations formed over past generations to resist harmful corporate behaviors are well positioned to take these logical next steps. How to press forward in the years ahead? That's what we want to consider with you.

## CHALLENGING CORPORATE AUTHORITY TO GOVERN

POCLAD is not building a big national membership operation. Rather, we are working with existing groups to launch democratic insurgencies to render corporations subordinate.

We are looking for people to invest time, energy and resources challenging judicial doctrines dealing with the Commerce clause, personhood, the business judgment rule, the prudent man rule, managerial prerogative, and corporate property rights. People who fancy extending the Bill of Rights to employees on company grounds; amending state corporation codes to end limited liability and to ban corporations from owning other corporations; excluding business corporations and their trade associations from elections, law-making, education and public debate over community values, legal philosophy and policy.

Activists will need to do what corporate

strategists have mastered: exploit the tensions of our federal system by creating crises of jurisdiction and authority between local, state and federal governments.

All this and more will happen as communities reject the idea that business corporations are private; as municipalities enact local ordinances defining corporations within their jurisdictions; as organized people instruct elected representatives to cease aiding and abetting corporate rule.

## CONSPIRE[1] WITH US

We see ourselves as instigators and provokers, as conveners and facilitators. Our work is to help organizers challenge the mass-producing and mass-marketing of culture and law by artificial entities called corporations. To help people contest the authority of corporations to govern. ■

## PROGRAM ON CORPORATIONS, LAW & DEMOCRACY

Bill Bachle
Greg Coleridge
Karen Coulter
Mike Ferner
Richard Grossman
Dave Henson

Peter Kellman
Ward Morehouse
Jane Anne Morris
Jim Price
Virginia Rasmussen
Mary Zepernick

## NOTES

[1] "Conspire" is constructed from the Latin *con-* "together with" + *spirare* "to breathe", meaning "to breathe together, to accord, harmonize, agree, combine or unite in a purpose." We use "conspire" based on this original construction.

# STARTING POINT

Corporations cause harms to life, liberty, and property every day. Most corporate harms are considered legal because corporate harm-doing is enabled and protected by law. Millions have organized courageously to prevent these harms or staunch their effects. But the harms keep coming, increasing in frequency and magnitude. Why are We the People always on the defensive?

What do we need *to know* in order to see that even when We the People win one defensive battle against a corporation we are closer neither to winning the next, nor to implementing *our own* vision of health, energy, food, monetary, military, trade, election, investment, technology, and other policies? What do we need *to do* to make these policy decisions? To define our communities' values?

Assessing our knowledge in the context of our experience is our starting point.

# "Help! I've Been Colonized and I Can't Get Up . . ."

## Take a Lawyer and an Expert to a Hearing and Call Me in a Decade

*by Jane Anne Morris*

---

A THIRD OF YOUR friends are locked down in an old growth grove or at a corporate headquarters, with law enforcement officers rubbing pepper spray in their eyes. Another third are preparing testimony so you can be persuasive at a generic regulatory agency hearing while you're begging them to enforce a tiny portion of our laws. The third third are trying to raise money to pay lawyers to get your friends out of jail (after they've been released from the hospital) or take the regulatory agency to court (after it declines to enforce the law).

The pepper spray, groveling and money-grubbing might not be so bad if we could honestly say that the earth is better off today than it was four years ago. I can't honestly say that.

This diatribe is an effort to take a hard look at what we're doing and insinuate some new elements into the debate. It's not intended to belittle any of our efforts, point fingers, or assign blame, so don't take it personally. We are all earthlings.

Our campaigns follow the gambling addiction model. The last bet didn't pay off but the next one might if . . . if . . . if we just had a new, improved tripod, three more experts, more labor or church support, ten more elected officials on our side, a hundred more people at the demo, or a thousand more letters in the mail . . . Who are we kidding? We are just doing the "same old thing" over and over again and fooling ourselves that it might work next time.

We are stuck in a feedback loop where our failures are interpreted as signs that we should repeat our failed tactics, but try harder. This is what it is to be colonized. The telltale sign is not that we're failing, but that we're fooling ourselves, and don't see it as a feedback loop.

If our minds are not colonized, then how come almost every *Earth First! Journal* action piece starts with a banner or a lockdown and ends with a plea to write a letter to a white male bigshot? (Go ahead, look through back issues. It goes on for years and years.)

Over at corporate headquarters they have a steeper learning curve.

Despite the occasional bag of guts on the committee table or clever banner, it must be reassuring for corporate executives and those who serve them to sit back and smile at the success of their containment efforts, and the predictability of our campaigns.

The issue of whose minds are colonized is a delicate one. We all know people whose minds have been colonized. Who are they? They are *other people*—people *out there*. They are somebody else. Not us.

---

It's time we did the unthinkable and asked ourselves if we have been colonized. What do we see when we compare our strategies to corporate strategies?

Many of our groups are organized to *save* wolves, butterflies, trees, prairie flowers, rivers, deserts, or estuaries. But corporation executives don't organize to *destroy* the wolves, butterflies . . . flowers . . . estuaries. Nor do they organize to pollute the air, spoil the rivers, or promote five-legged frogs.

This asymmetry should give us pause as we try to understand why corporations are on a roll while we're stuck in a feedback loop. Let's look again.

Corporate strategy leverages their power; their efforts reinforce and magnify each other. Our strategy splits our resources and dissipates our power.

Corporate strategy aims to increase the power that corporations have over people. That means that when a single corporation gets a victory, it helps all other corporations, too. They are all stronger, they all have more power, and the people have less.

We work on separate harms. When we lock down to one old growth stand, others go unprotected. When we protest about one chemical, others go unprotested. When we testify to preserve one watershed, others are not spoken for.

We have whole campaigns directed at one chemical, one corporation, one species, one grove of trees, one article of clothing.

In doing so, we fracture our resources. While we're out working on a "Chlorine is Bad" or "Wolves are Good" campaign, we're not working on all of the other chemicals, animals, trees, etc., that also need attention.

Some of us argue that this fracturing is inevitable, because there's so much wrong in the world. (Declaring a problem to be inevitable is a great way to justify not talking about it. Another gift to the corporate world view.)

Others of us think that the fracturing results from not being organized *enough*, or not being organized *right*. This opens the door for endless bickering about whether we should organize by bioregion or by article of clothing, by species or by chemical, by issue or by occupation. Either way, we're still fractured.

Being fractured is another way of being colonized.

Another sure sign of being colonized is when you censor yourself, and don't even wait for others to do it. Some of our self-imposed limitations are right off of a corporate wish list.

We have a strange "but it's the law" syndrome. Why can't we bring up important issues at EPA hearings? It's regulatory (administrative) law. Why can't we get our views accurately presented on TV? It's (corporate) private property law and FCC regulations. Why can't we imprison corporate executives for what their corporations do? It's liability law.

So what do we do? We toe the line at the EPA hearing. We dress up as animals to get a moment on TV. We let lying corporate executives lie.

That is, we work around the defining laws that are the groundwork for a rigged system. We're looking for favors, lucky breaks. We don't even dream of control, yet we call this a democracy.

This is being colonized.

Corporation representatives do not feel constrained in this way. Nothing is too destructive, too audacious, too outrageous for them to attempt. After all, they have most of us believing and not even objecting to the idea that corporations have "rights." In early 1998 an association of corporations (itself a corporation that supposedly has "free speech" rights, according to prevailing legal opinion) sued a talk show host in Texas for saying that she's going to stop eating hamburgers.[1]

Then there's the Zen of "Describing The Problem."

We need our storytellers, we need our scribes, we need our analysts, we need our own human fonts of crazy ideas. We needed *Silent Spring.*[2] By now we have the equivalent of *Son of Silent Spring, Daughter of Silent Spring, Second Cousin Once Removed of Silent Spring.* But habitat destruction continues as fast as we can describe it, if not faster. Our compulsion to Describe The Problem (something we do really well) serves a purpose, especially for people who think there's no problem, but the people who need to hear it the most aren't hearing it. We're Describing The Problem *to each other* in lavish detail, which crowds out efforts to rethink our whole strategy.

Are we doing anything other than lurching back and forth between Describing The Problem and then buckling the seatbelt on our feedback loop? I for one think I've heard enough "Bad Things About Corporations," and I'm pretty tired of working on campaigns that will not only fail, but fail *in predictable ways.*

How have we been colonized? Let me count the ways. We interpret failures as signals to do the same things over again. We are predictable. Our strategies and styles of organizing fracture and dilute our resources. We either accept this dilution as inevitable, or blame each other for not organizing right. We censor ourselves, in thought and action. We act as though if we Describe The Problem to each other enough, it might go away.

And now, we can argue about whether we've been colonized or not. Corporate management is popping extra popcorn for this one.

But enough of what *we* do. What do *corporations* do? (The question should be, "What do people do behind the fiction of corporations?" One of the signs of our being colonized is that we personify corporations. I've been trying to avoid that in this piece but . . . help, I've been colonized and I need help getting up . . .)

Corporate management figured out a hundred years ago that fighting against each other, competing and diluting their resources was weakening them and limiting their power. So they don't do that any more.

So what do people do while hiding behind the corporate shield? The short version is that they write a script for us, and we follow it. Then they write a script for themselves, and we don't even read it.

A big part of the script written for us involves Regulatory Law (including environmental and administrative law). It assumes that corporations have the rights of constitutional "persons."

It outlines procedures for what We the People can do (not much); what government can do (a little more); and what corporations can do (a lot).

At regulatory agencies *corporate* "persons" (that is, corporations) have constitutional rights to due process and equal protection that *human* persons, affected citizens, do not have. For non-corporate human citizens there's a "Democracy Theme Park" where we can pull levers on voting machines and talk into microphones at hearings. But don't worry, they're not connected to anything and nobody's listening 'cept us.

What Regulatory Law regulates is citizen input, not corporate behavior. So when we cooperate in regulatory law proceedings, we are following the script that corporation representatives wrote for us. We're either colonized, or we're collaborators. *That* the regulatory agencies fail to protect the public is clear. *Why* they fail is another matter.

One reason is that they were set up with the cooperation of and sometimes at the urging of big corporations. Today regulatory agencies and trade associations work together to do the work that the "trusts" of the last century were set up to do.

A second reason for regulatory failure concerns the nature of the corporation, to which we turn briefly.

Corporations are not natural entitles, like karner blue butterflies or white pines. Corporations are artificial creations that are set up by state corporation codes. These state laws, plus a bunch of court cases, form the basis for the notion that corporations have powers and "rights."

This law is Defining Law. This law is the script that corporate lawyers write for corporations. This law is the law that we don't even read.

It's right there in the law books in black and white, just like the "regs" that we spend so much time on. But this Defining Law is invisible to us because we've been colonized and have accepted it as a given. We leave this defining law—in corporation codes, bankruptcy law, insurance law, etc.—to corporation lawyers, who rewrite it every few years without so much as a whimper from citizen activists. Then we wonder why the parts-per-million regulations aren't enforced.

So, the second reason that regulatory agencies fail to protect the public is that we have allowed corporate lawyers to write the Defining Law of corporations. This law bestows upon corporations powers and rights that exceed those of human persons and sometimes of government as well. It seems pretty obvious, then, that we need to rewrite the Defining Law.

Sooner or later we come up against the claim that all this stuff about "rights" and so on is just too legalistic. None of us wants to be involved in narrow and excessively legalistic strategies. However, a glance through any *Earth First! Journal* will confirm that we're constantly dealing with The Law, whether we're filing testimony or engaged in direct action. As long as we're in the legal arena, we might as well be dealing with Defining Law, and not the regulatory frufru that we've allowed to distract us.

If the civil rights movement had been afraid to touch the deep defining "law of the land" we'd still be laboring under "separate but equal." For as long as we stick with Regulatory Law and leave Defining Law to corporate lawyers, we'll have corporate government.

What are we going to do tomorrow morning?

We could keep doing what hasn't worked in case it works next time; we could denounce people who suggest that what we're doing isn't working; we could declare victory so our folks won't get so depressed and discouraged. I'd like to steer clear of those options.

I'd also like to avoid "negotiating" with corporations as though they were persons with a role in a democratic system, and avoid doing anything else that accepts that corporations have the constitutional rights of human persons.

Here is one cluster of ideas for rewriting the Defining Law of corporations. It's not a 3-point plan, and it's not the beginning of a twenty point plan—just some ideas to think about.

1. Prohibit corporations from owning stock in other corporations. Owning stock in other corporations enables corporations to control huge markets and shift responsibility, liability, resources, assets and taxes back and forth among parent corporations, subsidiaries and other members of their unholy families. By defining corporations in such a way to prohibit such ownership, much of the anti-trust regulatory law becomes unnecessary and superfluous.

2. Prohibit corporations from being able to choose when to go out of business (in legalese, no voluntary dissolution). This would prevent corporations from dissolving themselves when it came time to pay

taxes, repay government loans, pay creditors, pay pensions, pay for health care, and pay for toxic cleanups.

3. Make stockholders liable for a corporation's debts. People who want to be stockholders would reallocate their resources to corporations that they knew something about, that weren't engaged in risky, toxic projects. (This would encourage local, sustainable businesses and healthy local economies. Imagine that.)

These three measures might seem "unrealistic" to some, but it beats the heck out of a voluntary code of conduct, or a wasted decade at a regulatory agency. All three of these provisions were once common features of state corporation codes. No wonder corporate apologists prefer that we hang around in the regulatory agencies with our heads spinning with parts per million and habitat conservation plans.

These three measures were quite effective, which is why corporation lawyers worked so hard to get rid of them. But they address only a tiny portion of what needs to be done.

Here's another cluster of ideas for ways to shape a democratic process that is about people. (The idea that corporations have "rights" would seem nonsensical to any but a colonized mind.)

1. No corporate participation in the democratic process. Democracy is for and about human beings. Corporations should be prohibited from paying for any political advertisements, making any campaign contributions, or seeking to influence the democratic process in any way.

2. Corporations have no constitutional rights.

A corporation is an artificial creation set up to serve a public need, not an independent entity with intrinsic "rights."

3. Corporations should be prohibited from making any civic, charitable, or educational donations. Such donations are used to warp the entire social and economic fabric of society, and make people afraid to speak out against corporations.

These probably seem even more "unrealistic" than the first batch. Imagine how good it is for corporate executives that we find these ideas "impractical." And by the way, these were all once law, too.

The final objection to be raised is that we'll never get anywhere as long as the "news media" are against us, refuse to cover our issues, and distort our views. Agreed.

But the "news media" are corporations, key players in a system of propaganda that encompasses not only television, radio and newspapers, but also the entire educational system. The "airwaves" belong to the public.

Why have we allowed a puppet federal agency to "lease" the public airwaves to huge corporations? Ya wanna lock down? Lock down to a TV or radio station and make the public airwaves public again. Not for a day but for a lifetime.

Ya like boycotts? What if a regulatory agency gave a hearing and nobody came? The outcome would be the same but we wouldn't have wasted all the time and resources, nor would we have helped grant an aura of legitimacy to a sham proceeding.

What could we do instead? We could get together with the lawyer and the expert and begin to figure out how to stop being collaborators. ∎

---

# Notes

[1] The talk show host was Oprah Winfrey. She had the financial resources and popularity to beat the lawsuit. —*Ed.*

[2] Carson 1962.

# PLAYING BY WHOSE RULES?

## A CHALLENGE TO ENVIRONMENTAL, CIVIL RIGHTS, AND OTHER ACTIVISTS

*by Richard L. Grossman*

---

WITH FEW EXCEPTIONS, people come out of law school without having questioned pro-corporate doctrines on property (for example, future profits are corporate property, the fruits of employees' labor are corporate property, the right to manage is corporate property, etc.). They accept today's giant corporations as inevitable. They don't seem to wonder how it came to pass that corporations became legal "persons" with free speech and other constitutional rights, while workers on company turf have no Bill of Rights protections.

They do not encourage the rest of us to ask why a sovereign people should permit corporate legal fictions to elect our representatives, write and pass our laws, or lie to the public on vital issues. Environmental and labor lawyers are trained to *not* challenge prevailing assumptions about the law, and *to* accept current legal doctrines. And then they train us.

Corporate lawyers, government lawyers, environmental lawyers—all have been funneling people's time, energy and resources into stacked-deck regulatory and administrative law arenas where even if we "win," we don't win much. And where there are few mechanisms we can use to shift rights and powers *from* corporations *to* people, communities and nature.

Movement lawyers should take their cues from activists on the ground. Local organizers should say:

> Such-and-such investment and production are destructive, uneconomical and wrong, but are protected by law and therefore by government. We will educate and organize to stop these harm doers. We need you lawyers to figure out how we can use the law and the courts to help us, or at least not to block us. Please don't lecture us about what we can't do. Don't come up with legal strategies which enable corporations to hide behind the privileges and immunities which corporations have taken from the people. And please don't tie our hands.

Today's leading environmental law groups—such as the Natural Resource Defense Council (NRDC)—were formed 20-30 years ago, mostly by young men just out of law school. When these men were law students, the Critical Legal Studies movement was not yet a presence within law schools.[1] So as students, they were not exposed to even the modest questioning of curriculum and law professor biases which goes on in some law schools today. Some of these environmental law groups received immediate support and finan-

---

©1994 by Richard L. Grossman. Previously published in *Daybreak* (vol. 4, no. 4, May 1995).

cial backing from powerful philanthropies like the Ford and Rockefeller foundations, and from law firms which represented large corporations.

Today, these groups define the agenda of environmentalism. They drive much of the environmental movement towards permitting and disclosure laws administered by federal and state regulatory and administrative agencies. Each wave of environmental activists has had to confront these legal groups eager to stop us from making investment and production decision-making a more public process. Instead, they have sought to determine acceptable amounts of corporate poisons and corporate clear-cuts, and to win compensation for corporate harms; they would have the public give greater profits to corporate leaders to encourage them to act more responsibly. As a result we've seen campaign after campaign for citizen authority over corporations diverted into regulatory agencies and the courts, where activists toe the line of managerial prerogative and other claimed corporate property rights.

As an anti-nuclear organizer in 1974 seeking to stop the construction of new nukes and to shut down existing nukes (not make nukes "safer") and to revise the legal relationship between people and energy corporations, I vividly recall the hostility I encountered in Washington D.C. when I inquired what help some of these groups would give us. I was astonished at their reaction, and it took some time before I began to understand it.

In fact, most popular struggles—labor, civil rights, environmental—have been taken out of the public's hands. Trade unionists allow their rights as organizers to be defined not by the power they could wield but by the National Labor Relations Act.[2] Years of protest by civil rights activists ended up with federal laws like the Voting Rights Act which

are much less than what people had organized and died for.

Decades ago, the American people accepted the alarms of activists and said: OK, we want clean air, clean water, wild lands preserved as national parks, forests and wilderness areas. Our movement lawyers and corporate lawyers wrote the laws. What did we get? Laws which legalized the poisoning of the air and water, which legalized clear-cutting, which left unchallenged the privileges and immunities which corporations had usurped during the past century, and which concentrated power in the hands of appointed regulators and administrators insulated from our reach.

Today, our regulatory and administrative laws are a stacked deck, granting corporations legal clout while disadvantaging peoples, communities and nature. The National Environmental Policy Act[3] does not mention corporations, and requires nothing of corporations. The Taft-Hartley Act[4] was written by corporate lawyers. Yet our environmental and labor lawyers let these laws define our arenas of struggle, our aspirations and our strategies. And now we let the lawyers shape what and how we think.

So much hope has been invested in creating, enforcing, and reforming these diversionary laws. So much time, energy, and resources.

Look at the roles in energy policy played by the Environmental Defense Fund, the Natural Resources Defense Council, and the Conservation Law Foundation. Under the banners of "demand side management" and energy efficiency, these groups—with philanthropic assistance and cover—have helped utility corporations get higher rates of return and decrease the powers of state public utility commissions to direct utility corporation executives to act. They have helped utility executives move decision-making behind closed doors, all in exchange for some (pathetically minute) voluntary corporation conservation efficiency investments.

Utility corporations such as the Pacific Gas & Electric Company and Southern California Edison Corporation—regulated monopolies which by law are required to serve the public interest—took their extra profits and set up subsidiary corporations in other countries to build big new fossil burners. Their executives flood state capitals and Washington D.C. with money to turn our elected officials against citizens' agendas. They spread their lies and intimidate people as they frame what little semblance of public policy debate we have.

Now they're backing off from their energy efficiency promises because they smell bigger profits from new "energy wheeling"[5] laws they wrote and enacted. And environmental law organizations remain these utility corporations' biggest defenders!

Over the past 25 years, environmental lawyers have been assuring the American people that with each new law the air and water and wilderness were being protected; that our children's health was being protected; that we were on the path to using energy efficiently and cleanly . . . not to worry. Snookered as we have been, we have not challenged corporations' claimed constitutional rights to make all the important investment and production decisions.

We have not made *people's constitutional rights* in economic and employment decision-making a movement goal, or placed this on *our* legal agenda. No wonder the public is vulnerable to corporate agitators and their "wise use" creatures inciting environmental and governmental backlash.

In the decades before the 1870s, the corporation was treated by the public—its creator—as a subordinate institution. At that time, both law and popular culture reflected that the use of natural resources—the commons—was very much a realm of *public decisions*. But railroad, banking, mining, grain and land speculator corporations began to steal the public lands and resources in vast amounts, and to change the law.

Today corporations exercise *governing* roles as they direct massive amounts of capital, control jobs, production, trade, technology and property. They dominate our elections, write and pass our laws, educate our judges in jurisprudence, shape public policy debate.

Corporations exert influence on law schools, law professors, law students, on our educational system, and on our culture as a whole.

The classic study of "bedrock" law is by Harvard Law School professor Morton Horwitz. It is called, appropriately, *The Transformation of American Law*, for that is precisely what corporate lawyers succeeded in doing by the end of the nineteenth century. Another scholar, Martin Sklar, called it a "corporate reorganization of the property production system."[6] This is what corporate leaders have been perfecting all during the twentieth century. It is what we face today.

Environmental and labor lawyers have placed our movements' hopes in regulatory and administrative agencies, and in appeals courts. In those political arenas, they work hard to limit corporate harms one-by-one, corporation-by-corporation. But the history of such laws suggests that, starting with the Interstate Commerce Act[7] in 1887 and the Sherman Anti-Trust Act[8] in 1890, they were used to divert angry people who had been organizing to get power over corporations.

Just at the time when the Supreme Court was bestowing legal personhood upon corporations, corporations were working children to death and using convicts to break strikes.

Carnage prevailed in the nation's mines and mills. By the 1890s, railroad corporations were killing 6000-7000 people a year and injuring over 30,000 people a year—employees, passengers and just people who happened to get in the way.

The owners of western railroad corporations had walked off with 180 million acres of public land. Federal judges were declaring unions to be criminal conspiracies. Corporate and government troops were bloodying and killing working people and Native Americans who dared to organize for their lives, liberties, rights and pursuits of happiness.

The working people and small business people who organized the Knights of Labor, and the farmers, urban workers, small merchants and intellectuals who built the Populist Movement sought ownership and control of railroads, banks, grain and telegraph corporations because they realized that federal regulatory laws and agencies would become barriers between the corporations and the people.

They understood they needed "democratic money" and an end to the crop lien system so they could break the grip of the cotton merchants, of tool and seed suppliers. They sought cooperation, cooperatives and sufficiency, instead of competition, hierarchy and maximum production of everything. They struggled but were defeated by the combined might of the state and the corporate class. After their defeat, claims to rights and powers by corporate executives were legitimated by legal doctrine, law, courts, historians, and law schools.

Populists left us important legacies, but the reality of these legacies has been distorted. Regulatory laws were declared great victories for the people. And for the past century, citizen struggles for justice have been channeled into regulatory and administrative law realms—and to the market—as if those are arenas where a sovereign people may redress grievances, or define a nation's values.

We have been playing too long by the rules of corporate exploiters and destroyers . . . by the rules they taught our lawyers, who have taught us well. ■

# NOTES

[1] The first national "Conference of Critical Legal Studies" was held in 1977.

[2] National Labor Relations Act of 1935, also called the "Wagner Act" after New York Senator Robert Wagner. —Ed.

[3] National Environmental Policy Act of 1969 created the Environmental Protection Agency (EPA), and expanded the use of regulations and the regulatory arena in setting and managing public environmental policy, and in managing the public's participation. See related articles "Sheep in Wolf's Clothing" and "Reaching Back, Digging Deep: Strategies in Context" in this volume. —Ed.

[4] Taft-Hartley Act, passed in 1947 over the veto of President Truman. It amended the National Labor Relations Act of 1935 and served to limit some of the rights established in the earlier act such as banning "secondary" boycotts. It required union officers to sign affidavits that they were not communists, and empowered employers to "give" their opinions on unionization elections. —Ed.

[5] "Energy wheeling" describes the transmission of large blocks of power from one region to another, or from one utility to another. This transmission occurs by way of the electrical power grids. Energy corporations often act as brokers in this exchange, and it provides profits with minimal costs or actions.

If the purpose of conservation is keeping demand below supply, then finding more supply (such as through energy wheeling) is an appropriate tactic. But if the purpose of conservation is about reducing demand and towards reaping the benefits associated with lower energy use, then energy wheeling is an inappropriate response. —Ed.

[6] Sklar 1988.

[7] Interstate Commerce Act of 1887 established the first federal regulatory agency, the Interstate Commerce Commission. See "Sheep in Wolf's Clothing" in this volume. —Ed.

[8] Sherman Anti-Trust Act of 1890 has a controversial, complex history. It is generally described as a response to public concerns stemming from the increasing power of corporations which coordinated activities and strategies within an industry to maximize profits. That particular "history" ignores the significant reality that in the 1890s activists defined "monopoly" as a political term, not an economic term. It was understood to mean *too much concentration of private power*, so much that democracy was not possible. Busting monopolies wasn't about keeping costs down to consumers; it was about the people owning and controlling the necessaries of life so that they could aspire to govern themselves.

# Unfinished Business

## Bhopal Ten Years After

### by Ward Morehouse

THE TENTH ANNIVERSARY of the world's worst industrial disaster—a poisonous gas leak from the Union Carbide Corporation[1] pesticide plant in Bhopal which killed as many as 15,000 people and injured hundreds of thousands more—occurred on December 3, 1994. The perpetrator of the disaster, Union Carbide, with the complicity of the Indian government, still refuses to take responsibility for the accident and has paid only token amounts of compensation. The judicial systems of both the U.S. and India have not delivered anything remotely resembling justice for the victims of the disaster, demonstrating that powerful multinational companies are beyond the reach of the law. The disaster's anniversary offers an opportunity to retell the tale.

## Responding to Tragedy

Since the disaster more than 600,000 claims have been filed with the Indian government against Union Carbide (with at least another 100,000 claims still unregistered). The company has fought tooth-and-nail to avoid paying anything more than a token amount of compensation—although by its own admission, it has spent about $50 million on legal fees.

The first objective of the corporation's lawyers was to get the proceedings for compensation transferred from New York—where the lawyers representing the claimants and government of India on behalf of all the victims first filed claims in 1985, and where the corporation is chartered—to India. The company argued that the U.S. courts were not the proper forum for the trial which should instead be held in Indian courts which, it claimed, were competent to decide the issue. After a year, the case was indeed transferred to India.

Once in India, Union Carbide switched its argument. It then claimed the Indian courts were not competent, and at every opportunity insisted that the company's rights to due process were being violated. It appealed virtually every decision of the trial court, even on minor procedural matters, not only to the High Court of Madhya Pradesh, the state in which Bhopal is located, but even to the Indian Supreme Court.

For example, when the Bhopal District Court ordered Union Carbide to pay interim relief of $270 million, Carbide refused to obey and appealed to the Madhya Pradesh High Court. When the High Court upheld the lower court ruling, the company again refused to obey the order and appealed to the Indian Supreme Court. This process lasted more than a year. The

©1994 by the Ecologist. This is an excerpt from an article published in *The Ecologist* (vol. 24, no. 5, September/October 1994).

company has also tried at different times to blame its Indian subsidiary, Union Carbide India Limited (UCIL), or a "disgruntled worker."

The litigation dragged on until February 1989 when unexpectedly the Indian government under Rajiv Gandhi agreed to a settlement "ordered" by the Indian Supreme Court of $470 million. This sum, equivalent to only $793 for each of the 592,000 who had by then filed claims, was not even sufficient to cover health care and monitoring of the gas-exposed population (conservatively estimated at $600 million over the next 20 to 30 years). The settlement was so favorable for Union Carbide that its stock price rose $2 a share on the New York Stock Exchange the very day it was announced.

The settlement provoked widespread public indignation and was immediately challenged in court by victim groups, and subsequently, by a new Indian government under V. P. Singh. It was upheld in October 1991 by the Indian Supreme Court. But this court also reinstated criminal charges of culpable homicide first made in 1985 against Union Carbide, its Indian subsidiary, and senior officials of both companies that had been quashed by the February 1989 settlement. These charges, if they are ever heard, remain the only prospect of a proper attempt to assign responsibility for the disaster.

## GOVERNMENT COMPLICITY

The Union Carbide Corporation's delaying tactics and its attempts to "blame the victim" have been predictable, but its success has been due to complicity from the Indian government and the Madhya Pradesh state government. In part, this complicity stems from the fact that the Indian government recognizes that Union Carbide will never be made fully accountable for the damage it has caused. Indeed, the Indian Supreme Court has held that if the settlement money should prove insufficient, the Indian government should make up the difference. The government, therefore, has an interest in minimizing the financial impact of the disaster, in demanding impossible types of medical evidence to substantiate claims, and in approving only trivial awards so that the settlement money is not exhausted.

There may, however, be other reasons for the Indian government's reluctance to prosecute vigorously the Union Carbide Corporation. The government's New Economic Policy is heavily influenced, if not imposed, by the World Bank and the International Monetary Fund (IMF). It has also signed the new General Agreement on Tarriffs and Trade (GATT), which critics see as a naked power grab by multinationals to facilitate their access to Southern economies, thereby shoring up the North's domination of the international economy.

Thus, in the last few years there has been a stampede of multinational companies to India through the open door provided by the Indian government. Companies such as Motorola, Hewlett Packard, General Electric, the General Motors Corporation, 3M, Honeywell, Kodak, Cargill, DuPont, Mitsubishi, Sumitomo, C. Itoh, Marubeni, BASF, ICI, Asea Brown Boveri, Royal Dutch Shell, McDonald's, Pepsico and Coca-Cola, have rapidly increased their investments in India, buying up formerly state-run enterprises for a song, or setting up new production facilities to take advantage of a highly-educated yet extremely cheap labor force. They are using India as a platform to produce cheap exports and sell products to the wealthiest ten per cent of the Indian population, a market of nearly 100 million people (roughly equivalent to the population of Germany, Switzerland, and the Netherlands combined). The only exception to this movement is Union Carbide, which for obvious reasons is trying to sever its last link with India by selling its shares in its Indian subsidiary, UCIL.

Prosecuting and forcing a realistic settlement out of Union Carbide might deter multinationals from investing in India, yet failure to do so raises further questions about the Indian government and its efforts to attract this investment. Although the Bhopal disaster provided the government with a powerful opportunity to force multinational companies to implement stricter safety and environmental precautions, the government has instead eliminated prohibitions against siting industrial facilities in ecologically sensitive zones, and "denotified" protected areas so that cement plants, oil refineries and dams can be built. According to Indian journalist Praful Bidwai:

> As far as environmental protection and management of hazards or disasters goes, no lessons [from Bhopal] have been learnt. Location policies for the chemical industries have not changed even one iota: Baroda, Patalganga, Lotfe Parashuram, Kalyani and other storehouses of chemical poisons continue to be promoted, built and expanded. The promise of strict regulation of toxic chemicals and an outright ban on the worst of them remains largely unfulfilled.

In fact, the government's vacillation and eventual capitulation on the question of compensation has given companies a free hand to forge their own policies. DuPont Corporation, for example, has a clause in its proposal to build a nylon plant in India that absolves it from all liability in the event of an accident.

## UNFINISHED BUSINESS

Not surprisingly, Bhopal has become a symbol of the corporate disregard for human welfare and environment in the drive for corporate profit. Union Carbide Corporation's success in avoiding prosecution underscores the present reality that transnational companies are lawless monsters roaming the earth, apparently beyond the reach of any judicial system but dominating the global political economy. Bhopal has exposed as myth the claim that these global giants—and Union Carbide Corporation is far from being the largest— are accountable to the governments of the countries in which they operate. Instead, experience and law show that multinational corporations are not subject to human rights and other standards in international law which apply to nation states.

The tenth anniversary of the Bhopal disaster presents an opportunity to focus attention on efforts to curb such corporations' power, making them accountable to those whose lives are most directly affected by their actions. This struggle must begin with the empowerment of those who bear the greatest risks—the workers and communities surrounding hazardous facilities which means effective political mobilization at the grassroots.

Indeed, the little positive treatment of those affected by the disaster has come about almost entirely as a result of the survivors' protests. Three of the victims' organizations—Bhopal Gas-Affected Women Workers Association, Poisonous Gas Disaster Struggle Front, Bhopal Gas-Affected

Women Stationery Workers Union—have drawn up an eleven-point list of demands for the tenth anniversary of the disaster. One of their demands is for the government of India to issue an extradition request for Warren Anderson, chief executive officer of Union Carbide at the time of the disaster, to face criminal proceedings in India. Union Carbide is at present hurriedly trying to evade jurisdiction of the criminal court in Bhopal by selling its shares in its Indian subsidiary under the guise of providing finance for a hospital for disaster victims in Bhopal. These shares are Union Carbide's last tangible asset in India; if it sells them all off, it will have severed all its connections with India.

National and international support of grassroots organizations is critically important. Bhopal support groups within India, especially in Delhi, have played an important part, as has the Bhopal Group for Information and Action in Bhopal itself. The International Coalition for Justice in Bhopal, a network of seven citizen activist groups based in Japan, Hong Kong, Malaysia, The Netherlands, Britain and the U.S., is one of the international links campaigning in support of the demands of the Bhopal victims. A number of international groups concerned with industrial pollution are calling for a "world day of action to fight toxics and corporate power" on the tenth anniversary of the disaster.

Not only do new standards of corporate ethical behavior need to be set, but effective techniques and institutional mechanisms need to be developed to ensure that standards are actually met and violators promptly and meaningfully held to account.

The "Permanent People's Tribunal on Industrial and Environmental Hazards and Human Rights" in Rome has started this work. The tribunal concluded in October 1992 in Bhopal that, on the basis of testimony from victims, workers, experts and others, the fundamental human rights of the victims and their rights under the Indian Constitution have been grossly violated by the Union Carbide Corporation, the government of India and the government of Madhya Pradesh. The final session of the tribunal will be held in Britain just prior to the tenth anniversary.[2]

In the United States, Union Carbide Corporation's role in Bhopal has stimulated efforts to reassert citizen sovereignty over corporations by demanding that company charters be rewritten to make them more directly answerable for their activities. Union Carbide, for instance, is incorporated in New York State, and New York's Business Corporation Law provides for dissolution when a corporation abuses its powers or acts "contrary to the public policy of the state." The law also calls for a jury trial in charter revocation cases, something Carbide strongly fought to deny its victims in Bhopal. A citizen petition is being drawn up to demand that the State Attorney General take action to rewrite Carbide's charter under the laws he is elected to uphold.[3] Several groups have also been busy preparing a large body of damning evidence against Union Carbide. For instance, Communities Concerned about Corporations has been documenting Union Carbide's environmental record in the United States, and will present it shortly before the tenth anniversary. The anniversary is also an opportunity to expose the myth that transnational corporations have a pivotal role to play in Third World development.

The words of the widow, Bano Bi, serve as a reminder that the people of Bhopal still have unfinished business.

> I believe that even if we have to starve, we must get the guilty officials of Union Carbide punished. They have killed someone's brother, someone's husband, someone's mother, someone's sister— how many tears can Union Carbide wipe? We will get Union Carbide punished. Till my last breath, I will not leave them.

The victims of the world's worst industrial disaster can never forget. We must not either. As Czech author Milan Kundera observed, "The struggle of people against power is the struggle of memory against forgetting." ■

## Notes

[1] The Union Carbide Corporation is now a subsidiary of the DOW Chemical Company (whose slogan is "Living. Improved Daily."). —Ed.

[2] That session of the Tribunal reaffirmed the decision of the 1992 "Bhopal Tribunal," as did another session of the "Permanent People's Tribunal on Global Corporations and Human Wrongs," held at the University of Warwick Law Faculty in the UK in March 2000.

[3] In the absence of widespread political pressure, the Attorney General ignored these demands. His successor has made public statements about his intention to use the power of his office to revoke charters of corporations causing great harm, but he has done little.

# ENDING CORPORATE GOVERNANCE

*by Richard L. Grossman*

---

TODAY FEW PLACES on Earth are free from corporate rule. Every day people are bravely resisting corporations. They are standing up to the bullying, blackmail, and violence corporate managers use to maintain their grip over our minds, our work, and our communities.

Yet most people still concede to corporations the broad property and constitutional rights which corporate leaders over the last century have claimed as their own. These rights disadvantage us every time we petition our elected officials, regulatory agencies or courts for justice. They enable corporations to use bastardized democratic rhetoric—and our own governments—to keep us smartly in line.

We have been trained to accept elected legislators and judges delegating our historical and constitutional sovereign authority over corporations to faceless institutions further and further away from our communities.

Even when corporations cause blood to run, national citizen groups generally limit their goals to curbing corporate excesses, or to requesting corporate managers to please act responsibly. While such efforts are important, they do not reduce significantly the destruction of communities, nature, and democracy by corporate leaders.

Resistance to corporate harms which does not challenge the legitimacy of corporate rule—valiant as such resistance may be—does not appreciably change the corporate laws or constitutional doctrines which bestow upon giant corporations our governments' support. It does not shift to people, communities and nature the power and authority over elections, law-making, and legal proceedings which corporations have consolidated over the past hundred years.

Indeed, the abdication of our social responsibilities as sovereign people has enabled many corporations chartered in our states to become larger, in financial terms, than most countries. The largest 300 corporations control about one-fourth of all the goods-producing assets in the world.[1] The largest 100 have incomes greater than half the member countries of the United Nations. Seventy percent of all international trade is directed by 500 corporations.

Today global corporations enter and leave communities at will, shaping the futures of people, ecosystems, and the Earth. Leaders of such corporations exercise sovereign control over vast lands (80 percent of all land used for export agriculture), species and minerals. They destroy local institutions of decision making, along with cultural traditions and regional self-sufficiency. They choose which products and technologies are researched and created, and how human beings are used as workers and then discarded. They tax unilaterally and invisibly, via administered pricing,

---

and spend huge sums to instruct us what to believe, what to buy, and how to vote.

Such concentrated corporate power that can manipulate our democratic processes is contrary to the theory of governance that is supposed to prevail in this republic. A revolution against tyrannical perpetual monarchy was waged in the name of this theory; that in the United States, all power must be constitutional, that is, answerable to the people.

But isn't it clear that We the People have little legal or moral authority over today's giant corporations? That many of us are not even conscious that people once exercised such authority with diligence and determination?

And as Cornel West suggests, hasn't it become "difficult even to imagine what a free and democratic society [without such concentrations of corporate power] would look like (or how it would operate)"?[2]

So what can we do? For starters, in our communities and in our states, we can begin doing our work to stop obvious corporate harms in ways which:

- Reveal today's large corporation as illegitimate for self-governing people, as contrary to community stability and ecological sanity.

- Enable us—via mass action, challenging law and custom—to assert local authority over corporations and over the Earth's assets which corporate managers claim.

- Contest legal doctrines which are currently in vogue—like the ones declaring corporations to be persons protected by our Bill of Rights, and granting to corporations the sole right to manage.

- Rewrite our state corporation laws to recharter corporations, that is, rework the legal relationships between our communities and the corporate fictions we allow to operate in our communities; and to redesign our institutions of enterprise.

- Freeze the assets and revoke the charters of harm-causing corporations whose managers and directors resist our constitutional authority over them.

None of this will be easy. But what alternatives do we have? Can we bring about the transitions our communities and the Earth cry out for by organizing chemical by chemical, forest by forest, dump by dump, technology by technology, product by product, outrageous act by outrageous corporate act?

We have enormous rethinking and organizing tasks ahead. But this is work which will be nurtured by struggle in communities and ecosystems where people and Nature experience corporate tyranny most keenly. And it is work which will be fueled by a growing realization that democracy will continue to be a delusion as long as we allow corporations to rule. ∎

---

## NOTES

[1] Barnet and Cavanagh 1994, p. 15.                    [2] West 1982, pp. 468-469.

# LETTER TO BARBARA DUDLEY

## GREENPEACE USA

*by Richard L. Grossman*

---

12 February 1994

Barbara Dudley, Executive Director
Greenpeace USA

Regarding:    11 Reasons Why Greenpeace Should Do Something Other than Organize Against the General Agreement on Tariffs and Trade (GATT) and the World Trade Organization (WTO)

1.    Don't worry, the major anti-NAFTA groups—especially the self-censoring union, church, and environmental institutions—will focus on reforming WTO. They will seek to make it more open, to create a predictable regulatory mechanism via which people and nature might have some limited standing. In the WTO context, they will seek WTO "codes of conduct" and "right to know." They will get thousands of pages of rules and the committees to match.

Instead, Greenpeace can choose goals which are commensurate with the sources of our problems. It can design campaigns which are conducive to global organizing and solidarity. Greenpeace can call for—and lead campaigns for—the abolition and conversion of the worst global corporations . . . *as steps towards eradicating from the Earth the global corporation as an institution.*

By so doing, Greenpeace will draw attention to important concepts which are camouflaged by custom, law, and propaganda, which have been neglected by too many organizers for justice since the days of the Populist Movement: sovereignty, human rights, illegitimate corporate powers under law, social compacts, commonwealth, privileges . . . not to mention *the nature of the corporation itself.*

If Greenpeace groups around the Earth pursued such goals and talked such talk, Greenpeace would gain leverage to inject into the "mainstream" efforts of church, labor, and environmental groups a different and empowering language. This language could help people imagine extricating our cultures, our minds and our nations from the grips of global corporations, could alter the nature of debate, and could strengthen the mainstream's efforts against the WTO.

2.    People need to control corporations. Control only comes from having the authority—backed by law and custom—to create and dissolve corporations without great effort, and at will. The WTO has nothing whatever to do with the creating and dissolving of corporations. From the standpoint of actually stopping current corporate harms, it is a diversion.

---

Our job is to identify the venues where people can take control, capture them, and uproot global corporations entirely. This will take a while. Why not start now?

3.    The WTO is steps removed from the corporations themselves. Corporate leaders *want* activists to focus on the WTO rather than on them and their corporations. Why should we do what they want us to do? Consider how much energy and effort people have already invested fighting other corporate stalking-horses: all the alphabet regulatory and administrative agencies in the U.S. (and cloning around the world); and all the taxpayer-subsidized corporate manipulating organizations, from the Business Roundtable to the Pharmaceutical Manufacturers Association, not to mention the peculiarities created by *our side*, such as the Ceres Principles[1] created by "responsible investors."

These organizations are not the sources of our problems. They are red herrings. They are barriers. They do not warrant the time and attention of radicals—except to understand their roles as agents of and apologists for corporations, and to figure out how to get beyond them.

The sources of our problems are the corporations themselves, their stolen rights and authorities under law, and their power over governments.

Simple as this seems, few citizen organizations act upon this self-evident reality. After 100 years of our being diverted and red herringed to death, Greenpeace's aiming for the eradication of global corporations—and the appropriation of their usable assets by global mass movements—would be a revolutionary and energizing act.

4.    If you target WTO, what would be your goal? To green it? Abolish it? Reform it? To have advisory committees made up of Fred Krupp, Alice Tepper Marlin, Ron Brown, Bruce Babbitt and Lane Kirkland, Paul Wellstone, Barbara Dudley, Heather Booth, Jesse Jackson? To set up rules for the appointment of WTO officials, for WTO operating procedures?

Struggles against GATT and WTO will have a few generals, many negotiators, and masses of "supporters." When after several years the International Chamber of Commerce or the World Council on Sustainable Development or the presidents of the World Bank, the IMF and the United States of America finally agree to negotiate with the leaders of major church, labor and environmental groups, will you announce a great victory? And what will you ask the masses of angry anti-corporate organizers to do—send telegrams?

Effectively, the people will be shut out by such a strategy, no matter how many briefing sessions, no matter how many authentic delegations foundations bring to New York or Geneva like for PrepCom,[2] no matter how many wonderful newsletters and films and *op ed* pieces you generate.

Why would you want to shut out and disempower the only real source of power and strength to confront corporations—millions and millions and millions of people every place where corporations are doing business?

5.    Suppose you WON the privilege of negotiations, and a few years later achieved what would be regarded as an acceptable agreement? You would announce victory.

But would *corporations* be any weaker than they are today? Would law and constitutional doctrines be less protective of alleged corporate rights and powers? Would people have greater ability to STOP corporate production, STOP their movement of capital, STOP their manipulating of governments, STOP their propagandizing, their violence, their blackmailing?

Would people have greater ability to create or dismantle corporations at will?

6. Suppose you achieved an agreement on rules and access. What would be your next steps? Based on our experience with American regulatory models, the next step would be monitoring and enforcement of the rules. Now wouldn't THAT be revolutionary work!

7. Major focus on WTO will not encourage or assist groups around the world (now fighting specific corporations) to raise their aims, escalate their tactics, or be more effective.

Where will be the loci of WTO battles? At the UN? In Switzerland? In national legislatures? All these sites are far removed from the neighborhoods where flesh-and-blood people are battling specific, tangible, real corporations; where people are suffering, where the Earth is crying out.

If you decide that the most important battle (or the most realistic, or whatever adjective) is against the WTO, if you decide that's where you will direct your intelligence and your resources, you will belittle peoples' current battles against actual, harm-causing corporations. You will question their judgments. And you will rouse false hopes that if Greenpeace and powerful groups like the AFL-CIO can successfully "tame" WTO, this will get the Cargill, the Union Carbide, Mitsubishi, Exxon,[3] and Chase Manhattan Bank corporations off communities' backs.

8. We need radical democratic upheavals within the ranks of unions, churches, environ-

mental groups, consumer groups, etc. From what are such upheavals more likely to be encouraged: focusing on WTO and GATT and the politicians/bureaucrats who staff/shill for such operations? Or campaigning for and supporting peoples' organizing to dismantle identifiable, undemocratic, global corporations, and dislocate the people who run them?

9. Local citizen groups are the foundation of potentially massive and creative solidarity movements against corporations around the world; *against the idea of the corporation* which has so perverted commerce, nature, culture, democracy, and the Earth itself. This massive and creative solidarity can be encouraged and nurtured by validating people's senses that today's global corporations—like yesterday's—are menaces, and that people can begin to take corporations apart in their own communities.

Massive resistance and creativity and solidarity will not be set in motion by diverting people's attentions and raising hopes in yet another drawn-out affair over another international forum which the corporations have set up.

But who better to validate alternate strategies, to encourage and nurture massive resistance to corporations, than Greenpeace... speaking—and acting upon—the truth?

10. Struggles which are about fundamentals—people's sovereignty over governing institutions, our rights to *create* and to *dismantle* oppressive and destructive organizations and *stop* their operations—resonate with what people know in their hearts is logical and necessary.

Such struggles reveal ideological contradictions; educate about the histories of people and places; energize and transform isolated individuals into powerful, brave, strategic conspiracies of citizens strong enough to take power, and wise enough to use power wisely. They spill out into the broader cultures, and affect the way people think and talk about community and solidarity, and how they act.

People around the globe have been steeped in confrontation with global corporations for the past 400 years. Fundamental struggle against institutional tyranny of all forms is in our marrow, in our unconscious, in our genes. If we tap into collective marrows and unconsciouses and genes, we release tremendous human energy for justice.

Do you imagine that a massive battle to make the WTO nice, or even to abolish it, could be transformational in such ways? So many struggles against regulatory bodies, against red herring corporation fronts, have been struggles against marshmallows. There is no collective, atavistic energy to be tapped by replicating such mush.

II. Even if people set out to dismantle a corporation and lose, we win. We win not only because *we* are transformed, but because we also set in motion so many forces that assume lives of their own. We will have changed the debate, changed the goals, gone from their terrain to our terrain, begun to put corporations on the defensive.

And the *idea* of the corporation will be forced onto the international public agenda.

If you set out to reform or even dismantle the WTO, and lose, what do you have? A complex, fragile, loose coalition of institutional leaders looking for another coalition campaign.

I agree that NAFTA had to be opposed. And out of the hard work of the past several years, important education and action have resulted. But NAFTA won, and now the big organizations are looking for the next campaign, while global corporations continue their daily ravaging of people, the Earth and sovereign governments before their eyes.

Except for Greenpeace and unions, most big institutions must go to foundations for money. You have the freedom to act as justice and logic dictate. Most American union officials would not even have read this far. But unions and others abroad might well be awakened and moved by Greenpeace's decision to declare the global corporation as an institution—and specific corporations—*non personae non gratae in terris.*[4]

The people who are resisting corporate harms up close today will be inspired and renewed. In return, they will launch Greenpeace on journeys beyond imagination . . . journeys that may, at last, be commensurate ones. Journeys for which Greenpeace has been preparing all these years—in spite of some of its own personnel and history.  ∎

# Notes

[1] The CERES principles describe measurable environmental practices which some corporations pledge to support. Regarding adherence to these principles, the CERES organization writes: "These Principles are not intended to create new legal liabilities, expand existing rights or obligations, waive legal defenses, or otherwise affect the legal position of any endorsing company, and are not intended to be used against an endorser in any legal proceeding for any purpose." In other words, this is just another public relations campaign, not a meaningful commitment to actual practices. —*Ed.*

[2] PrepCom refers to "Preparatory Committee" of the "United Nations Conference on Environment and Development" (UNCED), the global environmental forum held in Rio, Brazil in 1992. The PrepComs were a series of preparatory meetings in advance of the UNCED gathering. Each PrepCom (there were 4 or so) was attended by representatives from each country of the world, and a huge gathering of activist groups. —*Ed.*

[3] Now the ExxonMobil Corporation, following the largest merger ever of two petroleum corporations. —*Ed.*

[4] "*Non personae non gratae in terris*" is Latin for "non-persons not welcome in these lands."

# RETHINKING THE CORPORATION IN THE CONTEXT OF CITIZEN-ORGANIZING FOR JUSTICE

*by Richard L. Grossman*

## CORPORATION LAW AND ECONOMICS

JUDGE FRANK EASTERBROOK and law professor Daniel R. Fischel, in their 1981 book *The Economic Structure of Corporate Law*, describe the political and economic liberty which corporate money has been dripping into the nation's legal veins:

> Why does corporate law allow managers to set the terms under which they will administer corporate assets? Why do courts grant more discretion to self-interested managers than to disinterested regulators? Why do investors entrust such stupendous sums to managers whose acts are essentially unconstrained by legal rules?[1]

> The role of corporate law at any instant is to establish rights among participants in the venture . . . maximizing profits for equity investors assists the other "constituencies" automatically. The participants in the venture play complementary rather than antagonistic roles. In a market economy each party to a transaction is better off. A successful firm provides jobs to workers and goods and services for consumers. The more appealing the goods

to consumers, the more profit (and jobs). Prosperity for stockholders, workers and communities goes hand in glove with better products for consumers. Other objectives, too, come with profit. Wealthy firms provide better working conditions and clean up their outfalls; high profits produce social wealth that strengthens the demand for cleanliness. Environmental concerns are luxury goods; wealthy societies purchase much cleaner and healthier environments than do poorer nations—in part because well-to-do citizens want cleaner air and water, and in part because they can afford to pay for it.[2]

Frequently the harmony of interest between profit maximization and the other objectives escapes attention. Firms that close plants in one area while relocating production elsewhere are accused of lacking a sense of responsibility to affected workers and communities. Yet such a statement ignores the greater benefits that workers and communities in the new locale enjoy. (They must be greater, or there would be no profit in the move.) Firms that cause dislocations by moving their plants are no less ethical than firms that cause dislocations by inventing new products that cause their rivals to go out of business . . . All competition produces dislocation—all progress produces dislocation . . . and to try to stop the wrenching shifts of a capitalist economy is to try to stop economic growth.[3]

## CORPORATIONS AND THE PUBLIC AGENDA

In our and other nations, neither redefining the corporation nor redesigning corporate law is on the public agenda in a serious way, even among people who have difficulty detecting the harmony of interest between profit maximization and the other objectives. Unions occasionally seek labor law reform from a worker perspective. Not many people or groups talk corporation law reform—much less *corporation* reform—from a democracy perspective.

Why not? Legal theory, law, constitutional doctrines (e.g., managerial prerogative, the corporation as an artificial person) and our courts inhibit meaningful citizen involvement in corporate affairs.

There is an illogic behind much citizen organizing today. Injustices are caused by corporate decisions directing investment, production and the organization of work. But by law and precedent—supported by legal theory— We the People have few rights in such realms. So we engage in circular and indirect strategies, such as:

- Investing time and energy in regulatory arenas to which our elected legislators have delegated enormous powers, which have been dominated by corporations and corporate values, and are run by appointed attorneys answerable not to Congress but to the courts.

- *Proving* to corporate executives they can be profitable and efficient, for example by hiring union labor and by being "green."

- Giving corporate managers new incentives for doing the "right thing," that is, via utility demand side management schemes that circumvent democratic processes, and pollution prevention programs which do not alter power relationships between corporations and workers or communities.

A century ago Henry Demarest Lloyd concluded: "We are calling upon the owners of industrial power and property, as mankind called upon kings in their day, to be good and kind, wise and sweet, and we are calling upon them in vain . . . We have put power in their hands and ask them not to use it as power."[4]

We are still calling upon corporate leaders in vain . . . while corporations get richer, more powerful and more destructive, as they become more elusive and adaptive. Not surprisingly, they are helping Eastern European countries to rewrite corporation, liability and tort laws, just as corporations and the American Bar Association have helped American states rewrite corporation laws for the past half-century. Corporations and the U.S. government are also exporting the American regulatory model, and the United Nations is floating the idea of soliciting corporate contributions to support its peace keeping armies around the world.

People around the world may be forging transitions to democratic governance, but this democratic governance will not extend to our labor and our resources, to production, or to the swift flow of money and information, unless national and global citizen movements make it happen. All the more reason to talk about what people and the Earth actually *need*, and to think and plan how we get it.

We can't do this without talking about where power and authority lie.

We'll have to stop pretending that corporations do not govern, stop conceding unwarranted legitimacy to corporations and their mythologists, and stop limiting our goals and aspirations. We must put everything on the table.

## DIFFUSIONS AND DIVERSIONS

During the last 100 years, this has not been easy to do. Giant corporations have been ubiquitous, but their long arms have not always been visible even though the effects of their advertising and intimidation have been staggering. Corporations have shaped how we think; they have limited our hopes, dreams and aspirations regarding our ability to control our economic, political, and ecological futures.

Large corporations—via their advertising, trade associations, the press, universities and the government itself—have convinced many that today's corporations were inevitable, are ideal, and in whatever forms they choose to mutate *will forever be indispensable.*

From the days of the Interstate Commerce Commission[5] and the Sherman Act,[6] down through the NIRA,[7] the Employment Act of 1946, the Humphrey-Hawkins Act[8] and the 60-day notice for factory closings (WARN Act), politicians—together with corporate leaders and leaders of some national citizens' groups—have used weak laws as charades to defuse public anger and divert citizen organizing.

Corporate managers—with the help of politicians, academics and the press—have persuaded many people to regard citizen challenges to corporations and their government protectors, as attacks upon private property, jobs, freedom, democracy, all business, national security, and the American Way.

Corporate agents and propagandists have been able to count on questioning patriotism, dividing and conquering, self-censorship, as well as government action, to discipline and break popular movements for justice and democracy.

Since the Populist Era when there arose, in the words of historian Lawrence Goodwyn, "the flowering of the largest democratic mass movement in American history,"[9] citizen movements (with few exceptions) have not looked strategically at the institution which is the corporation, or at the laws which empower the corporation.

The post WWII decade turned out to be a disaster for workers' rights, civil rights, for public health, and the environment. Citizen-organizing for democracy and justice in the U.S., and by people in other countries seeking independence, justice and economic sovereignty—was crushed.

Maximum vaccuuming of global resources, combined with maximum production and maximum consumption under the direction of corporate-military-scientific leadership, were chosen to bring jobs, security and the "good life" to these shores. Cheap resources and cheap labor abroad plus taxpayers at home would subsidize the great American corporations to keep America free, and provide a high standard of living. Regulatory agencies would curb corporate excesses.

Corporate leaders locked up commercial, financial and industrial decision-making on investments, research and development, product choice, jobs, and the organization of work . . . cornering public capital in the process. Since jobs were supposed to come primarily from the corporations, the ability of corporations to use economic threats and job blackmail was assured.

Walls were erected between foreign policy and domestic policy, even as corporate executives moved in and out of government with ease, and corporations extended their reach and political involvement across Europe, the Middle East, and Asia.

For decades since WWII, corporate managers have been able to watch leaders of citizen organizations discipline their own members' thoughts, and channel civic organizing safely within acceptable boundaries.

But the nature of the corporation, the violations of national sovereignties fundamental to its operations—along with its enormous rights and powers—are not commonly discussed today. Rarely are giant harm-causing corporations the direct target of strategic citizen wrath and tactical organizing. More rarely do people question such corporations' right to exist. Even to many people self-consciously under corporate thumbs and suffering identifiable corporate harms, challenging the legitimacy of the corporation and organizing to limit its rights and powers under law are not regarded as obvious or logical.

Such ideas are often dismissed as unrealistic, utopian, and counter-productive.

During the last half-century especially, many proposed solutions for corporate-caused injustices have been grand diversions. They have sought not to stop but *to control* injustices by codifying them in law, and without ending the harm-doer's capacity to cause harm or requiring restoration and repair (for example, pollution permits, ecosystem sales in national forests, consent decrees where corporations pay fines but admit no guilt–such as the General Electric Corporation's poisoning of the Hudson River with PCBs).

Citizen groups have maintained single-issue perspectives and constituencies (for example, for years atomic bomb testing opponents and nuclear power protesters did not want to be associated with one another; currently labor and civil rights groups, and labor and environmental groups, still often define their interests so narrowly as to inhibit cross-constituency solidarity).

As corporate agents have encouraged people to blame themselves for corporate harms (note how often citizen group leaders and pundits quote Pogo's "We have met the enemy and it is us . . ."), citizen groups have mobilized popular support for corporate voluntary self-regulation and "codes of conduct." Examples of these include the chemical corporations' "Responsible Care," a traditional public relations exercise; the idea of "socially responsible" investors; and the CERES Principles which in the Principles' own words "are not intended to create new legal liabilities, expand existing rights or obligations, waive legal defenses, or otherwise affect the legal position of any signatory company."

Leadership groups have also settled for laws which were not intended to stop specific harms or weaken—much less dismantle—the harm-doers (for example, the Securities and Exchange Acts and the Toxic Substances Control Act, which are basically permitting and disclosure laws).

Corporations and corporate power are in the way of our nation achieving equal protection of the laws and justice for all people. They are preventing changes which we know in our hearts to be essential. So, We the People need to understand and reconsider the privileges and immunities we have allowed corporate legal fictions to wield against us.

The time is right for rethinking corporations, rethinking democracy and rethinking citizen-organizing. We can help one another envision alternatives to giant corporations, and convince ourselves that we can build a citizens' movement strong enough to end corporate rule.

This is what over a dozen "Rethinking the Corporation, Rethinking Democracy" meetings have been about—sovereign people gathering to break free from a century of corporate colonization of our minds; to raise our hopes, refashion our language, review the past, study the present, and choose new tactics . . . in order to shape our futures.

Ambitious? Perhaps. Unrealistic? No, logical and commensurate. ◼

## NOTES

[1] Easterbrook and Fischel 1991, p. 3.

[2] *Ibid.*, p. 14.

[3] *Ibid.*, p. 39.

[4] Lloyd 1894.

[5] Interstate Commerce Act of 1887 established the first federal regulatory agency, the Interstate Commerce Commission. See "Sheep in Wolf's Clothing" in this volume.

[6] Sherman Anti-Trust Act of 1890 established antitrust laws and regulations. *—Ed.*

[7] National Industrial Recovery Act of 1939, part of the New Deal program established under President Franklin Roosevelt. *—Ed.*

[8] Also known as the Full Employment and Balanced Growth Act of 1978. *—Ed.*

[9] Goodwyn 1978.

# CONSUMPTION, CIVIL ACTION, AND CORPORATE POWER

## LESSONS FROM THE PAST, STRATEGIES FOR THE FUTURE

*by Ward Morehouse*

S IMON ZADEK AND Franck Amalric in their essay, "Consumer Works!" argue that consumption-based civil activism can be one of the "transforming drivers" in the struggle to move the world onto a more sustainable path of development. They qualify this proposition with the words "at least in part." It is hard to disagree with their proposition so qualified. The key question then becomes how significant is that part attributable to consumption-based civil activism. Before turning to that critical question, it is necessary to understand some of the startling changes that have been occurring in the global political economy, and which have substantial impact on patterns of global consumption.

The picture that emerges is one of largely unmitigated bad news if the ultimate and overriding goal is to create a more environmentally and socially sustainable future. What has been happening in recent decades has been an accelerating drive toward creating a global consumer culture through the increasing concentration of wealth and power in giant corporations, larger than most nation states.[1]

## THE ROLE OF CORPORATIONS

The annual revenues of the 500 largest corporations in the world—the "Global 500"—are some $10 trillion, around twice the size of the gross domestic product of the United States, the biggest economy in the world. In a single year, 1994, the Global 500 revenues increased by 9 percent, and profits soared by a colossal 62 percent. The Global 500 in that same year eliminated 262,000 jobs.[2] Even more striking is the startling rate of capital accumulation among the top 200 global corporations. "The velocity of transnationalisation of capital as measured as a share of world GDP," writes Frederic Clairmont, "is stunning: from 17 percent in the mid-1960s to 24 percent in 1982 and over 32 percent in 1995."[3]

The drive to create a global consumer culture, and its impact on our increasingly stressed biosphere, have been well documented in a number of recent books.[4] Given the enormous concentration of wealth and power in the boardrooms of giant corporations, and their determined effort to lock us all into unsustainable patterns of consumption, resistance on a global scale has been largely incommensurate.

---

©1998 by Ward Morehouse. Excerpted from a paper published in *Development*, a journal of the Society for International Development.

## CIVIL ACTIVISM AND THE WATCHDOG ROLE

Zadek and Amalric suggest that civil activism may have played a not unimportant "watchdog role" in instances involving sweatshop labor by The Gap and Nike corporations; and environmental destruction and violations of the human rights of indigenous peoples by the British Petroleum Corporation in Colombia, and Shell Corporation in Nigeria. Since the thrust of their essay is to link consumption with civil action, I assume they have in mind boycotts in one form or another. While the threat of a consumer backlash—stimulated by unfavorable publicity—may have played some role in these cases, other strategies not necessarily linked to consumption have also been involved (for example, litigation in the case of British Petroleum and Shell, and governmentally sanctioned codes of conduct with monitoring—if not enforcement—mechanisms). But there seems to me to be little evidence, so far at least, of any "transforming" impact on these corporations.

Let us look at two other examples with a longer time horizon to illustrate a countervailing proposition—namely, that attempts to affect corporate behavior by making it less "unsustainable" (however that may be defined) are likely to be transitory in impact unless they diminish the structures of power that sustain these corporations.

## MAKING CORPORATE BEHAVIOR SUSTAINABLE?

Consider what happened after the Union Carbide Corporation caused the worst industrial disaster in history when its pesticide plant gassed the sleeping city of Bhopal in India, killing 10 to 20 thousand (we shall never know the exact number), and injuring hundreds of thousands more. After the disaster Carbide's management recognized that it was vulnerable to boycotts of the corporation's consumer products and, as one element in their response to this massive human tragedy, divested the corporation of its consumer products. This was done ostensibly as part of the Carbide management's defense against a hostile takeover bid by another chemical company. However, there is little doubt in the minds of those of us who have been supporting the struggle for justice by the Bhopal victims, that insulating the corporation from a possible consumer backlash over Bhopal was also a critical determinant in this divestment action. By the time these divestments were effected, Union Carbide Corporation announced to the world that it had become an "industrial company," meaning that it sold goods and services only to other industrial companies, which in effect screened Carbide from consumption-based civil activism.[5]

Of course, a divestment strategy as a means of insulating a corporation from consumption-based civil action is not equally available to all large corporations. But as long as corporations of this size are essentially sovereign entities, capable of transforming themselves into whatever form their management decides, they have the potential for defusing this type of civil action.

Or consider the case of Nestlé S.A. Corporation[6] and its infant formula products. During the early 1980s a worldwide campaign was mounted to prohibit Nestlé and other manufacturers of infant formula from marketing their products in an aggressive and deceptive manner in Third World countries. One of the seemingly great triumphs of consumer-based civil activism was the adoption of a code for marketing infant formula in developing countries by the World Health Organization, and its acceptance by Nestlé.

But what happened subsequently surely must have been discouraging to those who led this worldwide campaign. The Nestlé's S.A. Corporation "discovered" loopholes in the "code of conduct" large enough for them to resume the previously used deceptive marketing practices. Indeed, the Nestlé S.A. Corporation's actions had become so blatant that UNICEF felt compelled to initiate a "baby-friendly hospital initiative" to counter this behavior. The UNICEF initiative advocated that Third World countries adopt legislation prohibiting such marketing of infant formula, and establish public and professional education measures aimed at assuring effective implementation of such legislation.[7]

## LESSONS TO CONSIDER

The lesson which emerges from these and other similar examples is that consumption-based civil actions are not likely to become "transforming drivers" unless they address the roots of corporate power, and in some fundamental way alter the distribution of political and economic power in today's world.

Since corporations can continue to rule the world only as long as they are able to sell their goods and services, it seems entirely plausible, in theory, to argue that consumer-based civil actions could be "transforming drivers" in moving the world toward a more sustainable path of devel-opment. After all, we are, all of us as consumers, complicit in maintaining corporate dominance of the global political economy. If we would all simultaneously stop buying the products of a given corporation, we would put it out of business. The frequency with which consumer boycotts occur—only one form of consumer-based civil activism, to be sure, but a widely used form—is reflected in the pages of the U.S.-based publication *Boycott Quarterly*. It lists dozens, if not hundreds, of consumer boycotts in progress in any given moment. But few of them appear to achieve any "transforming effect" on their proclaimed targets. So, at least this form of consumption-based civil action remains attractive in theory, but extremely difficult in practice.

Nonetheless, ending corporate rule will need to reach well beyond consumption-based civil activism, even though such activism can certainly play a significant role. The largest corporations in the world today are simply too big to be subject to the meaningful democratic control which, I would argue, is essential to building a more just and sustainable social order. Any realistic strategy to achieve this goal must come to grips with the need for dismantling these global giants. ∎

---

## NOTES

[1] A comparison was made of the gross revenues of those corporations identified in "Fortune's Global 500: The World's Largest Corporations" published by *Fortune Magazine*, and the gross domestic product figures (GDP) of the nations of the world as published in the annual "World Development Report" by the World Bank. Corporations now comprise 50 of the 100 largest economies in the world.

[2] Clairmont 1996.

[3] Clairmont 1997.

[4] See Barnet and Cavanagh 1994, Korten 1995, Martin and Schumann 1997, and Karliner 1997.

[5] The struggle against the Union Carbide Corporation is described in Morehouse "And Not to Yield: The Long Struggle Against Union Carbide" 1997. See "Unfinished Business: Bhopal Ten Years After" in this volume.

[6] The "S.A." is a French-language acronym for "Société Anonyme," translated to English as "anonymous society." Consider this definition of the corporate form. —*Ed.*

[7] This information comes from remarks made by Leah Margulies at the "National Lawyers Guild Convention" (October 18, 1997). She played a leading role in the infant formula campaign and in UNICEF's baby friendly hospital initiative.

# CORPORATIONS MUST NOT SUPPLANT "WE THE PEOPLE"

*by Richard L. Grossman*

---

TALK OF CAMPAIGN finance has long been in the air. President Clinton and those rabid freshmen Republican congressmen—along with many others across the political spectrum—have been insisting they really and truly want to get big money out of elections. Impatient citizens in Maine and California have gathered enough signatures to place ballot measures before the voters next November, measures that attempt to limit campaign contributions.

It is healthy that so many are intent on fixing up this important part of our democratic process. But I believe the debate and the remedies so far have shied away from asking this basic question: Why should we, the sovereign people, permit giant corporations to contribute *any* money to candidates or referenda?

Corporations, after all, are not flesh and blood. Corporations are legal fictions, not included in "We The People," and not even mentioned in the federal Constitution. Corporations are chartered to conduct business, not to be political organizations. And a primary purpose of today's corporate form is to erect a legal shield between a corporate decision-maker and the people.

Nonetheless, the U.S. Supreme Court has decreed that corporations are artificial persons, with First Amendment—that is, free speech—rights. In *Buckley v. Valeo* (1976), a majority of the justices declared corporate cash a form of "free speech." Two years later, in *First National Bank v. Bellotti*, Justice Lewis Powell wrote that corporate spending to influence votes during a referendum campaign "is the type of speech indispensable to decision-making in a democracy, and this is no less true because the speech comes from a corporation rather than an individual."[1]

Because corporate fictions are now regarded under law as persons, their executives are free to use their corporations' power—and their stockholders' money—to further their own personal and political goals. Several Supreme Court justices in a number of cases have objected to this point of view, and their thoughts are instructive.

For example, Justices Byron White, William Brennan and Thurgood Marshall, dissenting in the *Bellotti* case, wrote:

> Corporations are artificial entities created by law for the purpose of furthering certain economic ends . . . It has long been recognized . . . that the special status of corporations has placed them in a position to control vast amounts of economic power which may . . . dominate not only the economy but also the very heart of our democracy, the election process . . . The State need not permit its own creation to consume it.

---

In a dissent from another Supreme Court majority opinion in 1986 expanding corporations' rights to interfere in elections, *Pacific Gas & Electric Co. v. Public Utilities Commission*, Chief Justice William Rehnquist wrote:

> To ascribe such artificial entities [corporations] an "intellect" or "mind" for freedom of conscience purposes is to confuse metaphor with reality.

Justice Brennan, in *Federal Election Committee v. Massachusetts Citizens For Life, Inc.*, wrote in 1986 that:

> Direct corporate spending on political activity raises the prospect that resources amassed in the economic marketplace may be used to provide an unfair advantage in the political marketplace . . . The resources in the treasury of a business corporation . . . are not an indication of popular support for the corporation's political ideas. The availability of these resources may make a corporation a formidable political presence, even though the power of the corporation may be no reflection of the power of its ideas.

Often, logical and rational dissents on the high court have eventually become the law of the land. I, for one, believe that in the not-too-distant future, the American people will insist that corporations must not be granted the rights of people, and that corporations will be barred from contributing any money whatsoever to candidates, to political parties, or on behalf of initiatives and referenda.

But that will only be a step toward claiming our democracy. We will also need to get corporations out of our city councils, our state houses, our Congress and our schools. This is because giant corporations—often global in reach—are awash in money, and have learned to use this money to flood us with misinformation, to distort basic values, and to shape public debate as their unelected executives see fit.

Between 1980 and 1992, the 500 largest U.S. industrial corporations more than doubled their assets, from $1.8 trillion to $2.57 trillion,[2] while shedding over 5 million jobs. The *Wall Street Journal* proclaimed that the first quarter of 1995 brought "the highest level of corporate profitability in the post-war era, and probably since the latter stages of the Bronze Age."[3]

And the rest of 1995 saw the money continue to roll in—enough to pay corporate CEOs an average compensation package of more than $3.5 million.

With over $100 billion spent in direct advertising each year (subsidized by the rest of us, given that corporate advertising is tax-deductible), our giant corporations can shape an awful lot of minds.

Increasingly, people are realizing that corporate wealth, in concert with corporate control over jobs and the economy, allows a relative handful of corporate executives in a few hundred giant corporations to promote some ideas while undermining others, to solidify certain values while neglecting or even ridiculing others.

With their ubiquitous lobbyists (also paid with tax-deductible money), direct access to elected officials, and ownership of radio, television, newspapers and magazines, corporations influence (and even write) our local, state and federal laws.

Corporations have been acting like We the People, exercising the political rights of flesh and blood citizens. The Program on Corporations, Law and Democracy has been convening meetings around the country at which people have been "Rethinking the Corporation, Rethinking Democracy." People have begun researching the corporate histories of their states, and asking why our politicians and our courts have granted so many rights and powers to legal fictions. We are finding that when people discover how earlier generations of Americans had forbidden corporations to interfere in our elections and our lawmaking, they are no longer content merely with placing a ceiling on campaign contributions.

It is not enough to get big money out of politics. Rather, We the People—the flesh and blood self-governing people in the tradition of those who came together to form a more perfect union—must now remove corporations entirely from our elections, our lawmaking, and from public education.

To accomplish this, we must challenge the absurd notion decreed by the United States Supreme Court in 1886[4] that corporations have the constitutional right to use their wealth, power and propaganda to overwhelm the sovereign people, and prevent the flowering of our democracy. ∎

## Notes

[1] This ruling legalized "advertorials." Corporations use them to influence public opinion and public policy, and to legitimate corporate "citizenship." —*Ed.*

[2] Statistical Abstract of the United States 1994, Table 870.

[3] Lowenstein 1995.

[4] *Santa Clara v. Southern Pacific Railroad Co.*

# Why We Research Corporate Law

*by Jane Anne Morris*

---

## Introduction

THIS PUBLICATION IS about how to use the dusty tomes in a law library to reconstruct part of the story of how corporations came to run this country.

This reconstruction will not be a rehash of tales of robber barons, swindlers, and the usual roster of ruthless greed mongers. It will be more like hearing about Adam and Eve, Isaac Newton, or apple pie—but from the apple's point of view.

The story you are researching is the story of the dismantling of democracy by corporations. Environmental lawyers don't know this story because they are busy with administrative law, chasing parts per million back and forth between the regulatory agencies and the courts. Corporate lawyers don't know this story because they work with current corporation law to increase profits further, and tighten corporations' already vise-like grip on the political process. Activists up to their eyeballs in crises find themselves rushing around trying to do what needs to be done, leaving little time to explore why we limit our activism to arenas defined and designed by the corporate opposition.

Your efforts to reconstitute the story of the dismantling of democracy will be easier if you know what you're looking for, and have some idea of how to use a law library. This guide provides some of both.

It is intended to be used in conjunction with other materials from the Program on Corporations, Law and Democracy. Taken together, they represent an effort to revitalize a perspective on the history of corporations in the U.S. that will help guide your research.

When people say that corporations are running the country (and the world), they mean that corporations have used their power to take over the role of governing that in a democracy belongs to the people.

But much current activism involves efforts to adjust corporate behavior without having to reduce corporate power. Adding a chemical to a list, taking a bird off a list, writing more letters to the Forest Service, putting a labor representative on a task force, or asking a corporation to employ more minorities in its quest to plunder the planet and enslave its inhabitants while enriching the fortunes of a few—will not alter the dominant governance role of corporations.

Even if we had time to address each harm one at a time, we would be no closer to having a democracy because we would still not be in control.

---

The free flow of information and the ferment of public debate are prerequisites for democratic self-governance. Self-governing people do not dump toxic chemicals into their water supply. They do not destroy the resources that their future depends on. They do not blame this or that minority for conditions arising from and sustaining the greed of a few. Corporations do all of these things and more.

If We the People are to live in a sane and just world, we must do more than slow or stop particular corporate harms. We must assume the power of governance that, in the United States, corporations have usurped over the last century and a half.

The story of how corporations accomplished this usurpation has been hidden but not obliterated. It lives in the traditions of Native Americans, in the songs of labor struggles, and in the lore of immigrant families. Fragments are scattered among footnotes in history books. Much of it is outlined in black and white in the constitutions, laws, and court cases that fill the shelves of law libraries.

Most people who use law libraries today do so in order to preserve, defend, and expand corporate "rights," corporate property, and corporate profits. Most current legal documents reflect the world view that it is "natural" that corporate "persons" have constitutional rights, that they play a governance role, and that they can and do make or break whole economies and topple governments.

But fifty years ago opinion wasn't nearly so harmonious. A century ago there was still real debate. And before that, the corporate view was a decidedly minority opinion.

For instance, the founding fathers of this nation deserve "Hall of Shame" membership for failing to recognize Native Americans, blacks, women, and unpropertied white males as possessing the rights of natural persons and citizens. But to their credit, it never occurred to the framers of the Constitution that corporations should have the right to due process and equal protection, or First Amendment rights, such rights belonging exclusively to "natural" (i.e., human) persons and having no sensible application to the legal fiction that is the corporation.

Similarly, it was once taken for granted that corporations exist only at the pleasure of the people, that their purpose is to fulfill a public need, and that if they exceed their specific purpose, or fail to adequately perform it, they are to be banished or dissolved.

That these ideas seem so shocking today only underlines how much ideological authority we have ceded to corporations.

In your research you will uncover laws that defined corporations as subordinate entities with limited powers, always subject to further amendment to better fit the public interest. Then you will see how corporations responded.

Over a period of many generations, corporate lawyers in drawing rooms, cloak rooms and court rooms, worked over our imperfect but promising democracy clause by clause. In all too many instances, when a law got in the way of corporate power, the corporations either got rid of it, weakened it, prevented it from being enforced, got it declared unconstitutional, or influenced the judicial interpretation of it so as to render it inconsequential.

While the rights of most human persons were denied or diminished, corporations acquired by sleight-of-hand the constitutional rights of "natural" persons. These newly anointed corporate "persons" claimed and gained constitutional protections for their "property," which was first construed to be something tangible, expanded to include the intangible, and now includes the imaginary.

And, just as the rights of "corporate" persons grew at the expense of the rights of "natural" persons, they grew also at the expense of the rights of "natural" persons who happened to have "jobs." Workers' rights to freedom of speech and of assembly, freedom of association, due process, and equal protection before the law, among others, were twisted and suppressed as corporations wrote the laws that defined not only themselves, but the labor "opposition."

Corporations, once strictly defined by people acting through their legislatures, have since the late nineteenth century been defining themselves and redefining us. They write the laws and shape the government that supposedly "regulates" them. Corporations essentially define our economy, our society, our jobs, our educational system, and our leisure time. Our state legislatures once defined corporations as subordinate entities, yet now We the People find every aspect of our lives subordinated to corporate "needs."

Corporation representatives worked a phrase at a time to deconstruct legal doctrines that protected persons, and transmute them through the alchemy of power into doctrines to protect and empower corporations.

In so doing they left a trail of tears in the fabric of democracy. The pattern of the violence they did to the democratic process is like a map that we can read to understand the nature of the damage, and then either work to repair it, or replace it with a more democratic weave.

What you can do in a law library is to trace this process in the context of your own state's history. ∎

# RECOVERING HISTORY

By what authority do corporations put pig genes in salmon; abandon Superfund sites; deny employees freedom of speech and assembly, and protection against unreasonable search and seizure; nullify laws passed by We the People's elected representatives?

From studying popular movements of the past we discover that men of property wrote their laws to protect themselves from *too much democracy*. We discover that large numbers of people organized to stop judges from endowing property with constitutional powers, and mobilized to fulfill the grand ideals of the American Revolution: "All political power is vested in and derived from the people. All government of right originates with the people, is founded upon their will only, and is instituted solely for the good of the whole."*

* Section I of the Montana state constitution of 1972.

# THE WORKING CLASS HISTORY TEST

*by Peter Kellman*

THE DOMINANT HISTORY taught in the United States today reinforces the notion that from 1776 to the present "We the People" have formed our own government, and this government has operated to protect and promote the interests of most of the people most of the time. Slavery and the denial of the right to vote for women are pointed to as exceptions that have been rectified through constitutional amendments.

Most working people today believe that the country is not run by We the People but by a small group of the very rich and powerful who manage large corporations. Many of us have in the back of our minds an image of this country, based on the history we have been taught, where the government was run to protect and promote the interests of most of the people. Therefore our vision of a better future is based on getting back to a time when things were better. The problem is that from its inception the United States government and economy have been run by and for the very wealthy.

If we are to build a society where the government is run to protect and promote the interests of We the People, we need to know the history of the elite who have always run this country, and the history of the working class that built it. The following test was put together to bring out some of the history that we have been denied. It is this denied history that should form the image of the past we carry around with us because we need to have a truthful understanding of the past to create a vision of the future.

We need to be clear about what it is we want to go back to. Do we want to go back to the vision of President James Madison—a slave owner and "Master Builder of the Constitution"—or to the vision of the people who built the early Abolition, Suffrage, and Labor Movements? Do we want to go back to the vision of President Hayes—who used Federal troops to break strikes, promote corporate interests and end Reconstruction—or to the Knights of Labor who demanded equal pay for equal work, and voting rights for all citizens regardless of race or gender?[1]

## THE TEST

Try the test. Answers at the end.

1. It is easy for citizens of the United States to form a corporation but very hard to form a union. Name three countries where it is as easy for workers to form a union as it is in the United States for investors to form a corporation.

2. In 1770, what percentage of the colonial population lived in slavery?

3. At the time of the War of Independence, what percentage of the people who made up the colonies of Pennsylvania, Maryland and Virginia were or had been indentured servants?

4. Who was the richest man in America at the time of the Revolution?

5. What percentage of We the People couldn't vote in 1776?

6. Who said, "The people who own the country ought to govern it."

7. What great American document was written behind closed doors in a meeting held in 1787, the minutes of which were only made public 53 years later?

8. What great American "told a British visitor shortly after the American Revolution that he could make $257 on every Negro in a year, and spend only $12 or $13 on his keep."

9. What were the demands of the Labor Movement in 1830?

10. The Fourteenth Amendment to the Constitution was ratified after the Civil War in 1868 to extend due process and equal protection of the law to African Americans. In the first 50 years after its adoption what percentage of the cases brought under it were on behalf of African Americans, and what percentage of the cases were brought on behalf of corporations?

11. The Supreme Court ruled in 1872 that women do not have the right to vote under the Fourteenth Amendment. What year did the Supreme Court rule "Corporations are persons within the meaning of the Fourteenth Amendment

to the Constitution of the United States"?

12. How can five people amend the Constitution?

13. Whose election to the presidency of the United States was determined by a special commission, controlled by the CEO of the Pennsylvania Railroad, made up of Supreme Court justices and members of Congress? In what year did that president pull the last of the Federal troops from the south ending Reconstruction and use those troops to put down the first national labor strike in the United States in which over 100 strikers were killed?

14. In 1886 the largest labor organization in the United States was the Knights of Labor. What issues did they advocate and fight for?

15. When was the labor movement politically powerful enough to prevent the Governor of Michigan and the president of the United States from sending troops to break up a strike in which workers were occupying corporate property?

16. Which president (John Kennedy, Franklin Roosevelt or Herbert Hoover) signed into law an act which included the following: it is necessary that he have full freedom of association, self-organization, and designation of representatives of his own choosing; to negotiate the terms and conditions of his employment; and that he shall be free from the interference, restraint, or coercion of employers of labor, or their agents, in the designation of such representatives or in self-organization or in other concerted activities for the purpose of collective bargaining or other mutual aid or protection.

17. In many countries workers have benefits like paid maternity leave, maximum hours of work, health care, paid holidays and vacations—defined by law. What do workers in these countries have that they don't have in the United States?

## ANSWERS

1. Sweden, Germany, Italy, Japan, Belgium, Ireland, and more.

2. 20%

3. 75%

4. According to historian Charles Beard in his book *An Economic Interpretation of the Constitution of the United States*, George "Washington of Virginia, was probably the richest man in the United States in his time, and his financial ability was not surpassed among his countrymen anywhere."

5. 75%

6. John Jay, first president of the Continental Congress and first chief justice of the Supreme Court.

7. The Constitution.

8. "Master Builder of the Constitution" and fourth president of the United States, James Madison.

9. The 10 hour day and public education.

10. African Americans 0.5% (one-half of one-percent), corporations 50%. Also of the 307 Fourteenth Amendment cases brought before the U.S. Supreme Court between 1890 and 1910, 19 dealt with the rights of African Americans and 288 dealt with corporations.

11. 1886

12. They become U.S. Supreme Court Justices.

13. Rutherford B. Hayes, 1877.

14. They advocated the creation of producer, consumer and distributive cooperatives; the prohibition of child labor; equal pay for equal work between the sexes and races; universal suffrage; the eight-hour day. And they opposed the concentration of wealth and power in the hands of a few, reasoning that as long as a few people controlled most of the wealth they would use their economic power politically to prevent the creation of a real democracy.

15. 1936-37

16. Norris-LaGuardia Act of 1932 was passed by Congress and signed into law by Herbert Hoover.

17. Strong working class political parties. ■

---

## NOTES

[1] Still, most "traditional" histories show events punctuated not with the actions of the ordinary but with the acts of the powerful: landed, privileged, and in control. One noted exception is Howard Zinn's book *A People's History of the United States: 1492 to Present.* —Ed.

# CITIZENS OVER CORPORATIONS
## A BRIEF HISTORY OF DEMOCRACY IN OHIO

*by Greg Coleridge*

HAVE CORPORATIONS BECOME too powerful? This is a relevant question during these times of rapid increase of corporate consolidations, movement of factories and money, lobbying and PAC contributions, tax breaks, and deregulation; of corporate internal regulation of pollution, involvement in health care, prisons, and education, and legal free speech and intellectual property protections.

With each passing day, corporations have a greater say in our lives: from the food we eat, to the products we buy, the health care we receive, the news we see, the ideas we think, the economic rules we follow, the entertainment we enjoy, the education we acquire, the laws we enact, the work we do, the politicians we elect, the policies we have, and the natural world we have left.

"Corporatization" of our society is not inevitable or irreversible. Corporations were not supposed to reign. The early history of the United States and of Ohio is of citizens clearly defining and closely controlling corporate behavior. It is a history that is outlined in the publication *Citizens over Corporations: A Brief History of Democracy in Ohio and Challenges to Freedom in the Future*, produced by the Ohio Committee on Corporations, Law and Democracy.

The American Revolution was not a revolution simply against a tax on tea or the King of England. It was also a revolution against the British "crown" corporations that ran the colonies—like the Massachusetts Bay Company, Maryland Company, Virginia Company and Carolina Company.

Following independence, the colonists transformed these corporations into constitutionalized states with elected representatives. From their experiences, the colonists knew to keep corporations on a short leash. Therefore, they entrusted the essential task of corporate control to the one group who was closest to the people—state legislators.

When Ohio became a state in 1803, the state legislature acting on behalf of the public used their power to create and define corporations. Early Ohio acts creating corporations one at a time stipulated rigid conditions. These privileges, not rights, included:

• Limited duration of charter or certificate of incorporation.

• Limitation on amount of land ownership.

• Limitation of amount of capitalization, or total investment of owners.

• Limitations of charter for a specific purpose (to amend its charter, a new corporation had to be formed).

©1999 by Greg Coleridge. This article summarizes the themes presented in the 56 page booklet titled *Citizens over Corporations*, published by the Ohio Committee on Corporations, Law and Democracy. That booklet is available for $3.50 (payable to "AFSC") from: The Ohio Committee on Corporations, Law & Democracy, 513 W. Exchange St., Akron, OH 44302.

And in keeping with a corporation's subordinate position to the state, the state reserved the right to amend the charters or to revoke them, and prohibited corporations from engaging in political activities.

In many instances, after a corporation built a turnpike and once the corporation recovered its costs and a fair profit, the charter or certificate of incorporation was dissolved and the turnpike became a public road. In other instances regarding turnpikes, the charter exempted the poor, voters, and church-goers from tolls.

A second way people exerted power and control over corporations through the Ohio legislature was by repealing all or a portion of a corporate charter of corporations which violated terms of their incorporation. From 1839-1849 the legislature effectively dissolved several enterprises. Turnpike corporations and banks were the most common targets; others included silk and insurance corporations.

In an 1842 act to repeal the charter of the German Bank of Wooster (40 Ohio Law 18), the state legislature stated:

> It shall be the duty of the court of common pleas . . . or any judge of the supreme court . . . to restrain said bank, its officers, agents and servants or assignees, from exercising any corporate rights, privileges, and franchises whatever . . . and force the bank commissioners to close the bank and deliver full possession of the banking house, keys, books, papers, lands, tenements, goods, chattels, moneys, property and effects of said bank, of every kind and description whatever . . .

From the 1830s through the 1912 Constitutional Convention, the Ohio Supreme Court and various lower courts ruled on hundreds of cases affirming the sovereign rights of people and their elected representatives to define corporations and their actions. Cases ranged from sweeping decisions on corporations in general to more specific decisions on an entire category of corporations (like railroads), and to very specific decisions addressing a particular corporation. Many decisions reinforced previously passed state laws or provisions of state constitutions. In *The state ex rel. Kohler v. Cincinnati W. & B. R. Co.*, the Ohio Supreme Court stated:

> The corporation has received vitality from the state; it continues during its existence to be the creature of the state; must live subservient to its laws, and has such powers and franchises as those laws have bestowed upon it, and none others. As the state was not bound to create it in the first place, it is not bound to maintain it after having done so, if it violates the laws or public policy of the state, or misuses its franchises to oppress the citizens thereof.

State courts imposed penalties for abuse or misuse of the corporate charter that were often more severe than a simple plea bargain or fine. They included ousting the corporation of its claimed privileges to perform certain actions. The most severe penalty, common from the mid-1800s through the 1920s, was to revoke the corporate charter and dissolve the corporation itself. The legal device used to achieve these penalties was a *quo warranto* (literally, "by what authority") proceeding.

The most well-known *quo warranto* case in Ohio history, *The State ex rel. Attorney General v. Standard Oil Co.*, involved the efforts by two Republican Ohio attorneys general to revoke the corporate charter of the Standard Oil Company, the most powerful U.S. corporation of the time, for forming a trust. In the 1892 argument to revoke its franchise Ohio Attorney General David Watson argued:

> Where a corporation, either directly or indirectly, submits to the domination of an agency unknown to the statute, or identifies itself with and unites in carrying out an agreement whose performance is injurious to the public, it thereby offends against the law of its creation and forfeits all right to its franchises, and judgment of ouster should be entered against it.

In a 1900 ruling to dissolve a dairy company, *State ex rel. Monnett v. Captial City Dairy Co.*, the Ohio Supreme Court said:

> The time has not yet arrived when the created is greater than the creator, and it still remains the duty of the courts to perform their office in the enforcement of the laws, no matter how ingenious the pretexts for their violation may be, nor the power of the violators in the commercial world. In the present case the acts of the defendant have been persistent, defiant and flagrant, and no other course is left to the court than to enter a judgment of ouster and to appoint trustees to wind up the business of the concern.

Corporations didn't take all this citizen self-governance and revocation business sitting down. Corporations fought back against legislative and judicial charter revocations and limitations, confronting the law at every point. They hired lawyers and created law firms. Corporations rewrote the laws governing their creation. They advocated replacing specific chartering rules with general incorporation laws (as Ohio did in 1842) with minimal reviews, perpetual life spans, limited liabilities, and decreased citizen authority. Judges rede-

fined "corporate profits" as property. The courts declared "corporate contracts" and the "rate of return on investment" as property. Judges and the legislature redefined the "common good" to mean corporate use of people and the earth to maximize production and profit.

In Ohio, laws and court cases favorable to corporations were passed and decided over a period of decades. If corporations couldn't get favorable treatment by the legislature, they focused their energies on the courts where they had a greater chance for success. The following story illustrates an extreme and ironic example of corporate power: corporations successfully revoking the charters of Ohio municipalities.

In 1902 the Ohio Supreme Court ousted, or dissolved, the Board of Control of the City of Cleveland. The people, city and its Board of Control, under the leadership of populist mayor Tom Johnson, sought to establish "three cent fares and universal transfers" for the city's street railways.

The regulations would have limited the power and profits of the street railway franchise owned by the wealthy and powerful corporate industrialist Mark Hanna. Hanna, a Republican, pressured the Republican state administration and Attorney General to file suit challenging the City of Cleveland's authority.

In a highly political decision and the only action like it in the nation, the state supreme court (several members of whom were pressured by Hanna and his friends) ruled against the City. The legal basis for the ruling was that Cleveland's existence, like all Ohio municipalities, was illegal since its charter was created years earlier by the Ohio General Assembly through a separate act (law). The incorporation of all municipalities at the time had been created one at a time by such acts of the General Assembly. Nonetheless, the Ohio Supreme Court ruled that these incorporations were "special" legislation which had been ruled unconstitutional by the 1851 state Constitution. Only "general" acts applying to all types of corporations were permitted under the Constitution.

With all the charters of all the municipalities of Ohio now unconstitutional, the state legislature was forced to meet in a special session in the fall of 1902 to adopt a single municipal code. No longer would some cities have certain powers that others did not have.

Once again, Hanna and other corporate heads exerted their influence. They pushed through a municipal code, still in place today, based on the model of the City of Cincinnati—a city run by one of the most powerful political bosses in the nation, George B. Cox, a Republican.

The "federal plan" of concentrated power and responsibilities, on which the charters of Cleveland and Columbus were based, was replaced by the Cincinnati "board plan" of scattered responsibility. In other words, the strong city structure that had let Mayors like Tom Johnson challenge corporate power was substituted by a weak structure that made it hard to confront corporations directly.

With corporate profits, consolidations, tax breaks and political influence at or near record levels today, it is time to reexamine the fundamental relationship between citizens and corporations. Challenging corporate "rights" is a legitimate and essential task of self-governing people. The time has still not yet arrived when the created is greater than the creator. We Ohioans must learn our history and use it to rethink and reassess our actions today. What is left of our democracy is at stake. ∎

# DOG DAYS AT COMPANY HEADQUARTERS

## BUSINESS ACCOUNTABILITY AND THE CORPORATE CHARTER

*by Richard L. Grossman & Frank T. Adams*

## THE CORPORATE CHARTER

CHARTERS HAVE BEEN used by kings and governments to select who organizes capital, labor, and natural resources, and who creates wealth. In the U.S. the Constitution gives this power to the states. Therefore, we, the people, have the constitutional authority—and a civic obligation—to grant *and* revoke charters.

Few states issue charters with anything more in mind than gathering statistics or taxes. So it is up to us in each state to force every corporation granted a charter in our name to operate in our—and the Earth's—best interest. Or to revoke that corporation's charter.

There is a rich, passionate but deliberately ignored history of U.S. citizens trying to protect themselves against corporations. The privilege of incorporation was widely distrusted in the nineteenth century, and often the subject of anti-charter agitation. As Justice Louis D. Brandeis wrote, "There was a sense of some insidious menace inherent in large aggregations of capital, particularly when held by corporations."

Nonetheless, during the last 150 years, we have been intimidated, snookered or outmaneuvered by our charterees and their apologists in the legislatures, courts and public relations firms. We have permitted corporations to become "persons" under the law. We have let them determine the "social definitions under which their own economic wrongdoing is differentiated from real crime," as one sociologist noted. Corporations invest, divest and destroy behind the cloaks of limited liability and business confidentiality. Like George III, they trace their powers virtually from Divine Right, equating corporate production and profits with our freedom and well-being.

The legal tools available to us, as Yale professor Martin Chirelstein has observed, become "blunt and clumsy" whenever management's "business judgement is placed at issue." Consequently, workplace health and environmental laws are inherently limited from the very moment of their legislative birth. As far back as 1941 the Temporary National Economic Committee, appointed by Congress, understood this when it concluded in its final report and recommendations:

> The principal instrument of concentration of economic power and wealth has been the corporate charter with unlimited power—charters which afforded a detour around every principle of fiduciary responsibility; charters which permitted promoters and managers to use the property of others for their own enrichment and to the detriment of the real owners; charters which made possible the violation of law without personal liability; charters which omitted every safeguard of individual and public welfare which common sense and experience alike have taught are necessary.

Today we need to ask one another if we haven't spent enough time, energy and money niggling with these well-guarded, intentionally-constructed, meticulously insulated corporations. Don't we harm ourselves and the Earth when we let the very real monster of corporate law block our paths? Don't we demean the tradition of active citizenship when we give our rights away? Wouldn't it be liberating and exhilarating to reclaim our civic rights?  ■

# CORPORATE SOCIAL RESPONSIBILITY

## KICK THE HABIT

### *by Jane Anne Morris*

WHAT TO EXPECT NEXT from corporate sponsors of the WTO? There's a well-thumbed page in the corporate playbook, ready to go. Whether or not it works depends on us. The last time there was a scuffle as worrisome as the Seattle demonstrations, Richard Milhous "Tricky Dick" Nixon was in the White House. Nearly everybody else was in the streets.

We were millions, and we demanded freedom, justice, equality, peace, clean air and water, and the right to choose our own hairstyles. We knew the joy of thinking it was all possible.

We also knew the raw fear wrought by the pop of tear gas canisters, the glint of sun on gunmetal, and the meltdown of a peaceable crowd being attacked by the forces of law and order.

But it is only at a distance of a quarter century that I begin to recognize the depths of another fear, just as visceral. As I pore over the writings by and about the corporate elite of that day, a simple fact stares out at me: they were scared witless.

While we wove our hopes into songs, and scrawled our demands onto placards, they spelled out their fears in journal articles and speeches at chambers of commerce.

The corporation was "under attack as never before,"[1] subject to a "tidal wave" of "dissident groups, structured into onslaught vehicles of unrelenting social action,"[2] according to corporate literature. The future looked "grim."[3] Corporations were about to "lose their autonomy, power and influence."[4] Some managers doubted that large corporations would even be "permitted"[5] in the future. The significance of profit margins shrank as the CEO of one of the largest corporations in the U.S. wondered whether "the corporation as we know it . . . will survive into the next century."[6]

For those whose greed commanded the rudder of the ship of state, the sight of people in the streets—and not for shopping, mind you—was terrifying.

What a difference a generation makes. Large corporations have more than survived the tumult of the Nixon era. Today, a tiny fraction of the human population, in its role as corporate managers, has been exceedingly successful in using the legal fiction of the corporation to expand its autonomy, power and influence. How did they accomplish this?

While we huddled in coffeehouses and church basements debating strategy, corporate managers plotted in boardrooms. Their diagnosis unfolded into a plan. From their perspective, a "Great Danger" threatened: government action spurred by public demands. A tried-and-true strategy beckoned:   make a show of voluntarily "Doing Something" and publicize it shamelessly.

This was a strategy with a thousand faces: corporations as socially responsible, corporations as "citizens" with civic duties, corporations as "good neighbors," corporate executives as "trustees" for the public interest, "business leaders" offering voluntary "codes of conduct," and so on.

There were three pillars to the corporate plan:   (1) placate; (2) co-opt; (3) reframe issues so that in the future, people would "demand" something that corporate managers want to "give."

Corporate donations and other forms of "corporate social responsibility" pacified portions of the community by softening the edges of some of the most egregious and most visible corporate harms.   In a quasi-behaviorist twist, they rewarded "good" behavior and disadvantaged "bad" behavior on the part of showcased community and charitable organizations.   But most of all they enabled corporate managers to reshape public "questions" so that the "answers" were to come not from a self-governing people but from "corporate good citizens."

Corporate executives were advised that they "should . . . be able to gauge with some accuracy the degree of social responsiveness that will satisfy the community . . . "[7] They were warned: "If corporations fail to exert considerably more social initiative, they will be com-

pelled to do so . . . ."[8] "The less voluntary social action U.S. companies take, the more it will be imposed by big government."[9] There were fears that public pressure would "compel legislative response."[10] (Heaven forbid that this should ever occur in a democracy.)

The beneficiaries of "corporate social responsibility" were selected for maximum effect. Corporate managers who lent financial support were well aware that they were "ingratiating themselves with recipients, or pacifying a pressuring public.   A corporate gift can be a bribe, paid in return for a gadfly group's promise to keep still and refrain from criticism of corporate policies."[11]

On the other hand, ". . . some business givers have . . . withheld grants from groups identified with causes they consider to be too militant, or unfriendly to corporate interests."[12]

For some, the success of another round of "corporate social responsibility" was a foregone conclusion.   "The social responsibility payoff has been attested to time and again. The most patent cost justification is a simple matter of good stickmanship—sidestepping the penalties of social irresponsibility."[13] The judicious distribution of corporate money "has allowed the managers to become brokers of social power, deciding which programs are supported and which are not."[14]

The language is vivid.      "Bribe." "Ingratiate."    "Satisfy the community." "Payoff."  "Brokers of Social Power."  How much plainer can it get?  In all cases, control was the goal; control not just of groups or movements, but of ideas and debates.

Coupled with brutal suppression, this three-step strategy—placate, co-opt, reframe debate—was used early and often.  It worked after the sixties-seventies wave of public uproar; before that it worked in the 1950s; it worked during the Depression; it worked during the wave of "unrest" immediately after World War I. In the late nineteenth century, an early version of it worked after corporate strategists got a glimpse of the Knights of Labor and the Populists.

The notions of corporate trusteeship, the civic duty of a corporation, corporate citizenship, corporate social responsibility and the corporate social audit—all originated in the desire of corporate managers to thwart unionization, forestall revolt, avoid government action, and above all retain control by shaping public debate.

Each time corporate managers, hiding behind the increasingly powerful shield of the legal fiction of "The Corporation," took another step toward becoming a more powerful "semi-autonomous managerial elite," they cranked up the public relations machinery to boast of The Corporation's deep concern and caring for the community. Increasingly, they doled out goodies—always on their terms. And *in* their terms.

So successfully have these terms become part of our political language that they often go unnoticed. Why is it, for instance, that when a government (using money collected for the public good) aids needy citizens, they're on the dole, a supposed disgrace, but when corporate managers give away other people's money to a soup kitchen, it's philanthropy?

If you doubt that corporate managers and not regular folks define the terms of public debate today, you might ask yourself these questions. Who defines *free trade*? What about *welfare reform*? Or those dubious twins, *tree harvest* and *deer harvest*? Remember *jobs-versus-environment*, a golden oldie that never seems to fade away? These terms, and the terms of the debate, were all brought to us by corporate managers.

Corporate managers are willing and eager to participate in the democratic process, but only if they are in charge of it. When it comes to being subject to it, they balk, and are in fact willing to do anything, anything—even give away a little corporate money—in order to avoid losing control over the way issues are framed, thus becoming subject to the democratic process.

Corporate managers of the seventies warned their comrades that failure to act would have horrific consequences. "The alternatives are not attractive. The likeliest possibility is the wholesale substitution of public for private goals, strategies, and actions . . . "15

The options were clear: either institute the three-point plan, or the country will succumb to . . . (I hope you're sitting down) . . . a people's democracy.

As night follows day, corporate managers experienced great surges of "corporate social responsibility" following each historic episode of social unrest. Such bouts of "corporate good citizenship" are voluntary, calculated, expedient, cheap and temporary. Far from reflecting democratic control, they frustrate it. Meaningless, unenforceable "side agreements" are not concessions to democracy on the part of corporate managers, but concessions to lack of democracy on the part of a not-sovereign people.

So it must be an especially sweet moment for corporate managers looking up from their Courvoisier-glazed snifters—to hear people clamoring for "corporate social responsibility," that strategy-with-a-thousand-faces that has served to solidify the grip of the corporate elite through a century of citizen protests.

With the echoes of "WTO Week in Seattle" still rumbling in our ears, we have another opportunity to firmly reject the "corporate social responsibility" ruse. A small but growing core of people is demanding not goodies or favors or good deeds but real self-governance. They know that receiving goodies from worried corporate managers is the real "dole," while a self-governing people controlling their community's resources in the interest of society as a whole—*that* is democracy. ∎

## NOTES

The author would like to thank Peter Kellman, J.M. Baime, Mary Zepernick and the POCLAD editorial board for comments on earlier versions of this article.

[1] Paluszek 1977, p. 3.

[2] Linowes 1974, p. 14.

[3] *Ibid.*, p. 43.

[4] Richman 1977, pp. 53-54.

[5] Paluszek 1977, p. 18.

[6] *Ibid.*, p. 3.

[7] Linowes 1974, p. 143.

[8] Richman 1977, p. 52.

[9] Linowes 1974, p. 9.

[10] Anshen 1974.

[11] Cohn 1971, p. 18.

[12] *Ibid.*, pp. 15-16.

[13] Linowes 1974, p. 43.

[14] Smith 1975, pp. 31-36.

[15] Anshen 1974.

# Taking Care of Business
## Citizenship and the Charter of Incorporation

*by Richard L. Grossman & Frank T. Adams*

---

Neither the claims of ownership nor those of control can stand against the paramount interests of the community. It remains only for the claims of the community to be put forward with clarity and force.

> \- A. A. Berle & Gardner C. Means
> *The Modern Corporation and Private Property*[1]

CORPORATIONS CAUSE HARM every day. Why do their harms go unchecked? How can they dictate what we produce, how we work, what we eat, drink and breathe? How did a self-governing people let this come to pass?

## A Hostile Takeover

The U.S. Constitution makes no mention of corporations. Yet the history of constitutional law is, as former Supreme Court Justice Felix Frankfurter said, "the history of the impact of the modern corporation upon the American scene."[2]

Today's business corporation is an artificial creation, shielding owners and managers while preserving corporate privilege and existence. Artificial or not, corporations have won more rights under law than people have—rights which government has protected with armed force.

Investment and production decisions that shape our communities and rule our lives are made in boardrooms, regulatory agencies, and courtrooms. Judges and legislators have made it possible for business to keep decisions about money, production, work and ownership beyond the reach of democracy. They have created a corporate system under law.

This is not what many early Americans had in mind.

People were determined to keep investment and production decisions local and democratic. They believed corporations were neither inevitable nor always appropriate. Our history is filled with successful worker-owned enterprises, cooperatives and neighborhood shops, efficient businesses owned by cities and towns. For a long time, even chartered corporations functioned well under sovereign citizen control.

But while they were weakening charter laws, corporate leaders also were manipulating the legal system to take our property rights. "Corporations confronted the law at every point. They hired lawyers and created whole law firms," according to law professor Lawrence M. Friedman. "They bought and sold governments."[3]

In law, property is not merely a piece of land, a house, a bicycle. Property is a bundle

---

of rights; property law determines who uses those rights. As legal scholar Morris Raphael Cohen said, property is "what each of us shall receive from our work, and from the natural resources of the Earth . . . the ownership of land and machinery, with the rights of drawing rent, interest, etc., [which] determine the future distribution of the goods . . ."[4]

Under pressure from industrialists and bankers, a handful of nineteenth century judges gave corporations more rights in property than human beings enjoyed in their persons. Reverend Reverdy Ransom, himself once a slave treated as property, was among the many to object, declaring "that the rights of men are more sacred than the rights of property."[5]

Undeterred by such common sense, judges redefined corporate profits as property. Corporations got courts to assume that huge, wealthy corporations competed on equal terms with neighborhood businesses or with individuals. The courts declared that corporate contracts and the rate of return on investment were property that could not be meddled with by citizens or by their elected representatives.

Within a few decades, judges redefined the common good to mean corporate use of humans and the Earth for maximum production and profit. Workers, cities and towns, states and nature were left with fewer and fewer rights corporations were bound to respect.

Wielding property rights through laws backed by government became an effective, reliable strategy to build and to sustain corporate mastery.

Some citizens reacted to this hostile takeover by organizing to maintain their rights over corporations. Mobilizing their cities and towns, citizens pressured legislators to protect states' economic rights for many decades.

Others turned to the federal government to guarantee worker and consumer justice, to standardize finance and stock issues, to prevent trusts and monopolies, to protect public health and the environment.

The major laws which resulted, creating regulatory and managing agencies, actually give corporations great advantages over citizens. Some, like the National Labor Relations Act and the National Labor Relations Board, intended that the government aid citizens against the corporation.

But these laws and agencies were shaped by corporate leaders, then diminished by judges. They neither prevent harms, nor correct wrongs, nor restore people and places. These regulatory laws were—and remain—reporting and permitting laws, laws to limit competition and to manage destruction.

Congress, betraying its obligation to preserve, protect and defend the U.S. Constitution, has been giving away citizen sovereignty to the EPAs, OSHAs, NLRBs, FTCs, NRCs, SECs, BLMs, RTCs.[6]

Agency administrators act under the assumption that corporations have prerogatives over labor, investment and production. They regard land, air and water as corporations' raw materials, and as lawful places to dump corporate poisons. Business leaders and politicians are given license to equate corporations' private goals with the public interest.

Regulators and regulatory laws treat labor as a cost and employees as disposable. They equate efficiency and freedom with maximum resource extraction, maximum production, and maximum profits. They shift what had been the corporate burden to "prove no harm" onto the citizen, who must prove harm.

Corporations chartered by our states are the cause of political, economic, and ecological injury around the globe. Little wonder so many citizens lament today, as Thomas Paine did two hundred years ago:

> Beneath the shade of our own vines are we
> attacked; in our own house, and on our
> own lands, is the violence committed
> against us.[7]

## A HIDDEN HISTORY

For one hundred years after the American Revolution, citizens and legislators fashioned the nation's economy by directing the chartering process.

The laborers, small farmers, traders, artisans, seamstresses, mechanics and landed gentry—who sent King George III packing—feared corporations. As pamphleteer Thomas Earle wrote:

> Chartered privileges are a burthen, under
> which the people of Britain, and other
> European nations, groan in misery.[8]

They knew that English kings chartered the East India Company, the Hudson's Bay Company and many American colonies in order to control property and commerce. Kings appointed governors and judges; dispatched soldiers; dictated taxes, investments, production, labor, and markets. The royal charter creating Maryland, for example, required that the colony's exports be shipped to or through England.

Having thrown off English rule, the revolutionaries did not give governors, judges or generals the authority to charter corporations. Citizens made certain that legislators issued charters, one at a time and for a limited number of years. They kept a tight hold on corporations by spelling out rules each business had to follow, by holding business owners

liable for harms or injuries, and by revoking charters.

Side by side with these legislative controls, they experimented with various forms of enterprise and finance. Artisans and mechanics owned and managed diverse businesses. Farmers and millers organized profitable cooperatives, shoemakers created unincorporated business associations. Joint-stock companies were formed.

The idea of limited partnerships was imported from France. Land companies used various and complex arrangements, and were not incorporated. None of these enterprises had the powers of today's corporations.

Towns routinely promoted agriculture and manufacture. They subsidized farmers, public warehouses and municipal markets, protected watersheds and discouraged over-planting. State legislatures issued not-for-profit charters to establish universities, libraries, firehouses, churches, charitable associations, along with new towns.

Legislatures also chartered profit-making corporations to build turnpikes, canals and bridges. By the beginning of the 1800s only some two hundred such charters had been granted. Even this handful issued for necessary public works raised many fears.

Some citizens argued that under the Constitution no business could be granted special privileges. Others worried that once incorporators amassed wealth, they would control jobs and production, buy the newspapers, dominate elections and the courts. Craft and industrial workers feared absentee corporate owners would turn them into "a commodity being as much an article of commerce as woolens, cotton, or yarn."[9]

Because of widespread public opposition, early legislators granted very few charters, and only after long, hard debate. Legislators usually denied charters to would-be incorporators when communities opposed their prospective business project.

Citizens shared the belief that granting charters was their exclusive right. Moreover, as the Supreme Court of Virginia reasoned in 1809:

> [If the applicants'] . . . object is merely private or selfish; if it is detrimental to, or not promotive of, the public good, they have no adequate claim upon the legislature for the privileges.[10]

Citizens governed corporations by detailing rules and operating conditions not just in the charters but also in state constitutions and in state laws. Incorporated businesses were prohibited from taking any action which legislators did not specifically allow.

States limited corporate charters to a set number of years. Maryland legislators restricted manufacturing charters to forty years, mining charters to fifty, and most others to thirty years. Pennsylvania limited manufacturing charters to twenty years. Unless a legislature renewed an expiring charter, the corporation was dissolved and its assets were divided among shareholders.

Citizen authority clauses dictated rules for issuing stock, for shareholder voting, for obtaining corporate information, for paying dividends and keeping records. They limited capitalization, debts, land holdings, and sometimes profits. They required a company's accounting books to be turned over to a legislature upon request.

The power of large shareholders was limited by scaled voting, so that large and small investors had equal voting rights. Interlocking directorates were outlawed. Shareholders had the right to remove directors at will.

Sometimes the rates which railroad, turnpike and bridge corporations could charge were set by legislators. Some legislatures required incorporators to be state citizens. Other legislatures bought corporate stock in order to stay closely engaged in a firm's operations.

Early in the nineteenth century, the New Jersey legislature declared its right to take over ownership and control of corporate properties. Pennsylvania established a fund from corporate profits which was used to buy private utilities to make them public. Many states followed suit.

Turnpike charters frequently exempted the poor, farmers, or worshippers from paying tolls. In Massachusetts the Turnpike Corporation Act of 1805 authorized the legislature to dissolve turnpike corporations when their receipts equaled the cost of construction plus 12 percent; then the road became public. In New York, turnpike gates were ". . . subject to be thrown open, and the company indicted and fined, if the road is not made and kept easy and safe for public use."[11]

Citizens kept banks on particularly short leashes. Their charters were limited from three to ten years. Banks had to get legislative approval to increase their capital stock, or to merge. Some state laws required banks to make loans for local manufacturing, fishing, agriculture enterprises, and to the states themselves. Banks were forbidden to engage in trade.

Private banking corporations were banned altogether by the Indiana constitution in 1816, and by the Illinois constitution in 1818. People did not want business owners hidden behind legal shields, but in clear sight. That is what they got. As the Pennsylvania legislature stated in 1834:

> A corporation in law is just what the
> incorporating act makes it. It is the crea-
> ture of the law and may be moulded to
> any shape or for any purpose that the
> Legislature may deem most conducive for
> the general good.[12]

In Europe charters protected directors and stockholders from liability for debts and harms caused by their corporations. American legislators rejected this corporate shield. Led by Massachusetts, most states refused to grant such protection. Massachusetts Bay State law in 1822 read:

> Every person who shall become a member
> of any manufacturing company . . . shall
> be liable, in his individual capacity, for all
> debts contracted during the time of his
> continuing a member of such
> corporation.[13]

The first constitution in California made each shareholder "individually and personally liable for his proportion of all [corporate] debts and liabilities."[14] Ohio, Missouri and Arkansas made stockholders liable over and above the stock they actually owned. In 1861 Kansas made stockholders individually liable "to an additional amount equal to the stock owned by each stockholder."[15]

Prior to the 1840s courts generally supported the concept that incorporators were responsible for corporate debts. Through the 1870s, seven state constitutions made bank shareholders doubly liable. Shareholders in manufacturing and utility companies were often liable for employees' wages.

Liability laws sometimes reflected the dominance of one political party or another. In Maine, for example, liability laws changed nine times from no liability to full liability between 1823 and 1857, depending on whether the Whigs or the Democrats controlled the legislature.

Until the Civil War most states enacted laws holding corporate investors and officials liable. As New Hampshire Governor Henry Hubbard argued in 1842:

> There is no good reason against this prin-
> ciple. In transactions which occur
> between man and man there exists a direct
> responsibility—and when capital is con-
> centrated . . . beyond the means of single
> individuals, the liability is continued.[16]

The penalty for abuse or misuse of the charter was not a plea bargain and a fine but revocation of the charter and dissolution of the corporation. Citizens believed it was society's inalienable right to abolish an evil.

Revocation clauses were written into Pennsylvania charters as early as 1784. The first revocation clauses were added to insurance charters in 1809, and to banking charters in 1814. Even when corporations met charter requirements, legislatures sometimes decided not to renew those charters.

States often revoked charters by using *quo warranto*—by what authority—proceedings. In 1815, Massachusetts Justice Joseph Story ruled in *Terrett v. Taylor*:

> A private corporation created by the
> legislature may lose its franchises by a
> misuser or nonuser of them . . . This is
> the common law of the land, and is a tacit
> condition annexed to the creation of every
> such corporation.[17]

Four years later the U.S. Supreme Court tried to strip states of this sovereign right. Overruling a lower court, Chief Justice John Marshall wrote in *Dartmouth College v. Woodward* that the U.S. Constitution prohibited New Hampshire from revoking a charter granted to the college in 1769 by King George III. That charter contained no reservation or revocation clauses, Marshall said.

The court's attack on state sovereignty outraged citizens. Protest pamphlets rolled off the presses. Thomas Earle wrote:

> It is aristocracy and despotism, to have a body of officers, whose decisions are, for a longtime, beyond the control of the people. The freemen of America ought not to rest contented, so long as their Supreme Court is a body of that character.[18]

Said Massachusetts legislator David Henshaw:

> Sure I am that, if the American people acquiesce in the principles laid down in this case, the Supreme Court will have effected what the whole power of the British Empire, after eight years of bloody conflict, failed to achieve against our fathers.[19]

Opponents of Marshall's decision believed the ruling cut out the heart of state sovereignty. They argued that a corporation's basic right to exist—and to wield property rights—came from a grant which only the state had the power to make. Therefore, the court exceeded its authority by declaring the corporation beyond the reach of the legislature which created it in the first place.

People also challenged the Supreme Court's decision by distinguishing between a corporation and an individual's private property. The corporation existed at the pleasure of the legislature to serve the common good, and was of a public nature. New Hampshire legislators and any other elected state legislators had the absolute legal right to dictate a corporation's property use by amending or repealing its charter.

State legislators were stung by citizen outrage. They were forced to write amending and revoking clauses into new charters, state laws and constitutions, along with detailed procedures for revocation.

In 1825 Pennsylvania legislators adopted broad powers to "revoke, alter or annul the charter"[20] at any time they thought proper. New York State's 1828 corporation law specified that every charter was subject to alteration or repeal. Section 320 declared that corporate acts not authorized by law were *ultra vires*, or beyond the rights of corporations, and grounds for charter revocation. The law gave the state authority to secure a temporary injunction to prevent corporations from resisting while legal action to dissolve them was under way.

Delaware voters passed a constitutional amendment in 1831 limiting all corporate charters to twenty years. Other states, including Louisiana and Michigan, passed constitutional amendments to place precise time limits on corporate charters.

President Andrew Jackson enjoyed wide popular support when he vetoed a law extending the charter of the Second Bank of the United States in 1832. That same year, Pennsylvania revoked the charters of ten banks.

During the 1840s citizens in New York, Delaware, Michigan, and Florida required a two-thirds vote of their state legislatures to create, continue, alter or renew charters. The New York legislature in 1849 instructed the attorney general to annul any charter whose applicants had concealed material facts, and to sue to revoke a charter on behalf of the people whenever he believed necessary.

Voters in Wisconsin and four other states rewrote constitutions so that popular votes had to be taken on every bank charter recommended by their legislatures. Rhode Island voters said charters for corporations in banking, mining, manufacturing, and transportation had to be approved by the next elected state legislature before being granted.

Over several decades starting in 1844, nineteen states amended their constitutions to make corporate charters subject to alteration or revocation by legislatures. Rhode Island declared in 1857 "the charter or acts of association of every corporation hereafter created may be amendable or repealed at the will of the general assembly."[21]

Pennsylvanians adopted a constitutional amendment in 1857 instructing legislators to "alter, revoke or annul any charter of a corporation hereafter conferred . . . whenever in their opinion it may be injurious to citizens of the community . . ."[22]

As late as 1855 citizens had support from some U.S. Supreme Court justices. In *Dodge v. Woolsey* dissenting judges declared that the people of the states have not:

> . . . released their powers over the artificial bodies which originate under the legislation of their representatives . . .
> Combinations of classes in society . . . united by the bond of a corporate spirit . . . unquestionably desire limitations upon the sovereignty of the people . . . But the framers of the Constitution were imbued with no desire to call into existence such combinations.[23]

## STRUGGLES FOR CONTROL

Massachusetts mechanics who opposed a charter request by the men who wanted to start the Amherst Carriage Company in 1838, told the legislature:

> We . . . do look forward with anticipation to a time when we shall be able to conduct the business upon our own responsibility and receive the proffits of our labor . . . we believe that incorporated bodies tend to crush all feable enterprise and compel us to Work out our dayes in the Service of others.[24]

Contests over charters and the chartering process were not abstractions. They were battles to control labor, resources, community rights, and political sovereignty. This was a major reason why members of the disbanded Working Men's Party formed the Equal Rights Party of New York state. The party's 1836 convention resolved that lawmakers:

> . . . legislate for the whole people and not for favored portions of our fellow-citizens . . . It is by such partial and unjust legislation that the productive classes of society are compelled by necessity, to form unions for mutual preservation . . . [lawmakers should reinstate us] in our equal and constitutional rights according to the fundamental truths in the Declaration of Independence, and as sanctioned by the Constitution of the United States . . .[25]

This political agenda had widespread support in the press. A New Jersey newspaper wrote in an editorial typical of the 1830s:

> . . . the Legislature ought cautiously to refrain from increasing the irresponsible power of any existing corporations, or from chartering new ones, . . . [else people would become] mere hewers of wood and drawers of water to jobbers, banks and stockbrokers.[26]

With these and other prophetic warnings still ringing in their ears, citizens began to feel control over their futures slipping out of their communities and out of their hands. Corporations were abusing their charters to become conglomerates and trusts. They were converting the nation's treasures into private fortunes, creating factory systems and company towns. Political power began flowing to absentee owners intent upon dominating people and nature.

As the nation moved closer to civil war, farmers were forced to become wage earners. Increasingly separated from their neighbors, farms and families, they became fearful of unemployment—a new fear which corporations quickly learned to exploit.

In factory towns, corporations set wages, hours, production processes and machine speeds. They kept blacklists of labor organizers and workers who spoke up for their rights. Corporate officials forced employees to accept humiliating conditions, while the corporations agreed to nothing.

Julianna, a Lowell, Massachusetts, factory worker, wrote:

> Incarcerated within the walls of a factory,
> while as yet mere children—drilled there
> from five till seven o'clock, year after year .
> . . what, we would ask, are we to expect,
> the same system of labor prevailing, will be
> the mental and intellectual character of the
> future generations . . . A race fit only for
> corporation tools and time-serving slaves?
> . . . Shall we not hear the response from
> every hill and vale, "EQUAL RIGHTS, or
> death to the corporations?"[27]

Recognizing that workers were building a social movement, industrialists and bankers pressed on, hiring private armies to keep workers in line. They bought newspapers and painted politicians as villains and businessmen as heroes. Bribing state legislators, they then

announced legislators were corrupt, that they used too much of the public's resources and time to scrutinize every charter application and corporate operation.

Corporate advocates campaigned to replace existing chartering laws with general incorporation laws that set up simple administrative procedures, claiming this would be more efficient. What they really wanted was the end of legislative authority over charters.

Cynically adopting the language of early charter opponents, corporate owners and their lawyers attacked existing legislative charters as special privileges. They called for equal opportunity for all entrepreneurs, making it seem as if they were asking that everyone have the same chance to compete.

But these corporations were not just ordinary individual entrepreneurs. They were large accumulations of capital, and getting larger. By 1860, thousands of corporations had been chartered—mostly factories, mines, railroads and banks.

Government spending during the Civil War brought these corporations fantastic wealth. Corporate managers developed the techniques and the ability to organize production on an ever grander scale. Many corporations used their wealth to take advantage of war and Reconstruction years to get the tariff, banking, railroad, labor and public lands legislation they wanted.

Flaunting new wealth and power, corporate executives paid "borers"[28] to infest Congress and state capitals, bribing elected and appointed officials alike. They pried loose from the public trust more and more land, minerals, timber and water. Railroad corporations alone obtained over 180 million free acres of public lands by the 1870s, along with many millions of dollars in direct subsidies.

Little by little, legislators gave corporations limited liability, decreased citizen authority over corporate structure, governance, production and labor, and ever longer terms for the charters themselves.

Corporations rewrote the laws governing their own creation. They "left few stones unturned to control those who made and interpreted the laws . . ."[29]

Even as businesses secured general incoporation laws for mining, agriculture, transportation, banking and manufacturing businesses, citizens held on to the authority to charter. Specifying company size, shareholder terms, and corporate undertakings remained a major citizen strategy.

During the 1840s and 1850s states revoked charters routinely. In Ohio, Pennsylvania and Mississippi, banks lost charters for frequently "committing serious violations . . . which were likely to leave them in an insolvent or financially unsound condition."[30] In Massachusetts and New York turnpike corporations lost charters for "not keeping their roads in repair."[31]

"No constitutional convention met, between 1860-1900, without considering the problems of the corporations,"[32] according to Friedman.

New York, Ohio, Michigan, and Nebraska revoked the charters of oil, match, sugar and whiskey trusts. Courts in each state declared these trusts illegal because the corporations— in creating the trusts—had exceeded the powers granted by their charters. "Roaming and piratical corporations"[33] like the Standard Oil Company of Ohio, then the most powerful corporation in the world, refused to comply and started searching for a "Snug Harbor" in another state.

Rhode Island enacted a law requiring corporate dissolution for "fraud, negligence, misconduct . . ."[34] Language was added to the Virginia constitution enabling "all charters and amendments of charters to be repealed at any time by special act."[35]

Farmers and rural communities, groaning in misery at the hands of railroad, grain and banking corporations, ran candidates for office who supported states' authority "to reverse or annul at any time any chartered privilege . . ."[36] The "Farmers' Anti-Monopoly Convention" meeting in Des Moines in 1873 resolved that:

> . . . all corporations are subject to legislative control; [such control] should be at all times so used as to prevent moneyed corporations from becoming engines of oppression.[37]

That same year, Minnesota Grangers resolved:

> We, the farmers, mechanics and laborers of Minnesota, deem the triumph of the people in this contest with monopolies essential to the perpetuation of our free institutions and the promotion of our private and national prosperity.[38]

Because these and other powerful resistance movements directly challenged the harmful corporations of their times, and because they kept pressure on state representatives, revocation and amendment clauses can be found in state charter laws today.

## JUDGE-MADE LAW

But keeping strong charter laws in place was ineffective once courts started aggressively applying legal doctrines which made protection of corporations and corporate property the center of constitutional law.

As corporations got stronger, government became easier prey; communities became more vulnerable to intimidation.

Following the Civil War, and well into the twentieth century, appointed judges gave privilege after privilege to corporations. They freely reinterpreted the U.S. Constitution and transformed common law doctrines.

Judges gave certain corporations the power of eminent domain—the right to take private property with minimal compensation to be determined by the courts. They eliminated jury trials to determine corporation-caused harm and to assess damages. Judges created the "right to contract," a doctrine which, according to law professor Arthur Selwyn Miller, was put forward as a "principle of eternal truth" in "one of the most remarkable feats of judicial law-making this nation has seen."[39]

By concocting the doctrine that contracts originated in the courts, judges then took away the right to oversee corporate rates of return and prices, a right previously entrusted to legislators by the U.S. Constitution. They laid the legal foundation for regulatory agencies to be primarily accountable to the courts—not to Congress.

Workers, the courts also ruled, were responsible for causing their own injuries on the job. The Kentucky Court of Appeals prefigured this doctrine in 1839: "Private injury and personal damage . . . must be expected" when one goes to work for a corporation bringing "progressive improvements."[40] This came to be called the assumption of risk, what professor Cohen dismissed as "a judicial invention."[41]

Traditionally under common law the burden of damage had been on the business causing harms. Courts had not permitted trespass or nuisance to be excused by the alleged good works a corporation might claim. Nor could a corporation's lack of intent to cause harm decrease its legal liability for injuries it caused to persons or the land.

Large corporations—especially railroad and steamship companies—pressured judges to reverse this tradition, too. Attentive to lawyers and growing commercial interests, judges creatively interpreted the commerce and due process clauses of the U.S. Constitution. Inventing a new concept which they called "substantive due process," they declared one state law after another unconstitutional. Wages and hours laws, along with rate laws for grain elevators and railroads, were tossed out.

Judges also established the managerial prerogative and business judgment doctrines, giving corporations legal justification to arrest civil rights at factory gates, and to blockade democracy at boardroom doors.

Corporations were enriched further when judges construed the common good to mean maximum production—no matter what was manufactured, who was hurt, or what was destroyed. Unfettered corporate competition without citizen interference became enshrined under law.

Another blow to citizen constitutional authority came in 1886. The Supreme Court ruled in *Santa Clara County v. Southern Pacific Railroad Co.* that a private corporation was an artificial "person" under the U.S. Constitution, sheltered by the Bill of Rights and the Fourteenth Amendment.

"There was no history, logic or reason given to support that view,"[42] Supreme Court Justice William O. Douglas was to write sixty years later.

But the Supreme Court had spoken. Using the Fourteenth Amendment, which had been added to the Constitution to protect freed slaves, the justices struck down hundreds more local, state and federal laws enacted to protect people from corporate harms. The high court ruled that elected legislators had been taking corporate property "without due process of law."

Emboldened, some judges went further, declaring unions were civil and criminal conspiracies, and enjoining workers from striking. Governors and presidents backed judges up with police and armies.

By establishing "new trends in legal doctrine and political-economic theory" permitting "the corporate reorganization of the property-production system,"[43] the Supreme Court effectively sabotaged blossoming social protest movements against incorporated wealth. Judges positioned the corporation to become "America's representative social institution, . . . an institutional expression of our way of life." [44]

Legislative "chartermongering"[45] attracted as many corporations as possible to their states. In exchange for taxes, fees, and whatever else they could get their hands on, some state governments happily provided new homes to Standard Oil and other corporations.

Led by New Jersey and Delaware, legislators watered down or removed citizen authority clauses. They limited the liability of corporate owners and managers, then started handing out charters that literally lasted forever. Corporations were given the right to operate in any fashion not explicitly prohibited by law.

After such losses of citizen sovereignty, twenty-six corporate trusts ended up controlling 80 percent or more of production in their markets by the early 1900s. There were trusts for almost everything—matches, whiskey, cotton, alcohol, corks, cement, stoves, ribbons, bread, beef.

During the Progressive Era corporations operated as ruthlessly as any colonial trading monopoly in the 1700s. Blood was often spilled resisting these legal fictions.

Jo Battley, a West Virginia miner, was beaten severely and stabbed trying to organize a union at the Consolidated Coal Company. Mother Jones, one of his rescuers, said, "We tried to get a warrant out for the arrest of the gunmen but we couldn't because the coal company controlled the judges and the courts."[46]

Corporations owned resources, production, commerce, trade, prices, jobs, politicians, judges and the law. Over the next half-century, as a United States congressional committee concluded in 1941:

> The principal instrument of the concentration of economic power and wealth has been the corporate charter with unlimited power . . .[47]

Today many U.S. corporations are transnational. No matter how piratical or where they roam, the corrupted charter remains the legal basis of their existence.

## TAKING BACK THE CHARTERS, TAKING BACK THE LAW

We are out of the habit of contesting the legitimacy of the corporation, or challenging concocted legal doctrines, or denying courts the final say over our economic lives.

For most of this century, citizens skirmished with corporations to stop doing harm, but failed to question the legitimacy of the harm-doers. We no longer use the charter and the chartering process to stop corporate harm, or to define the corporation on our terms. And what passes for political debate today is not about control, sovereignty, or the economic democracy which many American revolutionaries thought they were fighting to secure.

Too many organizing campaigns accept the corporations' rules, and wrangle on corporate turf. We lobby congress for limited laws. We have no faith in regulatory agencies, but turn to them for relief. We plead with corporations

to be socially responsible, then show them
how to increase profits by being a bit less
harmful.

How much more strength, time, and hope
will we invest in such dead ends?

When we limit our thinking only to existing
labor law, or only to existing environmental
law, or only to the courts, or only to
elections—or when we abide by corporate
agendas—we abandon our constitutional
claim on the corporate charter and the
chartering process.

When we forsake our constitutional claim,
we ignore historic tools we can use to define
and to control the corporation. We pass up
strategies which can inspire citizens to act. We
fail to demand what we know is right.

We must name and stop what harms us.
John H. Hunt, a member of the Equal Rights
Party, wrote this resolution in 1837:

> Whenever a people find themselves suf-
> fering under a weight of evils, destruc-
> tive not only to their happiness, but to
> their dignity and their virtues; when
> these evils go on increasing year after
> year, with accelerating rapidity, and
> threaten soon to reach that point at
> which peaceable endurance ceases to be
> possible; it becomes their solemn duty
> coolly to search out the causes of their
> suffering—to state those causes with
> plainness—and to apply a sufficient and
> a speedy remedy.[48]

His resolution was passed unanimously by
cheering mechanics, farmers and working people during a mass rally in a New York City park.

Around the nation, citizens are no less
willing—and are quite well prepared—to
educate, to organize, and to agitate.

Citizens who have been to folk schools or
labor colleges understand that by learning
together and teaching ourselves corporate history, we can hone the skills of citizen sovereignty and power.

We can read our state constitutions.
Libraries containing our states' constitutional
histories, corporate histories, and corporate
case law can provide details about what earlier
citizens demanded of corporations, what
precedents they established, and which of
their legal and organizing methods we can use
to our advantage.

We can demand to see the charters of every
corporation. We need to know what each
charter prohibits, especially if it is an old
charter. Armed with our states' rich legal
precedents, and with our evidence of corporate misuse or abuse, we can amend or revoke
charters and certificates of authority.

When corporations violate our constitutional guarantees, we can take them to court ourselves. Corporate officers can be forced to give
us depositions under oath, just as elected officials who spurned the Constitution were forced
to do by the civil rights movement—often in
courtrooms packed with angry citizens.

New Yorkers used to get sufficient and
speedy remedy through injunctions against
corporations. We can revive this tradition.
Surrounded by citizens and their peers, judges
can be encouraged to enjoin corporate officials from doing further harm, or from stripping the corporation's assets, or from moving
the company away.

Stockholders have authority to seek injunctions and file dissolution suits if they fear
managers are acting illegally, oppressively,
fraudulently, or are misusing or wasting corporate assets.

As in the first half of the nineteenth century,
would-be or ongoing incorporators must be

made to ask us for the privilege of a charter. We can set our own criteria: workers must own a significant or majority share of the company; the workforce must have democratic decision-making authority; charters must be renewed annually; corporate officers must prove all corporate harm has ceased . . . for starters.

Who defines the corporation controls the corporation. We cannot command the modern corporation with laws that require only a few days' notice before the corporation leaves town, or with laws that allow the corporation to spew so many toxic parts per million. If we expect to define the corporation using the charters and putting legislators on our civic leash, we must also challenge prevailing judicial doctrines. We cannot let courts stand in the way of our stopping corporate harm.

Legal doctrines are not inevitable or divine. When the liberty and property rights of citizens are at stake, as former Supreme Court Justice Louis D. Brandeis said:

> . . . the right of property and the liberty
> of the individual must be remoulded . . .
> to meet the changing needs of society.[49]

The corporation is an artificial creation, and must not enjoy the protections of the Bill of Rights. Corporate owners and officers must be liable for harms they cause. No corporation should exist forever. Both business judgment and managerial prerogative must meet the same end as the colonial trading companies' delusion of divine authority.

Our sovereign right to decide what is produced, to own and to organize our work, and to respect the Earth is as American as a self-governing peoples' right to vote.

In our democracy, we can shape the nation's economic life any way we want. ■

# NOTES

[1] Berle and Means 1933, p. 310.

[2] Felix Frankfurter quoted in Miller 1967, p. 1.

[3] Friedman 1973, p. 456.

[4] Cohen 1933, "Property and Sovereignty" p. 47.

[5] Reverdy Ransom quoted in Meier 1966.

[6] Environmental Protection Agency, Occupational Safety and Health Administration, National Labor Relations Board, Federal Trade Commission, Nuclear Regulatory Commission, Securities and Exchange Commission, Bureau of Land Management, and Resolution Trust Corporation. —Ed.

[7] Paine 1986, p. 124.

[8] Earle 1823, p. 19.

[9] Hartz 1948, p. 196.

[10] Virginia Supreme Court quoted in Horwitz 1977, p. 112.

[11] James Kent quoted in Dodd 1954, p. 44.

[12] Report of the Packer Committee of the Pennsylvania Legislature, quoted in Goodrich 1967, p. 374.

[13] Massachusetts law quoted in Berle 1929.

[14] First California Constitution quoted in Cadman 1949, p. 191.

[15] Ibid.

[16] Henry Hubbard quoted in Dodd 1954, p. 395.

[17] Joseph Story quoted in Ibid., p. 60.

[18] Earle 1823, p. 30.

[19] David Henshaw quoted in Blau 1947, p. 182.

[20] Hartz 1948, p. 239.

[21] Berle 1929.

[22] Hartz 1948, p. 240.

[23] Dodge v. Woolsey, U.S. Supreme Court quoted in Dodd 1954, p. 130.

[24] Amherst mechanics quoted in Handlin and Handlin 1947, p. 266.

[25] Equal Rights Party resolution quoted in Byrdsall 1967, p. 41.

[26] Trenton Emporium and True American quoted in Cadman 1949, p. 76.

[27] Juliana quoted in Baxandall, Gordon, and Reverby 1976, p. 68.

[28] Hartz 1948, p. 309.

[29] Ginsberg and Berg 1963, p. 8.

[30] Dodd 1954, p. 181.

[31] Ibid.

[32] Friedman 1973, p. 446.

[33] William W. Cook quoted in Ibid., p. 458.

[34] Rhode Island Law quoted in Berle 1929.

[35] Virginia Constitution quoted in Ibid.

[36] Martin 1873, p. 510.

[37] Ibid., p. 513.

[38] Ibid., p. 510.

[39] Miller 1967, p. 54.

[40] Kentucky Court of Appeals quoted Horwitz 1977, p. 75.

[41] Cohen 1933, "The Process of Judicial Legislation" p. 126.

[42] William O. Douglas in the dissenting opinion of Wheeling Steel Corp. v. Glander.

[43] Sklar 1988, p. 85.

[44] Ford Motor Company executive William T. Gossett, 1957, quoted in Williams 1961, p. 343.

[45] Nader, Green, and Seligman 1976, p. 44.

[46] Jones 1976, p. 44.

[47] Blair 1972, p. 667.

[48] Byrdsall 1967, p. 135.

[49] Louis D. Brandeis in Truax v. Corrigan.

# REGARDING "THE JOURNAL OF CORPORATE CITIZENSHIP"

*by Jim Price*

I RECENTLY RAN ACROSS a flyer advertising *The Journal of Corporate Citizenship*. Such terms as "corporate citizenship" and "corporate responsibility" reflect a deference to corporate language that I find disturbing.

Corporate executives like to throw around terms like "corporate citizenship" and "corporate citizen." Corporations cannot be citizens. Only natural persons can be citizens. Corporations are artificial entities created under the authority of laws enacted by natural persons—We the People—acting as citizens. Corporate officials also like to talk about "corporate responsibility." That term implies that We the People should leave to corporate managers the right to define what constitutes responsible corporate behavior. I believe that such determinations are solely the right of We the People, not of corporate officials.

We natural persons should determine the standards to be met by all economic enterprises whether those enterprises are organized in corporate, partnership, cooperative, or any other form. We the People, not corporate officials, should determine what constitutes "responsible" corporate behavior. Then corporations and their officials should be held accountable to the environmental, workplace safety, community health, worker rights, human rights, and other standards established by We the People.

We set the bar, we govern, not the corporations. We define the privileges which we will allow corporations to exercise, and the limits to those privileges. We hold them accountable to *our* defined standards, not *theirs*. This is the origin of the concept of "corporate accountability." This is why I think the language that is used in communicating about corporate abuses of wealth and power is very important.

Terms like "corporate citizenship" and "corporate responsibility" are corporate inventions; terms implying a deference by We the People to corporate officials of our right to define what constitutes citizenship and responsibility. "Corporate accountability" on the other hand retains that power in the hands of We the People, where it belongs.

We must be careful to not allow ourselves to become captive of corporate language, and to help others understand the distinctions among and the implications associated with the use of such terms as "corporate citizen," "corporate responsibility," and "corporate accountability." ∎

# MAN CORPORATE
# ON TOP OF THE WORLD

*by Mary Zepernick*

His eyes are the corporate eyes of the world, and he sees all that they see that is worth seeing; he hears all that all the individuals in the world hear that is worth hearing; he scents all that all the individual in the world scent; he tastes all that all the individuals in the world taste; he feels all that all the individuals in the world feel.

KING CAMP GILLETTE'S *World Corporation* was published in 1910, but the author could be describing "Man Corporate" at this century's end. Take Roberto Goizueta, the late chairman and CEO of the Coca-Cola Corporation.

One eulogizer at his recent funeral in Atlanta said Goizueta "was marketing more than a product. He was marketing a way of life. We are all better for having come under his influence." This, from Andrew Young, who was a protegé of Martin Luther King.

*Wall Street Journal* columnist Paul Gigot offered an even more fulsome farewell, lauding Goizueta for "seizing the global market and instilling a culture of competition . . . an engine of prosperity for millions." Gigot gleefully contended that "a CEO with vision and luck can have a larger impact on the world than just about any politician in Washington, maybe even a two-term president."

Sad but true. One can dispute that the world's people are better off and more prosperous for the Coca Cola Corporation's influence. But who can deny that Man Corporate

has increasingly determined our tastes, our sights, sounds and smells, and much of the world we reach out and touch? Or that corporations, like a giant Pac Man, have eclipsed (and bought) our elected officials?

If you doubt that our role has been effectively reduced from citizen to consumer, consider the refusal of all three major networks to run an ad for November 28's "Buy Nothing Day."[1] The vice-president of advertising standards at NBC, owned by the General Electric Corporation, explained that "We don't want to take any advertising that's inimical to our legitimate business interests." Even more explicit was the rejection letter from the Westinghouse Electric Corporation's CBS, declaring that Buy Nothing Day is "in opposition to the current economic policy in the United States."

Again, all too true, a policy of buy now and pay later: on your credit card bill; in the disempowerment of the sovereign people; and through damages to our life support systems. We've come a long way since We the People ordained and established the Constitution as a

---

compact among ourselves—not between us and corporations, or even us and our government—and since corporations were prohibited from owning other corporations.

A critical outcome of the American Revolution was the replacement of authoritarian corporations under royal charter, with corporations chartered by state legislatures for specific purposes, with explicit conditions and time limits, to serve the common good. As late as the 1890s states were revoking the charters of corporations which exceeded the authority granted to them. In one famous case, *People v. North River Sugar Refining Co.*, New York's highest court found the North River Sugar Refining Corporation "beyond its authority" and revoked its charter. "The judgement sought against the defendant is one of corporate death . . . The life of the corporation is, indeed, less than that of the humblest citizen."

Four years earlier, however, the U.S. Supreme Court had declared a private corporation a legal "person" under the Constitution, in a decision arrived at with no debate. The stage was set for a counter-revolution. Since then, corporations have used the rights and protections of "personhood" to concentrate wealth and power, reversing the proper relationship between a sovereign people and corporations—our created fictions—

and usurping the role of governance.

Today more than half of the world's largest economies are corporations, not countries, that increasingly run our lives and make a mockery of democratic process. Over the past century our minds have been so colonized that we collude in our own subordinate status, barely able to imagine, as Cornel West puts it, what a real democracy would look like.[2]

In place of the power to define our economy, we have a regulatory system of agencies unaccountable to the public. The few fines imposed either go unpaid or are deducted from already-shrinking corporate taxes as a cost of doing business. In other words, We the People pony up once again. All this in the name of "free enterprise," never mind the enormous government subsidies to corporations, past and present.

In *World Corporation*, Man Corporate is pictured as a seductive fellow in a toga-like garment, one hand on his hip, the other holding a globe. According to the caption "He absorbs, enfolds, encompasses, and makes the world his own."

Gargantuan multinational corporations are not persons, but they define our cultures, our economies, our politics, our very selves, even telling us how to measure our worth. Just what do we have to say about this? ■

## NOTES

[1] For more information on the Buy Nothing Day campaign, see www.adbusters.org. —*Ed.*

[2] West 1982, p. 469.

# LABOR ORGANIZING
# AND FREEDOM OF ASSOCIATION

*by Peter Kellman*

## THE PROBLEM

THE BAD NEWS is that since 1979 the percentage of union workers in the United States has declined from 24 to 14 percent.[1] The good news is that given the choice of joining a union or not, 48 percent of workers in this country would join.

Due to the exportation of jobs, outsourcing and automation, existing union jobs are being lost as fast as we bring new members in. The strategy of organizing workers—work site by work site—does bring in new members, but employer opposition still denies most workers union representation.

A case that makes the point is the healthcare industry in Massachusetts, which currently employs 400,000 workers, 10 percent of whom are union members. Unions put a fair amount of financial and human resources into organizing healthcare workers, and in 1997 organized 819 new members through the union certification process. At this rate it would take 434 years to organize the industry if the number of employed stayed at 400,000, but the industry is projected to grow another 250,000 in the next 45 years.

You see the problem; we have to do something different. In Sweden, for example, 83 percent of the workforce is represented by unions, and employers are prevented by law from interfering with the unionization process. Unlike U.S. workers, Swedish workers have the right to associate and bargain collectively. In Sweden, Japan, France, Germany and most countries with which U.S. corporate managers say we compete, the right to associate and bargain collectively is a basic human right recognized by the United Nations and stated in the Declaration of Human Rights of 1948 under Article 20: "Everyone has the right to freedom of peaceful assembly and association." This right is explained in the UN's International Labor Organization's Convention #87, "freedom of association and the right to organize," affirming the right of all workers to form and join organizations of their own choosing without prior authorization. Although 118 countries have ratified Convention #87, the U.S. Senate has steadfastly refused to do so over the past half-century.

Freedom of speech *plus* freedom of assembly *equals* freedom of association. It works like this: a group of people want to form a corporation. They call a meeting (freedom of assembly) and discuss (freedom of speech)

---

their options and decide they want corporate recognition. Then they send a representative to their state capital and file some papers. That's it. Their corporation is recognized by the rest of the society. No cards are signed; no campaign is waged; no one gets fired; and no election. Just recognition. In this country forming a corporation is a protected activity. It is a right.

Getting a corporation to recognize a union is not a right; it is not a protected activity. If it was, 48 percent of the workforce would be union members in a heart beat.

During a union campaign, in this country, the company will put up anti-union posters and hold captive audience meetings. But the union can't put up posters because it doesn't own the walls. The union can't bring a representative to the workplace to talk to workers in the private sector because the union doesn't own the building.

In this country we have freedom of speech and assembly on public property. On private property the owners of the property determine who can speak and assemble. Workers surrender their free speech rights to their employers when they enter the workplace.

If we want to associate, to organize, to exercise power, we need to change some fundamental relationships in our society. But first we need to understand how the fundamental relationships that now govern our lives were set. We need to know our own history.

He came to know . . . that history was not a page in a book, but something held in memory and in blood.[2]

## KNOWING HISTORY

Imagine a church without the Bible, a synagogue without the Torah, a mosque without the Koran or the Iroquois without the Creation Story. It is the teaching of the stories from these great books and oral traditions that holds the congregations and tribes of our people together. The wisdom acquired over the ages is passed down through the stories of the past. These stories guide us into the future, they give us our values, direction and strength. Without them we are rootless, have no direction and live only in the uninformed present.

The same is true for labor. We need a framework to view our history and connect the many stories of our great struggles. We need to learn from our past mistakes and victories. We need to take the best from the past and use it to help build our future. If not, we will forever live in the present and make the same mistakes over and over again.

It is often said in labor circles that we will never increase our numbers until we have better laws. The fact is that for most of our history, pro-labor laws have been the exception. Most laws relating to labor have been anti-labor, anti-union laws. It wasn't until 1937 that the National Labor Relations Act was found constitutional, though today that law is of more use to the employer than it is to us. But that is nothing new; U.S. law favored the wealthy in the 13 American colonies, and it still does in this country today.

George Washington didn't become the most powerful and one of the wealthiest men in America in 1776 by surveying house lots.[3] It is true that Washington did do some surveying for the Ohio Company, a company in which he was a major stockholder. George, and members of the planter and commercial class in colonial Virginia where he grew up, had a plan to exploit labor and make themselves even richer and more powerful. The plan was twofold. First, they had slaves to run their tobacco plantations; and second, they created the Ohio Company. The Ohio

Company was founded in 1748 by George's older brother Lawrence, and received from the King a grant of 200,000 acres of land west of the colony of Virginia.

Later, Virginia's Royal Governor Dindwiddie, himself an Ohio Company principal, "successfully appealed to the British authorities in London to offer ships passage to indentured servants who would work to clear and improve roads and farmsteads and build company trading posts for seven years in return for the right to remain on the lands as leaseholders afterward."[4] Pretty good plan. The King grants the company the land and then supplies unpaid workers to build the roads to access the land, and the forts to defend it. Then, if the workers survived their seven years of servitude, and many didn't, they had the privilege of renting land from the Ohio Company.

But it wasn't just Washington who was involved with this kind of scheme. The Ohio Company was in competition with the Loyal Land Company of Virginia, owned in part by Thomas Jefferson's dad, and the Vandalia Company, owned in part by Ben Franklin. We have heard a lot about Washington, Jefferson and Franklin, but who were these indentured servants and slaves? What was their history?

The history of the indentured servant, for our purposes, begins in 1500 when one-third of the land in England, France and Germany was owned by the Catholic Church. Much of this land was occupied by subsistence farmers. With the Protestant Reformation of the Church in 1517, Church land was taken over by nobles or sold to speculators who drove the tenant farmers off the land. Then in the 1600s and 1700s the "common lands"— which had been at the disposal of the poor in Europe—were enclosed, fenced off, and the people who lived on them driven off the land.

Finally, in the 1800s, in a process known as "clearing the estates," farmers were pushed off the land they rented to make room for sheep to provide wool for the growing textile industry.

As the rich stole the good farmland in Europe they passed laws that called for people without a place to live or work to be branded, punished, jailed, or sold into slavery. That is how a large pool of humanity, with an incentive to leave Europe and provide cheap labor in North America, was created.

Meanwhile in Africa, rich merchants from Europe organized an international slave trade in which they bought slaves from West African princes whose soldiers were armed with European weapons. The trade in African slaves spanned three centuries and "[b]efore it was over, ten to twelve million Africans would be transported to the New World."[5]

Indentured servants from Europe and slaves from Africa, people whose lives were contracts to be bought and sold, provided the founding fathers of our nation, men like George Washington, Thomas Jefferson, James Madison and Benjamin Franklin, the labor to exploit the natural resources of North America.

Roughly half the immigrants to colonial America were indentured servants. At the time of the war of Independence, three out of four persons in Pennsylvania, Maryland, and Virginia were or had been indentured servants. And by this time, roughly 20 percent of the colonial population was in slavery.[6] Slaves from Africa and indentured servants from Europe lived under the same fugitive slave laws, and their children were the property of the masters. These people were property to be bought and sold—property protected by colonial law, and later the United States Constitution.

For many in the United States the images of the colonial period are dominated by scenes of Thanksgiving, Pocahontas, Captain John Smith, and people seeking religious freedom. These images hide a colonial scheme that went like this: European adventurers "discovered America" and began the process of killing off the indigenous population. They were followed by European speculators who extracted profits from the new land primarily through the labor of African slaves and European indentured servants.

But the Americans who made great fortunes on the backs of slaves and indentured servants, weren't happy sharing their wealth with the English King.

## THE U.S. CONSTITUTION

In 1776 the 13 colonies declared their independence from the British Crown. In 1781 these former colonies—now states—ratified a set of rules called the Articles of Confederation which determined their relationship to each other. In 1787 the state legislatures sent delegates to a meeting to discuss amending the Articles of Confederation. This meeting is called the Constitutional Convention of 1787, and was held in Philadelphia, Pennsylvania. It was a closed meeting, the minutes of which were not made public until 53 years later.[7]

Much had happened between 1781 and 1787 that caused the class of people who fomented the revolution to be concerned about their future. Divisions within the propertied class surfaced in the state legislatures, and conflict between classes manifested itself in armed insurrections against the authority of state governments.

In the legislatures the interests of the small business owners and artisans clashed with those involved in national and international trade. The small businessmen wanted high

state tariffs to protect their small concerns, while those with large commercial interests demanded so-called "free trade" between the states. Meanwhile, the people who were clearing the land wanted to own it, and armed insurrection against state authority broke out in many places. For example, the rebellion of Vermont's Green Mountain Boys against their New York landlords eventually led to the establishment of Vermont as the fourteenth State in 1777. But it was Shays Rebellion, the armed 1786-87 insurrection of western Massachusetts farmers against the policies of the commercial class in Boston, that weighed most heavily upon the large property owners who sat down in 1787 to write the Constitution of the United States. Those who wanted free trade between the states saw the need to have a strong federal government, as well as a federal army that would always be available to put down rebellions which could not be suppressed with state militias.

The men who assembled in Philadelphia in 1787 to write the constitution were all men of property. The noted historian Charles Beard states that James Madison, primary author of the Constitution, "in more than one speech pointed out that the conflict of interests was inescapable. He told the convention that the greatest conflict of all in the country was between those who had property and those who had none."[8] Beard goes on to say:

> Leaders among the framers wanted, among other things, first to hold the Union together; second, to set up a government that would protect, regulate, and promote types of economic enterprise; third, to put brakes on the state legislatures which had been attacking the interests of protected classes.[9]

Here is some of what the founding fathers came up with.

## THE COMMERCE CLAUSE: THE FIRST NAFTA

The Commerce clause of the U.S. Constitution, Article I, Section 8, was written "To regulate Commerce with foreign Nations, and among the several States, and with the Indian Tribes," and was created to straighten out the conflict of interest between the small and large property owners. After the Constitution was ratified, independent state legislatures were no longer able to erect protective tariffs that "hindered" the flow of goods between the states. The big commercial interests of the day had triumphed over the small enterprises trying to "grow" local businesses.

Recently a similar event took place when the large transnational corporate interests triumphed over national business interests and labor with the passage of the North American Free Trade Agreement (NAFTA). The Commerce clause was the first "free trade" agreement in North America, and like NAFTA, it was negotiated at a closed meeting.[10]

## THE CONTRACTS CLAUSE

The Contracts clause of the U.S. Constitution, Article I, Section 10, states in part that "No State shall . . . pass any . . . Law impairing the Obligation of contracts." Legal theory holds that contracts are agreements made between equals, and therefore the state should not meddle.[11] If a state passes a *public* law that, for example, sets the maximum hours an employer can require people to work, it would be seen by the courts as *impairing* the right of individual citizens to negotiate contracts free from outside interference. Contracts are *private* laws. And thus most labor laws passed by state legislatures and Congress prior to 1937 were ruled unconstitutional by the U.S. Supreme Court because they violated the Contracts clause.

The reasoning was that contracts were *private* laws between individuals that were protected from state interference by the Contracts clause. Thus most state laws that were passed to protect or promote the interests of working people violated the Constitution, because they were *public* laws that violated *private* laws. The meaning is clear. The obligation of the government, as stated in the preamble to the Constitution, to promote the "general Welfare"[12] is secondary to the *private* law, the law of contracts.

Once again, the theory of contracts is based on the assumption that the contracting parties are equals. The founding fathers would have us believe that an indentured servant negotiating a contract with his master was somehow equal to the master at the negotiating table. The situation is similar to a small local union with 200 members negotiating a contract with a large employer who brings to the table enough resources to move the plant. In practice this can hardly be called a contract negotiated between equals. But this is the legal fiction; and the courts, the Congress, national guard, army, and police uphold this distortion of common sense.

The *Lochner v. New York* case of 1905 is a classic example of how the Contracts clause suppressed the democratic legislative activities of working class people. As a result of popular agitation, the New York State Legislature passed a law limiting the hours of work for people employed in bakeries to no more than 10 per day and 60 per week. The U.S. Supreme Court ruled, "Under such circumstances the freedom of master and employee to contract with each other in relation to their employment, and in defining the same, cannot be prohibited or interfered with, without violating the Federal Constitution."[13] Laws which limit the hours a person can work, and which today are found constitutional, generally apply to children or to where the public would be affected by tired workers, as in the case of people working in the railroad or trucking industry.

Dominance of the *private* law over the *public* law in our Constitution has made it very hard for working people to use the political process to better their conditions. This is true because the Constitution restricts our collective activity primarily to contractual relationships with employers, and the National Labor Relations Act serves to limit our activity even further. So much for "We the People" forming a government to "promote the general Welfare" that the Preamble to the Constitution promises. The question is: Who defines the "general Welfare"? So far it has been the lawyers of the elite who subsequently become Supreme Court justices—not shop stewards, teachers or home makers. When the constitutionality of a law is questioned, it is five Supreme Court justices who decide for the rest of us the resolution to issues like: Is a maximum 40 hour week constitutional? Do workers have free speech at work? Do employers have free speech rights in union certification elections? ∎

## NOTES

[1] All data on union membership are taken from publications of the U.S. Department of Labor's Bureau of Labor Statistics. From 1930 to 1980 the data were taken from surveys sent to unions. After 1980 the method of collection and interpreting the data changed and then changed again. Also the total number and percentage of organized workers varies regarding who is included or left out in a particular year, such as workers over 14 or 18 years of age, professional associations, farm and non-farm, civilian and non-civilian. In this document the percentage of union members is used to show trends, not to establish exactly how many workers were organized in a particular year.

[2] Papanikolas 1982, p. 259.

[3] Beard 1986, p. 144. Beard writes: "Washington of Virginia, was probably the richest man in the United States in his time, and his financial ability was not surpassed among his countrymen anywhere."

[4] Randall 1997, p. 68.

[5] Levine *et al.*, 1989, p. 25.

[6] Fresia 1988, p. 26. See also Smith *et al.* 1998.

[7] Fresia 1988, p. 47.

[8] Beard 1943, p. 285.

[9] *Ibid.*

[10] "Free trade" is the international equivalent of "right to work." As labor people know "right to work" means the right to work for less. The reality of "free trade" is that workers in one country are forced to work for less to compete with workers in another country. "Free trade" = right to work for less.

[11] A contract is an agreement between two or more parties. Contract law is private law enforceable through court action. When a union negotiates a contract with a private employer, the contract is not voted on by the state legislature. Yet if one party to a contract reneges, the aggrieved party will go to court to force the offending party to live up to the contract or "private law."

[12] Capitalization of "general Welfare" is as in the original, that is, the Constitution. –Ed.

[13] *Lochner v. New York*, p. 64.

# CORPORATIONS FOR THE SEVENTH GENERATION

## CHANGING THE GROUND RULES

*by Jane Anne Morris*

---

T HE PEOPLE WHO founded this nation didn't fight a war so that they could have a couple of "citizen representatives" sitting in on meetings of the British East India Company. They carried out a revolution in order to be free of oppression: corporate, governmental, or otherwise; and to replace it with democratic self-government.

It seems that things have slipped a little. Today, as soon as any group or movement puts together a coherent critique of the role of corporations, tongues start clucking. Politicians, mainstream reformers, degreed experts, and media commentators fall all over each other in an effort to dismiss such clear, practical, focused thinking as mere "conspiracy theories" cooked up by unbalanced "crackpots."

They forget that seventeenth century political philosopher Thomas Hobbes called corporations "worms in the body politic."[1] Adam Smith condemned them for their effect in curtailing "natural liberty."[2] And most of the so-called "founding fathers" of this nation shared an opinion of corporations that today would earn them the label "lunatic fringe" from the same mainstream tongue cluckers.[3]

Those who won independence from England hated corporations as much as they hated the King. For it was through state-chartered corporations that the British government carried out some of its most pernicious oppression. Governments extending their power by means of corporations, and corporations themselves taking on the powers of government, are not new problems.

Because they were well aware of the track record of government-chartered corporations, and because they guarded their freedom so jealously, citizens of the newly independent United States of America chartered only a handful of corporations in the several decades after independence.[4]

On those few occasions when states did charter a corporation, "the powers which the corporation might exercise in carrying out its purposes were sparingly conferred and strictly construed."[5]

But inevitably the generation that had fought against injustices perpetrated by corporations like the British East India Company and the Hudson's Bay Company was followed by others whose memories of corporate oppression were less vivid. Still, the warnings against corporations continued.

---

©1996 by Jane Anne Morris. Adapted from an article published in two parts in *Rachel's Environment & Health Weekly* (nos. 388 and 389, April 4 and April 11, 1996).

On the eve of his becoming Chief Justice of Wisconsin's Supreme Court, Edward G. Ryan said ominously in 1873:

> [There] is looming up a new and dark power . . . the enterprises of the country are aggregating vast corporate combinations of unexampled capital, boldly marching, not for economical conquests only, but for political power . . . The question will arise and arise in your day, though perhaps not fully in mine, which shall rule—wealth or man [sic]; which shall lead—money or intellect; who shall fill public stations—educated and patriotic freemen, or the feudal serfs of corporate capital . . .[6]

The feudal serfs of corporate capital made a lot of headway during the next fifteen years. In 1888 President Grover Cleveland echoed Justice Ryan's sentiments:

> Corporations, which should be the carefully restrained creatures of the law and the servants of the people, are fast becoming the people's masters.[7]

Well into the twentieth century corporate excesses were acknowledged and condemned by some pretty prominent persons. Louis D. Brandeis, a multimillionaire (from his own law practice and astute investments) by the time he became a Supreme Court Justice in 1916, referred to corporations as "the Frankenstein monster which States have created by their corporation laws."[8]

Far from being "radical," harsh criticism of corporations has a long, respectable, and mainstream political lineage. Now that you know you're in good company, let's dream a little. Imagine what grassroots environmental activism would be like if corporations were restructured to be responsive to the people and to serve the public interest.

What if...

- Corporations were required to have a clear purpose, to be fulfilled but not exceeded.[9]

- Corporations' licenses to do business were revocable by the state legislature if they exceeded or did not fulfill their chartered purpose(s).[10]

- The state legislature could revoke a corporation's charter for a particular reason, or for no reason at all.[11]

- The act of incorporation did not relieve corporate management or stockholders/owners of responsibility or liability for corporate acts.[12]

- As a matter of course, corporation officers, directors, or agents could be held criminally liable for violating the law.[13]

- State (not federal) courts heard cases where corporations or their agents were accused of breaking the law or harming the public.[14]

- Directors of the corporation were required to come from among stockholders.[15]

- Corporations had to have their headquarters and meetings in the state where their principal place of business was located.[16]

- Corporation charters were granted for a specific period of time, like 20 or 30 years (instead of being granted "in perpetuity," as is now the practice).[17]

- Corporations were prohibited from owning stock in other corporations in order to prevent them from extending their power inappropriately.[18]

- Corporations' real estate holdings were limited to what was necessary to carry out their specific purpose(s).[19]

• Corporations were prohibited from making any political contributions, direct or indirect.[20]

• Corporations were prohibited from making charitable or civic donations outside of their specific purposes.[21]

• State legislatures set the rates that corporations could charge for their products or services.[22]

• All corporation records and documents were open to the legislature or the state attorney general.[23]

All of these provisions were once law in the state of Wisconsin. And similar ones existed in most other states.

There is no reason why grassroots activists cannot insist that we once again impose similar laws to direct corporate actions. But because education and media corporations are silent about the power of the sovereign people literally to dictate terms to corporations, we instead spend our time fighting in regulatory agencies and courts where the odds are against us from the get-go.

Much activism today concerns itself with struggling to induce government agencies to enforce their own laws, or exerting superhuman efforts to close gaping loopholes in existing laws. When we're not doing that, we're perhaps trying to add an obviously toxic chemical to a list of prohibited substances. Or maybe we're trying to coax a corporation that profited greatly from poisoning our air and water to pay for even a small portion of the cleanup costs.

One reason that we the sovereign people don't know our own strength is that too often we think of corporations and business as more or less synonymous. But corporations are not simply big businesses. You don't need a corporate charter to sell apples on the corner, or to operate a widget factory. Individuals, sole proprietorships, partnerships and other business forms can do business without obtaining a corporate charter from a state. Corporations are a special case.

A corporate charter granted by a state gives special privileges not possessed by other businesses. And in return, the state retains the power to alter, amend, or repeal said charter. The legislature of a state thus possesses not only the power to grant charters but to revoke them. This power is laid out in what is called the reserved power clause, and is explicitly spelled out in the laws or constitution of almost every state. Corporations are all set up by states to serve a "public need" and act "in the public interest." This is a long established doctrine.

> [T]he corporation is a creature of the State. It is presumed to be incorporated for the benefit of the public.[24]

Corporations are instrumentalities of the state, not independent entities. How have we strayed so far from this notion?

In view of the historic provisions that used to govern corporations, their representatives must be pleased that at least in this country, boycotts and divestment strategies are considered radical, and "dialoguing" is the preferred mode of interaction. The rest of this article is an exploration of ways to restructure today's corporation so that citizen activist efforts to eliminate corporate wrongs can amount to more than just a few hard-won needles in a corporate haystack.

As we now know, corporations are a special form of business entity given a state charter and certain privileges in exchange for being subject to the will of the sovereign people as expressed through state legislatures.

Over the last half dozen generations, corporation representatives have managed to set up barriers to insulate the corporation from citizen influence. Several trends have made it more difficult to direct the corporation towards serving the public interest it was created to serve. Among them:

- Under cover of the U.S. Constitution's Commerce clause[25] as interpreted by the U.S. Supreme Court, federal regulatory agencies have usurped many of the powers once exercised regularly by state legislatures. Today's corporations are ideally suited to wage battles on the regulatory front, because it is so difficult for citizens' groups to match their resources.[26] (In many ways, the late nineteenth century ascendance of the "commerce" argument is an eerie foreshadowing of today's NAFTA and GATT controversies.)[27]

- Through a series of leveraged expansions of the "diversity clause" of the U.S. Constitution[28] (allowing "citizens" from two different states to be heard in federal court instead of the presumably more biased courts of either's home state), the U.S. Supreme Court "deemed" corporations "citizens" and thus gave them nearly unrestricted access to federal courts.[29] This saved corporations the trouble of defending themselves in the courts of the state where they actually cause the harms.

- In 1886 the U.S. Supreme Court decreed that corporations are "persons" under the Fourteenth amendment, thus granting them protection under the Bill of Rights.[30] Such guarantees of free speech, due process, and equal protection under the law were long considered to apply to human persons. This ruling gave corporations unprecedented "rights" to question almost any law applied to them, and frus-

trated the ability of the people to direct corporate action in service of the public good.

- Stockholders, who used to really run corporations, have seen their power dramatically reduced. Today the powerful corporate manager class is insulated from stockholder influence by a variety of stock voting tricks and governance structures that they themselves set up. They are protected from most liability by state corporation codes and lax laws and enforcement. And they write their own paychecks.[31]

In order to have a world that we would not be ashamed to bequeath to the Seventh Generation, we must make two major changes in the governance of the corporation. First, we must remove obstacles to citizen control of the corporation. Second, we must reinstate provisions such as those once governing corporations, and add others that are particularly suited to our times.

"Model" provisions can become part of 1) state constitutions, 2) state corporation codes and/or 3) the actual corporate "charters," which are the documents states give to corporations to formally bring them into existence.[32] A program to institute such changes would include areas such as the following.

- People's power over corporations.

a) We the People can demand that state legislatures, the most direct expression of the people's will, use their "reserved power" to revoke the charters of errant domestic corporations. (A domestic corporation is one chartered in that state.) The people of Delaware and a few other states with "easy" chartering policies would have a more exciting time than the rest of us here, since the overwhelming majority of offending

(U.S.) multinational corporations are chartered there.

b)   In other states, citizens can demand that their attorneys general (or whatever agent is specified in their state laws and constitutions) revoke the permission of errant foreign corporations to do business in their state. (A foreign corporation is one chartered in another state in the U.S. Those chartered in other countries are called alien corporations.) Such actions have already been initiated against Weyerhaeuser, WMX Technologies (formerly Waste Management, Inc.), and CSX corporations.[33]

• Annul "rights" given corporations by judge-made law. We can work for state constitutional amendments that underline corporations' status as subservient to the people and the legislatures, and assert that corporations are not legal constitutional "persons" and thus are not protected by the Bill of Rights of the U.S. Constitution.

• Re-open corporate affairs to legislative scrutiny. At one time, all corporate records and affairs were open to legislatures or other designated state officials so that state governments, on behalf of the people, could monitor and evaluate corporate actions. We can reinstate such provisions in state corporation codes.

• Reinstate stockholder/owner control over corporate management and policy. For decades, concerned stockholders have attempted to curb some of the worst excesses of corporate policies, only to find their efforts thwarted by corporate management. We can modify states' corporation codes to return a modicum of control

of corporations to their putative owners, the stockholders. Some basic provisions might include: a one stockholder, one vote policy; prohibitions against issuing non-voting stock; and removal of obstacles to stockholders' access to information, initiation of policies, and removal of unsatisfactory corporate management.

• Give state courts clear authority to hear all corporation cases. State courts, more sensitive to local needs and conditions and more accessible to citizens, once heard most corporation cases. During the last years of the nineteenth century, numerous unsuccessful attempts were made at the federal level to reinstate this practice. Both federal legislation and federal constitutional amendments were proposed. Either one would do the trick.

• Reinstate historic limits on corporations. State corporation codes and/or corporate charters can be amended to include provisions such as the following:

a)   Require corporations to have a specific purpose, with a penalty of charter revocation if said purpose is either not fulfilled or is exceeded. This would include a prohibition on the kind of "look how ethical we are" advertising that currently dissipates stockholders' dollars and discombobulates public perceptions.

b)   Require a percentage of stockholders to live within the chartering state.

c)   Prohibit corporations from owning stock in other corporations.

d)   Issue corporate charters for only a specific term of existence, perhaps ten or twenty years.

e)   Limit real estate holdings to that necessary for corporate purposes.

f) Prohibit any and all political donations by corporations.

g) Prohibit all civic, charitable, or educational donations not specifically provided for in the corporate purpose.

h) Impose strict liability for all corporate officers and/or stockholders.

- Initiate new limits on corporate activities. We can add provisions (to state codes, charters, and/or constitutions) that:

a) Forbid corporations from doing business under pseudonyms or alternative names.

b) Require corporations to use Earth-friendly materials in all stages of operations, and to list all ingredients.

c) Prohibit corporations from buying up patents for the purpose of preventing others from exploiting them.

d) Require every corporate document to be signed by a human being who thereby takes responsibility for the veracity of statements and the soundness of judgments therein.

e) Require a corporation to pay for periodic health, safety, and environmental audits by independent experts selected by workers and affected communities.

f) Require that in the event of bankruptcy, corporate management pay and perks be withheld until all other debts and creditors are paid, starting with workers and small businesses.

g) Require 95% recycling.

h) Prohibit corporations from seeking or accepting "incentive" packages from any government entity.

i) Establish a maximum ratio (like 1:5) between compensation of the lowest-paid worker and the highest-paid executive.

j) Establish a process similar to "recall" procedures for elected officials, so that citizens can initiate revocation referendums for corporate charters (in the case of domestic corporations) and for certificates of authority (that allow foreign corporations to do business in one's state).

k) Require uniformity of health benefits within each corporation for all corporation employees (from CEOs to wage-laborers).

This is just a sampling of some of the options open to us. Priorities might include working to revoke corporate charters, to end the privileges granted corporations under the judicial "corporate personhood" doctrine, and to prohibit political contributions. Most of the obstacles we face are in the arena of judge-made law, but historic legislation and constitutional provisions offer us a solid body of favorable precedents. Much debate lies ahead. But it is high time we shifted the controversy from whether we control corporations to how we do so.

The sky's the limit. What are we waiting for? ∎

## NOTES

[1] Thomas Hobbes (1588-1679), English philosopher.

[2] In his *Wealth of Nations* (1776), Adam Smith was concerned that people's liberty was being encroached upon through the use of corporations to restrain competition and establish monopolies.

[3] A discussion of this and related issues can be found in Grossman and Adams 1993. See "Taking Care of Business" in this volume.

[4] See note 2.

[5] Justice Louis Brandeis in *Liggett v. Lee.*

[6] From an 1873 address to the graduating class of the University of Wisconsin Law School published in Beitzinger 1960, pp. 115-116.

[7] Cleveland 1989, p. 773-774.

[8] On personal finances, see Urofsky 1981, p. 9; Justice Louis Brandeis in *Liggett v. Lee.*

[9] Wis. G.L 1864, Ch. 166, Sec. 7; Wis. R.S. 1878, Sec. 1767.

[10] See the "reserved power" clause.

[11] Wis. AG. Op. (1913), vol. 2, p. 169.

[12] Act of Aug. 21, 1848, Wis. Laws, p. 148 (Gen. Incorp. for Plank Roads).

[13] *State ex rel. Kropf v. Gilbert.*

[14] McGovney 1943, pp. 853-898, 1090-1124, 1125-1260.

[15] Wis. R.S. 1878, Sec. 1776; Wis. Stat. 1931, 180.13.

[16] Wis. G.L 1864, Ch. 166, Sec. 9.

[17] Wis. G.L 1864, Ch. 166, Secs. 4, 33.

[18] Wis. R.S. 1878, Sec. 1775.

[19] Wis. R.S. 1849, Ch. 54 Sec. 7; Wis. G.L 1864, Ch. 166, Secs. 6, 15.

[20] And it was a felony to do so. Wis. State 1953, Ch. 346.12-346.15.

[21] For example, Wis. G.L 1864, Ch. 166, Sec. 7.

[22] *Stone v. State of Wisc.*

[23] Wis. R.S. 1849, Ch. 54, Sec. 22.

[24] U.S. Supreme Court Justice Henry Billings Brown, in *Hale v. Henkel.*

[25] U.S. Constitution Art I, sec. 8.

[26] An excellent discussion of the difficulties of relying on a regulatory strategy to actually regulate corporate action can be found in Stone 1975. Also, see "Sheep in Wolf's Clothing" in this volume. —*Ed.*

[27] See section titled "The Commerce Clause: The First NAFTA" in the article "Labor Organizing and Freedom of Association" in this volume. —*Ed.*

[28] U.S. Constitution Art. III, sec. 2.

[29] See note 14.

[30] *Santa Clara v. Southern Pacific Railroad Co.*

[31] A discussion of the historical process of taking power from stockholders and giving it to a largely independent corporate management can be found in Berle 1950.

[32] See article "Creating a Model Corporation Code" in this volume. —*Ed.*

[33] *Corporate Crime Reporter,* June 28 1995, and *Rachel's Environmental Health Weekly,* no. 455.

# YOU'VE HEARD OF SANTA CLARA, NOW MEET DARTMOUTH

*by Peter Kellman*

WE HAVE A GREAT system of government. Amending the Constitution is a very different process for wealthy citizens as opposed to the majority of us. If the common people want to amend the U.S. Constitution, we must lobby Congress and get two-thirds of both Houses to propose an Amendment which must then be approved by three-quarters of the state's legislatures. Interestingly, freedom of speech, freedom of the press, freedom from unreasonable search and seizure, the right to a speedy trial, trial by jury, the ending of slavery, the right to vote, and the requirement that U.S. senators be elected by the people rather than appointed by state legislatures, all came into being through the amendment process.

The wealthy group of white men who gathered in a closed meeting in 1787 to write our Constitution didn't think any of these rights were important enough to be included. It was left to Anti-Federalists and mass movements of African Americans, Populists, workers and women—the mass movements of the common people—to amend the Constitution in ways they hoped would protect the majority of people from a wealthy minority.

There are four ways to change the Constitution. First, by revolution; second, by amending the Constitution (as described above); third, through a Constitutional Convention (which requires consent of two-thirds of the states); the fourth, by a process called "judge-made law."

A good example of judge-made law is the *Santa Clara* case of 1886, in which the Supreme Court ruled that a corporation is a person under the law and is therefore entitled to equal protection under the Fourteenth Amendment.[1]

An earlier example of judge-made law is the *Board of Trustees of Dartmouth College v. Woodward* from 1819. The word "corporation" is not mentioned in the Constitution or in any of its 27 amendments. However, Article I, Section 10, of the U.S. Constitution, known as the Contracts clause, declares that no state shall make any "Law impairing the Obligation of Contracts . . . " Chief Justice Marshall, writing for the majority in the *Dartmouth* case, stated in reference to the corporate status of the College that:

> The Opinion of the Court, after mature deliberation, is, that this is a contract, the obligation of which cannot be impaired, without violating the Constitution of the United States.

©2000 by Peter Kellman. Excerpted from an article published in *By What Authority* (vol. 2, no. 2, Spring 2000), a publication of POCLAD.

That is, a corporation is a *contractual entity*, and therefore is protected by the Constitution. But there is more to this story, a story which laid the legal ground work for the growth of corporate power at the expense of public education, and with it the future of our democracy.

In 1816 a class of small property owners and skilled artisans who, with Thomas Jefferson and many other founding revolutionaries, believed that the United States should have a republican form of government, elected a like-minded governor in the State of New Hampshire. The basis of Jeffersonian republicanism rests on a society primarily composed of small farmers who own their own land. An important component of republican philosophy is that a republican form of government requires an educated populace. These republicans wanted to insure that a college education would be available for their children, and that the content of education would be determined by a *public* process, not a *private* one.

However, colleges during that period were mainly private schools such as Yale, Harvard and Dartmouth; holdovers from the colonial days. These schools were linked to the past by class and religion. They were, by design, not republican in nature. Their purpose was to perpetuate the monarchy and class structure of the British empire, impose Christianity on native populations, train local clergy to keep the new populations in line, and educate the children of the elite.

Dartmouth College had been chartered by the King of England in 1769 as an Indian Charity School "with a view to spreading the knowledge of the great Redeemer among their savage tribes."[2] It soon evolved into a school "to promote learning among the English, and be a means to supply a great number of churches . . . with a learned and orthodox ministry."[3]

After the defeat of the British, American revolutionaries and Jeffersonian republicans led a movement to turn the colonial colleges into public schools. For example, the Colony of Pennsylvania had granted a charter to the University of Pennsylvania in 1755 under which the University would be run by a self-perpetuating board, similar to the Dartmouth College board. Following the revolution, in 1779 the legislature revoked the charter of the *private* University of Pennsylvania and in its place established the *public* University of the State of Pennsylvania.

In New Hampshire the newly elected Governor William Plumber, an ally of Thomas Jefferson, introduced "An Act To Amend The Charter And Enlarge And Improve The Corporation of Dartmouth College." The text of the law, passed on June 27, 1816, begins:

> Whereas knowledge and learning
> generally diffused through a Community
> are essential to the preservation of free
> Government, and extending the opportu-
> nities and advantages of education is
> highly conducive to promote this end . . .

The legislature made *private* Dartmouth College into *public* Dartmouth University, and ordered the new university to set up public colleges around the state. Governor Plumber promoted the change arguing that the original provisions of Dartmouth College "emanated from royalty and contained principles . . . hostile to the spirit and genius of free government."[4] The trustees of Dartmouth, however, objected to the charter change and took the state to court.

The New Hampshire State Supreme Court ruled that the legislature had the authority to change the charter of the college:

. . . because it is a matter of too great moment, too intimately connected with the public welfare and prosperity, to be thus entrusted in the hands of a few. The education of the rising generation is a matter of the highest public concerns, and is worthy of the best attention of every legislature.[5]

The decision was appealed to the U.S. Supreme Court; it reversed the state supreme court. As a result, the corporate form was given constitutional protection, and the formation of public colleges in the United States was set back for 50 years.

The U.S. Supreme Court was not interested in public education. The Court was set up to be the final protector of a propertied class. Think of it from a working class perspective. A group of wealthy white men goes behind closed doors for a couple of months and come up with a form of government to protect and promote whom? The people they fear most? Slaves, women, indentured servants, Native peoples, and people with little or no property? Not likely. The founders set up a government with a legislature composed of two bodies: the House of Representatives, elected by the people (the people at that time being, for the most part, white men who owned property); and the Senate, with members appointed by state legislatures.

So, if the "people's house" passed legislation that benefited the common people at the expense of the ruling elite, it could be pre-

vented from becoming law by the Senate. And should legislation promoting the interests of the majority over the interests of the wealthy minority be passed in both House and Senate, there was a president elected by an electoral college, not directly by the people, who could veto the legislation. If all this failed, and the House, Senate and president—or a state legislature—passed laws detrimental to the ruling elite, the case against this legislation could be taken to the Supreme Court. The justices of this court are lawyers appointed for life, lawyers who, for the most part, had distinguished careers representing the wealthy.

Imagine how the Supreme Court would have ruled in *Dartmouth* if the Court were composed of shop stewards, teachers, homemakers and librarians. But it wasn't. The Supreme Court delivered for the ruling elite, arguing that a corporation is a private contract, not a public law. The Court decreed that although the state creates the corporation when it issues a charter, it is not sovereign over that charter but is simply a party to the contract. All of which means that the corporation is protected from state interference by the Contracts clause of the Constitution because the relationship is a *private* not a *public* one. And so, Dartmouth University, a public school, once again became private. The republican notion that We the People needed to be educated in the democratic arts if we were to have a truly republican form of government was defeated, at least temporarily. ∎

---

## Notes

See *The Bank of Toledo v. The City of Toledo and John R. Bond*. In this case the Ohio Supreme Court took on the U.S. Supreme Court's *Dartmouth* decision, finding both the decision and its interpretation wanting. The *Bank of Toledo* case is a must read for anyone who wants to challenge the legal concept of the corporation.

[1] *Santa Clara v. Southern Pacific Railroad Co.*
[2] Clews 1899, p. 171.
[3] *Ibid.*, p. 173.
[4] Governor William Plumber, in a message to the New Hampshire legislature, June 6, 1816.
[5] Adams 1819, p. 135.

# CORPORATIONS AND THE PUBLIC INTEREST

## THE DEVELOPMENT OF PROPERTY CONCEPTS IN THE U.S. "JUST US" SYSTEM

*by Karen Coulter*

## LAW AS A MANUFACTURED ASSUMPTION

CONTEMPORARY EXPLANATIONS OF law seem to proceed on the assumption that the framers of the Constitution and the Bill of Rights were alone responsible for its content. Yet their authors represented a privileged class immersed in the public political tumult of a vigorous new State, with people prolifically espousing ideals, debating law and policy, and trying to obtain promised rights and freedoms.

Likewise, critical turning points in court doctrine are perceived as only due to particular cases and decisions, as if judges are merely arbitrators whose decisions are somehow kept pure and separate from their context of societal values and class biases.

This perception of judicial isolation is reinforced by a manufactured "assumption" that the U.S. public has been a static entity. People in the eighteenth and nineteenth centuries are presumed to have been passive and uninterested in personally engaging in the interpretation of law and political policy-making, as the majority are now disengaged in our current context of mind-numbing com-mercial media, abandonment of relinquished civic responsibilities to a technical elite, and well-advanced corporate takeover of governance, public life and culture. The omission in academic texts of the historical reality of significant public engagement in shaping law, policy and culture sets people on the dangerous path of believing law to be fixed in stone except for occasional inexplicable aberrations at the discretion of judges alone.

Corporate rule, thus, has been made to appear inevitable and too immense and unfathomable to overthrow. The individual's freedoms and abilities have been narrowly circumscribed as the courts have increasingly given corporations more powers. The torrent of ongoing abuses of wealth and power are seen as the *status quo*, regarded as normal costs of doing business, and as nothing that can ever be subject to more than limited reforms.

These are some of the basic perceptions which have generated current public apathy (along with a great confusion of mass-produced goods and parasitic consumerism with the source of happiness). However, court doctrine is mutable, with tremendous reversals and new precedents that come about as a

This article is provided without copyright. It is an excerpt from the author's presentation at the "Rebellious Lawyering Conference" at Yale Law School (February 1999), subsequently delivered at the University of Oregon's annual "Environmental Law Conference" in Eugene, Oregon (March 1999).

result of public agitation and consequent shifts in the political climate. And there are ways to shift the locus of power from arbitrary judicial fiat based on outdated elevation of private property rights as the highest good back to popular mandates protecting the overall welfare of real human beings and the Earth.

Our biggest stumbling block to lasting, systemic social change is our perceptions—ourselves—not physical impediments. So, let's think about some historical and legal history as a way of breaking through these perceptual barriers, to come out on the other side with a clearer vision of how to effectively challenge corporate rule.

## REVOLUTIONARY IDEAS

The bedrock of U.S. law lies in concepts of property rights and their defense, so let's start with a re-evaluation of property. The meaning of the word "property" has changed over the course of the twentieth century. In most cultures of the world, property typically meant only personal property such as clothing and household goods. Land was considered to be held in common, to be shared by all, or was thought to be part of God or Nature, inseparable. Under Native American Iroquois confederacy law, the buying, selling and monopolizing of land was illegal and immoral. In English history, it was not until the enclosure movement that land titles were transformed from leasehold, or use, to freehold property. Nobles seized the land of the commons for themselves, fencing it off in their names only, even when they had no use for it. Enclosures were a revolution of the rich against the poor which left a large class of people with no land base and no commons from which to procure food. This forced dependency on the nobles for payment in exchange for labor, much as whole classes of

people are now dependent on corporations to provide for their basic needs in exchange for labor.

English common law can be seen as a reaction to the extensive collapse of the corrupt Roman empire and feudal and money-based speculative economies. Much as with today's globalization of finance and neoliberal imperialism, the competing monopolists of the Roman Empire left Rome for lower tax, labor, resource and environmental costs. Money flowed out of the imperial realm. Common law and Native Confederacy law, by contrast, limited the effects of greed by placing the commonwealth beyond the reach of speculative individuals, kings and corporations.

However, in the mid-1500s, the English monarchy regressed to imperial Roman ways. Royalty used so-called "equity" courts to give urban commercial interests access to rural community lands and resources denied to them by common law courts. In return, merchant taxes financed military colonizing conquests and opened the way for merchant and military influence-dealing in government policy-making. Again, we have an equivalent situation in the U.S. today, where corporations seek "equity" through use of the Fifth Amendment "due process" clause and through general use of federal courts to change the law of the land and gain greater wealth and power, redefining themselves through court doctrine and using their growing political rights and economic influence to govern the nation.

Many of the early colonists in the U.S. were disillusioned by the wretched poverty of England caused by enclosures, displacements and growing industrialism. They were impressed by the wealth and beauty of many Native American societies, and recognized the similarity between Iroquois Confederacy laws and English common law. To protect themselves from the economic and political subjugation they had experienced in England, they placed strong constraints in many of the early states' constitutions (once the "states" became constitutionalized after the American Revolution, as they had originated as corporations serving the British monarch). For example, the Massachusetts Constitution of 1780, Part I, Article VI, states:

> No man, nor corporation, or association of men, have any other title to obtain advantages, or particular and exclusive privileges, distinct from those of the community, than what arises from the consideration of services rendered to the public.

Likewise, due to the colonists' experience with British crown corporations, original corporate charters issued after the American Revolution strictly defined corporations as under the authority of the sovereign citizens. American revolutionists overthrew the British monarch and instead put newly enfranchised citizens (although they were all white men of property) in the King's place to rule. Corporations were only allowed to do what they were chartered to do: a paper-making corporation could only make paper, not lobby or pay off elected officials or improve its public image through charitable donations. Corporations were only given a limited time frame in which to exist, then were automatically dissolved. They were not allowed to own other corporations. Most importantly, a citizen could institute legal proceedings called *quo warranto*, literally "by what authority," for the revocation of corporate charters, the dissolution of the corporation, and disbursement of its assets, if the corporation either exceeded the authority given to it by citizens or failed to act on behalf of the public welfare.

## MEN OF PROPERTY WRITE THE LAW

Yet as the concept of property changed, the rights of corporations expanded. From the first application of the common land law of the English settlers, there has been a gradual extension of private control over land, first to simple use, then to benefit and ultimately to the idea of gain made by selling land. Land speculation radically transformed New England's quasi-democratic town pattern. (Actually most people, including Native people, women, children, indentured servants, slaves and poor vagrants were considered property or non-persons under New England's much touted "democracy," and insubordination to the ruling elite was met with severe bodily punishment, branding, increased length of servitude or slave-for-life status. There was active trading and selling of white servants (including at public auctions, and orphans or unclaimed children were sometimes forced into labor as "apprentices" or indentured servants.)

As land was transferred to the wealthy elite and usurped under title in "fee simple,"[1] it came to be regarded as a private financial asset. Earlier (especially in Native American tradition) land was considered part of Nature, like air, wind, water, and weather. Property concepts have been continuously extended so that today even much of our air, water, wind and sunlight have been privatized. Such privatization has led to the extension of private and corporate property rights to "intangible property" such as: so-called commercial free speech, the corporate ability to spend money to influence the outcome of public referenda, access to government contracts and subsidies and even the empty space in utility bill envelopes.[2]

Since land, resource wealth, and political

power are virtually inseparable in practice, the conversion of land into capital can be seen as one of the greatest paradigm shifts in the evolution of social philosophy. Traditionally, sovereignty is a concept of political or public law, and property is part of civil or private law. Montesquieu, the eighteenth century philosopher and jurist, said that:

> . . . by political laws we acquire liberty and by civil law we acquire property, and that we must not apply the principles of one to the other.[3]

That distinction has surely been blurred considerably now that U.S. courts have defined individual rights and liberties under the Constitution as corporate property, so that property no longer means just physical things. By the acquisition of such intangible property, in addition to amassing great physical wealth far beyond the means of all but the wealthiest individuals in the world, corporations have acquired most of the rights of individuals with virtually none of the responsibilities or liabilities (such as disparate taxation, and no death penalty or incarceration for serious crimes, and limitations on liability for actions). This creates a very unequal playing field. Yet Montesquieu's now outdated view that political laws must in no way impinge on private property—because no public good is supposed to be greater than the maintenance of private property—still forms the basis of legal thought in the U.S.

Legal and moral philosopher Morris Cohen has much to say on this issue. He writes:

> In making a private property right out of the freedom to contract, the Supreme Court has stretched the meaning of "property" to include what it has never before signified in the law or jurisprudence of any civilized country. But whether this extension is justified or not, it certainly means the passing of a certain domain of sovereignty from the state to the private employer of labour, who now has the absolute right to discharge and threaten to discharge any employee who wants to join a trade-union, and the absolute right to pay a wage that is unjurious to a basic social interest.[4]

Meanwhile, the sovereignty of the state is limited by the manner in which the courts interpret the term "property" [as well as "personhood"] with regard to the Fifth and Fourteenth Amendments to the Federal Constitution.[5]

Any one who frees himself from the crudest materialism readily recognizes that as a legal term, "property" does not denote material things, but rather certain rights. In the world of nature . . . there are things but clearly no property rights.

Further reflection shows that a property right is not to be identified with the fact of physical possession. Whatever technical definition of property we may prefer, we must recognize that a property right is a relation not between an owner and a thing, but between the owner and individuals with reference to things.[6]

This becomes unmistakable if we consider intangible property, which constitutes an ever increasing part of the capitalized assets of corporations. "[T]he essence of private property is always the right to exclude others."[7] Corporate private property rights exclude individuals and communities from access to commonwealth and power.

The money needed for purchasing things in the corporate commercial economy must be acquired by long labor and disagreeable service to those to whom the law has granted dominion over the things necessary for subsistence.[8]

Thus, not only medieval landlords, but the owners of all revenue-producing property are granted by the law certain powers to tax the future social product.[9]

The future social product constitutes natural resources once held in common and individual labor once used directly for family and community subsistence.

When to this power of taxation there is added the power to command the services of large numbers [of people] who are not economically independent, we have the essence of what historically has constituted political sovereignty.[10]

Thus the modern corporation has been given political sovereignty—the right to rule over individuals and communities.

In addition to indirect ways which the wealthy few use to determine the parameters of culture and freedoms for the many—such as commercial advertising to direct patterns of material consumption, and corporate control of media to limit the scope of political analysis—there is also the more direct mode of control that bankers and financial speculators exercise when they determine the flow of investment. This power becomes especially obvious when an economically poor country has to borrow foreign capital to develop its resources. The corporate-directed World Trade Organization and International Monetary Fund now exploit countries with the neocolonial practice of requiring "structural adjustments" in return for loans. These "adjustments" mandate severe decreases in domestic spending for public welfare and environmental protection, effectively impoverishing the debtor country and opening the countries door to their greater vulnerability and to their further exploitation by transnational corporations.

Thus, as Cohen points out, "it is necessary to apply to the law of property all those considerations of social ethics and enlightened public policy which ought to be brought to the discussion of any just form of government."[11] For that is what the largest corporations are doing—governing—just as the British crown corporations governed when they colonized other parts of the world with an explicit mission to destroy existing cultures and exploit the natural wealth of the land. The Crown corporations were granted authority by the British monarch to govern the conquered territories. The difference is that now the corporations are almost completely sovereign in themselves.

As transnational corporations have liquidated most of the natural resources and destroyed most of the cultural and biodiversity in colonial "new frontiers" abroad, they are now tightening their stranglehold over domestic policy, culture and labor in their countries of origin (witness the effects of NAFTA: the gutting of domestic regulatory laws, the blackmail of widespread downsizing of domestic workers with the threat of shipping jobs and factories overseas, pitting states against each other in a downward economic spiral). Transnational corporations' use of violence via foreign military actions and donated corporate equipment such as helicopters (from which to gun down indigenous protesters) and bulldozers (with which to bury the bodies) has also become more blatant (witness Shell and Chevron corporate-sponsored massacres of indigenous people in Nigeria to make way for oil pipelines).

## CORPORATE RULE IS RULE BY PROPERTY

Many corporations are now larger in gross economic revenues than most of the nations of the world. Corporations now make decisions behind closed doors that extend their governance (dictatorship) to a global scale. It is necessary to move beyond generally accepted justifications of the preeminence of property rights in order to free ourselves of the growing reality of global enslavement by the wealthy few. Cohen's refutations of some of the standard justifications for elevating property rights over all other values are worth considering.

First, it is as "absurd to argue that the distribution of property must never be modified by law as it would be to argue that the distribution of political power should never be changed."[12]

Second, as "not all things produced are ultimately good, as even good things may be produced at an unjustified expense in human life and worth, it is obvious that other principles beside that of labour or productivity are needed for an adequate basis or justification of any system of property law . . . [A]ll things being equal, property should be distributed with due regard to the productive needs of the community."[13]

Third, "the primary effect of private property on a large scale is to limit freedom."[14] A private corporate regime is too likely to sacrifice social interests for its own short-term or immediate monetary profits to itself. There are also inherent sources of waste in a regime of private enterprise and so-called "free" competition (which is actually heavily subsidized by taxpayers who benefit little or not at all, as well as being subsi-

dized by depletion of the commons—existing and future social wealth.) There is a finite, limited common supply of many resources that form the basis of corporate profit, such as land, minerals and fossil fuels. Thus a government that limits the rights of property-owners such as corporate entities may be promoting real freedom for individuals and communities and preserving social wealth for common use and future generations. As Cohen points out:

> [P]roperty, being only one among other human interests, cannot be pursued without detriment to human life. Hence we can no longer maintain Montesquieu's view that private property is sacrosanct and that the general government must in no way interfere with or retrench its domain.[15]

However, in the U.S. the last word on law comes from judges, who as lawyers are mostly trained in private rather than public law. This is why absolutist concepts of property prevail over obvious national interests such as the freedom of workers to organize, the necessity of preserving sufficient standards of living, and the need to prevent destruction of ecological necessities such as pure air, pure water and food, fertile soil, and a diversity of native plants and wildlife.

## CORPORATIONS AS PUBLIC, NOT PRIVATE

After all, it should be considered: what private corporate interest is not really a public interest? Most private property rights now claimed by corporations involve some part of the public domain, whether it be public lands, minerals and ocean fish, or what is to be public media and our right to have government free of corporate influence, to be a self-governing people.

When slavery is abolished by law, the owners have their property taken away but compensation is paid to the slaves, not the slave owners. Likewise, when a corporation's charter is revoked for exceeding its authority or acting against the public-welfare, corporate property must be taken away and its assets redistributed among the people and for the good of the land that suffered damages. Let's get the relationship straight—people must put themselves back in charge of the institutions society created to serve the public interest.

With these considerations in mind, it becomes clear that there is no unjustifiable taking when corporations are prohibited from firing their employees if they engage in union activity, and there is no property taken away without due process of law when a corporation is compelled to pay its workers a living wage instead of subsistence wages, or being downsized so that the corporation can exploit workers overseas at starvation wages.

Throughout history, experience has shown societies the necessity for "communal control to prevent the abuses of private enterprise"[16] arising from the accumulation and concentration of wealth. The subordination of all our societal values to the single unrealistic aim of somehow maintaining endless economic growth and ever greater short-term profit for the wealthy few (no matter the cost) puts corporations in the position of an imperial, dictatorial power. Life is far too rich and complex to hand over sovereignty and governance to those who are systematically rewarded for placing money above everything else. ∎

## NOTES

[1] "Fee simple" is an estate of a free person, of virtually infinite duration, and without restriction as to whom that free person may transfer the estate.  —Ed.

[2] *Pacific Gas & Electric Co. v. Public Utility Commission.*

[3] Cohen 1933, "Property and Sovereignty" p. 41.

[4] *Ibid.*, pp. 44-45.

[5] *Ibid.*, p. 45.

[6] *Ibid.*

[7] *Ibid.*, p. 46.

[8] *Ibid.*

[9] *Ibid.*, p. 47.

[10] *Ibid.*

[11] *Ibid.*, p. 49.

[12] *Ibid.*, p. 51.

[13] *Ibid.*, p. 52.

[14] *Ibid.*, p. 54.

[15] *Ibid.*, pp. 56-57.

[16] *Ibid.*, p. 65.

# SHEEP IN WOLF'S CLOTHING

*by Jane Anne Morris*

---

IF YOU'RE HAVING trouble getting to sleep, you can count sheep, or read a book about the history of regulatory agencies. It may turn out to be the same thing.

The nation's first federal regulatory agency, the Interstate Commerce Commission (ICC), was established in 1887. Concerned citizens, having failed to solve their difficulties in more traditional ways, sought the intervention and assistance of the federal government. Over the next three decades, these mavericks worked to defend the ICC's existence and increase its powers to regulate the railroad corporations.

Who were these pioneers who dared to go where no one had gone before, to urge the formation of and expand the powers of the first federal regulatory agency?

Prominent among them were the director and general counsel for several of Vanderbilt's railroad corporations, including the New York Central Railroad Company, Chauncey M. Depew; the president of the Union Pacific Railroad Company and former chairman of the Massachusetts Railroad Commission, Charles F. Adams; the president of the Minnesota and Northwestern Railroad Company, and president and chairman of the board of the Chicago and Great Western Railway Company, A. B. Stickney; the vice president, General Manager, director, and president of the Chicago, Burlington & Quincy Railroad Company and later, presi-dent of the Burlington & Missouri River Railroad Company, Charles E. Perkins; the vice president, general manager, director, and president of the Pennsylvania Railroad Company, Alexander J. Cassatt; Andrew Carnegie (Man of Steel); the prominent J. P. Morgan, banker, associated with the rise of the International Harvester Company and U.S. Steel Corporation; and 1912 chairman of the national executive committee of the Progressive Party, George W. Perkins.

The role of these and other railroad corporation men has been explored by historians whose research into primary materials led them to things you'll never read on the back of a cereal box. One such historian, Gabriel Kolko, made use of letters, speeches, testimony before Congressional committees, and trade journal articles in his efforts to piece together the story of what amounts to a regulatory revolution in the U.S.[1]

That such a revolution occurred is historical fact. After a slow start, an alphabet soup of regulatory agencies proliferated like lawyers on the national scene. But that the midwives of this revolution were railroad men and other corporate executives is a reality less widely appreciated, and at odds with current regulatory agency creation myths.

Late nineteenth century railroad companies were troubled by too much competition: waves of fierce rate cutting and rate wars, the

---

use of discriminatory rebates (a form of dis-count—actually a bribe—used by rival com-panies to steal each other's customers), and major bankruptcies. This is hardly the sce-nario that would have existed had the railroad companies succeeded in fixing prices, estab-lishing monopolies, and controlling the mar-ket. But they tried.

Corporate mergers, trusts, pools, and trade associations were all methods through which corporations sought to eliminate competition. Each ran into glitches, however.

Until the late 1880s, many mergers were effectively illegal because most states had laws prohibiting a corporation from owning stock in other corporations. Trusts, an effort to finesse this prohibition, were made technically illegal by the 1890 Sherman Anti-trust Act (subject to spotty enforcement and soon ren-dered nearly useless by judicial monkey-wrenching). Pools—sometimes illegal, some-times not—ultimately failed to maintain price levels for their members because they lacked enforcement powers (to sanction a member that broke ranks and cut prices, for instance). Trade associations tried to control the market by means of informal price agreements, stan-dards, and licenses, but as with pools, such agreements lacked the force of law.

So, throughout the late nineteenth and early twentieth centuries, mergers, trusts, pools, and trade associations all failed to meet the needs of large corporations eager to crush competition in order to maintain price levels.

Railroad companies wanted to fix rates among themselves, and then enforce these rates. (That is, they wanted legally enforce-able price-fixing). They wanted a shield against a tide of public activism that was showing itself in the form of tough state laws, increased populism, calls for government own-ership of railroads and other public utilities,

and a resurgence of socialist movements.

They wanted the public to pay the costs of coordinating an industry and maintaining quality control (standards, inspection, enforcement), while guaranteeing the railroad corporations a basic (and profitable) rate of return. Despite all of this government invest-ment, however, profits were to go to corporate coffers and stockholder wallets.

Railroad executives wanted the ICC to enforce rates. But enforcing rates did not mean capping rates in order to protect the public. Enforcing rates meant prohibiting upstart companies from offering lower rates and thus undercutting the profits of the established railroad companies. Enforcing rates was a means of protecting large corpo-rations from what John D. Rockefeller called "ruinous competition."

A. B. Stickney (Chicago & Great Western Railway Co.) explained about rates: "Let the law name the rates, and let the law maintain and protect their integrity." The Railroad Gazette expressed a hope that the ICC would "go ahead and catch every law-breaking rate-cutter in the country."

The 1906 Hepburn Act (augmenting ICC powers) has frequently been cited as a victory for "reformers." However, Railway World stated, ". . . we can see nothing in the measure threatening the interests of the railroads." In Railway and Engineering Review, G. J. Grammar of the New York Central Railroad Company concurred: "The enforcement of the new rate law will, I believe, be of the great-est benefit to all the railroads."

One such benefit was protection from what historian Lawrence Goodwyn called "the largest democratic mass movement in American history."[2] A railroad man wrote to the ICC in 1897, "Oh Lord pity us in Nebraska and preserve us from the results of a populist legislature and State government." Richard Olney, President Cleveland's Attorney General, explained to railroad corporation executives that the ICC was to be "a sort of barrier between the railroad corporations and the people . . . "

From the early days of the ICC, Charles F. Adams (later President of the Union Pacific Railroad Co.) saw what was needed to solve the railroad corporations' problems. "What is desired . . ." Adams wrote, "is something having a good sound, but quite harmless, which will impress the popular mind with the idea that a great deal is being done, when, in reality, very little is intended to be done."

The public was to be pacified with laws that sounded tough but placed much discretion in the hands of regulators. As Charles E. Perkins (Chicago, Burlington & Quincy Railroad Company) said succinctly in 1888, "Let us ask the [ICC] Commissioners to enforce the law when its violation by others hurts us."

In this context, federal regulatory agencies emerged like the Promised Land from a wilderness torn by rate wars, strewn with the carcasses of bankrupt corporations, clouded over with competition and uncertainty, and ringed by the howls of an outraged public.

Regulatory agencies like the ICC transformed activities once illegal (such as price-fixing and market control) into practices that were now not only legal but mandatory—with the government doing the enforcing and taxpayers bearing the infrastructure costs, while business corporations, investors and speculators reaped the profits.

By 1920 railroad corporations pretty much had it all, courtesy of the U.S. government and the ICC. The Transportation Act of 1920 gave the railroads what they had dreamed of since the 1890s if not before:

legalized pooling (i.e., price-fixing), guaranteed prices, exemption from anti-trust laws and an assured rate of return.

Thus emerged the ICC over its first decades as coordinator and guarantor of a government-enforced, regulated monopoly. The ICC had been exceedingly flexible in using its discretionary powers; its commissioners had been exceedingly sensitive to the views of railroad corporation officials. In short, it had been a good sheep, in wolf's clothing. Its actions had become so vital to railroad corporations' well-being that others could not help but notice. And so—you guessed it—this sheep was cloned. The ICC, considered to be a successful model commission, became a template for the next dozen or so regulatory agencies, effectively establishing the U.S. regulatory system pattern.

The argument will be made that the ICC is only one regulatory agency, that the railroad industry is different from other industries, and that the railroads are, well, a special case. With due respect to the railroads (which went into decline because corporation executives decided they could make more money from steel, rubber, and oil transformed into the polluting profit-makers known as automobiles), and to the ICC (abolished by an act of Congress in 1995), all industries are "special."

Kolko describes how regulation came to corporations in a host of industries in the decades around the turn of the century—including insurance, meat packing, food, banking, and communications (telephone and telegraph). The parallels to the railroad industry are striking. The big corporate players in various industries sought an escape from the rigors of competition through control of markets, government-borne costs of infrastructure and quality control, and direct or indirect price maintenance or guaranteed rates of return. Special, indeed.

No sooner had a flock of regulatory agencies been established than critiques began to appear. Every generation or so there arises a great hue and cry about how corrupt and/or ineffective they are. Soon after World War II one wave of criticism receded and left behind the Administrative Procedures Act (1946), which outlined measures that would supposedly make regulatory agencies less arbitrary by making them more like courts. Marver Bernstein followed up in 1955 with a classic critique that concluded, "Because [the regulatory agency idea] is based upon a mistaken concept of the political process which undermines the political theory of democracy, [it] has significant antidemocratic implications."[3] In 1960 James Landis, a regulatory agency veteran, made a report on regulatory agencies to President-elect John F. Kennedy. Landis, a supporter of the regulatory agency concept, nevertheless conceded that regulatory agencies were mired in "Alice in Wonderland" procedures; the costs were "staggering"; the delays "inordinate"; and the failures sometimes "spectacular." Then in 1975 Christopher D. Stone's *Where the Law Ends*[4] delivered an updated and still devastating analysis, this one encompassing the newer 1970s crop of regulatory agencies, many of them concerned with the environment.

It is difficult to say which is more discouraging: that the criticisms have changed very little over time, or, that the suggested changes are clearly unequal to the task. Some of the recurring criticisms are that:

1. Regulatory agencies have too much discretionary authority, which is almost invariably abused.

2. They combine legislative, executive, and judicial power in one place.

3. Their personnel and outlook reflect the views of the corporations they are supposed to be regulating.

4. Since individuals and small businesses can't afford the time and expense to fully participate, large corporations dominate.

5. Procedural considerations are so intricate and demanding that matters of fairness, justice, and overall policy questions, not to mention common sense, are ruled irrelevant if they come up at all.

Any one of these five would present a serious obstacle to democratic control. Together, they are so formidably anti-democratic that it's a wonder we can keep a straight face while claiming that by tinkering with regulatory agencies, we might "reform" them. There is nothing new about these problems, of course; they are why federal regulatory agencies were established.

Regulatory agencies are the corporations' response to people's calls for democracy and self-governance. Corporate officials who once hired Pinkerton's goons to do their dirty work and protect them from an activist public can now rest assured that much of that burden has been assumed by regulatory agencies. They work as the barriers they were designed to be.

Over the last century the regulatory regime did something else, something that receives too little of our attention. It replaced, and seemingly erased from memory, a myriad of imperfect but promising democratic measures that defined the corporation at the outset as a subordinate entity chartered to serve the public good. Many of these measures were straightforward, effective, and even clever, and did not require arcane administrative structures for their implementation and enforcement.

In contrast, our current system heaps huge helpings of powers, privileges, property protections, grants, exemptions, subsidies, and favors upon the corporate form, and then, as if in an afterthought, adds: "And, by the way, now we'll go through the motions of regulating you."

And what great targets these regulatory agencies make. Corporate public relations teams blame them for economic ills, and the public blames them for "not doing their jobs." Attention is deflected away from corporations as the source of problems, and toward efforts to "reform" regulatory agencies. *The idea that the concept of the regulatory agency is inherently flawed doesn't even make it onto the table.*

Moving this idea to the center of our debates opens up new strategies, more democratic goals, and opportunities for activism that have long been obscured by regulatory minutiae.

What would it take for us to discuss this possibility openly?

We have heard the howl of the regulatory agencies: a resounding "Baa-a-a, baa-a-a."

We've had a century to watch them fail to work for the public interest. Corporate lawyers might as well have put up billboards: "Do people think your factory stinks? Hire an expert to prove they're wrong!" "State legislature too democratic? Escape to a federal regulatory agency. And then to the courts!"

Why is so much of today's activism confined to what Harper's editor Lewis Lapham calls "clean and well-lit regulatory agencies"? What lies outside the regulatory realm?

Some of what lies beyond that realm can be found in the lore of labor struggles and the nineteenth century Populist movement. Some is between the lines in the convoluted prose of state corporation laws. Much lies dormant but frustrated, drowned out by the clanking machinery of our current democracy theme park. But we won't see or use any of it until we step out of the glare of the "Alice in Wonderland" regulatory realm, and let our eyes adjust to the unfamiliar light of democratic conversations and actions.

A sheep is a sheep is a sheep. Pulling the wool over our eyes won't change that. ∎

## NOTES

The bulk of background materials for this article, including quotations, can be found in Gabriel Kolko's excellent books, *Railroads and Regulation*, and *The Triumph of Conservatism*. Both are readable and widely available. Lawrence Goodwyn's *The Populist Moment* and R. Jeffrey Lustig's *Corporate Liberalism* are also indispensable in providing background on this critical period of U.S. history. The Bernstein,

Landis, and Stone critiques are all classics in the regulatory agency genre.

[1] Kolko 1963, 1965.
[2] Goodwyn 1978.
[3] Bernstein 1955.
[4] Stone 1975.

# CONQUERING FIBS

It's a big fib that this nation is a democracy. But such lies often assume lives of their own, become obstacles to change. This lie of "democracy achieved" warps thinking and organizing by encouraging people to believe that if enough of us bring enough accurate information to enough elected officials, they will set things straight.

This lie camouflages continuing efforts of the wealthy few to govern, for example, by redefining Earth's genes as *their* property; by enacting corporate property rights agreements masqueraded as trade agreements; by extending constitutional powers to corporations.

The democratic ideals so many have struggled for, generation after generation, cannot be reached by squabbles over how much poison corporations may legally discharge; over how much corporate campaign money; over how much corporate hog manure per square meter; over voluntary codes of conduct and corporate "social responsibility." The real struggle has always been over who has authority: the few, or the many.

Magnificent efforts over such diversions reinforce the lie, they don't expose, confront, and uproot.

# March of Folly

## CORPORATE PERVERSION OF THE
## FOURTEENTH AMENDMENT

*by Greg Coleridge*

"**M**ARCHING TOWARD JUSTICE: The History of the Fourteenth Amendment" is an impressive collection of pictures, quotations and chronological descriptions currently on display at the U.S. Court House in Cleveland. The exhibit, part of the Damon J. Keith Law Collection of African-American Legal History at Wayne State University in Michigan, examines the history of African-Americans in the United States from pre-Revolutionary times through the civil rights era.

The display revolves around the Fourteenth Amendment to the U.S. Constitution. Passed in 1868, the Amendment, as the exhibit's introduction states, "created a dramatic and fundamental break from the past by providing full protection for all American citizens, regardless of race. It redefined the nature of citizenship, solidified the system of federal government and, most of all, fulfilled the American Revolution's promise that all men are created equal and entitled to full and equal protection under the law. After its adoption, the Fourteenth Amendment became the chief weapon used by African-Americans to achieve citizens' rights."

As informative and broad as the exhibit is, there is a glaring vacuum in this historical account with important implications for all of us today, regardless of race. This is the absence of any mention of how corporations perverted the Fourteenth Amendment for their own benefit.

Following the Civil War, corporate agents were eager to translate their increased economic wealth into political power. From early days in many states, including Ohio, corporations were closely controlled and rigidly defined by the public through their elected officials, and by state courts. Corporations had no "rights," only "privileges" to do what individual corporate charters and state laws allowed. The Fourteenth Amendment provided a crucial tool for corporations to become "artificial" persons, to be no longer subordinate to human persons.

Applying the Fourteenth Amendment, a railroad corporation in California claimed that its due process and equal protection "rights" were being violated. In *Santa Clara v. Southern Pacific Railroad Co.*, in 1886, the U.S. Supreme Court—including three Ohioans— without deliberation agreed. Thus, corporations gained the constitutional shield of equal protection as persons. This meant that corporations, in important ways, could no longer be controlled. Hundreds of state laws defining corporate conduct—including many in Ohio—were overturned following *Santa Clara*;

and one can imagine that *Santa Clara* also had a chilling effect on much needed legislation in this area.

Eleven years earlier, in *Minor v. Happersett* in 1875, women in Ohio argued before the U.S. Supreme Court that the denial of their right to vote was an infringement of their due process rights under the Fourteenth Amendment. The Court did not agree. It took 48 more years and another constitutional amendment before this human right was won. Thus, corporations, legal fictions which exist in large part to protect directors, officers and wealthy investors with shields against liability, gained important constitutional protections that women, Native Americans and, as it turned out, most African-Americans, did not have. To the United States Supreme Court, property rights were more sacred than human rights.

The Fourteenth Amendment was not only perverted by corporate agents to gain initial "personhood" rights, but also to expand them. As Supreme Court Justice Hugo Black pointed out in *Connecticut General Life Insurance Company v.*

*Johnson, Treasurer of California* in 1938:

> Of the cases in this court in which the Fourteenth Amendment was applied during the first fifty years after its adoption, less than one-half of one percent invoked it in protection of the Negro race, and more than fifty percent asked that its benefits be extended to corporations.

"Marching Toward Justice" should have included not only the intention of the Fourteenth Amendment, but its actual impact. In significant ways, the Fourteenth Amendment became the chief weapon used by corporations to achieve personhood rights. Then again, given that the sponsor of the exhibit is the General Motors Corporation, and that sponsors of the Damon J. Keith Law Collection are the Ford Corporation, Charity Motors Corporation, Chrysler Corporation, General Motors Corporation, and Ameritech Corporation, the glaring omission of the corporate perversion of the Fourteenth Amendment may not be accidental. ■

# Coming Soon

## Futures Market in Constitutional Rights?

*by Jane Anne Morris*

---

I'T'S THE BEST of times, if you're a rapacious corporation with money. It's the worst of times, if you're a citizen with democratic pretensions, or a living thing. Or a rock. Especially if you contain ore.

Feeling cash-poor? Already sold your organs? Had your crop seeds patented by a transnational? Don't miss out on the growing market for selling your rights, individually or as a community. And the prospective buyers are. . . you guessed it, transnational corporations.

In Wisconsin, under the homey phrase "local agreement," corporations have found a way to buy up the constitutional rights of whole cities and counties, once and for all. This is how it works:

MegaMining Corporation (MMC) proposes a contract to a local government body, city council, county board, Native American tribal council, whatever. Then the corporation runs roughshod over open-government laws and exerts all the pressure that a multibillion-dollar corporation can bring to bear on a handful of local officials.

After months or years of pressure, the officials sign the local agreement and the following provisions become law:

- The local government gives MMC the right to mine, as long as it obtains state and federal permits (a breeze, if history is any guide).

- The local government promises to say that MMC "conforms with all local ordinances" when asked about MMC's mine permit changes or the adequacy of the company's reclamation plan.

- The local government promises not to renounce or repudiate this agreement.

And here's the good part:

- The local government agrees that this contract replaces, and constitutes compliance with, all local regulations, laws, permit requirements, licensing conditions, ordinances etc.—both in terms of substance and procedure. (READ THAT AGAIN. The local government has just given up all authority to govern or to represent its citizens. Local citizens have just lost their rights to enforce any local ordinances or regulations that were put in place to protect their environment or way of life. This goes for future laws, as well.)

It gets even better.

- If the local government is party to any proceeding that questions the validity of the contract, it agrees to allow MMC to represent it. (MMC will not charge for its legal services in this case. What a deal.)

---

• The local government is assured that it can sue MMC at any time so long as that action is consistent with the agreement. (But the agreement states that MMC is in compliance with all local laws and that the local government won't question the agreement, so what's left to sue about?)

In exchange, the local government gets a load of empty, unenforceable promises from the corporation—and a yearly payment. (Nashville, Wisconsin, a town of less than 1,000 people, stands to receive nearly $1 million over the first six years of its local agreement with a mining corporation.)

In a nutshell, this makes it legal for a local government to abandon all of its governmental and regulatory functions regarding mining activities by promising in a contract not to exercise its governance functions.

(It also may be possible for a corporation to transfer or sell the contract to another corporation. The contract is a form of property, and stranger things have happened in property law.)

If the local government somehow does end up in court over a dispute about conditions for renegotiating part of the contract, the local agreement stipulates that whatever else happens, "the court may not directly or indirectly prohibit . . . mining." (I'm not a lawyer, but it seems downright odd that a contract between a local government and a corporation could stipulate what action a court may take.)

Wisconsin passed one of the first local agreement laws in 1987, right after Exxon Corporation lost its first attempt to turn Wisconsin's North Woods into a mining district. Several local governments already have signed local agreements with mining corporations, despite sustained and persistent protests by area residents. Other government entities are under heavy pressure to do the same. (Of course, they have a "signing bonus" to look forward to. Nashville was set to receive $450,000 up front for signing.) The fact that the Wisconsin law has not yet been judged unconstitutional sets a decade-long precedent.

The Wisconsin law specifically permits local agreements regarding mining. But if the reference to "mining" were deleted from the law (which is simple enough to do), this would permit any corporation to buy off any local government on any pretext.

Imagine a JunkMart Corporation or a Toxic Mismanagement Corporation buying off the governance functions of a town or city, thereby gaining "legal" rights to do whatever the state department of natural resources and the feds would allow.

All such "local agreement" laws, under whatever name, should be located, identified and repealed. ■

# JUSTICE FOR SALE

## SHORTCHANGING THE PUBLIC INTEREST FOR PRIVATE GAIN

*by Richard L. Grossman*

---

J USTICE FOR SALE describes a "multi-faceted, comprehensive, and integrated campaign" coordinated over the past 20 years by large corporations and "ideologically-compatible foundations" to create taxpayer subsidized law firms, to change the civil justice system, to shape law school curriculum, to organize and reward law students, and to affect the minds and decisions of sitting judges.

The goal of this "relatively quiet but significant effort" was "to rewrite American jurisprudence . . . advanc[e] their agenda before judges, lawyers, legal scholars, and government policy makers. In addition, by focussing extensively on law schools and the next generation of lawyers, they have sought to assure control over the future direction of the law."

In 1971 Virginia attorney (and future justice of the Supreme Court) Lewis Powell wrote a memorandum for the United States Chamber of Commerce. As *Justice For Sale* describes it, Powell warned against zealous environmentalists, consumer activists and others who "propagandize against the system, seeking insidiously and constantly to sabotage it." It was time, Powell said, "for the wisdom, ingenuity and resources of American business

to be marshaled against those who would destroy it."

A successful corporate counterattack, in Powell's view, would require broad-based and coordinated activism on campuses, in the media, in political arenas and—most importantly—in the courts: "Under our constitutional system, especially with an activist-minded Supreme Court, the judiciary may be the most important instrument for social, economic and political change," Powell wrote.

Among Powell's recommendations, *Justice For Sale* notes, was to establish a business-sponsored legal center that would promote business interests and not hesitate to "attack the Naders" and others who "seek destruction of the system."

Soon the California Chamber of Commerce would propose what would become in 1973 the Pacific Legal Foundation, a nonprofit set up in Sacramento, California, from seed money raised by J. Simon Fluor of the Fluor Corporation. And in 1975 the National Legal Center for the Public Interest (NLCPI) was formed "to assist in the establishment of independent regional litigation foundations dedicated to a balanced view of the role of law in achieving economic and social progress."

---

©1993 by Richard L. Grossman. This article originally appeared as a book review in *The Workbook* (vol. 18, no. 3, Fall 1993). The book *Justice For Sale* is available from The Alliance for Justice at www.afj.org.

NLCPI helped create seven more such firms around the country, six of which operate today with money from the Olin, Scaife, Bradley, and Smith Richardson Foundations. In courts around the nation, they are challenging Superfund hazardous waste programs, environmental regulations, and rent control statutes—all of which they regard as grave challenges to economic freedom. They are also designing litigation around "takings"— the doctrine that some government regulations constitute takings of private property without due process and just compensation, thereby violating the Fifth Amendment. With this tactic they are seeking not merely to invalidate specific laws or to argue interpretations of laws. Rather, they are seeking to eradicate categories of laws by changing prevailing legal theory and establishing new precedents.

These legal foundations claim they are expanding the property rights and resource access rights of persons. But because the corporation under law is considered to be a person, with every victory they actually expand the property and resource access rights of corporations.

Olin Foundation president William Simon, a former secretary of the U.S. Treasury, has been a major player in these efforts. He is quoted in *Justice For Sale*: "Funds generated by business . . . must rush by multi-millions to the aid of liberty . . . to funnel desperately needed funds to scholars, social scientists, writers and journalists who understand the relationship between political and economic liberty."

Simon and many others have orchestrated and coordinated "sophisticated media offensives, academic research, and advocacy efforts" with lavish funding from Aetna Life And Casualty Corporation, Exxon Corporation, Pfizer Corporation, RJR Nabisco Corporation, General Electric Corporation, Dow Chemical Corporation, Monsanto Corporation and other legal fictions chartered in our names and in our states.

Corporate money has also been rushed by multi-millions to corporate fronts such as the American Enterprise Institute, the Heritage Foundation, the Manhattan Institute for Policy Research, the Insurance Information Institute, the Product Liability Coordinating Committee, and the American Tort Reform Association (ATRA). (The ATRA is made up of corporation trade groups such as the National Association of Manufacturers, the Chemical Manufacturers Association, the Pharmaceutical Manufacturers Association— thus giving corporations a decoy and accomplice group two full steps removed from their board rooms.) Judge Robert Bork, Irving Kristol, and law schools at Stanford, Yale, Columbia, George Mason, Chicago and Virginia universities have also been beneficiaries of this corporate largess.

Corporate money created the Federalist Society in 1982, helping it to gather 10,000 members at 120 law schools. "Dedicated to purging law schools and the legal system of the "orthodox liberal ideology which advocates a centralized and uniform society," declares *Justice For Sale*:

> . . . the Society is now the principal organization for recruiting, educating and mobilizing conservative students on law school campuses and showcasing conservative legal scholarship . . . The group's influence is perhaps best exemplified by the success of its three cofounders. As a member of the White House Office of Legal Counsel, Lee Liberman was considered the "ideological gatekeeper for the Bush Administration's process for selecting judges." David McIntosh served as

Executive Director of Vice President Quayle's Council on Competitiveness, and Steven Calabresi, now a professor at Northwestern University School of Law, was a special assistant to Reagan Attorney General Ed Meese.

In sum, paying for and orchestrating law and economics professors and curricula at the nation's elite schools; sponsoring conferences, "Continuing Legal Education" workshops, legal research and theoretical writing; and funding massive advertising and strategic litigation "to make conservative economic theory the cornerstone of legal decision-making," they have set up an "institutional network that will advance and sustain their cause well into the future. Integrated and intergenerational, this infrastructure includes representatives from all segments of the legal establishment—judges, scholars, practitioners, and young apprentices hailing from the Federalist Society."

*Justice For Sale* is a frightening report, meticulously documented with references to the professors, theorists, and foundations behind this campaign. "Intended to provoke debate" and "instigate true reform of the legal system," it should be a catalyst for public debate and strategizing. Read it.

Readers, however, should consider this report in a broader political and historical context than the one the Alliance establishes for its hue and cry.

For example, as former Supreme Court Justice Felix Frankfurter pointed out decades ago, the history of constitutional law is "the history of the impact of the modern corporation upon the American scene."[1] But *Justice For Sale* interprets current corporate efforts as seeking "to shift the law from its traditional foundations of public justice and equity . . . to elevate corporate profits and private wealth

over social justice and individual rights as the cornerstones of our legal process." Alas, such shifts and elevations were engineered by the forbears of today's corporations over a century ago and steadily extended ever since.

*Justice For Sale* also posits as our public policy choices only government regulation, on the one hand, and unregulated markets on the other. It makes no mention of alternatives to private corporations—public ownership of enterprises, cooperatives or worker- and municipally-owned businesses—well within American traditions.

The report does not discuss how corporations shaped and dominated the operations of (to cite only a few) the Interstate Commerce Commission, the Employment Act of 1946, the Taft-Hartley Act, the Wilderness Act of 1964, the Atomic Energy and Nuclear Regulatory Commission, and the latest Clean Air Act amendments. We must therefore inquire, after Harvard Law School professor Morton J. Horwitz, what evidence is there for this report "characterizing most forms of government activity as a promotion of the public interest?"[2]

Lastly, this report stops far short of where its own internal logic clearly points: the need for major, coordinated, well-funded citizen counter strategies directed at the public, law schools and the courts, and which challenge the legitimacy and existence of today's corporations.

From a strategic perspective, it is vital to understand that Justice Powell wasn't just whistling Dixie when he counseled the Chamber of Commerce in 1971 that "the judiciary may be the most important instrument for social, economic and political change." As Professor Horwitz has observed in his book on legal history from the ratification of the Constitution to the Civil War:

A major transformation of the legal system took place . . . it enabled emergent entrepreneurial and commercial groups to win a disproportionate share of wealth and power in American society . . . [T]he law had come simply to ratify those forms of inequality that the market system produced . . . [T]he American judiciary—especially aggressively procommercial [and not-elected] federal judges—managed to overthrow earlier anticommercial legal rules . . . [A]s political and economic power shifted to merchant and entrepreneurial groups . . . they began to forge an alliance with the legal profession to advance their own interests through a transformation of the legal system . . . to create legal doctrines that simply mirrored the market.[3]

Despite such accomplishments, the judiciary did not rest from its labors. Throughout the rest of the nineteenth and well into the twentieth centuries, appointed judges gave privilege after privilege to corporations. They invented new doctrines such as freedom of contract, substantive due process, and managerial prerogative, which they used to overturn state laws asserting even limited citizen sovereignty over corporations, and to bestow upon corporations constitutional authority over investment, production, and the organization of work.

According to Professor Martin J. Sklar, by establishing "new trends in legal doctrine and political-economic theory" allowing "the corporate reorganization of the property-production system," the Supreme Court helped to sabotage blossoming social protest movements against corporate power and corporate harms.

So the law had already been stacked on behalf of corporations when attorney Lewis Powell penned his memorandum to the Chamber of Commerce in 1971 and when former Treasury Secretary William Simon started soliciting corporate millions. *Justice For Sale* describes what is only the latest in a long history of corporate efforts to use judges and the law to shape constitutional doctrines governing investment, production, natural resources, the rights of workers, the rights of stockholders, the liabilities of corporations and their executives. Simon's initiative is but another corporate campaign to limit citizens' fundamental rights, to close off the courts as a means of redress against concentrations of capital defined as *private*.

By virtue of their claimed right to influence the electoral process (upheld by the courts under the doctrine of "commercial free speech"), corporations have been major opponents of citizen referenda and initiatives to stop corporate harms, and major proponents of referenda and initiatives to shape pro-corporate government intervention in the economy. Via contributions to House and Senate candidates, they have bought the best Congress money can buy. Via campaign contributions to state legislators and with help from the American Bar Association and state bar associations, they have been rewriting corporation, tort, contract, property and liability laws. Never known for thinking small, they are today unabashedly writing such laws for former Soviet Union and Eastern European countries—places where these same corporations are seeking natural resources, cheap labor and vast markets.

*Justice For Sale* has correctly identified a major strategy of large and powerful corporations to undermine citizen efforts to establish worker, community, and constitutional rights; protect biological diversity, and the Earth itself. But if we intend to "instigate true reform of the legal system and a return to a process that seeks to secure justice for all," we must go well beyond this report's recommendations.

Three hundred years ago the corporation was understood to be a convenience devised by monarchs, merchants, explorers and men of wealth. It was a legal device to gather up resources and hold property, to exploit and dominate people. After the American Revolution, it was generally understood that the people were—and desired to remain—sovereign over corporations. Accordingly, Americans limited corporate existence to a set number of years and spelled out rules each corporation had to follow.

Today the 15 largest global corporations have gross incomes greater than the gross domestic products of over 120 countries. The 100 largest global corporations have incomes greater than half the member nations of the United Nations.

The havoc such corporations cause—documented in every issue of *The Workbook*, combined with the research reported in *Justice For Sale*—make clear that people must again extend our inquiries, political debates and active citizenship beyond "government regulation," on the one hand, and "the free market" on the other.

We can challenge the legitimacy—and the existence—of large corporations doing harm. As Paul Hawken, a founder of Smith and Hawken Corporation, recently offered as a first step toward a sustainable world economy:

> Take Back The Charter . . . Although corporate charters may seem to have little to do with sustainability, they are critical to any long-term movement toward restoration of the planet . . .
> Corporations are chartered by, and exist at the behest of, citizens. Incorporation is not a right but a privilege granted by the state that includes certain considerations

such as limited liability. Corporations are supposed to be under our ultimate authority, not the other way around. The charter of incorporation is a revocable dispensation that was supposed to ensure accountability of the corporation to the society as a whole . . . We should remember that citizens of this country originally envisioned corporations to be part of a public-private partnership, which is why the relationship between the chartering authority of state legislatures and the corporation was kept alive and active. They had it right.[4]

*Justice For Sale* concludes by reiterating that the direction in which the legal system is moving and the corporate forces propelling it raise "troubling and provocative concerns." In order to protect academic freedom, as well as our system of justice, the authors maintain, there must be "informed debate within law schools" and "full disclosure." Further, legislators, judges, and juries must "apply exacting scrutiny to the message and messengers of the so-called civil justice reform movement," and any "fine-tuning" of the civil justice system must depend on "accurate, relevant data." Finally:

> . . . the litigation strategy pursued by the business-funded "public interest law firms," complemented by the scholarship flowing from law schools and think tanks
> . . . mandate a corresponding vigilance of their actions in the courts, in "judicial seminars," in the law schools and in the legislatures.

Troubling and provocative concerns? Full disclosure and informed debate? Exacting scrutiny? Fine-tuning? Accurate, relevant data? Corresponding vigilance? Well, yes, of course.

But fantastically wealthy and powerful corporations have a long head start on expanding the legal rights and powers they usurped over the previous 150 years. So We the People need ambitious, well-planned, coordinated, public counter-strategies in each of the realms the report details, plus the real money to extend and expand these strategies over several decades.

We need law professors, law students, tacticians and organizers, unions and environmental groups, civil rights and consumer groups, garden clubs, students and enlightened business people, plus the growing locally-based movement for environmental and economic justice here and around the world, to organize an array of coordinated short- and long-term efforts.

The Alliance For Justice and other organizations should convene meetings to plan for more than fine-tuning the law, for more than restoring the legal system to what it was in 1970. Starting with denying the corporation personhood under the Constitution and reformulating managerial prerogative and liability, we need to reverse the transformation of the law that corporations accomplished well over a century ago.

These counter-strategies also need to redesign the corporations—which throughout U.S. history have been rewriting the rules of their own existence—to redefine in fundamental ways those legal fictions that Thomas Hobbes labeled "worms in the body politic." ∎

## Notes

1 Felix Frankfurter quoted in Miller 1967, p. 1.
2 Horwitz 1977.
3 Ibid.
4 Hawken 1993.

# THE CORPORATE CRUNCH IN VERMONT

*by Richard L. Grossman*

---

The whole premise of this silly law is that we can only get corporations to come to Vermont by prostituting ourselves like Delaware; that we can only get them to come here by giving away as many privileges as possible to corporate directors and managers, by showing them they can screw employees and the natural environment and Vermonters and get away with it.

DAVID BRIARS, A Vermont piano rebuilder and activist, is referring to SI, a bill enacted by the Vermont General Assembly early Sunday morning, May 15, and signed by the governor along with other economic development legislation. "There are Vermonters who have a different view. We wanted to rewrite Vermont's corporation law to attract responsible entrepreneurs and sensible investment to this state," says Briars. "We tried to raise the idea that we could use the corporate law to create preferred Vermont corporations which would meet high standards with regard to shareholders' and employees' rights, the environment, the community and citizens."

Briars had been working on telecommunication issues in the state legislature, but only got wind of SI in February 1993. "I thought it must be dangerous since it was written in impossible lawyer language, had no table of contents and a bunch of Republicans was trying to ram it through. So I read it. I was unimpressed and surprised

that it was regarded with such reverence by the people advocating it."

Briars spent hours putting SI into a readable format, integrating Senate and House amendments into the text, preparing a table of contents to the bill and soliciting comments. Along with a handful of other concerned citizens, he formed "The Committee To Comprehend SI" (CTCSI), seeking to stimulate debate over Vermont corporate law and citizen control over the economy. They convened meetings of citizens and legislators and circulated annotated copies of the bill.

## THE "HANDS-OFF" APPROACH

By the 1930s, U.S. judges, laws and regulatory processes had granted vast rights and powers to corporate entities. But a problem remained for corporations. Many state corporation laws, constitutional amendments and legal precedents which citizens had used to control corporations were still on the books. State laws and state constitutions still extended to citizens and their elected officials legal

---

authority to define corporate privilege, to grant and revoke charters, to set criteria for corporate existence, to hold managers, directors and stockholders liable for their corporations' abuses, to safeguard minority stockholders and to dictate the internal structure of corporations.

Enter the American Bar Association (ABA). For the past 60 years, the ABA has been aggressively peddling its "Model Corporation Act," which has become the basis of corporation law in most states. Every few years ABA lawyers come up with a revised model and work with more states to "modernize" their corporate law.[1] To the ABA, modernizing means transforming what had been "defining" state corporation laws into "enabling" statutes. According to *Economic Structure of Corporation Law* by Frank Easterbrook and Daniel Fischell, enabling statutes allow "managers and investors to write their own tickets, to establish systems of governance without substantive scrutiny from a regulator. [This is] a 'hands-off' approach."

In Vermont the effort was headed by Laura O. Smiddy, associate professor of law at the Vermont Law School, chair of the Vermont Bar Association's Business Association Law Committee and chair of the committee that drafted SI.

In a Fall 1992 *Vermont Law Journal* article Smiddy argued that Vermont's corporate law was "seriously outdated, [making] other states more desirable." She wrote, "If the Reform Act [SI] is passed, it will modernize Vermont's corporation law, provide the flexibility needed to adapt to changing business practice, and make Vermont's law consistent with the law of other jurisdictions." Smiddy's clear intent was to bring Vermont's corporate law in line with states such as Delaware, West Virginia and Nevada where officials eagerly granted charters to corporations with few questions asked.

In introducing SI, officially titled *An Act Relating To Business Corporations*, Republican Senator John Bloomer of Rutland County said that the bill's purpose is "to comprehensively revise and recodify Vermont law relating to business corporations" chartered in Vermont, or chartered elsewhere and doing business in Vermont. Originally introduced in 1991 as HB 265, the bill passed the House unanimously but died in the Senate when the legislative session ended. According to Representative Tom Smith of Burlington, "There had been no real public discussion, and no opposition was raised. Basically, corporate lawyers seemed to run the show." Reintroduced this session as "SI"—190 pages of what the *Burlington Free Press* called "a mogul field of jargon"—it picked up 106 amendments in the Senate and 60 amendments in the House on its way to the House-Senate conference.

Advocates described SI simply as a modernization of Vermont's 1960 corporation law, last amended in 1970. When pressed for details, they referred the curious to Smiddy's law journal article, where in 106 pages and 384 footnotes she contended that the state's existing corporation law was "unsuitable to modern business transactions," that it was "organized poorly, lack[ed] clarity and certainty," and was "overly rigid and inefficient." Robert Martin, a state official who lobbied for SI, summed up the official line at a March 1993 meeting with the Committee to Comprehend SI: "There is nothing more here than an effort to update the law. This law merely tells would-be incorporators where their corporation's birth certificate should be filed. If you are looking for corporations to be more environmentally sensitive, for example, this law has nothing to do with that."

Others argue, however, that SI is far more than a simple update of corporate law. Jerry Colby, a freelance journalist and former co-chair of the Vermont Coalition for Bank Reform, says that SI is "about consolidating corporate life and power in Vermont's economic life." Colby explains that the SI prevents small shareholders—even if they make up the majority—from exercising rights which have been traditional under Vermont law. It strengthens corporate managers' and directors' protection from stockholder lawsuits and public liabilities. It decreases the ability of shareholders in Vermont corporations to stave off hostile takeovers. It also removes stockholders' and citizens' ability "to delay corporate actions which might later be seen as harmful to shareholders or the public," and weakens legislators' traditional power to dissolve harmful corporations. "The whole question of engaging in unlawful business—where are the sanctions?" asks Colby. "This law not only encourages financial services and Walmart-type corporations to come in by removing obstacles, but more importantly, it will contribute to corporate takeovers in our small state."

Briars and his allies argued against granting more power to incorporators through SI, declaring that Vermont's *citizens* had the responsibility for planning and shaping the state's economic and social future. But these arguments were drowned out by official choruses claiming that Vermont had to become a more "hospitable" domicile to corporations in order to foster economic development and progress. As progressive Representative Terry Bouricius of Burlington says, "The concept of reining in the corporation was exactly the opposite of what the authors sought in this legislation . . . All this bill was trying to do was to accommodate this corporate world as

neatly and efficiently as possible."

The Vermont General Assembly passed Governor Harold Dean's Economic Policy Act along with SI. The Act's primary goal is to attract corporations to the state by giving them tax breaks and subsidies, in tandem with SI which offers business corporation law that, in the words of Professor Smiddy, "permit[s] corporations to operate without undue restraint."

The Vermont Progressive Economic Development Task Force, a citizens group made up of academics, planners and organizers, was also concerned about the direction in which the governor's Economic Policy Act would take the economic development of the state. In an April 1993 report the Task Force said that the Act's focus on public subsidies for "large (often out-of-state or foreign) employers is demonstrably short-sighted and naive. These are companies . . . over which we, as a small state, have no control . . . We need look no further than GE, IBM, Simmonds and Digital to see the fragility of a job base dominated by such giants." The Task Force concluded, "The Economic Policy Act ignores one of the fundamental causes of our continuing decline, which is a loss of control over our economy."

## CITIZEN SOVEREIGNTY

Task Force member and University of Vermont economics associate professor Jane Knodell says the Task Force had a sense that SI "would reduce the state's capacity to regulate private corporations . . . [and] would make all the alternate polices we are proposing not possible." But the Task Force did not pay much attention to SI as it made its way through the Vermont legislature.

That task was left to the small group of Vermonters who became The Committee To Comprehend SI. They attempted to make SI accessible to all citizens, focusing on the need for citizen sovereignty over corporations. It framed its meetings with citizens, legislators and the press around corporation-state-citizen relationships: Should each state set criteria for issuing corporate charters and corporation performance, and regularly review a corporation's record? Should states exercise their historic rights to prevent corporations which cause harm from doing business in their states? Why shouldn't states revoke the charters of harmful corporations? Why shouldn't employees, shareholders and corporate neighbors have as many rights as corporate directors and managers? If taxpayers subsidize a corporation, why shouldn't those taxpayers have ownership rights in that corporation?

The group's last-minute efforts—including a meeting at the State House in the same room where the Senate Judiciary Committee had polished up SI—enabled a handful of progressive legislators to startle the legislative leadership by posing a few amendments to strengthen shareholder and employee power. They opened up discussion about the relationship between Vermonters and corporations, and about the state's economic future.

But Briars and his Committee to Comprehend SI received little help from organizations and citizen leaders traditionally concerned with issues relating to giant out-of-state financial, agribusiness, energy, retail, information and timber corporations. No consumer, labor or other citizens' organization—from the Vermont Public Interest Research Group (VPIRG), to the Progressive Economic Development Task Force, to the Vermont Business Association for Social Responsibility—was active in fighting SI. Vermont's U.S. Representative Bernie Sanders—the nation's only Socialist member of Congress—chose to keep his state-wide

political organization at a distance. "I had assumed some of the private, non-profit groups involved in public advocacy would express interest, but they did not, even though the way corporations misbehave is at the core of what they are fighting," Briars says.

However, Briars does note, "I was astounded that there were so many people interested in this concept, ordinary people as well as lawyers . . . They regarded corporate law with the same horror I regarded it, did not want to look at SI any more than I did. But they read it. They felt it was essential for ordinary people in our society to understand and to think about stuff like this."

But the legislative process was stacked against them. Briars says of legislators who came to the citizens' meetings, "I got the clear impression that they were already overwhelmed, were just trying to sort out smaller bills, and were at their wits end, and here was this huge bill. Even in the form we had created, it was difficult for conscientious legislators to digest. After all, they are part-time lawmakers, with no staffs."

Representative Smith echoes Briars. "This spring, because of a little citizen organizing, different perspectives were put forward. At least there was some sort of debate on a number of items." Smith adds, however, "I think real debate over something like SI requires a preexisting body of knowledge. That takes time . . . I had an amendment on putting employee representatives on the board of corporations . . . [T]here was some sympathy for this in the House, but not enough . . . Hopefully, this was the beginning of a debate."

Representative Bouricius also notes the impact of the small public revolt against SI. "We had this yeoman's citizen group which . . . played a positive role, allowing a few progressive legislators to formulate amendments on the floor. They gave us good ideas for bills next year, on workers' rights and related issues," he says. Bouricius acknowledges the need for greater mobilization on this issue. "If citizen groups could have persuaded the secretary of state to take a consumerist, populist position, that would have helped. But our hope to restructure debate on 'what are corporations?' needed to have outside mobilizations—unions and other citizen groups writing letters, organizing, talking about corporations, history and alternatives. We needed a mobilized organization ready to go, along with a [corporate] scandal that forces these issues to be newsworthy."

Bouricius views the fight for greater citizen control over corporations and the economy as a long-term struggle. "I'm in it for the long haul," he says. "This spring, I offered quite a few amendments, a few got through, rather minor ones but more than just what we progressives wanted . . . We tried to make SI more shareholder-friendly, less director-friendly. But we could not raise the issue of greater state democratic control over corporations. We keep pushing, believing there will be an historic shift . . . It can be done."

## CORPORATE POWER

Without stepped-up citizen involvement, corporate manipulation of state legislatures and the law will continue. In state after state, large corporations are gaining tax abatements and other subsidies, and putting the latest version of the ABA's hands-off corporation law on the books. Dangling tax payments and promises of jobs as incentives, corporations rule as state politicians compete for corporate favor.

Corporate lawyers and sympathetic politicians have defined the terrain, the language, the agenda, the role of citizens and the legislative process. As Bouricius explains, "Even once legislators wade through bills like SI, few have the time or experience to understand the implications and compare it with the existing law or with norms in other states, to put each section into context."

In Vermont, with SI, corporations have rewritten the law which governs their own creation and operation. Activist organizations, struggling against many different corporations, were overwhelmed and caught napping. But a few citizens and legislators spoke out and organized a long-overdue effort to assert citizen sovereignty over the modern corporation. ∎

## NOTES

[1] For examples of "modernization" efforts in other states, see "A Quick Look at What Happened in New Mexico" and "Wrong Turn in Ohio" in this volume. —*Ed*

# WRONG TURN IN OHIO

## A WAKE-UP CALL FOR OTHER STATES

*by Greg Coleridge*

---

WITH ATTENTION OF citizen activists in Ohio focused this past fall on day-to-day battles against corporate harms or the World Trade Organization (WTO) meeting in Seattle, legislation to further reduce citizen authority over corporations was passed by the state with virtually no public awareness.

The Ohio General Assembly approved in October, with Governor Taft signing in December, House Bill 78, titled "Modernization of the Ohio General Corporation Law" (H.B. 78). The bill allows the withholding of listing a corporation's purpose and names of corporate directors at the time of incorporation, permits important corporate meetings to be held outside Ohio, and reduces the legal liability of corporate officials for corporate debts, obligations, and liabilities.

This stealth legislation should be a wake up call to citizen groups in other states struggling to strengthen democratic values and processes. The price of liberty is eternal vigilance, to paraphrase one of our founding fathers.

Promoted by the Corporations Committee of the Ohio State Bar Association, composed of corporate attorneys from across the state, H.B. 78 is the first major revision of Ohio's corporate code since 1955. At the very least, such a bill should have been voted on only after significant public debate from diverse groups and individuals across the state concerned about environmental, health, farm, labor, consumer, and citizen democracy issues. Better still would have been these same groups and individuals writing the bill in the first place.

Many of the H.B. 78's provisions came from the state of Delaware. Like desperados of old who used to run south of the border to escape prosecution, Delaware has been for decades the safe refuge for corporations seeking the absolute lowest level of accountability to citizens and public officials.

For several generations leading up to the 1930s, U.S. judges, laws and regulatory agencies had granted expansive rights and powers to corporations. But a problem remained for corporate agents. Still on the books were many state corporation laws, legal precedents and constitutional amendments which citizens over decades had used to define corporations. State laws, precedents and constitutions, like those in Ohio, still extended to citizens and their elected officials legal rights to set criteria for corporate existence: to grant and revoke charters; to hold managers, directors and stockholders liable and accountable for their corporation's abuses; to safeguard minority stockholders; and to govern the internal structure of corporations.

"It's a trend," says Richard Grossman of the Program on Corporations, Law and Democracy. "The American Bar Association's corporate attorneys target state legislatures. They call it 'modernizing,' but they're writing significant changes in the law, and they keep doing this in state after state. It just happened to be Ohio's turn."[1]

By the time a few environmental, labor and consumer organizations around the state learned about this stealth legislation, it had passed the Ohio House of Representatives 94-1 and had three hearings before the Senate Judiciary Committee. The bill was labeled by corporate attorneys and other promoters as simple "housekeeping" and "updating antiquated laws." The bill's chief proponent in the House called the legislation "a straightforward but dull piece of legislation . . . not likely to generate widespread interest in the corridors of the House and Senate but is offered for the benefit of Ohio's strong corporate community."

Many legislators in the Ohio House and Senate admitted they didn't know the bill's contents but voted for it anyway. So much for representative government.

When inquiring about testifying on the bill at the fourth and final public hearing before the Senate Judiciary Committee, I was asked if I was a corporate attorney. Greg Finnerty, legislative counsel for the Ohio State Bar Association said publicly, "It's not the most interesting topic in the world . . . It's only of interest to those engaging in corporate interests. I can't believe anyone cares." Apparently only corporate attorneys, not ordinary people or citizen organizations, should be interested in whether corporations should be even granted greater powers to define themselves.

With one minor change, the Judiciary Committee voted the bill out of Committee

unanimously. The following week, the bill passed the full State Senate 28-5.

The corporate media did not serve the public well on this issue—or maybe it did its job *all too well*. No major newspaper or electronic media outlet in the state even bothered to report the bill's basic contents. Alas, only a few community newspapers were interested.

The Ohio Committee on Corporations, Law and Democracy—an American Friends Service Committee-sponsored group of citizens statewide concerned about the illegitimate authority of corporations to govern, and the dangers this poses to democracy—mobilized against the bill at the last minute. The Ohio Sierra Club and the United Steelworkers of America in Ohio came out against the bill. In addition, the Ohio AFL-CIO sent a letter to every State Senator calling for further investigation into the bill before a vote.

At a time when seemingly everything is being "privatized" or "corporatized" in our society—health care, prisons, education, social services, ideas, cultural values, agriculture, media, and elections—giving up citizen authority over corporations deserves timely public information and debate. Unfortunately, neither our elected representatives nor the mainstream press felt that this bill was important enough to seriously examine and question. And unfortunately, a critical mass of Ohio's people were not organized well enough to know that this bill was in the pipeline, resist it once introduced, or force our elected representatives to amend it in ways that would have strengthened citizen authority over corporations.

H.B. 78 was a "Wrong Turn in Ohio" (WTO) for those striving to achieve democratic control over corporations. It represents a victory for the ABA corporate road show, and for strengthening corporate power in the U.S.

While important follow-up work to the Seattle World Trade Organization meetings and actions must be done, the same goes for our own "WTO." Citizens in every state face a daunting, yet exciting, challenge ahead: to understand and reverse the constitutional doctrines and laws in our states and at the federal level passed or constructed to insulate corporations from meaningful democratic control.

Activists must begin solid ground work now in preparation for the ABA corporate road show visiting their state, and for other potential wrong turns off the path to true citizen authority over corporations and their assaults on democracy. ∎

## NOTES

[1] For examples of "modernization" efforts in other states, see "A Quick Look at What Happened in New Mexico" and "The Corporate Crunch in Vermont" in this volume. —Ed

# A Quick Look at
# What Happened in New Mexico

*by Richard L. Grossman*

## Defining vs. Regulating

THROUGH MOST OF the nineteenth century in the U.S., the mechanisms people used to define corporations were:

- Actively debating and redefining the society's values and principles—including the basic concept that corporations were subordinate entities with no role in the mechanics of democracy (elections, lawmaking, jurisprudence, and education on values and public policy).

- Writing, issuing, amending and enforcing corporate charters.

- Writing, amending and enforcing state corporation codes and state constitutional provisions.

- Convening *quo warranto* ("by what authority") hearings to dissolve corporations which had become cancers upon the body politic.

By World War I corporations had by and large replaced these mechanisms of *sovereignty* with administrative statutes they wrote which conceded fundamental civil and property rights to corporations and aspired only to control corporate excesses, to regulate some of their behaviors. These laws instructed governments—often through regulatory and administrative commissions—to do the corporations' heavy lifting.[1]

Consequently, the people's authority to *define* the nature of our corporate bodies was replaced with rules which sought instead to *regulate* corporations' behavior, one harm at a time, and usually after the fact. We see the results of this in regulatory commissions—from public utility commissions to the Federal Communications Commission, Securities and Exchange Commission, Environmental Protection Agency, National Labor Relations Board, etc., which serve as barriers between the corporations and the people. (In Pennsylvania, the Department of Environmental Protection actually calls the regulated corporate polluters—not people, flora and fauna—their "clients.")

During the twentieth century, corporations worked diligently to divert movements for justice from taking their struggles into political arenas of authority—of sovereignty—to prevent people from using the *defining* mechanisms (like constitutions) to strip corporations of their privileges and immunities. In New Mexico in 1998 it is obvious that the corporations are still hard at work.

©1997 by Richard L. Grossman. This memo responded to a request of the author to provide critical analysis of, and suggest responses to, then-current legislation for a constitutional amendment in New Mexico known as House Joint Resolution 16. The legislation sought to amend the New Mexico constitution to abolish the state Corporation Commission (whose members were elected by the public) and replace it with a single regulatory agency administered by the legislature. This excerpt includes three of the six sections of that analysis.

## COMPARING LANGUAGE, THEN AND NOW

The reader can compare the language of the 1912 constitution and the amendment and consider the implications of these changes.

A. It is essential to know some recent history here: When was the last time the various (for example, insurance, communications, transportation, banking, energy, etc.) New Mexico corporation codes were rewritten, amended, or modernized? What institutions and persons were behind *those* efforts in New Mexico?

In many states, energy corporations are busy rewriting energy codes; telecommunication corporations are rewriting *their* laws. What institutions and persons were/are behind this current effort?

Over the past half-century, large corporations, with the assistance of the American Bar Association, have been orchestrating rewrites of state corporation laws under the banner of "modernization."[2] Usually, these efforts receive very little publicity, with no or *pro forma* public hearings, with the heavy work having been done quietly and behind the scenes (often by "liberal" attorneys and law professors). Their productions resemble this legislation: long, with no index or table of contents, consumed with details. The citizenry in general are not involved in planning or writing the new laws.

William Greider, in his 1993 book *Who Will Tell the People*, coined the phrase "deep lobbying":

> The larger point is that an informal alliance [is] formed by important players . . . to massage a subject several years before it would become a visible political debate . . . [T]he process that defines the scope of the public problem is often where the terms of the solution are predetermined. That is the purpose of deep lobbying—to draw boundaries around the public debate.

It is likely that the constitutional amendment and this draft legislation are the result of just such deep lobbying by major New Mexico corporate officials and their associates and hirelings.

B. The original state Corporation Commission created by the constitution of 1912 had some constitutional authority independent of the legislature. For example, it had the "right at all times to inspect the books, papers and records of all such companies and common carriers doing business in this state," and to require from them "special reports and statements, under oath, concerning their business."[3] It was the duty of the commissioners to be informed about rates and charges and to take appropriate action when the public welfare was involved.[4]

The new commission will be totally a creature of the legislature: "The public regulation commission shall have responsibility for chartering and regulating business corporations in such manner as the legislature shall provide."[5]

How did the original language get into the New Mexico constitution? What was going on at the time of statehood that Article XI was inserted in the constitution? Who organized and mobilized to get some of this defining language into the document?

Did the old state Corporation Commission ever use its authority to advocate for the people? Did it ever support the public against the power and wealth of great corporations doing business in New Mexico? Was there an opportunity for environmental justice, labor and low-income activists to take over the

Commission, and to use its constitutional authority to bring about meaningful changes in the rights and powers of New Mexico corporations?

C. Over the past few years I have suggested to friends in New Mexico that campaigns to elect people's commissioners to the old state Corporation Commission could serve as organizing vehicles for raising basic questions about the illegitimacy of the modern large corporation. Such campaigns could educate and mobilize people (and then state power) to define the corporation as a subordinate entity, without legal authority to shape public policy, influence elections, law-making and education, and the culture in general.

Imagine such a campaign. Imagine a majority of new commissioners opening their tenure by:

• Demanding that Intel, and other large corporations operating in New Mexico, surrender all their books and records.

• Scrutinizing past charters and licenses to foreign corporations.

• Convening public hearings about corporations and democracy.

• Issuing subpoenas to corporate executives to testify and supply essential corporate information.

• Prescribing the form of all corporate reports.

• Carrying out "all the provisions of this constitution relating to corporations and the laws made in pursuance thereof." [6]

The new commission, as cumbersomely constituted in the draft legislation, will not offer a like opportunity. Instead, it will be a giant, all-purpose bureaucracy focusing on regulat-

ing corporate behaviors. This draft law is quintessential "regulatoryese," administrative legalese. It is endlessly procedural, as will be the new agency it brings into being. There are no values here, no reflections on relationships, on historical evolution.

Life, health, wealth and democracy will be shaped by this piece of legislation . . . yet the language here is as antiseptic as can be.

## CONCLUDING THOUGHTS

Given that few New Mexican activists seemed knowledgeable about the old Corporation Commission, or sought to explore and invoke its constitutional authority and helpful precedents, the changes brought about by the constitutional amendment and the reorganization of regulatory bureaucracies probably will not make a hell of a lot of difference as to how things work. The relationship between large corporations, the state and the people will continue to be defined and dominated by the corporations.

What concerns me is that a major restructuring of the way New Mexico will deal with its people, and with corporate existence and behavior, has been under way for quite some time with (I've been led to believe) hardly any public input or awareness; that activists have not regarded this process as important, and therefore have not forced their way into it. They have not prepared by digging up relevant history and learning the law. Nor have they sought to take the offensive by using this amending or rewriting process as an opportunity to instigate a different debate about the proper relationship between the people of New Mexico and the corporate bodies they allow into their state.

Clearly, some people and organizations have gone to great lengths to arrange for the state constitution to be amended, and to restructure the regulatory agencies as they see fit. It looks as if they pretty much have had a free hand, and that they will get just what they wanted.

For environmental justice and other activists at this late date to inject values, principles and definitions establishing the proper subordinate role of corporations into a democratic New Mexico, and assert the proper sovereign role of people into this entire revision and future governing, will be a stretch. This is because the forces behind the scenes have obviously greased a great many skids via well-planned deep lobbying, and now have the momentum. The new draft legislation—without an index, without a table of contents—is a study in administrative and procedural minutiae. But it is possible, and I believe essential, for people interested in New Mexico's future to interrupt the corporate steamroller by forcing debate on the core issues glossed over during this process:

- What was going on in New Mexico in 1912 that people were able to get strong provisions subordinating corporations in the New Mexico constitution? What is the history of corporations, corporate law, and human opposition to corporate concentration of power in this state?

- Who should be in charge in New Mexico, the people or the corporations?

- What will be the mechanisms for We the People *defining* all corporations which seek to do business in the state? The new commission will essentially be a permitting agency, occasionally addressing specific corporate behaviors—after the fact and no doubt over and over again. OK, so who in the state is going to define corporate nature? Or do we just leave that to the corporate lawyers and public relations experts?

- Our states' elected officers are not empowered to create corporations (or help existing corporations) to cause harms to life, place, species or democracy. So, how will your state deal with corporations which persist in causing harms? (In other states, for example, corporations which have been convicted time after time of violating labor, environmental and other regulatory law cite these convictions as "proof" that the regulatory system works.[7] Which activist groups are prepared to challenge this insanity?)

- Corporations should not be regarded as persons under the law, with the ability to lobby, participate in elections, influence education and public policy, to shape the culture of the state.

- What about labor, environmental and other organizations of people? Why should they have fewer rights than the organizations of capital?

Without intentional efforts to educate and create a ferment around fundamentals, what has been a corporate-controlled process from the beginning will produce the desired corporate result, with no increase in public awareness, or will, or practical authority. Activists will experience this in the years ahead when they appeal to the new regulatory commission for justice.

What could have been an occasion for a statewide ferment about democracy and the institutions people create or allow will pass into history as having resulted in yet one more efficient "modernization" of law and regulation.

And in the future, when people realize that the harmful behaviors of giant corporations are forever, and start mobilizing to define corporate natures as limited and subordinate, plenty of official voices will be able to reply:

"You had your chance. There was a constitutional amendment on the ballot for you people to discuss and vote on; new legislation was circulated across the state, and then voted on by the people's representatives. Where were you? We've *done* corporations." And the new regulatory commission will loom large before you.

I therefore suggest that some organized group or groups begin agitating for statewide teach-ins on the nature and role of giant corporations created in our names, or allowed to do business in our states; for public hearings across the state on the nature and role of giant corporations; and for a large-scale public offensive—centered around *people's* draft legislation limiting the civil, political and property rights of corporations which do business in New Mexico—as a counter to the current 94 page draft drivel.

Please note that I am not proposing arguing over the procedural minutiae that characterizes the draft legislation. Indeed, contesting its procedural and explanatory minutiae would be like punching a marshmallow, and end up being an extraordinary waste of time and energy.

Rather, activists can provoke discussion and debate around the big issues of We the People: self-governance, democracy, and our responsibility as sovereign people not to allow the subordinate institutions we create to destroy the vital legacies of the people who struggled before us or to overpower the body politic, the land, and future generations.

There are ample precedents across the nation—and no doubt in New Mexico and across the southwest—for such an offensive. There are even major and potentially powerful historical traditions (which courts once respected) against granting to corporations governing powers. For example, the United

States Supreme Court, in *West Virginia State Board of Education v. Barnette*, 1943, noted that:

> The Fourteenth Amendment, as now applied to the States, protects the citizen against the State itself and all its creatures . . . There is no mysticism in the American concept of State or of the nature or origin of its authority. We set up government by consent of the governed, and the Bill of Rights denies those in power any legal opportunity to coerce that consent. Authority here is to be controlled by public opinion, not public opinion by authority.

In *Nebbia v. New York*, 1934, the U.S. Supreme Court declared:

> Under our form of government, the use of property and the making of contract are normally matters of private and not of public concern. The general rule is that both shall be free of government interference. But neither property rights not contract rights are absolute; for government cannot exist if the citizen may at will use his property to the detriment of his fellows; or exercise his freedom of contract to work harm . . . The Constitution does not secure to anyone liberty to conduct his business in such fashion as to inflict injury upon the public at large, or upon any substantial group of people . . .

In *Central Railroad Co. v. Collins*, a late nineteenth century decision, the Supreme Court of Georgia noted that:

> All experience has shown that large accumulations of property in hands likely to keep it intact for a long period are dangerous to the public weal. Having perpetual succession, any kind of a corporation has peculiar faculties for such accumulation, and most governments have found it nec-

essary to exercise great caution in their grants of corporate powers. Even religious corporations, professing and in the main, truly, nothing but the general good, have proven obnoxious to this objection, so that in England it was long ago found necessary to restrict them in their powers of acquiring real estate. Freed, as such bodies are, from the sure bounds to the schemes of individuals—the grave—they are able to add field to field, and power to power, until they become entirely too strong for that society which is made up of those whose plans are limited to a single life . . .

Without awareness and action by people in our communities and states, such lofty statements of principle—and the alleged laws of the land—are nothing but empty words.

There is still an opportunity here. But without intentional preparation and intervention, future efforts for justice in New Mexico will be made more difficult by the freedom given to corporations to amend your constitution and erect great bureaucratic barriers against democracy and self-governance. ∎

---

# Notes

[1] Kolko 1963. See also Weinstein 1968.

[2] For examples of "modernization" efforts in other states, see "Wrong Turn in Ohio" and "The Corporate Crunch In Vermont" in this volume. —Ed.

[3] Article XI, section 11, of the 1912 New Mexico Constitution.

[4] Article XI, section 9, of the 1912 New Mexico Constitution.

[5] Section 3 of the proposed amendment.

[6] Article II, section 6, of the 1912 New Mexico Constitution.

[7] See endnote 5 of "Some Lessons Learned" in this volume. —Ed.

# LETTER TO THE
# NEW YORK TIMES CORPORATION

*by Richard L. Grossman*

---

THE HEADLINE OF the Times' lengthy obituary[1] of Supreme Court Justice Lewis Powell labeled Powell a "Crucial Centrist Justice." But Justice Powell did not represent the "center" when the issue was human and environmental rights in conflict with the market economy, or people in conflict with corporate privilege having proper access to the civil justice system.

The obituary, by Linda Greenhouse, closed with President Clinton's unexamined comment that Powell "approached each case without an ideological agenda . . ." But when the United States Chamber of Commerce, on behalf of the nation's giant corporations, sought Powell's advice in 1971, Powell recommended the creation of nonprofit law corporations "to attack the Naders and others who openly seek destruction of the system." As justification, he railed about environmentalists, consumer activists and others who "propagandize against the system, seeking insidiously and constantly to sabotage it." It is time, wrote Powell in his memo entitled *Attacks On the American Free Enterprise System*, "for the wisdom, ingenuity and resources of American business to be marshaled against those who would destroy it."

Advising corporate counterattack at university campuses and in the press, he urged corporate leaders to devote special attention and resources to the courts. "Under our constitutional system, especially with an activist-minded Supreme Court, the judiciary may be the most important instrument for social, economic and political change." Powell's advice led to the creation of the Pacific Legal Foundation in 1973 (with seed money from anti-environmental, anti-human rights corporate mogul J. Simon Flour), and similar non-profit corporations specializing in advantaging corporate property interests over human rights. (A 1993 report by the Alliance for Justice, *Justice For Sale: Shortchanging the Public Interest For Private Gain*, described in detail Powell's memo and the Chamber's strategy.[2])

Where on the political spectrum did Mr. Justice Powell sit? Readers of *The Times* could have decided this for themselves if Linda Greenhouse had examined Powell as corporate ideologue, and had explored his role in helping the United States Supreme Court expand the privileges of business corporations while diluting the constitutional rights of people. ∎

---

[1] Published August 26, 1998.

[2] See "Justice for Sale" in this volume.

# Out on Our Own

If not for lavish corporate fairy tales and democratic myths, would anyone believe the idea of building a sane society based upon endless production and consumption; based upon corporate managers wielding the Constitution against us; based upon the routine destruction of the biological building blocks of life; based upon corporations pitting worker against worker, community against community, nation against nation?

It takes work—intentional educational organizing and collective work—to liberate ourselves from big lies and nice myths. But in the process of liberation we see, hear, feel, taste, touch. We think for ourselves. We trust our own experiences. We ask and answer relevant questions, like: How do we make the rules? How can we make laws about equal justice and consent of the governed; about cooperation over competition, and human rights over property interests; about people living in harmony with other species and the Earth; about honoring "enough" over endless "more"?

# REVOKING THE CORPORATION

*by Richard L. Grossman*

IN 1894 HENRY DEMAREST LLOYD, who was an agitator and orator during the peak years of the Populist revolt against corporations, wrote a wonderful book called *Wealth Against Commonwealth*. In that book he declared:

> We are calling upon [those who wield corporate] power and property, as mankind called upon kings of their day, to be good and kind, wise and sweet, and we are calling in vain. We are asking them not to be what we have made them to be. We have put power into their hands and ask them not to use it as power.[1]

Throughout this century many people have been asking the same thing. So we are here today at this law school. We the People are gathering and assembling, talking and listening, trying to figure out our situation. Over the past couple of days, in the workshops and in the halls, much of what is being said is that people are no longer functioning as We the People. Large corporations govern us. Corporations are defining our society, telling us how to think, and how to live.

If we assess the situation properly it becomes clear that we must do more than stop the obvious or even the subtle harms, like corporate poisoning and destroying. It becomes clear that it is what corporations are designed to do that is our problem, and that should command our attention.

So if what large corporations do well, do efficiently, is the problem, what should be our goals? What political arenas do we have to move into? What new tactics and strategies can we employ? Those are the key questions we will need to address tomorrow, and over the coming months and years.

For me, the question "What should our goals be?" has changed and evolved over the last couple of years. My sense now is that our goal is for the United States to become socially responsible. *We* must fulfill our social contract with one another and with the Earth. *We* need to struggle with what self-governance means, with what freedom means. We the People need to be the ones to define our communities, to define our work, to define our society. It is *We* who must take responsibility for acting like a free people and governing ourselves.

Thomas Berry, who has written about the history of the universe, met with my colleague Ward Morehouse and me a few months ago. We told him what we thought we were doing—that one of our goals was to begin building a global movement of human beings to dismantle the thousand largest corporations on the Earth.

Thomas, in his 80s, is a contemplative man. He stared at us for a while with his cerulean blue cosmic eyes, and he paused for what seemed to be eons. Then he said: "Why are you guys settling for such a limited goal?"

©1996 by Richard L. Grossman. This is an excerpt from his keynote address at the 14th annual "Public Interest Environmental Law Conference" at the University of Oregon School of Law, Eugene, Oregon (March 1996) which POCLAD convened and staffed.

It has taken me a while to figure out what Thomas meant. I think it is something like this: for billions of years, the universe has been exploding and unfolding. Vast, unimaginable events occurred across unthinkable amounts of time, across millions of light years. Out of that primordial energy emerged new stars and planets, the Earth with its mountains and seas and rivers and trees and diverse species . . . and human beings. For thousands of years these creatures have interacted, and people have struggled to figure out who they are and what is going on and how to live and how to cooperate, to think, to build.

This cosmic convulsion has been under way for billions of years . . . for what? So that in the course of a few generations we can turn it all over to the Walt Disney Corporation? To the Time Warner Corporation? So that it can be destroyed by the Weyerhaeuser Company? The Georgia-Pacific Corporation? Union Carbide Corporation? Exxon Corporation? Philip Morris Corporation? Microsoft Corporation?

Again, we are faced with the question: What are we going to do? How can we take humankind's enormous productive capacity, this enormous technological capacity, this enormous intelligence—how do we take our nimble fingers and our facile brains, and standing upon the shoulders of people who came before us, build the self-governing, just, and sensible societies which so many people in every generation since life began have sought?

Over this century, and certainly in my own lifetime, people have been resisting harms and waging wonderful struggles for justice. We have built an enormously strong foundation to take the next big leaps, the logical and commensurate leaps, to assume control over our lives, over our communities, and over our country.

What people are talking about at this conference is what people are beginning to talk about all over. We are educating ourselves about our histories—of our places, of the law, of this continent, even of the cosmos.

And people are organizing. They are organizing "Rethinking the Corporation, Rethinking Democracy" meetings, and other types of meetings, as they research and plan for appropriate action.

More people are trying to be intentional, logical. They want the next generations to be spared efforts that are off the point, that mostly camouflage who is in charge and what has to change. The people are focusing on our own responsibility, on our strengths, on our rights. In a real way, people in many places are continuing struggles for democracy and freedom and self-governance that began thousands and thousands of years ago.

What people are concentrating on now is not that there are a few rogue corporations, and that if we could just rein them in things would be better. It is not that there are a few overpaid CEOs. It is not that we need to put a few token workers or neighbors on corporate boards, or pass new regulatory laws.

People are demanding changes in legal doctrines like personhood, managerial prerogative, and intangible property rights. We are focusing on property and liability and the many counterintuitive doctrines which comprise corporate law. We are saying that it is illegitimate for corporate fictions to divide and conquer us, to define our labor, control our wealth, demarcate the commons, write our laws, elect our officials, poison our food, indoctrinate our children; to use job blackmail and control of information, the press, and money to run our local, state, and federal governments.

We are *not* aspiring to bring about "good corporate citizenship"—corporations are fictions, not citizens. We are not looking for "corporate responsibility" either. As subordinate entities, corporations must do what We the People tell them to do. *We* are the ones who must act responsibly.

We do not use the term "corporate America"—that is a basic contradiction in terms. We are not talking about meaningless voluntary codes of corporate conduct, corporate environmental management or equal poisoning under law.[2]

We are not calling for new labor law reform, or lobby law reform, or campaign finance reform. We are not aspiring to those alleged great days of the 1970s and 1980s when labor, environmental, health and safety, and consumer laws supposedly safe-guarded the public interest.

We are not suggesting that folks work harder to resist each chemical one at a time, each clear-cut one at a time, each mass lay-off one at a time, each toxic dump one at a time, each corporate purchase of a law or an election one at a time.

We are advocating citizen authority over the subordinate entity which is the modern, giant corporation. We are demanding repeal of judge-made doctrines; withdrawal of privileges and immunities which corporations have taken from the people and from the Earth.

⊚

For thousands of years, people have sought to live and die in harmony with place and other species. Thanks to the energy of the universe, to the richness of this Earth, and to the human beings who lived and struggled before us, we have the ability to analyze our present, to imagine many futures, and to take appropriate action.

It is time for us to embrace the responsibility for our lives. We can reject the dependency and phony security that accompanies all subservience to power, including corporate power. We can continue the historic struggle—the cosmic struggle—to create democratic societies.

As Gary Snyder has encouraged us, in *The Practice of the Wild*:

> To be truly free, one must take on the basic conditions as they are—painful, impermanent, imperfect—and then be grateful for the impermanence and the freedom it grants us. For in a fixed universe there would be no freedom. And with that freedom we improve the campsite, teach children, oust tyrants.[3] ∎

---

## Notes

[1] Lloyd 1894, p. 517.

[2] "Equal poisoning under law" is an ironic reference to the environmental regulatory system. Agencies, such as the EPA, define the levels of acceptable poisoning to the environment; for example 50 parts-per-billion (of arsenic in drinking) is *legal* poisoning, but 51 parts-per-billion would be *illegal* poisoning. The question is, should any amount of poisoning be legal?

Activists working on environmental justice issues note that all people, regardless of race, ethnicity, etc., should be poisoned equally. They are not saying that corporations cannot poison anyone, they are not challenging corporate authority to poison. The absence of such statements makes visible the prespective of POCLAD. *—Ed.*

[3] Snyder 1990, p. 5.

# THE POLITICS OF CHALLENGING CORPORATE POWER

## NOTE ON ISSUES AND STRATEGIES

*by Ward Morehouse*

## COLONIZATION OF OUR MINDS

A GREAT OBSTACLE TO asserting genuine democratic control over our lives is the corporate domination of American culture, our political economy, and the long-term corporate colonization of our minds.

Following the homely wisdom that fish discover water last, there is still strikingly little awareness of the extent to which our institutions and values are dominated by the corporate cultural paradigm. Cornel West expresses it this way:

> American society is disproportionately shaped by the outlooks, interest, and aims of the business community—especially that of big business. The sheer power of corporate capital is extraordinary. This power makes it difficult even to imagine what a free and democratic society would look like (or how it would operate) if there were publicly accountable mechanisms that alleviated the vast disparities in resources, wealth, and income oweing in part to the vast influence of big business on the U.S. government and its legal institutions.[1]

This dominance in Cornel West's view yields "a profoundly conservative culture" which in turn results in an emasculated American liberalism, the sacred cow of which—economic growth achieved by the actions of major corporations—is never seriously examined or questioned. Those who do are relegated to what West calls "the margins of political culture."[2]

These difficulties are compounded by a massive mythology surrounding the U.S. political culture. All societies entertain myths about themselves, and the U.S. is no exception. It is widely believed, and constantly reinforced by the mass media, schools, and other institutions which shape and transmit our political and social values, that we live in a political democracy. The reality is not political democracy but plutocracy—government by the wealthy.

## ACCOMMODATION AND CO-OPTATION

Another problem is the disposition of often well-intentioned persons and groups to indulge in accommodation with corporate power. This poses a real dilemma for those committed to going for the "corporate jugular" by attacking the roots of corporate power. "Accommodationists" often share with "jugularists" common values and concern with fighting economic and environmental injustice. Yet by the very act of accommodation they weaken their own efforts by suggesting that it is possible to change corporate leaders' behavior without changing the dominant role which corporations play in our society.

The whole social investment movement is a good illustration of accommodation in confronting corporate power. A glance at the *Newsletter of the Social Investment Forum* reveals hopeful initiatives involving the social investment community such as community development banks, and resistance to corporate attacks (through the Security and Exchange Commission) on shareholders' rights to raise social and environmental issues.[3] Within the religious community, the Interfaith Center for Corporate Responsibility has played a major role over a number of years in raising important questions about corporate performance, but its commitment to maintaining dialogue with corporate management makes this group hesitant about taking confrontational positions.

Related in character is the work of the Council on Economic Priorities (CEP) with its "Campaign for Cleaner Corporations." CEP's evaluations of corporate performance are frequently at variance with those of grassroots organizations fighting the same corporations in their own front yards.[4]

In a similar vein is the "social audit" movement which has gathered more ground in Britain than it has in the U.S., in part through the efforts of the New Economics Foundation in London. But even in the U.S., the idea has gained at least a foothold among what are generally regarded as more progressively managed corporations such as Ben and Jerry's, which engaged the services of Paul Hawken to conduct its "social audit."[5]

Closely related to social auditing is the "business ethics" movement—redemption from within, so to speak. Some of us in the struggle against corporation power think that when the chips are down (and much more often even when they are not) "business ethics" is an oxymoron.[6]

There is a fine line between accommodation and co-optation. The latter phenomenon is widely perceived, certainly by grassroots activists, to have destroyed much of the credibility of the major environmental organizations in this country. A recent report by an organ of the corporate-dominated "wise use" movement, paradoxically, documents the extent of this co-optation by listing major corporate contributors to the big environmental groups. The list is a roll call of some of the most environmentally destructive and socially abusive U.S.-based corporations in the world, including Exxon Corporation, Mobil Oil Corporation,[7] DuPont, Monsanto Corporation, Dow Chemical Corporation, General Electric Corporation, Amoco Corporation, ARCO Corporation, Weyerhaeuser Company, WMX Technologies (formerly Waste Management, Inc.), and dozens of others.[8]

For those of us committed to working toward genuine democratic control of corporations, this situation poses a dilemma. In many cases, as I have suggested, those involved in accommodation with, or co-opted by, corporate power also share with us many common values and goals. They are, at one and the same time, both our friends and our enemies. Serious thought needs to be given to engaging these persons and groups, sharpening the definition of co-optation so that this practice is immediately clear and can be readily labeled for what it is.

Given the foregoing discussion of accommodation and co-optation, coalition-building would appear to be dubious organizing strategy. Yet the task we are tackling involves a fundamental redistribution of power in our society, and we can hardly accomplish that alone. The problems of building coalitions and maintaining them, at any meaningful level of common action, are formidable, and almost certainly going to involve some measure of accommodation, if not co-optation.

## WE'LL NEVER WIN IF WE PLAY BY THEIR RULES

That is a truism. The rules of the game have been established by corporations, and by the institutions which they have increasingly dominated, including legislative bodies, bureaucracies, and courts. Thus, most of us would readily enough agree that a legal challenge to a charter of a major corporation would be unlikely to go very far without widespread political organizing.

Indeed, we should ponder one of the major lessons of the long, frustrating struggle of the victims of the world's worst industrial disaster. While the Bhopal victims' and groups supporting their struggle within India and elsewhere around the world used a variety of tactics (including recourse to the courts), in almost every instance in which they got some response, their tactics had been coupled with various forms of direct action, including hundreds of street demonstrations over the last decade in Bhopal and India's capital city of Delhi.[9]

So direct action needs to be part of this millennial struggle against corporate power. Just what kind of direct action and under what circumstances are matters that demand serious and careful consideration. And where do we draw the line? My long association with India may have put me under Gandhi's spell with a strong commitment to non-violence. But does that preclude destruction of

corporate property, such as that carried out by enraged farmers of the Indian State of Karnataka who destroyed the offices of the U.S.-based multinational corporate grain company, Cargill?

## ANTICIPATING THE CORPORATE COUNTER ATTACK

In the beginning, I think it most likely that we will be ignored, because to respond to our challenges to corporate power would only lend credibility to those challenges. But in time, challenges become more formidable as a movement gathers momentum. Once our adversaries begin to take us seriously, counter attack will be vigorous and vicious.

We need to give careful attention to our vulnerabilities and develop anticipatory and protective strategies to the extent possible. We also need to keep in mind that the stakes in this struggle are very high and may lead to more antisocial and destructive responses.

## THE LESSONS OF HISTORY

Of course, we know that reasserting citizen sovereignty over corporations—involving as it does such a profound redistribution of political and economic power—will not be easily or quickly achieved. But we should not lose hope in the face of such an awesome challenge. The big lessons of twentieth century history tell us we should not lose hope. As Howard Zinn reminds us:

> . . . the struggle for justice should never be abandoned because of the apparent overwhelming power of those who have the guns and the money and who seem invincible in their determination to hold on to it. That apparent power has, again and again, proved vulnerable to human qualities less measurable than bombs and dollars: moral fervor, ingenuity, courage,

patience—whether by blacks in Alabama and South Africa, peasants in El Salvador, Nicaragua, and Vietnam, or workers and intellectuals in Poland, Hungary, and the Soviet Union itself. No cold calculation of the balance of power need deter people who are persuaded that their cause is just.[10] ∎

## NOTES

[1] West 1982, pp. 468-469.

[2] *Ibid.*, p. 469.

[3] See, for example, "News, Views and Commentary," *Social Investment Forum Newsletter*, Winter 1995.

[4] For analysis of the CEP "Campaign for Cleaner Corporations" see Epstein 1994.

[5] Simon Zadek and others at the New Economics Foundation have produced several papers on social auditing; see, for example, Zadek 1994.

[6] Morehouse 1993.

[7] See endnote 3 of "Letter to Barbara Dudley" in this volume.

[8] Center for Defense of Free Enterprise 1994.

[9] Morehouse 1994. An excerpt of this article appears as "Unfinished Business" in this volume.

[10] Zinn 1993, p. 27.

# CORPORATIONS, ACCOUNTABILITY, AND RESPONSIBILITY

*by Richard L. Grossman*

---

IN 1628 KING CHARLES I granted a charter to the Massachusetts Bay Company. In 1664 the King sent his commissioners to see whether this company had been complying with the terms of the charter. The governors of the company objected, declaring that this investigation infringed upon their rights. On behalf of the King, his commissioners responded:

> The King did not grant away his sovereignty over you when he made you a corporation. When His Majesty gave you power to make wholesome laws, and to administer justice by them, he parted not with his right of judging whether justice was administered accordingly or not. When His Majesty gave you authority over such subjects as live within your jurisdiction, he made them not *your* subjects, nor *you* their supreme authority.[1]

From childhood this King had been trained to act as a sovereign should. What about us?

By means of the American Revolution, colonists took sovereignty from the English monarchy and invested it in themselves. Emerging triumphant from their struggle with King George and Parliament they decided they would figure out how to govern themselves.

Alas, a minority of colonists were united and wealthy enough to define *most* of the human beings in the 13 colonies as property or as non-persons before the law and within the society, with no rights any legal person was bound to respect. Ours was a terribly screwed-up sovereignty from the beginning.

Because of this immoral, atrocious structural mess, whole classes of people had to organize and struggle over centuries to gain recognition as part of the sovereign people— that is, they had to get strong enough as a class to define themselves and not let other people or institutions define them: African Americans, Native peoples, women, debtors, indentured servants, immigrants. To this day, many still must struggle to exercise the rights of persons, to be recognized as persons by law and by society.

Throughout this nation's history there has always been plenty of genuflecting to democracy and self-governance—check out politicians' Fourth of July orations and corporate advertisements. But the further each generation gets from the Revolution, the less the majority acts like sovereign people. And when it comes to establishing the proper relationship between sovereign people and the corporations we create, recent generations seem to be at a total loss.

Yet, earlier generations were quite clear that a corporation was an artificial, subordinate entity with no inherent rights of its own, and that incorporation was a privilege

---

©1997 by Richard L. Grossman. This article comes from a POCLAD memorandum.

bestowed by the sovereign. In 1834, for example, the Pennsylvania legislature declared:

> A corporation in law is just what the incorporation act makes it. It is the creature of the law and may be moulded to any shape or for any purpose that the Legislature may deem most conducive for the common good.[2]

During the nineteenth century both law and culture reflected this relationship between sovereign people and their institutions. People understood that they had a civic responsibility not to create artificial entities which could harm the body politic, interfere with the mechanisms of self-governance, or assault their sovereignty.

They also understood that they did not elect their agents to positions in government to sell off the sovereignty of the people.

In other words, these were human beings who tried to act as sovereign people. One thing they did was to define the *nature* of the corporate bodies they created. If we look at mechanisms of chartering, and at the language in corporate charters, state general incorporation laws and even state constitutions prior to the twentieth century, we find precise, defining language, mandatory and prohibitory language, often self-executory in nature. These mechanisms *defined* corporations by denying corporations political and civil rights, by limiting their size, capitalization and duration, by specifying their tasks, and by declaring the people's right to remove from the body politic any corporations which dared to rebel.

Here is an example of language which sovereign people, responding to the rise of corporations after the Civil War, placed in the California Constitution of 1879, and which appears in other state constitutions at about that time:

> All power is inherent in the people… (Article I, section 2)

> The people shall have the right freely to assemble together to consult for the common good, to instruct their representatives… (Article I, section 10)

> The exercise of the right of eminent domain shall never be so abridged or construed as to prevent the Legislature from taking the property and franchises of incorporated companies and subjecting them to public use the same as the property of individuals, and the exercise of the police power of the State shall never be so abridged or construed as to permit corporations to conduct their business in such manner as to infringe the rights of individuals or the general well-being of the State. (Article XII, section 8)

The principal mechanism which sovereign people used during the nineteenth century to assess whether their corporate creations were of a suitably subordinate nature was called *quo warranto*. The *quo warranto* form of action, as attorney Thomas Linzey has noted, "is one of the most ancient of the prerogative writs. In the words of the Delaware Court of Chancery, the remedy of *quo warranto* extends back to 'time whereof the memory of man runneth not to the contrary.'"[3]

*Quo warranto* simply means "by what authority." All monarchs understood how to use this tool in self-defense. They realized that when a subordinate entity they had created acted *beyond its authority*, it was guilty of rebellion and must be terminated.

Sovereignty is in *our* hands now, but the logic is the same: when the people running a corporation assume rights and powers which the sovereign had not bestowed or when they assault the sovereign people, this entity becomes an affront to our body politic. And like a cancer ravaging a human body, such a rebellious corporation must be cut out of our body politic.

During the first hundred years of these United States, people mobilized so that legislatures, attorneys general and judges would summon corporations to appear and answer to *quo warranto*. In 1890 with *People v. North River Sugar Refining Co.*, the highest court in New York State revoked the charter of the North River Sugar Refining Corporation with these words:

> The judgment sought against the defendant is one of corporate death. The state which created, asks us to destroy, and the penalty invoked represents the extreme rigor of the law. The life of a corporation is, indeed, less than that of the humblest citizen, and yet it envelopes great accumulations of property, moves and carries in large volume the business and enterprise of the people, and may not be destroyed without clear and abundant reason . . . Corporations may, and often do, exceed their authority only where private rights are affected. When these are adjusted, all mischief ends and all harm is averted. But where the transgression has a wider scope, and threatens the welfare of the people, they may summon the offender to answer for the abuse of its franchise and the violation of its corporate duty . . . The abstract idea of a corporation, the legal entity, the impalpable and intangible creation of human thought, is itself a fiction, and has been appropriately described as a figure of speech . . . The state permits in many ways an aggregation of capital, but, mindful of the possible dangers to the people, overbalancing the benefits, keeps

upon it a restraining hand, and maintains over it a prudent supervision, where such aggregation depends upon its permission and grows out of its corporate grants . . . [T]he state, by the creation of the artificial persons constituting the elements of the combination and failing to limit and restrain their powers, becomes itself the responsible creator, the voluntary cause, of an aggregation of capital . . . the defendant corporation has violated its charter, and failed in the performance of its corporate duties, and that in respects so material and important as to justify a judgment of dissolution . . . All concur.

Such a judgment should not be regarded as punishment of the corporation, but rather a vindication of the sovereign people. When our sovereignty has been harmed, we are the ones who must be made whole. The concept is similar to what Hannah Arendt described in her book *Eichmann in Jerusalem*:

> The wrongdoer is brought to justice because his act has disturbed and gravely endangered the community as a whole, and not because, as in civil suits, damage has been done to individuals who are entitled to reparation. The reparation effected in criminal cases is of an altogether different nature; it is the body politic itself that stands in need of being "repaired," and it is the general public order that has been thrown out of gear and must be restored, as it were. It is, in other words, the law, not the plaintiff, that must prevail.

There is no shortage of court decisions affirming the sovereignty of the American people over corporate fictions, and the need to restore the general public order. In *Richardson v. Buhl*, the Nebraska Supreme Court in the late nineteenth century declared:

Indeed, it is doubtful if free government can long exist in a country where such enormous amounts of money are . . . accumulated in the vaults of corporations, to be used at discretion in controlling the property and business of the country against the interest of the public and that of the people, for the personal gain and aggrandizement of a few individuals.

The Illinois Supreme Court in an 1889 case, *People ex. rel. Peabody v. Chicago Gas Trust Co.* wrote:

When a corporation is formed under the general incorporation act for the purpose of carrying on a lawful business, the law, and not the statement or the license of the certificate must determine what powers can be exercised as incidents of such business . . . To create one corporation that it may destroy the energies of all other corporations of a given kind, and suck their life blood out of them, is not a "lawful purpose."

The Supreme Court of Georgia, in *Central Railroad Co. v. Collins*, at about the same time:

All experience has shown that large accumulations of property in hands likely to keep it intact for a long period are dangerous to the public weal. Having perpetual succession, any kind of corporation has peculiar facilities for such accumulation, and most governments have found it necessary to exercise great caution in their grants of corporate charters. Even religious corporations, professing and in the main, truly, nothing but the general good, have proven obnoxious to this objection, so that in England it was long ago found necessary to restrict them in their powers of acquiring real estate. Freed, as such bodies are, from the sure bounds to the schemes of

individuals—the grave—they are able to add field to field, and power to power, until they become entirely too strong for that society which is made of up those whose plans are limited by a single life.

Justices White, Brennan and Marshall, dissenting in a 1976 case, *Bucklely v. Valeo*:

It has long been recognized, however, that the special status of corporations has placed them in a position to control vast amount of economic power which may, if not regulated, dominate not only the economy but also the very heart of our democracy, the electoral process . . . The State need not permit its own creation to consume it.

Chief Justice Rehnquist, dissenting in the same case:

. . . the blessing of potentially perpetual life and limited liability . . . so beneficial in the economic sphere [sic], pose special dangers in the political sphere.

A great achievement of corporations, as they set out towards the end of the nineteenth century to transform the law and recreate themselves, was to replace basic tools of sovereign people— chartering, defining incorporation laws, *quo warranto* proceedings and charter revocation— with regulatory and administrative law, new legal doctrines, and fines as corporate punishment. The Populists understood that these changes amounted to a counter-revolution, and so they resisted with great passion and energy.

Populist farmers and workers were not willing to concede that the corporate form would define "work" and "money" and "progress" and "efficiency" and "productivity" and "unions" and "justice" and "ethical conduct" and "sustainability" and "food" and "harm" and "personhood" and "reasonable."

They were not willing to concede that corporations should have the rights and privileges of persons.

So they organized, educated, resisted. They were crushed by giant corporations' ability to use state and federal government to take rights away from people and bestow them upon corporations.

Along came the Progressives. *They* were willing for the corporate form to become dominant, to shape our culture, to define work and our communities. They and their followers (and descendants) conceded to the corporation the rights and privileges it had taken from the sovereign people (via violence and via the decisions of federal judges): personhood, and a long list of civil and political rights such as free speech, and property rights such as the right to control investment, production and the organization of work.

By the beginning of the twentieth century, corporations had become sovereign, and they had turned people into consumers or workers or whatever the corporation of the moment chose to define humans as.

Public memory of the Populists' analysis and their efforts was rapidly wiped clean, while the Progressives were fulsomely legitimated and praised. Corporations did such a good job of rewriting history that when the Supreme Court finally began to hold New Deal legislation constitutional in the late 1930s, few understood that it was not the Populist agenda of sovereignty over corporations which was being affirmed, but rather the Progressive agenda of conceding power and privilege to corporations as a form of property, of tinkering with corporate behavior at the margins, curbing corporate excess, and perfecting the market.

As a result, most people do not acknowledge the massive corporate rebellion which took place; and most citizen efforts against corporations in this century have been struggles against the symptoms of corporate domination in regulatory and administrative law arenas.

But these are *not* arenas of sovereignty. These are stacked deck proceedings where people, communities and nature are fundamentally disadvantaged to the constitutional rights of corporations. Here, we cannot demand: *By what authority* has corporation X engaged in a pattern of behavior which constitutes an assault upon the sovereign people. Here, we cannot declare a corporation *ultra vires,* or *"beyond its authority."*

To the contrary, regulatory and administrative law only enables us to question specific corporate behaviors, one at a time, usually after the harm has been done— over and over and over again.

In these regulatory and administrative proceedings, both the law and the culture concede to the corporation rights, privileges and powers which earlier generations knew were illegitimate for corporations to possess. In addition, in these proceedings the corporation has the rights of natural persons: a human and a corporation meet head on, in a "fair" fight

Today our law and culture concede our sovereignty to corporations. So do most of our own citizen organizations dedicated to justice and environmental protection and worker rights and human rights. Consequently, our organizations use their energy and resources to study each corporation as if it were unique, and to contest corporate acts one at a time, as if that could change the nature of corporations.

Folks relentlessly tally corporate assaults, study the regulatory agencies and try to strengthen them. We try to make corporate toxic chemicals and corporate radiation and corporate energy and corporate banking and corporate agriculture and corporate transportation and corporate buying of elections and corporate writing of legislation and corporate educating our judges and corporate distorting of our schools, a little less bad.

But we don't study who We the People are; how sovereign people should regard ourselves; how sovereign people should act. We need to realize what power and authority we possess, and how we can use it *to define the nature of corporations*, so that we don't have to mobilize around each and every corporate decision that affects our communities, our lives, the planet. So that we don't have to wage a revolution every time we must remove a corporate cancer from our midst.

There is much talk today about the need for corporate responsibility and corporate accountability. The focus is on changing corporate behavior, primarily by voluntary codes of corporate conduct, education of corporate officers, pressure by consumers, etc.

Such discussions are diversionary. The reason corporations are so dominant and so destructive to life and democracy today is that a century ago corporations took rights and powers away from people. For example, corporations made themselves into persons under the law and created the category of "worker" with limited human rights. This was *before* most human beings had won their civil and political rights. Corporations' "right to manage" and "free speech" are currently safeguarded by the U.S. Constitution, thanks to legal doctrines concocted by the appointed judges of the federal judiciary.

Isn't it an old story? People create what looks to be a nifty machine, a robot, called the corporation. Over time the robots get together and overpower the people. They redesign themselves and reconstruct law and culture so that people don't remember they created the robots in the first place, that the robots are machines, are not alive.

For a century the robots propagandize and indoctrinate each generation so it grows up believing that robots are people too, gifts from God and Mother Nature; that they are inevitable, and the source of all that is good. How gullible we've been. How docile. How obedient.

But in the face of what we experience about corporations, of what we know to be true, why are so many people so obedient? Why do we hang on to the hope that the corporation can be made socially responsible? Isn't this an absurd notion? After all, organizations cannot be responsible. This is simply not a relevant concept, because a principal purpose of corporations is to shield the managers and directors who run them, and shareholders who profit, from responsibility for what the corporation actually does.

But people can declare organizations criminal, or vile—take a look at the Nuremberg Trials and at American history. And people can define organizations, business or government. Again, see the Nuremberg Trials, and American history.

But only people can be responsible. How? By exercising our sovereign authority over *all* the institutions we create. We the People are the ones who must be accountable. We are not accountable when we create monster robots which run rampant in our communities, and which in our names sally forth across the world to wreak havoc upon other places and upon other people's self-governance.

We are not being socially responsible or civically accountable when we don't act like sovereign people.

We are not being socially responsible or civically accountable when we play in corporate arenas by corporate rules.

We are not being socially responsible or civically accountable when we permit our agents in government to bestow our sovereignty upon machines.

We are not being socially responsible or civically accountable when we go to corporate executives and to the hacks who run corporate front groups and ask them please to cause a little less harm; or when we offer them even more rewards for being a little less dominating.

Sovereign people do not beg of, or negotiate with, subordinate entities which we created.

Sovereign people *instruct* subordinate entities. Sovereign people *define* all entities we create. And when a subordinate entity violates the terms of its creation, and undermines our ability to govern ourselves, we are required to move in responsibly and accountably to cut this cancer out of the body politic.

With such deeds do we honor the millions of people who struggled before us to wrest power from tyrants, to define themselves in the face of terror and violence. And we make all struggles for justice and democracy easier by weakening the ability of corporations to make the rules, and to rule over us.

Some might say this is not a practical way to think and act. Why? Because corporations will take away our jobs? Our food? Our toilet paper? Our hospitals? Because we don't know how to run our towns and cities and nation without global corporations? Because they will run away to another state, to another country? Because the Supreme Court has spoken? Because philanthropic corporations won't give us money? Because it's scary? Because it's too late to learn to act as sovereign people? Because in 1997 it is not realistic for people across the nation and around the world to take away the civil and political rights of all corporations, to take the property rights and real property corporations have seized from human beings, and from the Earth?

Yeah, and it *is* realistic to keep conceding sovereign powers to corporations; to keep fighting industrial corporations and banking corporations and telemedia corporations and resource extraction corporations and public relations corporations and transportation corporations and educational corporations and insurance corporations and agribusiness corporations and energy corporations and stock market corporations one at a time forever and ever?

Our president is realistic and practical. On January 10, 1997, President William Jefferson Clinton sent a letter to the mayor of Toledo, Ohio. The mayor had asked the president for help in getting the Chrysler Corporation to build a new Jeep factory within Toledo city limits to replace the ancient one which Chrysler Corporation was closing.[4]

The President of the United States, leader of the most powerful nation the world has ever known, elected head of a government always eager to celebrate the uniqueness of its democracy to the point of forcing it upon other nations, wrote:

> As I am sure you know, my Administration cannot endorse any potential location for the new production site. My Intergovernmental Affairs staff will be happy to work with you once the Chrysler Board of Directors has made its decision.[5]

Our president may not have a clue, but We the People did not grant away our sovereignty when we made Chrysler into a corporation.

When we gave the Chrysler Corporation authority to manufacture automobiles, we made the people of Toledo not its subjects, nor Chrysler Corporation their supreme authority.

How long shall We the People, the sovereign people, stand hat in hand outside corporate boardrooms waiting to be told our fate? How long until we instruct our representatives to do their constitutional duty?

How long until *we* become responsible; until *we* become accountable, to our forebears, to ourselves, to our children, to other peoples and species, and to the Earth?  ■

## NOTES

[1] Berman 1995.

[2] Goodrich 1967, p. 84.

[3] Thomas Linzey *et. al.*, Brief in Support of Motion for Peremptory Judgment," *CELDF v. Thomas Corbett, Attorney General of PA et. al.*, citing *Wilmington City*

*Railway Co. v. People's Railway Co.*

[4] For more details on this story, see "What Is The Purpose of Public Education?" in this volume.  *—Ed.*

[5] President Bill Clinton quoted in a letter to Mayor Carty Finkbiner, January 10, 1997.

# THE WTO, THE U.S. CONSTITUTION, AND SELF-GOVERNMENT

*by Richard L. Grossman*

---

I F THE WORLD Trade Organization (WTO) disappeared tomorrow, many people in other nations would feel a bit of relief. But nothing fundamental would change in the U.S. This is because corporations already have the special privilege (which lawyers call their "right") to make basic governing decisions. WTO or no WTO, corporations are protected by our Constitution and our Supreme Court, and therefore by the police, army, navy, air force, CIA . . .

In late November thousands from around the world will join people across the Pacific Northwest to protest WTO maneuvers in Seattle. Outside the United States, WTO decrees will inflict great harms upon human life and biological systems. We in the U.S. have a responsibility to support efforts by activists from other lands to neutralize and abolish the WTO. So POCLAD is participating in and supporting efforts to raise hell in Seattle.

But after Seattle, we in the U.S. have a formidable challenge: to identify and undo over 200 years of constitutional doctrines and laws designed to clothe corporate property with the power of government.

One example (among a zillion) of how these doctrines work: a few years ago a Massachusetts people's movement got a law passed restricting state officials from buying goods or services from corporations trafficking with Burmese dictators. Corporate directors did not like this public assault upon their "rights." But they did not have to summon the WTO into action. Why? Because men of property in the U.S. have long relied on the federal courts as their very own safety net. So they expected federal judges to nullify this law. And these judges did not disappoint, declaring simply that it was beyond the authority of the Massachusetts people to legislate such matters.

We have a long history of corporations vetoing people's laws and making their own. And the idea of merchants using some kind of world trade organization to do this work is nothing new. Towards the end of the seventeenth century, a new class of global merchants—architects of the expanding British Empire—realized their need "to create or adapt agencies to enforce British law on the one hand and restrain colonial legislatures on the other." So they set up a Board of Trade and Plantations to "scrutinize [the] colonial economy with an eagle eye . . . [and] recommend . . . with firm insistence the annulment of objectionable bills passed by colonial legislatures."[1]

The American Revolution unleashed a great democratic spirit. This led to struggles

---

©1999 by Richard L. Grossman. Previously published in *By What Authority* (vol. 2, no. 1, Fall 1999), a publication of POCLAD. Mike Ferner, Dave Henson, Peter Kellman, Ward Morehouse, David Cobb, and Mary Zepernick contributed to this article.

between the more-propertied and the less-propertied. In a number of states activists were able to qualify more white men to vote, increase the authority of lower legislative houses, lessen the ability of creditors to milk their debtors forever and ever, and limit the veto powers of governors and judges.

This of course is not what the wealthy, landed men who helped lead the revolution had in mind. They were, after all, a small minority of 20 percent: European and Colonial class structures had already defined the majority—women, slaves, Native peoples, indentured servants and workers in general—as *non-legal persons;* indeed as property. So in self-defense, Washington, Hamilton, Madison and other leaders of this minority wrote and fixed in place a constitution "to contain the threat of the people rather than to embrace their participation and their competence."[2] Committed to "preventing popular liberty from destroying itself" because "the anarchy of the property-less would give way to despotism,"[3] they made it extremely difficult for the majority to use the Constitution to make basic changes in law even if and when they should ever win the civil and political rights of persons.

In addition, these Federalist[4] founders defined decisions about investment, production, labor and technology as private property's "rights." They believed such decisions were proper matters only for the wealthy landed gentry and commercial class (the corporate managers of today). Accordingly, at the 1787 constitutional convention in Philadelphia, Federalist delegates maneuvered a leap from the Articles of Confederation—which had kept power and authority in state legislatures—to a totally new constitution erecting a powerful central government. In the constitution's Commerce clause (Article I, section 8), they forbade majorities, through state legislatures,

from making rules for production, commerce and trade; and to appointed Supreme Court justices, they gave the authority of kings.

So when today's corporate managers assemble at a meeting of the World Trade Organization, it is in this triumphant Federalist tradition that they deny legislatures representing communities, states, provinces and national governments the right to make decisions over what shall be produced, where it will be produced, and who shall produce it under what conditions.

Photographs of the blue-green Earth floating in space help people see our planet's fragile place in the Cosmos. A decade's experience with the North American Free Trade Agreement (NAFTA), the proposed Multilateral Agreement on Investment (MAI) and the World Trade Organization can help us examine our country's camouflaged histories.

With critics properly identifying the Seattle WTO meeting as an illegitimate global constitutional convention, we can now recognize the U.S. constitution as the first NAFTA. Sent to Philadelphia by their states to address some problems of interstate commerce under the Articles of Confederation, the (mostly Federalist) delegates pledged themselves to secrecy. Once behind closed doors, they replaced the Articles with a new plan, and denied the public any details about their deliberations for 53 years.[5] Their constitution turned a cooperative venture among sovereign states into a set up where Congress would decide commerce, an unelected Senate[6] would approve treaties, a Supreme Court would dictate the law of the land, and an indirectly-elected president[7] would command a standing army.

There are many similarities in the critiques put forward by the foes of the 1787 Constitution and by foes of today's corporate

WTO:

- Ultimate authority to govern should be in the hands of elected legislators meeting in decidedly public processes, not given to appointed judges.

- Government should promote democracy, community and public virtue, not special privileges for the few, not a commercial empire based on aggressive accumulation of wealth; property should not translate into privilege and political power.

- Communities and states should not give up their authority to distant, absentee rulers—especially to an appointed Supreme Court or to tribunals of corporate lawyers and trade bureaucrats.

- The majority must be able to amend bedrock doctrines and laws without waging a revolution every time.

- Mechanisms must exist to cut out of the body politic all institutions which improperly seize property and governing authority, or cause vast harms.

Overpowered and outmaneuvered by the Federalist founders, critics of the Constitution yielded when promised a Bill of Rights. With spotlights on global production and trade deals revealing our Constitution as the first NAFTA, our Bill of Rights stands exposed as the first diversionary "side agreement"! This is because, just as the labor and environmental "side agreements" did not alter NAFTA's basic undemocratic design, the Bill of Rights did nothing to change the very specific language of the constitution which empowered the propertied minority to rule. In addition, the state ratification process—during which the text of the constitution itself could not be changed—was the continent's first "fast track" vote.

For two centuries, people—especially those disinherited by the Federalist founders—have sought to use these first ten amendments to gain their rights and stop assaults by the wealthy and powerful. But to this day the courts have not used the Bill of Rights to protect people from entities defined as *private*—such as corporations. That is why, for example, workers on corporate property enjoy no Bill of Rights powers such as freedom of speech and assembly. Indeed, the Bill of Rights has been used to give even greater powers to the propertied—as with the Supreme Court's creation and expansion of corporate "free speech."

What's more, invoking the Bill of Rights frequently requires appeals to property's safety net—the federal courts. Such appeals legitimate federal court authority—particularly the Supreme Court's—to nullify the laws of towns, cities and states (just as we legitimate the whole cockamamie NAFTA structure by invoking a NAFTA "side agreement" to save a worker or a tree). In other words, we empower the Supreme Court (or NAFTA) to amend the constitution. This is what Supreme Court justices did by ruling that the slave Dred Scott had no rights a court must respect because he was someone's property;[8] that states could not control railroad corporations within their borders; that unions were criminal conspiracies; that the Fourteenth Amendment made the corporation a legal "person";[9] that speaking out against war was a crime.[10]

The surface language of the U.S. constitution is about We the People, our delegated authority, consent of the governed, the blessings of liberty. But the coercive power of the constitution is directed to limiting authority of the majority to make the rules for governing this country.

The surface language of the WTO is about the free trade of goods and services across national borders. But the coercive power of the WTO is directed to limiting the authority of the majority in every country to govern— that is, to control their own labor, steward their natural wealth, use their property, conserve their resources, structure their communities, define their institutions, choose their technologies. Backed by the military power of governments controlled by men of property (especially by the United States), the WTO is about enabling a few to rule over multitudes.

Let us all help get the WTO off the backs of other countries. But after Seattle, we'd best start changing the rules which the propertied minority put into our constitution two hundred years ago. Growing numbers of people have been exploring this challenge, but a definitive blueprint is yet to emerge. So there is great need for creative people from all walks of life to help frame this work.

As throughout human history, our collective task is protecting human rights over property privileges; empowering local, elected and public authority against private and distant unilateral decree; nurturing democracy, equal opportunity and the Earth, as opposed to protecting the wealthy minority's "property rights" in governing, accumulating, and denying others.

This minority uses elections, mayors, governors, legislatures, regulatory agencies, courts, police, armed forces and the president to keep the people from assembling to make the rules for investment, production, work, property and self-governance. We can replace the legal codes, judicial precedents and corporate culture which enable them to do so.

It is up to We the People—which now includes whole classes (such as women, African Americans, workers and Native peoples) who the culture, law and the Federalist founders once defined as *property*—to define corporations as *public instruments* subordinate to the people, and not as *private contracts*.[11] Let us break the hold which dead Federalists and Supreme Court justices have maintained over our lives and this fragile Earth. ∎

## NOTES

[1] Beard and Beard 1927, pp. 197-198.

[2] Nedelsky 1990, p. 159.

[3] *Ibid.*, pp. 27-28.

[4] Wealthy planters, land speculators, bondholders and slaveholders like Washington and Madison who sought a strong central government, and who organized states to ratify the constitution (written largely by Madison), were known as "Federalists." Those who opposed these men and their constitution were labeled "Anti-Federalists." Among the most famous were Patrick Henry, Richard Henry Lee, and Mercy Otis Warren.

[5] Only after Madison's death were his detailed notes on the constitutional convention published.

[6] The Seventeenth Amendment, ratified in 1913, replaced selection of senators by state legislators with direct election.

[7] Electors appointed by each state—comprising the so-called "electoral college"—technically control selection of the president.

[8] *Dred Scott v. Sandford*

[9] *Santa Clara v. Southern Pacific Railroad Co.*

[10] See various court decisions supporting the legality of sedition laws punishing speech and assembly during World War I. *—Ed.*

[11] In an 1819 decision, *The Board of Trustees of Dartmouth College v. Woodward,* the Supreme Court wrote corporations into the Constitution, declaring that corporate charters were contracts which legislatures could not change. See "You've Heard of *Santa Clara,* Now Meet *Dartmouth*" in this volume.

# Rumors of USA Democracy Discovered to be Counterfeit

*by Greg Coleridge, Richard L. Grossman, & Mary Zepernick*

---

*Disbelief and Sadness Sweep the Nation...*
*Land of Plenty Run By and For a Few...*

HOW MANY PEOPLE would be shocked to read these headlines in the morning newspaper? How many would cancel their subscription in outrage? Scratch their heads and think? Perhaps even be relieved to find they aren't crazy after all?

Along with Santa Claus, the Easter Bunny and the Tooth Fairy, an enduring myth of our society is the belief that the United States is a democracy. We learn it in school and hear it all the time in our popular culture, especially during this and every election year. While it is true that people have significantly expanded justice, equality and opportunity since the nation's founding, most such gains actually came about only as a result of great popular movements. At every step these movements confronted a Constitution and government institutions arrayed against them, as do organizers for justice today.

For six years we in POCLAD have been talking and writing about the relentless corporate seizure of the people's authority to govern. Over the past year we have focused on the undemocratic nature of the Constitutional Convention, the Constitution itself, and the subsequent denial of the people's governing authority by federal courts and legislatures. It may be painful to say "Uncle Sam has no clothes!" Yet all the digging and grappling, the discussing and analyzing, point in this direction.

For example, in many gatherings we have asked participants to identify and share a "democratic experience." Just a handful of people among scores came up with examples having to do with governing institutions and processes. It has been in family meetings, civic groups or volunteer projects in which people said they have participated fully in discussions and decisions. Clearly, elections do not a democracy make.

A protest sign outside the Republican convention warned: "The most serious threat to democracy is the notion that it has already been achieved." Let's face it: for many the cat has long been out of the bag.

## A Stolen Birthright

C. Douglas Lummis has noted, "Democracy was once a word of the people, a critical word, a revolutionary word. It has been stolen by those who would rule over the people, to add legitimacy to their rule."[1]

---

However defined, democracy surely is a *process* whereby decisions that shape life, work, community and the Earth are *public* decisions, framed, debated and made by diverse human persons in open forums not dominated and warped by wealth; whereby all institutions that shape ideas or make governing decisions are public in nature. How does the U.S. of A. stack up?

This nation was born in revolution against authoritarian absentee rule. Its first and second constitutions set up very different governments. The first—the league established by the Articles of Confederation—did not create a strong central government, and left ultimate authority in state legislatures rather than courts. Although far from perfect, it was good enough to enable 13 loosely-knit colonies to defeat the greatest global power of the day. Yet it has been cavalierly dismissed by historians, politicians and corporate apologists as cumbersome and inappropriate. George Washington revealed something about his values when he observed that "We probably had too good an opinion of human nature in forming our confederation. Experience has taught us that men will not adopt and carry into execution measures the best calculated for their own good, without the intervention of a coercive power."[2]

The second government—established by the Constitution of 1787—reflects Washington's perspective. Celebrated in fable and song, its founding rhetoric extols liberty, equality and justice. However, much of its language made the United States government complicit in denying the rights of millions of people, and hedging the power of the electorate. The presidency and Senate were not directly elected. The separation of powers and checks and balances kept the House of Representatives, the unit of government closest to the people, weak. The federal judiciary was insulated by presi-

dential lifetime appointment and Senate confirmation. Constitutional amendment was made difficult, and there was no provision for national referendum or initiative. Not surprisingly, constitutional provisions like the Commerce and Contracts clauses have been used to magnify corporate power, deny human rights and community authority, and generally stack the deck in favor of privilege.

The Bill of Rights, added to the Constitution by anti-Federalists as the price of ratification, was intended to safeguard citizens from government abuses of power. However limited this protection has been in reality (thanks to the Supreme Court), it never purported to safeguard people from non-governmental power. What's more, the Bill of Rights has been hijacked by corporations to turn government against human persons, communities and the Earth.

> To a large degree, the court was intended to enforce the lines of division set down in the Constitution, in order to ensure that the areas marked off from politics would not be subject to political revision. The boundaries set in the Constitution were thus to be unrevisable by electoral majorities—a safeguard that would buttress the other institutional checks.[3]

The men who wrote the Constitution, and the men who refined it through the courts, have done a wonderful job of privatizing government—until just about every decision of importance is considered beyond the authority of the people. And what does the law most zealously protect? The constant corporate usurpation of people's rights, the relentless corporate denial of people's authority to govern, the absolute corporate squashing of working people's First Amendment freedoms of speech and association.

We in POCLAD have not studied all this history simply as an academic exercise, but to help us provoke conversation and debate among activists into rethinking organizational goals and strategies. We have been doing this work because, as pragmatists, we concluded that despite the successes that hard working people and civic groups have achieved, We the People still have not gained the promised authority to govern ourselves.

Ask yourself: are the decisions which define our communities' energy, transportation, agriculture, health care, land use, education, work, money supply, etc., really made by We the People? Is foreign policy? Government spying? The production and sale of weapons of mass destruction? Do elections, law-making, legal proceedings, and education nurture vigorous public debate about history and the real choices the nation can make? Are institutions actually defined and controlled by the people? Do all people enjoy liberty—that is, freedom of speech, freedom of association, equal protection, due process of law?

Who framed the issues in the recent presidential campaign? What do you conclude when the Democratic and Republican candidates for president and vice-president supported existing global trade agreements and fast track authority to create even more? When despite escalating popular protest the corporate press dismissed global "corporatization" as a campaign issue?

Why do state laws make it so difficult for third, fourth, fifth political parties to get on the ballot?

Do your congressional representative or senators take your views, or the views of your organizations, seriously? Do your state representatives? Do they treat you as they treat the CEO of the General Motors Corporation or the heads of the National Association of Broadcasters or the U.S. Chamber of Commerce?

## A DIFFERENT VISION

POCLAD has been looking at two historical streams: one is about the decentralization of power, about public decision-making and self-governance—about democracy; the other stream is about the concentration of power, private decision-making, governance by the few, and the corporation as their governing institution. We have been looking for and piecing together people's histories, like a tapestry—in pieces, not necessarily chronological, with different threads and strands waiting to be uncovered and connected.

Our hope is that a critical mass of people will develop a clearer sense of how previous generations have struggled—*not* to make rulers a little less destructive, a little kinder and gentler—but *for* democracy. We sense that more people are now tracing the tensions that have long raged between government by the many and government by the few, and asking fundamental questions about who's in charge.

To foster this process, we think it is vital to understand that the nation's great popular movements—the American Revolution and the Abolition, Populist, Women's, Labor, Civil Rights, and Native people's struggles—were not simply defensive efforts. Again and again, whole classes of people, many originally defined as *property* by the Federalist founders, organized to gain basic human and constitutional rights. In so doing, they put forth visions of this nation quite different from the visions of those propertied few who sought to keep power in their own hands.

Look at the Knights of Labor in the 1880s. They were clear that the "transportation of knowledge," meaning the new communications inventions, must be public. Similarly, the millions of late nineteenth century Populists understood that *all* the "necessaries of life" belonged in the hands of the people. However, we know that knowledge—like land, money, food, health care, energy, and our very government—has from the beginning been controlled by a small number of people. The propertied founders, Robber Barons and their descendants in today's corporate boardrooms and halls of government have consistently elevated property interests over human and species rights. The result is a global empire built on military force, expanding production and consumption without end—all cloaked in the myth of democracy.

## IMPLICATIONS FOR ACTIVISTS

To those who have looked at U.S. history it is evident that simply regulating the authority of propertied men and their corporations to dictate the rules diverts people from the age-old struggle for democracy. So it should come as no surprise to find that creating and running organizations to *build* democracy is quite different from creating organizations to pry better terms from those in charge. There are hidden histories of past organizations to uncover, and there are people's organizations—formed in response to relentless assaults on life, liberty, property, and the Earth—which need to retool into strategic vehicles for forcing government to disperse power and foster democratic institutions.

How can activists stop investing in hopes and strategies based on rules stacked against us? How do we evolve into a democracy *movement*, whose participants make clear that it's not labor and environmental side agreements, or better judges, or a tougher National Labor Relations Act, or public financing of campaigns that are needed, but rather the authority as a people to make all the decisions required to govern ourselves?

As a *By What Authority* reader recently asked, "What steps can the average citizen take to help in the process of securing and maintaining democracy . . . Divided as we are, how can this amorphous mass ever be defined as a sovereign people?"

Perhaps the first challenge is convincing ourselves that we are capable of self-governance. After all, the very Father of our Country chided himself and his compatriots on an overblown faith in human nature. Alexander Hamilton dubbed us the "mob at the gate." Leaders throughout U.S. history have denigrated, denied and disregarded the aspirations and sovereignty of the people, all the while singing the praises of our counterfeit democracy.

For that matter, all of us—ruler and ruled alike—are infected by a millennia-old patriarchal world view that defines power as something exercised over others. This paradigm assigns to human differences dominant and subordinate status and parcels out power and privilege accordingly. Ruling minorities in every era have capitalized on such differences to divide and conquer. In the United States, for instance, race was socially constructed to justify slavery and keep the disenfranchised from making common cause. Racism, along with other forms of oppression, perpetuates inequity and continues to divide those who struggle to change the *status quo*.

No wonder we citizens harbor a colonized and oppressive self-image.

So the USA is not a democracy—let's move on. After all, who among us collapsed when we learned there was no Santa Claus? We can free ourselves, and our liberation will pick up steam as we stop talking about and structuring our organizations around reclaiming, revitalizing or renewing something that never existed; as we analyze, plan and carry out strategies to uproot concentrations of so-called private power and build democratic institutions in their place.

POCLAD is cooperating with organizations seeking to make such a shift. For example, the U.S. Section of the Women's International League for Peace & Freedom (WILPF) has launched a three-year campaign to Challenge Corporate Power, Assert the People's Rights. Phase one is a study group curriculum featuring readings and discussion guidelines on the U.S. corporate power grab and on global corporatization; phase two is about crafting commensurate strategies in WILPF communities and coalitions.

This is hard work for all concerned:

- In an activist organization around which a mythology has grown as a means of survival, leaders often treat internal debate on mission and tactics as threats to their authority.

- Given that most organizations were created to gain relief from corporate and government assaults—either in progress or looming—money, time and even the inclination to "rethink" are generally in short supply.

- Whether the impetus for change comes from membership, staff, officers, board of directors, or funders, all must be involved in analyses and deliberations around how the organization can evolve; yet few activist organizations are really structured democratically, and many actually replicate the very hierarchical corporate model they purport to resist.

- People in existing and new organizations committed to building democracy need to study models throughout history and to practice the "democratic arts."

- When sufficiently pressured, the ruling class may concede some ground to unionization, higher minimum wages, limits to their spewing of poisons, etc.; however, they draw the line when it comes to sharing power and authority under law with those whom they, like Hamilton, regard as the mob, the rabble.

If people cannot make our own civic organizations democratic, we will be unable to gain our rightful power. As the late poet Audre Lorde put it, "You can't dismantle the master's house using the master's tools!"

When more and more people adopt democracy as their goal, it will become easier to see that the logical and efficient way to end corporate assaults is by contesting illegitimate corporate power; the logical and efficient way to right government wrongs is by challenging government's relentless denial of people's fundamental rights; and the logical and efficient way to practice democracy is not by making the bad less bad but by rewriting the rules of governance.

We can let C. Douglas Lummis cheer us on:

> The basic idea of democracy is simple . . . Democracy is a word that joins *demos*—the people—with *krakia*—power . . . It describes an ideal, not a method for achieving it. It is not a kind of government, but an end of government; not a historically existing institution, but a historical project . . . if people take it up as such and struggle for it.[4]

That's a tall order, folks.
What do you think? ∎

# NOTES

[1] Lummis 1996, p. 15.
[2] Fresia 1988, p. 23.
[3] Stone, Seidman, *et al.* 1996, p. 19.
[4] Lummis 1996, p. 22.

# RIGHT SIDE UP

When a minority rules, when corporations govern, when We the People let corporations define us as "taxpayers" and "consumers," we let them turn us upside down. Setting ourselves "right side up," we examine important issues of public concern: the environment, human health, energy, labor, and economic and political power.

Now right side up, on our feet, what would we see? What would we do? The prospects are exhilarating.

# Rally Against the "Contract On America"

*by Mike Ferner*

THANK YOU AND congratulations to each of you who came out today to stand up for justice in America. Today I want to make two points: First, the United States is not going broke. Second, the Contract On America is not ultimately about balancing the budget or about reforming welfare. The Contract is about who runs our country.

Let me explain.

Recently, during all the hoopla over the commissioning of the $750 million nuclear sub, USS Toledo, two amazing stories appeared on the evening news. Seventh-graders from Byrnedale Jr. High marched into the glare of TV lights and saluted a 10-ft. model of the sub their class had built. The announcer spoke of the excitement shared by all Toledoans.

The very next story was that the U.S. House of Representatives had just voted to eliminate the federal entitlement for school lunches—giving up responsibility for a program started in 1946. We could run the school lunch *and* breakfast program throughout Ohio for five years for what the USS Toledo cost.

With the school lunch program, and in 1935 with the Aid for Families with Dependent Children (AFDC) program and other programs, we decided as a nation that our fellow citizens were entitled to a certain minimum existence just because they were people.

This is not just about compassion. It's also about investing in democracy. For how can citizens participate in a democracy if they are too hungry to study; or must work three minimum wage jobs to make ends meet, never having time for public affairs?

Compare what Congress did to the kids eating school lunches, with what it did for corporations anxious to limit liability suits for damage done to consumers and the environment.

For school kids, the battle cry was "reduce Federal bureaucracy; let states administer the program." For corporations wanting reform of state tort laws—it was another matter altogether. Preempt states, stack the deck. And Congress did their bidding.

Think about the ways the Contract On America has increased corporate power. Is this debate about reducing the deficit? Or is it about who runs our country?

Again, our country is not going broke. Wealth is simply being taken out of the commons; stolen from the public trust.

Twenty-five years ago, corporations paid 36% of all federal income taxes. Now they pay 20%, a reduction by almost half in their share of income tax payments. During

Ronald Reagan's first term, with Democrats controlling the House of Representatives, 130 of the largest corporations in America received $6 billion in tax rebates! In 1986, Congress finally plugged this loophole, but last month the House put it back in. That corporate favor will cost the treasury $125 billion over the next ten years.

But when budget-cutters in Congress wield the knife, they do so like skilled sleight-of-hand experts, distracting our attention. They use code words like "family values," and "personal responsibility," as they try to convince us that this nation is in danger of collapse because black teenagers have too many babies; because food stamp recipients spend too much on corn flakes and peanut butter.

They patronizingly proclaim we must think of the "poor" and of the "consumers"—welfare destroys motivation to work; product liability laws cause higher prices.

But ask them to eliminate the subsidies handed out routinely to corporations and they fall suddenly silent. Is this debate about budget deficits? Or is it about who really runs our country?

When the U.S. Department of Agriculture gave McDonald's, Pillsbury and other multinational corporations $1.25 billion to "encourage export of agricultural products," didn't this contribute to the deficit?

When one family with several large sugarcane farms in the Florida Everglades receives $60 million a year in profits from price supports and import quotas, and then contributes $350,000 to political campaigns in one year, is this debate about reducing deficits? Or is it about who runs our country?

Congressman George Miller estimates several billion dollars a year can easily be raised by charging fair market rates to corporations that profit handsomely on our commons: our public forests, grazing lands, and minerals. But instead, even more attacks on our commons are planned: turning national forests over to private landowners; scrapping renewable energy programs; and turning the Arctic National Wildlife Refuge over to energy companies. Woody Guthrie said it all: "some will rob you with a six-gun, and some with a fountain pen."

The right-wing corporate-funded Heritage Foundation recommends dropping 3 million children from AFDC because their fathers are unknown; that cutting welfare "reduces the subsidizing of dysfunctional behavior." Don't let anyone tell you this debate is about budget deficits.

We must all stand together in this fight. Will our representatives protect us, or will they protect the wealthy? Will Congress fight to preserve the democratic rights of citizens to be the sovereign power in America, or shift even more economic and political power to corporations?

These are truly fundamental questions. As we answer them, we have immediate work before us: to stand shoulder-to-shoulder with our fellow citizens who deserve a share of this nation's wealth; to make clear to elected officials who care more about corporations than about democracy, that they will pay a political price. Congratulations for standing up for justice in America. ■

# THE GREAT CORPORATE SOCIAL SECURITY STING

*by Virginia Rasmussen*

WATCH OUT! There's a giant sting operation underway. It comes to us as "the crisis" in Social Security. "Sting" is slang for a meticulously planned and carried out confidence game. Who could be up to such a stunt? That's easy. It's those who defined and promoted the problem. The very same who now offer to come to the rescue, whose private power and purses will swell if any one of *their* solutions is enacted.

## THE REAL STORY

Sixty-four years after the passage of the Social Security Act of 1935, the Social Security system's performance is nothing less than a success story. It was designed as an insurance program, not a tax-sheltered investment plan seeking highest returns. It is a pooled system, not one of individual accounts. This national pension program involves pay-as-you-go funding which means that each generation of retirees is supported by the country's present generation of workers. That is, the FICA (Federal Insurance Contribution Act) amount you pay this month will be used to pay your grandmother's benefits this month. Such a system is inflation-proof because pay-in and pay-out are in same-valued dollars. The surplus is what is left of the amount collected through FICA taxes each year that is not paid out in benefits that same year. Surpluses have

accumulated in recent years and are known as the Social Security Trust Funds, or simply the reserves.

The nation's objective was to build a level of future financial stability in most workers' lives, and to do it in a way that connects people of different generations, backgrounds and incomes in the spirit of community. Since the program is backed by a national commitment, it is able to respond to changing conditions of national dimension, thus offering a kind of security that no market-based plan can claim.

About 147 million workers, 96 percent of the workforce, pay into Social Security and will receive benefits in later years. For 60 percent of older Americans, benefits make up more than half of their income, lifting 56 percent of the country's elderly out of poverty. This is a result of the program's progressive structure in which low wage earners receive a greater proportion of their lifetime earnings in benefits than do high wage earners. The system provides a disability policy equivalent to $200,000 and survivor insurance when a wage earner dies. Today more than 7 million people, many of them children, receive survivor benefits.

Is the program in fiscal danger? Not at all. It is remarkably efficient, with administrative costs under one percent of benefits paid (this compares with 20 to 35 percent for corporate insurers). The fund is currently taking in nearly $100 billion a year more than it pays out to recipients. The accumulated reserve peaks at over $3 trillion in 2020 and, according to present estimates, will gradually be used up by 2034. Any future low reserves would not be the result of a retiring baby boom generation, as this bulge in the number receiving benefits was accounted for in earlier adjustments through a regular public process. Rather, they would be due to people living longer and to workers having experienced stagnant wages between 1974 and 1994 while corporations were hauling in record-setting profits. Those less-than-anticipated wages, the consequence of corporate decisions defined as beyond the authority of public action, brought less-than-anticipated payroll taxes into the reserves.

It is important to note that an actual shortfall will result only if we assume a very low economic growth-rate in the coming decades, lower even than that during the Great Depression. Using this assumption, annual payroll taxes in 2034 will cover only 75 percent of benefits owed. However, if we use mid-range economic assumptions, Social Security would remain solvent as far as the eye can see.

"This is a crisis," claims Dean Baker of the Economic Policy Institute, "in the same way that a car headed westward in the middle of Kansas faces a crisis. If it doesn't stop or turn, the car will eventually fall into the Pacific Ocean."

Yet, contrary to common sense, we are told that to "save" Social Security we must privatize it. That is, remove it, in part or in whole, from public control and transfer it to decision-makers in corporate boardrooms. This counsel comes from those very same boardrooms and from their shills in corporate-funded think tanks and political circles.

Brokerage, investment, insurance, advertising and manufacturing corporations will be sweepstakes winners if even a portion of the yearly payroll tax (FICA) is diverted to the stock market. Investment company officials drool at the thought of a possible 130 million new investment accounts and billions of dollars in transaction fees each year, the heavy overhead costs of a privatized system. This in itself is sufficient reason for people to suspect the corporate call for a rescue, but it is not the only reason. It is not even the most important reason.

## CORPORATE "TAKINGS" OF PUBLIC WEALTH AND POWER

This is a move not only on individual and public wealth but also on public democratic process—on the power of the people to conduct our political and economic life free from corporate influence and distortion. This is not a new maneuver, but merely the latest example of an old practice. The corporate form has long been the vehicle of a powerful minority to control the property and governance rights of the majority.

We should be asking ourselves: Why do corporations—inanimate bodies given existence by the people to serve the people—claim to have any say about the Social Security system? The system is, after all, a compact among self-governing people. If it needs attention, it is not our corporate creations but We the People who are responsible for taking action. By what authority do these nonbeings sound alarms, shape debates, instill fear, drive bargains, suppress truth and covet our retirement funds?

On reflection, the larger significance of this proposed "taking" becomes clear. Putting money into the stock market enhances the power of corporations. What will happen to public protest against corporate violations of workers, communities, environmental and public health, justice and democracy, when most workers have Social Security retirement funds in the stock market? And how will the relationship between our government and corporations be further affected should a percentage of our Social Security Trust Funds be invested privately?

You can be sure these questions were raised by those in corporate boardrooms and answered to their satisfaction: protest will be quieted; government "meddling" relaxed.

## THE STING

Should the nation choose to address any Social Security shortfall we can do so without imposing burdens on lower-income employees. There are four million government workers not included in the Social Security program. The shortfall shrinks if we add them. There is presently a cap on earnings subject to the FICA tax. All wages and salaries above $72,600 are exempt. As we raise the cap, the shortfall will be proportionately reduced.

And does it make sense that unearned income—stock dividends, interest, currency speculation winnings—should go untouched with regard to Social Security contributions? Or why not tax burgeoning corporate profits? After all, it was the low wages paid to labor that contributed to the shortfall in the first place. The latest report of the General Accounting Office (GAO), a Congressional research arm, brings the astonishing news that in each year from 1990 through 1994, nearly one-third of all major corporations operating in the United States paid no U.S. income tax! More than six out of 10 of those same corporations paid less than a million dollars in federal income tax in 1995.

These options would solve any future problems while taking nothing away from lower income earners. Yet they are rarely mentioned as politicians wrangle over reform

choices all of which would directly harm wage earners. They include:

• Increasing the FICA tax on earnings.

• Raising the retirement age.

• Reducing spousal benefits.

• Taxing benefits received in excess of contributions made; trimming the inflation adjustment or cost of living allowance (COLA).

• Increasing the computation period used to derive benefit amounts from 35 to 38 years. This means more lower wage years will be averaged into the monthly benefit determination, thus shrinking the payment.

In the bargain, the centerpiece of this corporate-driven rescue would place a portion of a worker's retirement funds in the stock market, either in individual accounts or by government officials investing a percentage of the Social Security Trust Funds in the market. *Retirement security would be left to Wall Street*, the volatile market painted as a sure and steady thing. But playing it carries risks, especially for the untutored. The wealthy who already have stock holdings would experience handsome gains during the initial and hugely expanded investment period. But low and middle income families, often lacking best advice or driven by fear, would be vulnerable to market fluctuations. In these flush times the buy-in price is high. Is it really smart to bet our Social Security benefits on the present market continuing to climb through the 2020s?

Add to this trepidation the foolhardiness of fueling a corporate growth-machine that imposes ever greater ecological harm, social injustice, and illegitimate government, and one wonders why these proposals have any credibility.

It's also true that a poor future economy would leave vulnerable not only Social Security, but the *stock market as well*—that alternative the corporate rescuers offer with a promise of great returns. Surely they must know we can't have it both ways.

Putting this ruse over on the public and its elected representatives required the best of "sting doctors" and a dozen years of painstaking strategy, dogged tactics and generous financing. The privatizers created and funded think tanks, convened panels, wrote books, formed institutes, shaped coalitions. They did "research," created stories, supplied slants, swayed young voters, lobbied Congress, saturated airwaves, and otherwise seeded insecurity about Social Security. The detractors' message is filled with fabrication and hyperbole. Examples follow:

- *Fear language* is rampant: "an economic problem to dwarf all other national issues"; "a system in "dire jeopardy"; a program "on the skids." *The Atlantic Monthly*, *Time*, and *The New Republic* are among publications in the chorus.

- The *increasing cost of Social Security and Medicare is bankrupting the nation*, privatizers say. True, the combination of Social Security and the mounting health care bill totals an alarming figure (any number added to a huge number is a huge number). The problem is health care, which requires a separate discussion and solution.

- *Social Security trust funds are used irresponsibly*, opponents say, to cover other government projects and reduce the reported annual budget deficit. Yes, the surplus is lent to the Treasury to finance the Federal deficit with bonds that receive the highest credit rating. If the funds did not exist, the government would be borrowing from private sources at greater interest rates. In the future, should the government have difficulty meeting its Social Security obligations, it is not the fault of the Social Security System that its reserves have been used elsewhere. It is the nation's taxing, interest and spending policies that must be questioned.

- *Many rich elderly are ripping off young people*, they claim. The reality is that the median household income of the elderly is $18,000. Fifty percent of those receiving Social Security have incomes under $15,000. More than 10 percent of seniors live in poverty, with women and people of color composing the majority of them. Underpaid and often unemployed during their working lives, women have paid less into the system and receive less in return. The figures fall to $8,579 for white women, $6,200 for Black women, and $5,968 for Hispanic women.

- *It's all a big Ponzi scheme*, critics charge. A Ponzi or pyramid scheme is a con game in which the first person gets money from two people who then receive money from four, and so on. The first in are winners, but when its participants can no longer entice new members those at the bottom of the pyramid lose their money. The analogy derives from the retiring of the baby boomers, when there will be fewer workers per retiree. But that situation was largely accounted for, as noted earlier. The problem is not boomers so much as it is increasing longevity, and those twenty years of sluggish wages that fed record corporate profits.

The real Ponzi scheme is the stock market itself. Designed on the gambling motif, it carries no assurances. Should a corporation go bankrupt, the largest investors receive first payoff, and preferred stock is honored before common stock.

As the privatizers peddle these unfounded "problems" of the current program, they are mum on the pitfalls of a privatized system:

- the vagaries of the stock market and a global economy;

- the loss of retirement savings for many as a result of bad investments;

- a further widening of the economic gap between rich and poor; and

- total costs far in excess of the present system (these include not only all that "corporate overhead" accompanying new investment arrangements, but also the funds necessary to pay present and pending Social Security recipients caught in the lengthy transition period).

## THINKING FORWARD

So where does this leave us?

- Corporations, having seen in workers' yearly FICA contributions a profitable financial asset, are claiming a portion as their own. But that's only the beginning. It's also the co-opting of a compact We the People made with one another. The prescribed "debate" and "solutions" steal from us an opportunity to evaluate our own program, to define language and analysis suitable to the issue. We are deliberately led past a discussion of values; and of commitment to community, our elders and the vulnerable in society.

- The right to be in charge is the people's. The responsibility for uncovering a well hidden history of corporate "takings" of law and culture is also ours. The work in coming years is to bring this history to light, to understand its pivotal meaning for reframing the language and strategy of popular struggles against illegitimate corporate authority.

- The Social Security debate is rich with opportunity for a different kind of activism. We can take up this challenge in many venues—in city councils, state legislatures and election campaigns, in organizations and classrooms, through newsletters and newspapers, in public squares, workplaces, union halls and pool halls, in synagogues, churches, mosques, and around pagan campfires.

It's only people who can save Social Security from its corporate saviors. ■

# WHAT IS THE PURPOSE OF PUBLIC EDUCATION?

*by Mike Ferner*

WHAT IS THE purpose of public education? To teach students to read and write so they can discover this beautiful world; to think critically so they can then help change it for the better? Or to prepare them for their prescribed places in a society where the few govern the many in a "corporatized" world?

From yesterday's effort to make Dartmouth a public college[1] to today's efforts to keep corporations out of public education, the fundamental question is who designs our institutions and shapes our common life. This question is obscured, however, by politicians' and media focus on school uniforms, standards and discipline.

Take "America 2000," for instance, the six national goals for public education unveiled by President George Bush in 1989. Depending on your perspective, these would save the U.S. educational system from imminent collapse, or dangerously accelerate private influence over public education. Arkansas Governor Bill Clinton supported America 2000, and as president added two goals and convinced Congress to pass the "Goals 2000: Educate America Act" in March, 1994.

Within a month of its passage, the ideological foundation of Goals 2000 was revealed in "Reinventing Education: Entrepreneurship in America's Public Schools," co-authored by Louis Gerstner. A renowned educator with 30 years experience in public schools? No, the CEO of the IBM Corporation. Gerstner *et al.* defined students as "human capital," and urged schools to compare themselves to each other as "Xerox compares itself to L.L. Bean for inventory control."

A Goals 2000 follow-up meeting held in 1996 at IBM Corporation headquarters boasted a Fortune 500 planning committee from the IBM, AT&T, Eastman Kodak, and Procter and Gamble corporations. Officials from the American Enterprise Institute and the Heritage Foundation think tanks, formed to push a corporate agenda, were invited as "resources."

In his address to this gathering, President Clinton repeatedly urged the adoption of "standards" for students and schools—a concept that, like education itself, depends on who does the defining. Significantly, Clinton agreed with Gerstner that business execs should "know what reforms to speak out for . . . as well as how to help local school districts change some of the things they are now doing so they have a reasonable chance at meeting those standards."[2]

In a number of states, the standards are measured by high-stakes tests that decide the fates of individual students and whole school

---

districts. Yet the people who grade them are often college-educated temp workers who read 200 hand-written essays per shift for $8.50 an hour.[3] Their job is to do what many parents, teachers, and public officials assume is done by trained educators: decide whether your child receives a high school diploma.

## DEBATE WHAT?

Will the growing debate over such standards and tests illuminate the core purpose of public education? Will more and more people realize we've been had? David Stratman, a former educator and the founder of New Democracy, believes the 1983 book, *A Nation at Risk*,[4] helped create the impression that public education is crumbling, an impression he calls as fraudulent as the Social Security "crisis" promoted by those who would corporatize the people's covenant with one another.

> It's a little like the con-artist in The Music Man, who declares, "We've got trouble, right here in River City..." and the chorus repeats, "trouble, trouble, trouble, trouble..." How do you sell radical changes that would have been completely unacceptable a decade or two ago? You tell people over and over that their institutions have failed, and that only the solutions you are peddling offer any way out of their "troubles."

This corporate-manufactured trouble makes it difficult to identify real problems and solutions, and the resulting conflict underlies debates over school funding and policy. To Stratman, the essence of this debate is:

> What are we educating our students for? We can prepare students for unrewarding jobs in an increasingly unequal society, or ... to understand their world and to change it. The first is education to meet

the needs of the corporate economy. The second is education for democracy.[5]

In the debate over the purpose of education and the means to achieve it, money is not the only measure of what schools need, but without adequate funding, such proven reforms as reducing class sizes and paying higher salaries are impossible. In states such as Ohio, courts have ordered the legislature to come up with a more equitable funding method than property taxes. You might think that grappling with such a fundamental challenge would cause politicians, educators, reporters, parents, and taxpayers to examine every conceivable revenue source. Think again. Ending corporate tax breaks and subsidies is not even on the agenda.

Let's look at where school money *doesn't* come from. The Ohio Department of Taxation reported that in 1998, local governments exempted nearly $3 billion worth of corporate-owned property (land itself) from taxes in Ohio. Conservatively estimated, at least that much and probably more in "personal" property (buildings, equipment, machinery) has been exempted. State officials, telling us that revealing the actual numbers would compromise a company's competitive position, declare such figures private—beyond the people's authority.

The following examples from my hometown indicate how such staggering ransom is collected. When Owens-Corning Corporation officials threatened to move company headquarters just outside the city limits, Toledo taxpayers coughed up a $25 million tax break, worth $1.2 million annually, plus a $10 million cash grant. Company directors used the first two years' tax savings to pay CEO Glen Hiner's bonus.

DaimlerChrysler Corporation officials, sitting on $8.6 billion in cash reserves, proposed to rebuild Toledo's existing Jeep factory. In exchange they demanded and got $281,000,000 in public assistance from local and state governments.[6] Included were tax abatements that robbed two local school districts of $86 million. Barely a year after the deal, one of the districts announced that to repair leaking school roofs it needed voters to pass a levy to raise an amount similar to the abatement. The other district proposed canceling bus service after voters defeated an operating levy.

## THE LESSON PLAN

As an elected official in Toledo, I used to see two big problems with such corporate tax relief: school revenues took big hits and we hapless human persons remaining on the tax rolls had to make up the difference. But what I see now troubles me even more. As the public purse is pauperized, so is self-governance. We citizens spiral downward into an ever-diminishing democracy, exercising less and less political power until it appears there's no solution but corporate charity to rescue and thus define our "failing public institutions."

Like many reversals, it happens little by little. In Toledo's hardscrabble south end, administrators affix a sign to Jones Junior High, thanking the bank that "adopted" the school. At a Chamber of Commerce breakfast, three school officials approach the head table and reach up with outstretched hands to accept their $10,000 gifts from eminent local tax dodgers Owens-Corning Corporation, DaimlerChrysler Corporation, and other Chamber members.

Of course, when schools need more than mere handouts, they ask voters to raise taxes. With astounding audacity, the boldest corporate tax evaders then help bankroll the campaign to pass the levy—to raise taxes for everyone else!

How is it that corporate officials now decide which levies are supported and which

schools get desperately needed funds? What if DaimlerChrysler's corporate board graciously offers "free" transportation to those grade school students left without bus service? By what authority could they even make such an offer? And what do students learn at Jones Jr. High? That We the People are sovereign over schools, government, and corporations? Or that supposedly democratic institutions are in fact orphans, grateful to be adopted by generous and powerful business benefactors?

Schools around the nation are subjected to similar corporate onslaughts. One district sponsored "art contests," grade school students designing ads for soft drink and hamburger companies, with winning entries painted onto school buses. Hundreds of districts have signed chump change contracts with soft drink companies that trade student health for priceless brand loyalty. In one bizarre example of municipal fascism, a student was suspended for wearing a Pepsi Cola t-shirt on "Coca Cola Day."

For-profit corporations now run 200 schools with 100,000 students. Edison Schools, Inc. operates 79 of these, leading the effort to cash in on a $700 billion "education industry." Edison founder Christopher Wittle introduced Channel I, a mix of cable TV news and commercials wired into thousands of schools seeking a "free" supplement for shrinking budgets in return for a guaranteed student audience for corporate programming.

The corporate assault on public education, like the corporate assault on democracy itself, has the single-mindedness of a steamroller. However, public resistance to it is building. As with other such assaults, from toxic chemicals to toxic organizations like the WTO, demands for public education must address the illegitimate power of corporations and challenge the public officials who are complicit in the usurpation of our democracy. ∎

## Notes

1 See "You've Heard of Santa Clara, Now Meet Dartmouth" in this volume. —*Ed.*

2 As quoted by Susan Ohanian in *Kappan*, the journal of Phi Delta Kappa International, January 2000.

3 Cleveland Plain Dealer, February 25, 2000.

4 United States 1983.

5 David Stratman quoted in his Keynote to Massachusetts Association of Superintendents, 1997.

6 These "incentives" were given with the belief that the corporation would retain 4,900 jobs in the Toledo area. The development agreement signed with the city in 1997 states only that employment at the company's Toledo assembly operations is "currently anticipated to be about 4,900 Chrysler employees." In April of 2001, DaimlerChrysler corporation announced that it would cut up to 2,035 jobs. Ralph Nader commented on this situation that the city "doesn't have any legal remedies. [The city] is in a one-sided contract, and Chrysler has plenty of escape clauses to make sure that they couldn't be brought to justice." —*Ed.*

# THE RISING COSTS OF INEQUALITY IN THE U.S.

## DEMOCRACY IN CRISIS

*by Ward Morehouse & David Dembo*

THE CLINTON IMPEACHMENT spectacle has hardly helped to alleviate the crisis in our democracy, generating cynicism about the political process and the role of government in late twentieth century America. But far more powerful is the relentless mantra from corporate public relations and advertising campaigns and the giant global conglomerates which dominate the mass media: "Corporations: efficient, good. Government: wasteful, bad."

Nor is the decline in voter turnout the main cause of the crisis, although it is hardly a cause for celebration. The class bias in electoral participation has an even more dismaying impact on democratic values in the United States. Because most rich people vote and most poor people do not, the outcome of national elections is effectively determined by the richest 20 percent of the population.

And the candidates presented to those of us who do vote are selected by a very much smaller percentage—the corporate tycoons and fat cats who provide most of the cash necessary to run effective campaigns in a political culture dominated by sound bites. The harsh reality is that we live in a plutocracy, not a democracy.

A real crisis in U.S. society, effectively vitiating the democratic process, is economic inequality. And this inequality is growing. The numbers are striking. In the first three decades after the Second World War, various segments of U.S. society grew together, and the gap between the rich and the poor actually declined a little.

But for the next two decades (1980s and 1990s) something very different happened. The share of family income going to the bottom 20 percent of the population dropped 7%, the second 20 percent stood still, the middle 20 percent grew only 5% and the fourth 20 percent just 1%. The top 20 percent (with family income of $80,000 or more) increased 3%, and the top one percent (family incomes of $243,000 and more) increased by a whopping 106%!

These numbers come from a Boston-based group, United for a Fair Economy, which is fighting economic inequality in the United States, and which has joined hands with the Council on Public Affairs in publishing a quarterly newsletter tracking inequality in our society entitled *Too Much*. Bad as these numbers are, chances are that the real situation is even worse. The numbers are drawn from the Current

Population Survey of the U.S. Census which, as Professor Seymour Melman of Columbia University has pointed out, severely understates income concentration at the very top of the scale.

The picture gets still worse if we consider the distribution of wealth in the U.S. America's richest one half percent—families worth at least $4 million—own 42 percent of all U.S. wealth. Bill Gates, the CEO of Microsoft and arguably America's richest person, now owns more wealth than the bottom 45 percent of American households. The leading tracker of wealth distribution in the United States is a New York University Professor, Edward Wolff. "Financial wealth is the key to political power," observes Wolff. "Given the fractured state of political parties and the lack of real leadership, it's monetary muscle that makes the difference."

Now, so-called middle class households are barely holding their own. With incomes stagnating, fewer and fewer families without homes can afford to buy one. Home ownership rates in the U.S. have not risen for a quarter of a century. And in fact if you exclude mobile homes, home ownership rates in America have actually declined.

"We are becoming an oligarchic society, with an extreme concentration of wealth," states Wolff. "This concentration of wealth is protected through a political process that's making it difficult for anyone but the monied class to have a voice." This harsh reality is increasingly shaping the cultural outlook of future generations. Consider this observation by a Princeton University Professor, Uwe E. Reinhardt, in commenting on the snobbery and exclusion practiced by one of Princeton's undergraduate "eating clubs":

> In a way the Ivy Club is certainly in tune with current trends if not even ahead of the curve. We are . . . sliding back toward a [country] dominated by corporate society. I think in our corporate elite that there is a Marie Antoinette complex and that percolates down to Princeton.

The modern corporation has become the principal vehicle through which great wealth is accumulated and gross inequality generated. So any way out of our predicament must come to grips with this enormity of corporate power—financial and political. Until We the People exercise our sovereignty over these artificial entities,[1] democracy will remain an empty phrase, a cruel hoax trotted out in Fourth of July speeches. ∎

## NOTES

[1] The articles of section seven of this volume provide examples of citizens exercising, or at least acting as if they have, sovereignty over these artificial entities. —Ed.

# UTILITIES GET THEIR WAY
## THE FRAUD OF ENERGY DEREGULATION
### by Richard L. Grossman

*COUNTRY CONNECTIONS:* Many environmentalists think energy deregulation is a good thing. Why do you disagree?

*Richard Grossman:* We the People—and environmentalists especially—have been sold a bill of goods about energy deregulation. This is because people have not been paying enough attention to community and corporate histories.

Early in this century robber barons like Sam Insull in electricity, and August Belmont in street cars, were busily taking over small, local systems—many of which were municipally owned—and creating giant holding companies. Their methods were ruthless, and angry people began to organize and mobilize in opposition.

To put down this popular resistance the barons went to state politicians and said something like, "To maximize efficiency and keep costs down, we have to minimize competition. We want the state to create utility corporations. You guarantee us a satisfactory rate of return and protect us from the anarchist, communist, socialist, grassroots, public ownership rabble, and our utility corporations will serve the public. Trust us."

Civic leaders of labor, business and the press, who saw themselves as part of the Progressive Movement, no doubt believed that a relatively small number of regulated "public service corporations" would be an improvement over many independent and locally owned systems. They therefore used their influence as "reformers" and worked with the electricity barons to create new utility corporations.

Given the privileges and immunities which corporations in general had attained by the time (such as perpetual existence, legal personhood, and favorable changes in property laws), I am sure that utility corporation leaders were quite confident that they would be able to use this category of corporation to their advantage.

For most of this century utility corporations, such as the Pacific Gas & Electric Company and Southern California Edison Corporation in California, along with construction and manufacturing corporations like Stone & Webster, Westinghouse, General Electric, oil and coal corporations have defined the nation's investment and technology policies around energy.

In other words, they decided how to spend ratepayers' money and taxpayers' money, choose the technologies to research and develop, and educate the nation about energy "choices." Like the leaders of other corporations, their leaders quickly figured out how to influence government officials, dominate and manipulate state public utility commissions, and control public debate.

And the history of vigorous community resistance to corporate consolidation— major grass roots efforts for municipal ownership and control over energy, and indeed, of successful municipal ownership—faded from public memory.

Going into the 1970s, corporations— shielded by utility and other laws and legal doctrines—were firmly in charge. The nation's goal was the corporate goal: perpetual expansion of energy use via large, complex, costly, wasteful, environmentally destructive and dangerous systems. This was, according to corporate experts, the key to economic expansion, the good life and, of course, jobs.

But people started educating themselves about energy, economics and the law. They began to question the corporate wisdom. For example, people across the nation joined to defeat utility corporations' plan to build 1000 nuclear power plants by the century's end. Their goal was to direct investment to increasing energy efficiencies and planned transitions to renewables.

When a large number of Californians advocated an end to nuclear power and a shift to efficiency and solar via a ballot initiative in the mid-1970s, California utilities, along with energy corporations from around the country, spent great sums of their ratepayers' money to discredit them and their ideas, and to defeat their legal challenges. I was part of this No Nuke effort. I recall vividly the steady stream of corporate lies asserting that without fifty nuclear power plants in California the people of the state would be freezing and starving, jobless, in the dark. I also saw the great pressure that these corpo-

rations exerted upon good people and organizations across the state.

By the end of the 1970s, a great safe energy movement had emerged nationwide. The corporations' nuclear plans had been revealed as absurd on economic, efficiency and health grounds. Almost 800 nuclear plants had been canceled. And the energy corporation leaders started pretending they would move on to decentralization and renewable energy.

Alas, the safe energy movement never used its power to pick up the early twentieth century struggle for public ownership, and to challenge the vast authority which utility and other energy corporations were claiming under the law. And over the past generation, these corporations have been able to use state and federal government regulation and regulatory agencies to tighten their grip even more over our money, our legislatures, the nation's resources and our minds.

Here's where we need to be clear: the previous regulatory laws served as shields for these great corporations, and they used these laws as tools to maintain their control over public policy and public money. Today's so-called "deregulation" laws, including the 1996 Telecommunications Act, are merely the next generation of laws which the corporations have written in order to continue their domination.

Behind the charade of increasing competition and giving customers choice and lower prices, utility corporations in California enacted AB 1890 in 1996. This law requires ratepayers—not corporate stockholders—to fork over $30 billion to cover the stupidity costs of the utility corporations. They call these their "stranded costs," a euphemism for their investments in nuclear power plants that are not paying off, and for their other dumb investments which so many people at the time quite properly opposed.

The theory of capitalism is that you invest your money and you take your chances. You then either make money or lose it. But this is not how it works for these utility corporations, which used the State of California to help them vacuum up $30 billion of the people's money there, several billion in my state of Massachusetts, and billions more in states around the nation.

Your California utilities also got the state to float bonds, which will be paid off by the taxpayers, so that they can pretend to offer ratepayers a temporary cut in rates.

Still, Californians are paying 50 percent above the national average. And the corporations are throwing in all kinds of extra fees, like "competition transition charges," and "direct access service request charges," if a customer dares to choose a different supplier.

So, to call what's happening today "deregulation," an encouragement of competition and the path to lower energy prices, is nonsense. Energy corporations across the nation are orchestrating a new assault upon democracy and against people's ability to define what happens within their communities.

The utilities have done a terrific propaganda job. Even the California watchdog group, Toward Utility Reform Now (TURN) supported AB 1890 at first. Later, it acknowledged that it had made a terrible mistake. The Natural Resources Defense Council (NRDC), a national environmental legal group, has been working closely with these utility corporations for a long time. With the help of the Environmental Defense Fund, it has sold these utility plans to the general public, and particularly to environmentalists.

*CC:* The people of Davis, California, are doing something different in terms of energy.

*RG:* Not just in terms of energy, also in terms of self-governance. One of their models is the city of Sacramento. Sacramento owns its own utility system, called a municipal utility district, SMUD. It had built a nuclear power plant, Rancho Seco, twenty or twenty-five years ago. Because the people of Sacramento owned and controlled SMUD, they were able to order its directors, via a ballot initiative, to shut Rancho Seco down and redirect its investment and technology policies to become the premier solar and energy efficiency supplier in the country. And SMUD has done so.

It is offering low-interest loans to people for solar panels and energy efficiency retrofits. It is planting trees all over the city. It is saving energy, decreasing pollution and saving money.

There are people in Davis who want to set up a Davis Municipal Utility District DMUD, also owned and controlled by the people. And they want to pool their community's resources with other communities to buy electricity and other necessities in bulk, at cheaper price

They are clear about investing in a major transition to energy efficiency and solar. So they plan to set aside five percent of revenues to create a Community Solar Bank to lend money for home, business, farm and government retrofits and for new technologies. They also want to provide rate relief for low-income people and small businesses, and to make water,[1] electricity, gas and trash services more efficient and economical.

They understand the need to assert civic authority over all these decisions. But they face the reality that energy financing and production have been controlled by the giant corporations now for over a century, and that these corporations have essentially written the laws and shaped how people think.

It is wonderful that folks in Davis are working to establish a locally-owned system, and will seek to buy electricity from corporations that are a cut above average. It certainly will make a difference if communities can begin to set their own standards for energy production and use. But in the process, they will have to grapple with the reality of great corporate privilege and power under law. So the underlying challenge is: how can the people of Davis undertake this effort in ways that contest the authority of utility and other energy corporations to write the laws, to elect our representatives, to shape the culture—to govern?

*CC:* What is the best way to accomplish that?

*RG:* This is the challenge facing all organizers for justice around the country. And it will require all of us to rethink who we are as "We the People," and to learn how to act like the sovereign people we are supposed to be. We will also have to uncover our communities' and states' histories, and be open to refashioning our goals and strategies.

We are the ones, after all, who must be accountable to one another and to prior generations, as well as to the people who come after us. We must, therefore, take back from giant corporations the authority they have stolen from the people—the authority to decide the criteria and values for energy investments and technologies, and to control the money needed to set up the energy systems which communities believe most appropriate and desirable.

For me, the bottom line is: how do we address the seemingly endless corporate assaults upon our ability to govern ourselves as free people in ways that contest corporate privilege; that encourage people to believe that we can govern ourselves; that strip away the self-censorship and the laws that sustain illegitimate corporate rule?

It's been over one hundred years since giant corporations assumed the authority to govern in this country. So long, that for many people our current predicament appears to be the way it has always been, or the way it must be. But people have waged valiant campaigns, and sometimes—as in Sacramento—have triumphed, have won control and authority.

What is happening today under the so-called banner of "deregulation" is nothing new. We must not be deceived. It's just corporations running the show, as usual.  ∎

## NOTES

[1] Water use, especially in California where it is pumped all across the state—including up mountains—is exceedingly energy intensive.

# THE MULTILATERAL AGREEMENT ON INVESTMENT

## AN INTERNATIONAL HUMAN RIGHTS CRISIS

*by Ward Morehouse*

THE MULTILATERAL AGREEMENT on Investment (MAI) is an audacious attempt by giant global corporations larger than most nation states to consolidate their power by making capital mobility a legally enforceable property right. It is, in the words of the Director General of the World Trade Organization, "the constitution of a single global economy." Or as Tony Clarke of the Polaris Institute and Canadian Centre for Policy Alternatives in Ottawa characterizes it, "a bill of rights and freedoms for transnational corporations . . . a declaration of corporate rule."[1] And this global property right will transcend internationally recognized human rights because it will be legally enforceable at the international level while human rights have historically not been.

For working people and local communities the MAI is nothing but bad news. It will exert downward pressure on wages and increase job insecurity by making it easier for corporations to move their operations anywhere in the world. It will be harder to insist on high standards for workplace safety and protection of surrounding communities from "normal" industrial pollution and catastrophic accidents like the world's worst industrial disaster in

Bhopal, India. It will make illegal those efforts by states and municipalities to encourage locally owned enterprises. And it will certainly lead to even greater concentration of wealth and power in the boardrooms of giant anti-democratic corporations.

Under negotiation—in secret until a draft text was leaked and put on the Internet in January 1997—at the Organization for Economic Cooperation and Development (OECD) in Paris, the MAI is supposed to be completed and ready for government approval by spring 1998. The choice of venue for negotiations is a clever tactic, designed to exclude participation by governments representing most of the world's population.

The OECD is a rich man's club composed of 29 industrialized countries. Once approved by the governments of these countries, it will then be presented to the rest of the world as a *fait accompli*. If the rest of the world wants access to principal world capital markets, they will have no choice but to sign on. And the compulsion will be intense if the *Wall Street Journal's* view of the rest of the world as "money hungry" while "the global competition for capital heats up" is anywhere near the mark.[2]

---

The MAI is several hundred pages of turgid text and commentary organized into half a dozen major segments on such topics as "Treatment of Investors and Investments," "Investment Protection," and "Dispute Settlement." But the overriding purpose is simple and clear: to establish mobility of capital as a global, legally enforceable private property right.

In doing so the MAI takes a giant step toward affirming constituting corporations as sovereign instruments of governance. It replicates at the international level the regimen of corporate rule now well established in the United States through such constitutional provisions and judicial doctrines as interstate commerce, contracts, managerial prerogative, and the business judgment rule. Its dispute settlement and investor protection sections accord corporations judicial standing similar to that of nation states

## RAPID CHANGES IN THE GLOBAL POLITICAL ECONOMY

The MAI comes amid rapid changes in the global political economy. The annual revenues of the 500 largest corporations in the world are some $10 trillion, around twice the size of the gross domestic product of the United States, the biggest economy in the world today. In a single year, 1994, the Global 500 revenues increased by 9 percent and profits soared by a colossal 62 percent. But notwithstanding such huge profits, or perhaps to achieve them, the Global 500 in that same year eliminated 262,000 jobs.[3]

Even more striking still is the startling rate of capital accumulation among the top 200 global corporations. "The velocity of transnationalisation of capital as measured as a share of world GDP is stunning: from 17 percent in the mid-1960s to 24 percent in 1982 and over 32 percent in 1995."[4]

So if the central purpose of the MAI is to establish capital mobility as a global private property right, its fundamental effect will be the rapid acceleration in the concentration of wealth and power in the forms of giant, globe-encircling conglomerates, and further erosion of democratic institutions and values worldwide.

## A GOVERNMENT THAT CAN'T SAY "NO"

The men who run global corporations and serve as their agents, and the national governments of the OECD member countries, are well aware of these underlying realities. Hence they attempted to negotiate this grab of power in secret before popular opposition could organize. The Clinton Administration is in sync by seeking "fast track" legislation in the U.S. that will limit Congress to voting the MAI up or down without amendments if the Administration chooses to treat the MAI as an agreement rather than a treaty.[5]

As in the case of Third World governments hungry for foreign capital, Congress will be under strong compulsion to approve the MAI, since the only alternative is the "unthinkable" one of rejecting it and thus denying United States-based corporations access to world capital markets.

However, the underlying rationale for Clinton's fast track proposal and for the MAI when it is submitted to Congress—that recent trade and investment agreements have brought unprecedented prosperity to the American people—is contradicted by a recently released report, *The Underbelly of the U.S. Economy*.[6] There were more than 14 million jobless people in the U.S. in 1996, resulting in a jobless rate of 11.0 percent—more than twice the official figure. Nor is this all the bad news for the victims of past trade agreements. Real wages of American workers are well below what they were 25 years ago. Poverty is substantially higher than official figures from Washington indicate.

So the first step in the U.S. is to defeat fast track legislation by whatever it takes: a judicial challenge to its constitutionality; filibuster in the Senate because it strikes at the very foundation of our constitution—the sovereignty of "We the People"; massive nonviolent civil disobedience or a general strike.

Democratic forces won the first round through grass roots lobbying when "fast track" legislation was withdrawn by the Clinton Administration in early November 1997, once it became clear the bill would not pass the House of Representatives. But the fight is not over. The Business Roundtable and its allies in big business have vowed to regroup their lobby initiative, ALOT (America Leads On Trade), to raise a new war chest and to kick off a "grassroots" lobbying effort of their own in early 1998.[7]

## DEFEAT THE MAI, NOT THE CONSTITUTION

The next step is to defeat the MAI. Make no mistake about it: the MAI cannot be salvaged through "side agreements" on labor and environment, a point which thus far seems to have eluded U.S. trade union leadership and members of Congress who claim to be opposed to fast track legislation.[8] It is designed to serve the few at the expense of the many, and stands in direct opposition to the democratic ideals which peoples in every generation have aspired for—no matter how elusive their realization has been.

A third and most important step is proactive: to use the MAI as the launching pad for a truly vigorous and searching debate on property rights and democratic values. For too long we have allowed advocates of corporate hegemony to define the future, to appropriate language and minimize or confuse public discourse (such as calling environmental destruction "wise use"). It is time to start a "fair use" movement which recognizes the "reliance interest" of workers and community in the creation of capital, and the transcendence of public property rights of people and the Earth over private property rights when they are in conflict.[9]

## HUMAN RIGHTS AS THE FOUNDATION OF OUR FUTURE

The time has come to recapture the spirit of the American revolution and claim the sovereignty of "We the People" who did, after all, in the compelling words of the Preamble to the Constitution, "ordain and establish this Constitution for the United States of America."

The time has also come to move beyond the United States Constitution to the international human rights arena where the MAI must be recognized for what it is—a monumental assault on internationally recognized human rights, especially that most fundamental of all rights, the "right to be human."[10] ■

# Notes

[1] Clarke 1997.

[2] Lehner 1997.

[3] Clairmont 1996.

[4] Clairmont 1997.

[5] Like the ratification process for the U.S. Constitution in 1787. *—Ed.*

[6] Written by the author and David Dembo, published annually by The Apex Press.

[7] *National Journal*, November 21, 1997.

[8] Greenhouse 1997.

[9] On the "reliance interest," see Singler 1988. On public vs. private property, see Benson 1997. Why not use as a tool for consciousness raising and political mobilization the call for a common property rights amendment to the United States Constitution by Winona LaDuke, one of the most articulate and forceful advocates of the rights of indigenous peoples?

[10] Baxi 1989. See also Pereira 1997.

# CANCER IS A POLITICAL DISEASE

*by Mary Zepernick*

I N 1958 RACHEL CARSON, a scientist retired from the U.S. Fish and Wildlife Service and a best-selling author of nature books, received a letter from a friend in Massachusetts telling of a nearby DDT-based mosquito control program.

The woman described the mass death around her birdbath, birds convulsed, beaks agape. Thus does Sandra Steingraber portray in her book, *Living Downstream: An Ecologist Looks at Cancer and the Environment*, the inspiration for Carson's investigation of pesticides, resulting in the 1962 publication of *Silent Spring*. The title referred to the absence of bird song in a world poisoned by chemicals, but Carson was also concerned with two other forms of silence.

One was the failure of the government to include the public in important ecological debates going on within federal agencies. And the other was the complicity of scientists who didn't speak publicly about the growing chemical hazards around us. Two years after her book galvanized concern about "the environment," Rachel Carson died of breast cancer.

Some 36 years after she raised the alarm, what's the status of the disease that killed her? Breast cancer, the most frequently diagnosed cancer in women, has continued to increase 1 percent a year, as it has done since 1940. According to Steingraber, a breast cancer survivor, "women born in the United States between 1947 and 1958 have almost three times the rates of breast cancer that their great-grandmothers did when they were the same age."

And according to *Rachel's Environment & Health Weekly* (named for Carson), more U.S. women have died of breast cancer in the past two decades than all the country's dead in both World Wars, Korea, and Vietnam.[1]

How well have we come to grips with the poisons Rachel Carson saw silencing the spring? Pesticide use in this country has doubled since her book was published, and *Rachel's* reports that only 1.5 to 3 percent of some 75,000 chemicals now in use have been tested for carcinogenicity. "Currently, our government regulates fewer than 200 chemicals on the basis of their carcinogenicity—and we add roughly 2,000 new untested chemicals into commercial use each year now."[2]

Steingraber quotes Philip Landrigan, a pediatrician and public health researcher who believes the quest for the causes of elevated cancer rates must include environmental inquiry. "The possible contribution to recent cancer trends of the substantial worldwide increases in chemical production that have occurred since World War II (and the resulting increases in human exposure to toxic chemicals in the environment) has not been adequately addressed. It needs to be systematically evaluated."

The Silent Spring Institute has taken on this task. Formed when activists from the

---

Massachusetts Breast Cancer Coalition demanded a scientific investigation of elevated breast cancer rates on Cape Cod, the Institute has just finished a three-year study, funded by the Massachusetts Department of Public Health. While not yet identifying specific causes, researchers have developed new methods for tracking and mapping environmental data, establishing a foundation for the next phase of the study.

The Silent Spring Institute has also pioneered in its goal of prevention, since breast cancer research, centered at the National Cancer Institute, has focused almost exclusively on treatment. The Breast Cancer Awareness Month slogan, "Early Detection is Your Best Prevention," illustrates the priority to date. After all, notwithstanding the importance of detection and cure, once cancer is found it has hardly been prevented!

The history of Breast Cancer Awareness Month also tells a tale. Imperial Chemical Industries, a British chemical conglomerate, initiated the annual event in the mid-1980s, and it is now funded and controlled by Zeneca Pharmaceuticals, a spin-off of ICI.

*Rachel's* identifies Zeneca's "dual role in the cancer business. On the one hand it earns $300 million each year from sales of the carcinogenic herbicide acetochlor. At the same time the corporation earns $470 million each year marketing the world's best-selling cancer therapy drug, tamoxifen citrate, and operates a chain of 11 U.S. cancer treatment centers. Clearly, cancer prevention would conflict with Zeneca's business plan."[3]

*Rachel's Environment & Health Weekly* concludes its five-part series on breast cancer with the contention that "Cancer—including breast cancer—is a political disease. Corporations have hijacked our sovereign power and are using it against us, contaminating our air, water and food with cancer-causing, hormone-disrupting chemicals. If we are to survive as a species, we will need to reassert the sovereign power of the people to 'promote the general welfare.'"[4]

Nothing else will do it. ∎

## NOTES

[1] *Rachel's Environment & Health Weekly no. 571.*

[2] *Rachel's Environment & Health Weekly no. 573.*

[3] *Rachel's Environment & Health Weekly no. 572.*

[4] *Rachel's Environment & Health Weekly no. 575.*

# WELFARE REFORM
# COMES TO TOLEDO

*by Mike Ferner*

THESE ARE FUNNY times. If you're poor, it's not the "ha-ha" kind of funny, but these are indeed funny times. Toledoans may recall the effort last summer to place the Owens-Corning property tax abatement on the ballot. Ten-thousand signatures gathered in a month were a lot, but not enough. Voters did not get an opportunity to decide on the abatement—$1.3 million a year for 20 years—passed by city council last June. The company retained its tax break by convincing city leaders that the abatement, on top of a $10 million grant from city taxpayers, and a $1 million grant plus low interest loans from state taxpayers, was essential to keep the firm downtown.

So where's the humor? Recently, Owens-Corning officials released figures on 1994 corporate profits and executive compensation. A picture emerges of a company sorely in need of public assistance.

As reported by Toledo's daily newspaper, sales increased by $400 million to $3.35 billion. Profits were up 5% to $159 million. Glen "Captain of Industry" Hiner's compensation totaled $1.9 million plus stock options of about $1.75 million. He did a swell job getting us to pay the company's taxes, so his bonus went up last year by 41% to just under a cool million. In 1994, the top five corporate officers received compensation packages, including the median value of stock options, worth $8.7 million. Officials announced plans to open two plants in China, one in Argentina, double the one in Africa, and "explore opportunities" in Colombia and India. A new manufacturing plant will even be built in Ohio—but not Toledo.

Hiner's $986,000 bonus last year is not far from what the company would have paid in property taxes to our schools, library, zoo, mental health and other agencies in one year without the abatement. These guys gotta be laughing—all the way to the bank!

Meanwhile, our governor signed a bill eliminating the $100 a month general assistance payment to 61,000 Ohioans—4,373 in Lucas County. Eligible citizens received that princely sum six months out of the year, but no more. The cut will save the state less than 0.3 of 1% of a $33 billion state budget, and if Michigan's experience is any indication, will do little to move people into productive jobs. A study done by the University of Michigan found that after Governor Engler ended general assistance for "able-bodied" adults in that state, a whopping 20% of them were working full time a year later.

The moral to the story? If you're on the dole big time, you qualify as a captain of industry and get hefty bonuses. If you only get $100 a month, you're an expendable pain in the neck. ∎

# GENDER AND GLOBAL CORPORATIZATION

*by Molly Morgan,*

*Virginia Rasmussen & Mary Zepernick*

WHILE THE POWER wielded by giant corporations and its resulting extremes of wealth and poverty are unprecedented in scale, the worldview that supports it reaches back between five and 10 millennia.

Starhawk, a sponsor of the Women's International League for Peace and Freedom, as well as Riane Eisler and others, describe the "power-over" model of society, which replaced more egalitarian cultures in the transition to large centers of population, with the accumulation of surplus and its accompanying rule-based structures. As Starhawk puts it in *Dreaming the Dark*:

> We like to tell ourselves that there once was a time when we were free, that "power-over" is a human invention, not an imperative of nature. The story of the rise of power-over is the story of the literal dismemberment of the world, the tearing apart of the fabric of living interrelationships that once governed human life.

The power-over model, because it is a human invention, arbitrarily assigns unequal value to human difference, establishing dominant and subordinate categories and the political concept of "other" as the basis for discrimination and exploitation. Though rooted in male dominance, patriarchal behavior applies to all of us when we exercise power over others and the Earth. Global "corporatization" is a logical extension of the "dismemberment" that accompanied the development of "civilization." Far from being natural and inevitable, the transnational corporation, with its vast supporting infrastructure, is the most virulent manifestation of power-over to date.

The standard teaching of U.S. history emphasizes wars, land acquisition and industrial "progress" rather than the ongoing struggle of people of color, women, the working class and poor. As these oppressed groups slowly gained ground, the wealthy changed the nature of corporations, whose operations for the first century were restricted and enforced by state-issued charters. After the Supreme Court in 1886 declared the corporate form equivalent to a natural person under the law (in *Santa Clara v. Southern Pacific Railroad Co.*), people's already limited sovereignty was further subordinated to the large corporation. Thus, a major corporate achievement has been to convert the corporate form *from* that of a publicly defined institution *to* one that receives constitutional protection from effective public control.

The primary defining of markets and investments today is controlled by the international institutions that serve the interests of transnational corporations rather than people and planet. Out of the Uruguay Round of negotiations under the General Agreement on Tariffs and Trade (GATT), the profoundly anti-democratic World Trade Organization (WTO) was established in 1995. Its authority on behalf of unlimited mobility for capital and production has the legislative, judicial and enforcement power to undermine, in the name of "free trade," national and even local laws passed to protect workers, communities and the environment. What is the impact upon women of so much power vested in a single institution?

Today, what author bell hooks calls the "white supremacist capitalist patriarchy" dominates not only its own people, but also the less developed nations of the global South. Within all countries, females are the most disadvantaged and exploited, particularly women of color, the poor and lesbians. The Women's Caucus of organizations from the South and North attending the "Third Ministerial Meeting of the WTO" in Seattle made this statement:

> [T]he majority of the world's women and girls are adversely affected by the unequal power relations created at the national, regional and international levels by the new trade regime . . . We believe the WTO undermines major international agreements that women have worked hard to get their governments to commit to.

The corporate form and its national and international institutional protectors are especially damaging to the lives of women, who comprise the majority of the poor in every country. In the United States, many women work in low-wage categories that are particularly vulnerable to downsizing as corporations compete for ideal profit-yielding conditions.

State and local governments, held hostage by corporations seeking tax relief and subsidies, are strapped for funds to meet social program obligations, with much of the resulting slack taken up by already overworked women.

The same phenomena are infinitely more disastrous for women in the debtor nations on which the International Monetary Fund and World Bank have imposed Structural Adjustment Program (SAP) policies. SAPs demand that nations reduce their own economic planning in favor of a commodity-based, export-oriented economy, and a "liberalization" that includes deep cuts in expenditures on social programs, the privatization of state-run industries and services, and increased labor flexibility.

When SAP policies result in recession, the resultant wage and job cuts most drastically affect women, for whom the "informal economy" is their last resort. Alicia Sepulveda, Foreign Secretary of the Mexican Telephone Workers Union, describes the "explosion in the number of street sellers, most of them women," with nearly a quarter of employed women earning less than the daily minimum wage of $3.50. Women who migrate as domestic workers, caregivers, or farm workers are particularly vulnerable to sexual as well as financial exploitation.

Reduced social services adds to women's responsibility for the functioning of their families and communities. Throughout the world women work more hours than men— the so-called double burden—but much of their labor is not reflected in official statistics; according to a recent United Nations Development Program's Human Index

Report, women contribute $11 trillion annually in unpaid "household work" to the global economy.

Most of the sweatshop workers in developing countries are women, who put in long hours for below minimum or living wages, and receive no overtime pay, sick leave or medical benefits. Susan Tompson of the Colombia Justice and Peace Society says:

> You can see it in Mexico, in Honduras, and in a number of other countries where women—particularly young women—are working in the maquiladoras, the factories that put together clothes or electronics. Because the country desperately needs export dollars, officials often turn a blind eye to the abuses suffered by the women in the factories.

Author, activist and researcher Vandana Shiva declared that "all domestic issues have been drawn into the global economy, bringing women into direct collision with global patriarchal institutions." Because patriarchal economic institutions are international, so must be people's movements to resist and replace systems that benefit a few at the expense of the majority of the world's populations. The quest for the rights and powers of self-governance requires us to grapple with who we are as human beings. Do we really believe that power over others is so embedded in "human nature" that the best we can do is picket sweat-shop owners, one by one, imploring them to respect voluntary codes of conduct? Or can we rise to the challenge of being self-determining, exercising authority over the institutions and policies that affect our lives?

Vandana Shiva points out that:

> For more than two centuries, patriarchal, eurocentric, and anthropocentric scientific discourse has treated women, other cultures, and other species as objects. Experts have been treated as the only legitimate knowers. For more than two decades, feminist movements, Third World and indigenous people's movements, and ecological and animal-rights movements have questioned this objectification and denial of subjecthood.

The late twentieth century growth of a global feminist movement has brought women together in common cause. A widespread expression and tool of women's organizing is the Beijing Platform for Action, a solid indictment of corporate oppression and a democratic agenda for people and their institutions of governance.

From village centers to U.N. forums, women's ideas, processes and relationships are important models for the world we seek to create. As African-American lesbian poet Audre Lorde put it, "You can't dismantle the master's house using the master's tools." ■

# IS TRUTH FOR SALE?

## CORPORATE POWER ON CAMPUS AND THE FUTURE OF STUDENT ACTIVISM

*by Rob Inerfeld*

FOR STUDENTS ACROSS the country this is an uncertain but exciting time. Since last fall's elections there has been a surge in student activism as Congress—no longer with any pretense—abandons the notion that our government should protect the common good.

In the fall of 1994 hundreds of students mobilized against racism at Rutgers University, and thousands of youth walked out of classes to protest Proposition 187 in California. In late February of 1995 nearly 2,000 youth activists converged on Philadelphia for the "Free the Planet Conference." On March 23rd over ten thousand students took to the streets of New York City to protest education funding cuts and tuition hikes. Thousands of students at over 100 campuses across the country turned out on March 29th for protests coordinated by the Center for Campus Organizing against the "Contract on America."

This is a sign of a great awakening on our campuses. However, these and other actions were reactive—they were instances of people coming together to denounce what the Republicans and many Democrats are doing in Congress.

It has become increasingly clear to many activists that our democracy is not functioning because of the interference of large corporations in the democratic process. Many of these corporations are enjoying record profits, yet they are ordering Congress to dismantle laws that protect people and nature from corporate harm. Corporate lobbyists not only lobby members of Congress, but actually write many of the proposed laws for our elected "representatives."

Reactive efforts in opposition to the Contract on America may prevent passage of parts of it and convince Clinton to veto other parts of it. But unless activists from different movements come together to take power away from corporations, worse things will happen in the future as corporations become even more powerful and wield more control over our nation's public policy.

Unfortunately, many colleges and universities are no better models for democratic participation than is our federal government. At most universities, power is concentrated in the hands of school presidents and boards of trustees, many of whom are executives at large corporations. Our colleges and universities were not designed as democracies. How can we learn about participation in a democracy when our schools are such hierarchical institutions?

©1995 Center for Campus Organizing. Previously published in *Infusion* (Fall 1995), a publication of the Center for Campus Organizing. Author Rob Inerfeld worked for POCLAD from 1995 to 1997 as a researcher and campus organizer.

The influence of corporations at colleges and universities is increasing. Many university departments have become research and development arms for corporations. Universities are spending millions of dollars building facilities and seeking business, science, and engineering professors so that they can draw corporate research to their schools. These increasing costs have led many university presidents to raise tuition, making schools even more inaccessible to poor and working-class students.

Given this, how can we challenge corporate power on our campuses with power-building and multi-issue campaigns?

One way is to organize campaigns to shift college and university investments from harmful corporations to community investments. Our academic institutions often invest in large, polluting, democracy-corrupting corporations, while at the same time our urban communities are suffering from an under-investment crisis.

Many campuses are situated near low-income communities that have economic, environmental, and social problems, including under-investment and a dearth of good jobs. Over the last twenty years hundreds of community development corporations have been established to channel money into the economic development of low-income areas. Although these efforts have made a difference in the lives of millions of Americans, additional funds are needed for community investments if we are to conquer poverty in the United States.

A national campaign to shift campus investments from harmful multinational corporations to communities could have many advantages over other national campaigns. Unlike national legislative campaigns or boycotts which are only win-or-lose, there could be victories at individual schools which would inspire students elsewhere. There could also

be individual victories along the way as students gain access to investment information and establish boards elected by students, staff, faculty, and alumni, to oversee investments.

This would be a campaign about doing good—it would focus on revitalizing impoverished areas rather than just withdrawing funds from investments in harmful corporations. However, there will be strong resistance to these ideas from those with power. We should expect that university administrators will say that shifting to investments which have lower returns will necessitate tuition increases. This is an issue that we have to address in all our divestment activism.

The campaigns to divest from South Africa and Hydro-Québec effectively connect U.S. students to the efforts of other people struggling to take control of their lives. Similarly, campaigns against corporate power could build solidarity among students, workers, the poor, indigenous people, and communities in the U.S. and in other countries.

A new surge of student activism around divestment could bring the discussion of important issues about corporations and democracy to college campuses and help students develop an analysis of the root causes of environmental, economic, and social problems in society. Students could begin discussing the following questions:

- How much authority should we grant to corporations to make decisions that affect our lives and communities?

- What roles should students play in school curriculum, investment and purchasing decisions?

- What alternatives are there to working for big corporations?

- How can we make our universities democratic?

- Why is an increasing amount of university research done for corporations?

- How is this perverting the original purposes of our universities? How is this related to tuition increases?

In every era, student movements have inspired and been essential to national movements. Today many adults feel lost and are searching for new directions. A multi-issue campaign against corporate power would be a galvanizing force for positive change. ■

# SPEAKING TRUTH TO POWER ABOUT CAMPAIGN REFORM

*by Jane Anne Morris*

---

THE WORD "REFORM" has lost some of its luster lately. Remember regulatory "reform"? Health care "reform"? And then welfare "reform"?

As we stand today, up to our armpits in schemes for campaign finance "reform," we need to make sure that proposals are grounded in principles that we at least recognize. All the better if they are explicitly democratic. A bit of history will provide some perspective on how "campaign finance reform" efforts came to assume their current form.

A generation ago, public disgust at the way elections were run reached one of its periodic peaks. That last big wave of "campaign finance reform" was set into motion by corruption at CREEP (the Committee to Re-Elect the President) during the Nixon years. Responding to a public outcry, Congress passed the Federal Election Campaign Act (FEC Act, 1971; amended 1974).

What washed ashore shortly thereafter were corporate political action committees (PACs) and the now-legendary *Buckley v. Valeo* (hereafter, "*Valeo*") Supreme Court decision of 1976. Conditions being optimal, the scum left behind at reform's high water mark has ripened into the sleaze that is now rotting all around us.

Even more disturbing than the failure of the Watergate-era "reforms" to restore some sense of integrity to our election process is the growing evidence that very little has been learned in the last quarter century. What is the sense of making a mistake if you're just going to repeat it?

While what little democracy we have goes down the tubes, we are avidly arguing about precisely what formula corporate managers and the very wealthy must use to funnel millions of dollars to targeted candidates.

While corporate speech saturates the legally public airwaves, we're debating about whether or not we dare to restrict independent expenditures. Nay, we're debating about how to even *define* independent expenditures.

Meanwhile, we're not confronting issues such as . . .

- Is money speech?

- Should a corporation have the same rights as a human person to participate in the democratic process?

- If this is a democracy then shouldn't all citizens, regardless of their economic status, be equally able to run for office?

- What should be the nature of our public policy discussions and our elections?

It may be another generation before as much momentum and outrage is again built up around this issue. It would be nice to leave a

---

©1998 by Jane Anne Morris. Many of these issues have been discussed by Maine labor activist Peter Kellman. Thanks also to Richard L. Grossman, and J.M. Baime of the Gray Panthers.

more democratic heritage than the seventies left us in the form of the FEC Act and the *Valeo* decision. That is possible only if we first understand the assumptions gently but insidiously folded in the FEC Act/*Valeo* package, now the "law of the land."

## MONEY AND SPEECH

First, let's examine the issue of viewing money as a form of speech.

Starting out with "separate but equal" ends up with counting drinking fountains to measure equality. Today, starting with "money is speech," we are doing little more than counting dollars to measure democracy. We've missed the point.

How did we come to such a state that we can talk about free speech only by talking about money?

The money-equals-speech equation derives from the Supreme Court's 1976 *Valeo* decision. In a nutshell, in that decision the Court held that as far as campaign expenditures were concerned, money is speech. Therefore, limits on expenditures were limits on free speech, which is a constitutional no-no unless "compelling" circumstances are demonstrated.

To complicate the picture further, the Court in *Valeo* also ruled that though *spending* money is free speech and cannot be limited (as the original FEC Act provided), *donating* money is a slightly different kind of free speech that can be limited.

So, while demand (expenditures) was unlimited, supply (contributions) was limited, thus creating a perfect setting for creative "bundling" of contributions, the opening up of numerous "conduits" for funds, the use of "independent" expenditures, and the proliferation of other kinds of "soft money" (unregulated expenditures). And that is what happened.

The near unanimity of opinion in the *Valeo* decision concurring that money equals speech is striking:

> One of the points on which all Members of the Court agree is that money is essential for effective communication in a political campaign.[1]

> [V]irtually all meaningful political communications in the modern setting involve the expenditure of money.[2]

> [C]ontributions and expenditures are at the very core of political speech.[3]

> [V]irtually every means of communicating ideas in today's mass society requires the expenditure of money.[4]

This assumption is echoed in today's debate.

> Money in politics is not evil. It would be impossible to have a good democracy without paying for candidates to talk with voters . . .[5]

It was not always so. In the early days of the First Amendment in this republic, all information and discussion was either by word of mouth—"live"—or by means of reading the printed word. Informal talks, handbills, newspapers, and songs were all part of the public debate. Much later, the airwaves—radio and television—became available as media for communication.

Other changes occurred as well. The open marketplace at the crossroads was replaced by the shopping mall. Time once spent in public areas exchanging news and views is now spent in front of the blue glow of the television set.

The meaning of free speech rights has been altered correspondingly. The First Amendment rights of human persons have been progressively restricted, primarily through a steady expansion of the concept of private property rights and an ever-growing laundry list of what the government may prohibit by sweeping it into the category of "public safety" laws.

What this means in practical terms is that a human person's free speech rights are severely restricted in the workplace, at the shopping center, and on the street corner. But in these same contexts, First Amendment rights of corporate "persons," as interpreted by the courts, are almost limitless.

So as we human persons work and shop, we are bombarded by corporate "free speech" but may not exercise our own First Amendment rights much beyond asking where the bathroom is or what something costs.

From here on out the magic works by itself. You need money to be heard in the only places that matter. Corporations have both First Amendment rights and ample funds; hence, only their views are heard. But any "person" (that means you the reader, or a transnational corporation) is equally free to take out a full-page advertisement in the New York Times or buy a minute of air time for a half a million bucks.

There is a further twist. The airwaves belong to the public, but our federal regulatory regime has leased them to private corporations for a song. These media corporations use them to make huge profits partly by selling the public's own air waves back to them through public financing of campaigns.

Free civic forums where people can speak truth and debate ideas without fear of harassment are almost nonexistent. Potential forums that remain (like the news media, malls and workplaces) are private property where, with the help of court declarations, free speech by human persons is either forbidden, severely limited, or costs money.

If the only way to speak freely and be heard is to pay the powerful corporations for a forum, and be subject to their censorship whims, then speech is not free.

## CORPORATIONS AND FIRST AMENDMENT RIGHTS

Now to the second issue that we are not debating: Should a corporation have the same rights as a human person to participate in the processes of democratic governance?

The absence of this issue from the current debate is disturbing. When we neglect to even question whether corporations should have the constitutional rights of human persons, we are drifting far afield from any real sense of democracy.

The word democracy, it should not need to be pointed out, means rule by the *people*: self-rule, self-governance. It is one of the shameful aspects of our history that it took great ferment to establish (at least theoretically) that "people" means all human beings, and not just the wealthy white males who framed the Constitution. How is it then that corporations have for a century possessed the core constitutional rights of natural persons? Shouldn't we debate this, or at least mention it, before embedding corporations even more deeply in our political process?

The FEC Act, like most discussions of "campaign finance reform," does not distinguish between the rights of "natural persons" (legal parlance for human beings) and other entities such as corporations and committees.

How can we fail to distinguish people from corporations in laws about the democratic process itself? Our laws distinguish species of birds from each other; we have separate laws for all manner of fish and reptiles. Trees in our yard, trees on federal land, trees along rivers, and trees whose corporate "owners" are involved in leveraged buyouts of other corporations fall into different legal categories. But we lump people and corporations together as constitutional "persons."

People didn't always think that corporations were entitled to constitutional rights. Since the late nineteenth century the Supreme Court has been handing corporations many of the protections guaranteed to "persons" by the U.S. Constitution. But it wasn't until the "reforms" of the 1970s that the idea that corporations had free speech "rights" began to be widely accepted.

If corporations have such constitutional rights, perhaps they ought to vote and have their own named representatives in the halls of Congress. "The Chair recognizes the Senator from Union Carbide Corporation . . . from Waste Management Corporation . . . from the British East India Company . . ." etc.

Democracy is not a matter of people negotiating with a corporate management team, or with an administrative board, or with a king. It is a matter of We the People talking *with each other* and deciding what our community, society and economy should look like. We should do it more often.

Imagine a law that prohibited corporations from engaging in *any* form of political activity. Imagine that breaking such a law was a felony, and that a corporation could be dissolved or kicked out of a state for disobeying it.

Wisconsin had such a law from 1905 until 1953. Check out this language:

> No corporation doing business in this state shall pay or contribute, or offer consent or agree to pay or contribute, directly or indirectly, any money, property, free service of its officers or employees or thing of value to any political party, organization, committee or individual for any political purpose whatsoever, or for the purpose of influencing legislation of any kind, or

to promote or defeat the candidacy of any person for nomination, appointment or election to any political office.[6]

The law was still on the books, with lessened penalties, until the early 1970s when the new improved FEC Act took effect, making PACs legal.

It was not so long ago that corporations were not viewed as appropriate participants in elections. Democracy and free speech were for humans. Dare we think that way again? If we don't speak truth to power about free speech, what grounds have we for democracy?

## WHO SHOULD BE ABLE TO RUN?

And now the third issue that we seem unwilling to raise: If this is a democracy then shouldn't all citizens, regardless of their economic status, be equally able to run for office?

Today, even with some "public funding" of campaigns, perhaps 80% of the population cannot even consider running for office. That we accept this as "normal" is a stinging indictment of how low our standards for measuring democracy have fallen.

Not surprisingly, most of the reasons why only a small percentage of U.S. citizens can even dream of running for office revolve around money. Who can take time off from work to campaign? Who is assured that after a campaign, or a term served, that they can return to a job? How many public offices provide only a token salary, thereby limiting those who can serve to the independently wealthy?

If we want free and fair elections, and not just "campaign finance reform," we are going to have to think about and debate these issues.

## TODAY'S DEBATE: ENTER MAINE

Against this historical and conceptual backdrop we can view current reform efforts through a distant mirror.

The recent upsurge of interest in what's being termed "campaign finance reform" reflects people's growing awareness that big corporations dominate our political process, and with it our economic and social lives. As Sir John Colepepper put it in the early seventeenth century, corporations sip from our cup, they dip in our dish, they sit by our fire.

If you said this only a few years ago, people called you a conspiracy theorist. Now they say either "So what else is new?" or "But there's nothing we can do about it."

All over the nation, people are trying to do something about it. Their efforts are termed "campaign finance reform" and many are hailing Maine's new election law (the Maine Elections Act, passed by initiative in November 1996) as the pot of gold at the end of the campaign finance reform rainbow.

A cursory review of news clippings and editorials about the Maine Act speak of it as a "model," as a "standard against which all other reform efforts are judged." It is "far-reaching," it is "revolutionary." It "addresses nearly every problem that exists in the campaign world." One commentator noted that the people of Maine had "reached for the stars." Another stated flatly, "Maine is the future . . . We have to figure out how to do Maine everywhere."

One would expect that such an initiative would represent a fearful threat to entrenched corporations in Maine, and nationwide. One would expect that such an initiative would be fought tooth and nail by the same powerful corporations that launched a successful media barrage to crush the anti-clear-cutting initiative on the same ballot.

Instead, it was a real ho-hummer. There was no organized opposition to the Maine "campaign finance reform" initiative. According to Maine labor activist Peter Kellman who followed the campaign closely for the Program on Corporations, Law and Democracy (and voted for the initiative), the only visible opposition was from the American Civil Liberties Union (ACLU).

(The ACLU has embraced the "money equals speech" doctrine, and has accepted the extension of constitutional rights to corporate "persons." Corporate donations and expenditures for political purposes thus appear as "free speech" issues.)

This great gaping corporate silence—remember how they handled Clinton's hardly radical health care plan—should be an alarm bell for us. Pretend you're a corporate CEO and see if you feel threatened by the Maine Act's provisions.

The Maine Act was intentionally drafted to avoid challenging the *Valeo* decision:

- It accepts the equation money equals speech.

- It accepts the equivalence of human beings and corporations for most legal purposes relating to the mechanisms of democracy.

- It does not address most of the obstacles preventing most people from running for office. That is, it's not about democracy, it's about money.

As to how it would affect current campaigns, consider these points:

- It does not prevent a wealthy candidate from using family or personal wealth to outspend a publicly financed opponent ten-to-one, or a thousand-to-one.

- It does not prevent a corporation from setting up scores or thousands of PACs (political action committees), each of which can collect the maximum amount of money for a candidate.

- It does not prevent dozens or hundreds of "independent" individuals or groups from spending unlimited amounts of money advocating a particular candidate or position.

The Maine Act is not only not about democracy, it's not very much about money, as many so-called current "abuses" will continue.

What the Maine Act does, however, under the guise of "public financing," is set up a system that collects money from the many, passes it quickly through the hands of the hopeful (candidates), into the coffers of the few (media corporations). Misleadingly termed "public financing," this scheme is a redistribution of wealth in which We the People pay huge media corporations to allow us limited use of the airwaves we own.

For such a non-solution, scores of citizen organizations around the U.S. are receiving financial infusions from philanthropic foundations to pursue measures much like the Maine Act.

Many proponents of such "reform" admit it's "not perfect," but assert that it's the best we can do at this time. This "best" amounts to accepting the *Valeo* and FEC Act assumptions as the natural order of things. We say with a sigh ... We live in an imperfect world. For reasons of money only a small proportion of us can even think of running for office. Among those privileged few campaigns are corrupt by any measure. But We the People are severely limited in what we can do about it because of the Constitution. The best we can do is to limit money in campaigns enough to temper the corruption to tolerable levels but we certainly can't do anything to chill corporate free speech.

The 1970s electoral "reforms" did not usher in an era of clean and open democratic elections by any means. It follows, then, that if we do want to work toward such a goal, we need to do something *different*.

If we expect to get beyond the tinkering stage in dealing with the campaign reform issue, we will have to face each of the following three issues:

- People can recognize and reject the profoundly anti-democratic equation of money and speech, and identify the root causes that make it seem to be "natural."

- People can reject the notion that persons and corporations are legal or constitutional equivalents, and that corporations have "rights" at all, other than those limited capacities specifically granted them by the sovereign people.

- People can debate not campaign "finance" but campaigns themselves, and decide how We the People want to hold our elections and make public policy decisions.

## RE-FRAMING THE DEBATE

A debate that confronts the fundamental issues underlying current proposals for "campaign finance reform" would begin by recognizing that we need wholesale *election reform*, not just campaign "finance" reform. The authors of the *Valeo* decision stated that:

> ... in the free society ordained by our Constitution, it is not the government but the people ... who must retain control over the quantity and range of debate on public issues in a political campaign. (*Valeo* p. 56)

If they meant all people and not just the self-styled elites in power at the moment, we can agree with them. If they meant human persons and not corporate "persons," then we can agree with them.

What we're seeking here isn't changing the laws of gravity or finding the fountain of youth. It's self-governance, by all of the people. It is self-governance in a context of the free flow of ideas and information, sparked by debate and discussion. And it is fairness—plain, ordinary fairness, something that any child can detect.

We seek the "unfettered interchange of ideas for the bringing about of political and social changes desired by the people."[7] Obviously this is not possible where corporations dominate the election process and election opportunities are not equal for all.

Chances are that we won't achieve this goal by next year's elections, but if we can't even imagine it, much less talk about it, we'll never achieve it. The word campaign comes from the word for open, level field, and that's what we're after.

We can start with six basic democratic principles.

1.  Free speech is a prerequisite for democracy.

2.  Money is not speech.

Participation in the democratic process should not in any way or to any degree be dependent on money. (Note: There is a move afoot to reverse the *Valeo* decision, but on grounds of "compelling" government interest, as opposed to a refutation of the money-equals-speech equation.)

3.  Natural persons (citizens—the "demos" of democracy) should be distinguished from corporations in all laws regarding the political process.

Since democracy is about people, corporations should not have First Amendment rights. (Note: In view of the fact that the legal term corporation covers municipalities, many environmental groups, media corporations, corporate trade associations, some Native American tribes, some unions and transnational corporations, among other entities, obviously some fine-tuning is needed here. But there are ways of handling this issue so as to avoid jeopardizing the First Amendment rights of human persons to associate.)

4.  Public forums (such as the airwaves, our newspapers and magazines, our workplaces, malls and street corners) should be free from corporate control.

5.  Election provisions should be mandatory and apply to all.

"Voluntary" programs should be avoided because they allow rich candidates to buy their way out of conditions imposed on lower and middle income candidates (We can call it the Perot-Forbes Syndrome.)

6.  Under no circumstances should public money be paid to media corporations for use of the airwaves that we already own.

Measures to apply these principles might include the following:

• Prohibit all paid political advertisements on radio and television.

• Use the public airwaves for debate and discussion of candidates, issues and concerns. Don't ask, tell. Corporations are legal fictions granted special powers in order to serve a public need. Corporations that fail to comply shall have their corporate charters or certificates of authority revoked.

• Do not require monetary contributions to qualify a candidate for public financing or an issue to appear on a ballot. Signatures are enough. Current attempts to justify a dollar contribution to demonstrate "seriousness" or "commitment" parallel the arguments offered in previous eras in support of the poll tax, and the "property" requirements of 1789.

• Workplaces, malls and street corners should be made into free speech and free assembly zones. As a general rule, any space where we "hear" corporate speech without asking for it should be a place where human persons can express their ideas freely, and have the right to hear others' views, without fear of harassment or retribution.

- Election opportunities should be the same for all, regardless of wealth. Provisions for time off during campaigns, the guarantee of a job to return to after an election or a term served, and a living wage for both candidates and elected officials will help

remove the built-in advantages that now exist for wealthy persons who run for political office.

We are a long way from the "unfettered interchange of ideas" described as desirable in the *Valeo* decision. We need the courage, and the space, to challenge the prevailing wisdom of our age. There is much to discuss, debate, work out, and experiment with. But if we fail on our first try, or succeed only partially, it will be because we spoke truth to power, and not because we worked only for measures that were "achievable" but changed little. ∎

## NOTES

[1] Justice Marshall in *Valeo* p. 288; Marshall concurred in part and dissented in part.

[2] *Valeo* p. 11, describing appellants' views.

[3] *Valeo* p. 56, describing appellants' views.

[4] *Valeo* p. 19.

[5] Donald F. Kettl, director of the La Follette Institute of Public Affairs, University of Wisconsin at Madison, 26 Jan. 1997 in the *Wisconsin State Journal*.

[6] Wis. Laws, Section 4479a. (Sec. I, ch 492, 1905).

[7] *Valeo* p. 49, quoting *New York Times v. Sullivan*, quoting *Assoc. Press v. US.*

# HUMAN RIGHTS VS. CORPORATE "RIGHTS"

*by Mary Zepernick*

---

[T]he right of property in a slave is distinctly and expressly affirmed in the Constitution.[1]

-Chief Justice Taney

I N 1857 THE U.S. Supreme Court found against Dred Scott's right to freedom, despite the fact that his owner had taken him to a free state and territory before returning with him to Missouri, a slave state.

The court also declared the Missouri Compromise[2] unconstitutional on the grounds that Congress had no authority to exclude slavery from the territories.

> [N]o word can be found in the Constitution which gives Congress a greater power over slave property; or which entitles property of that kind to less protection than property of any other description. The only power conferred is the power coupled with the duty of guarding and protecting the owner in his rights.[3]

Thus did the highest court come down foursquare on the side of property over people. As for human freedom, Abraham Lincoln, born 190 years ago today, wrote in a letter to journalist Horace Greeley in 1862 that "My paramount object in this struggle is to save the Union and is not either to save or destroy Slavery. If I could save the Union without freeing any slave, I would do it and if I could save it by freeing all the slaves, I would

do it and if I could do it by freeing some and leaving others alone, I would also do that." Lincoln's humanitarian impulses took a back seat to practical politics.

For example, the Emancipation Proclamation, issued the first day of 1863, freed only those slaves behind enemy lines, where Lincoln had no authority. However, soon after the Union won the Civil War (or "War of Northern Aggression" to those who believe the South will rise again), the Thirteenth Amendment to the Constitution abolished slavery. Three years later, the Fourteenth Amendment extended citizenship to African-Americans. The "due process" and "equal protection of the laws" clauses prohibited states from depriving any person of guaranteed civil liberties and equal treatment.

President Grover Cleveland had made note of another threat to this beloved Union.

> Corporations, which should be the carefully restrained creatures of the law and the servants of the people, are fast becoming the people's masters.

Upon this nation's founding, conditions of corporate operations were clearly defined by state-issued charters. However, with the

---

growth of railroads, banking and manufacturing in the mid-nineteenth century, corporate barons and lawyers figured their fortunes would be better served if their institutions gained the rights of people.

In 1886, after decades of corporate maneuvering and corrupting those in high places, the Supreme Court issued a watershed decision in *Santa Clara County v. Southern Pacific Railroad Co.*, declaring the corporation a legal "person" under the Constitution, entitled to the protection of the Fourteenth Amendment.

Sixty years later, Justice William O. Douglas wrote that "There was no history, logic or reason given to support that view."[5]

In 1896, a decade after giving corporations legal personhood, the court stripped it from African-Americans in *Plessy v. Ferguson* (establishing the doctrine of "separate but equal"), putting the Supreme seal of approval on segregation.

Between 1890 and 1910, 307 Fourteenth Amendment cases came before the Supreme Court, 19 dealing with African-Americans, and 288 with corporations. It took 58 years of freedom struggles before the court reversed Plessy, with *Brown v. Board of Education* finding in 1954 that separate is inherently unequal.

Referring to the mid-twentieth century civil rights movement, researcher Jeff Kaplan writes that "these attempts by real human beings to assert their rights threatened the prerogatives of the corporations. Corporate lawyers responded by seeking to expand the standing of corporate persons to include a number of protections under the Bill of Rights which previously had been granted only to human beings. In other words the Court has endorsed a counter attack by property against the assertion of human rights by the public in general, and people of color and women in particular."

Consequently, at the turn of another century we witness the grotesquerie of corporate "free speech;" of Omnipoint Corporation suing the citizens of Wellfleet over the placement of cell towers for allegedly violating the corporate entity's civil rights under the Civil Rights Act of 1964,[6] and the Wells Fargo Corporation threatening a suit against the people of Santa Cruz for denying them a piece of public land; of activists and the government negotiating "voluntary" codes of corporate conduct rather than insisting that the people's representatives once again define the nature and activities of our legal fictions.

Some folks, alarmed by the corporate usurpation of our power to govern, seek to "level the playing field." But this is not the *people v. corporations* suiting up for a contest between two equal teams. Becoming self-governing, in charge of our common life and institutions, isn't a game; it's the work of We the People.

Grover Cleveland had it right. Corporations should be servants of the people, not their masters. ■

---

## NOTES

[1] *Dred Scott v. Sandford*

[2] This was a compromise worked out in Congress in 1820 which granted statehood to Missouri without restrictions on slavery, and statehood to Maine as a free state. Also part of this agreement was a federal decree declaring all territories north of Missouri's southern boarder to be free territories. —*Ed.*

[3] *Ibid.*

[4] Fourth Annual Message to Congress, 3 December 1888.

[5] William O. Douglas in the dissenting opinion of *Wheeling Steel Corp. v. Glander*.

[6] See *Omnipoint Communications Enterprises L.p. v. Zoning Hearing Board of Chadds Ford Township*. —*Ed.*

# DISAPPEARING RAILROAD BLUES?

*by Mike Ferner*

---

*My heart is warm with the friends I make,*
*And better friends I'll not be knowing.*
*Yet there isn't a train I wouldn't take,*
*No matter where it's going.*
*- Edna St. Vincent Millay*

ABOARD THE TEXAS EAGLE. Pulling out of Chicago's Union Station, perched in the upper deck of an Amtrak Superliner, the car's immense weight begins to slowly rock from side to side as the train picks up speed. It's a uniquely comforting feeling—one you'll not feel in a car or bus, and certainly never on a plane.

Quickly, we're going fast enough to catch, and then pass, cars clogging 12 lanes of freeway at 6:30 on a Friday night. Through the wintry darkness I peer at the lines of traffic. I know that at least some of the commuters are glancing back, looking into the warm interior lights of the train and feeling just like Edna St. Vincent Millay. For once, I'm on the inside, beginning a marvelous journey by rail.

The sleeping car attendant makes his rounds, taking dinner reservations for the dining car and asking what time I'd like to get up in the morning. When he leaves, I have to pinch myself to be sure that enjoying this height of civilized travel isn't just a dream.

A fresh carnation, linen, and china grace the dining-car table. The menu ranges from steamed vegetables and brown rice to NY strip steak, salad and baked potato. Railroad dining cars are never spacious, but it only adds to the adventure as I'm seated with an anxious Chicago grandmother-to-be, going to visit her daughter in Phoenix. Suddenly, my 22-hour trip to Fort Worth to visit friends doesn't seem nearly so arduous.

Later, sandwiched into the aptly-named "economy-size" bunk, I pull up the crisp, white sheets and listen to the frozen steel rails sing. We hurtle across the snowy prairies of western Illinois at what seems at least the official speed limit of 79 mph. Locomotive power great enough to make diner, baggage, lounge, coach, and sleeper cars fly through the night at that rate does not terminate in the cars, it courses all through you. You feel it into your bones. The rhythm of the rails rocks me to sleep.

The sweet dreams about train travel I've had since that night are always in danger of becoming a nightmare in America. Even though passenger rail travel is beloved by millions and is the safest, most fuel efficient, and environmentally friendly form of transport, it has not been a priority with our government in this century. The mighty highway lobby has steamrolled its way over legislators from the

---

local to the national level for decades. Once it was even caught red-handed.

In a case brought by the federal government in 1947, General Motors Corporation, Firestone Corporation, and Standard Oil Corporation were found guilty of criminally conspiring to put local trolley companies out of business. It was proven that those corporations and others were behind an effort to dismantle streetcar lines in 45 cities between 1936 and 1946. For these loathsome crimes against the public interest, corporate officers were fined a dollar each, and the corporations were fined $5,000—a pittance compared to the millions made from selling buses, fuel, and tires once the tracks were ripped up.

In other areas, electric "interurbans" carrying passengers and freight safely and quietly between cities declined from negligent public policy if not downright criminal conspiracy. Until 1938, you could travel a dozen times a day between Toledo and Cleveland on an interurban. This privately-owned form of public transport had to raise capital from freight and passenger revenues, while "private" autos and the growing truck freight traffic benefited from some of the largest government investments since the building of the pyramids.

Later and much larger investments in the interstate highway system have forever changed our national landscape, brutalized our downtown areas and inner cities, created the largest single source of urban air pollution, and robbed our people of the joy of travelling by train. And yet, our highways are always jammed.

Austin Coates, president of the United Rail Passenger Alliance, put it well. "You can't build highways as fast as they can build cars ... you just can't pour concrete that fast." Referring to a long section of I-95 from Miami to West Palm Beach, Florida, Coates said it has just been upgraded to six lanes, with a 12-lane freeway projected within 10 years.

The very term "freeway" gets Russ Capon's blood up. Capon, head of the National Association of Railroad Passengers, quickly points out that gas taxes paid by American motorists don't come close to the total bill for highway construction and maintenance. He cites reports from the Worldwatch Institute and other think tanks that estimate gas taxes cover only about 60% of the tens of billions of dollars spent annually by all levels of government on road construction and repair in the U.S. The rest is subsidized by federal, state, and city taxpayers.

Amtrak, targeted by Congressional fanatics as a black hole for tax dollars, covered 81 percent of operating costs from its revenues last year, up from 48 percent in 1981. Still, Congress is in a mood to end all help to intercity rail, and not likely to give Amtrak the half cent of the 18-cent-per-gallon federal gas tax it desperately needs for new rolling stock.

"The U.S. is 36th in the world in per capita investment in rail," Capon decried. "Bangladesh spends more per person on its train system than we do. I'm sick of this country being a throwaway society ... we now have to 'reinvent the wheel' in streetcars and light rail, and I don't want the same thing to happen to long haul trains."

Does America have the disappearing railroad blues? If everyone could hear the rails' song on a winter's night, the answer would be a resounding "no." ∎

# QUESTIONS, QUESTIONS

Governing ourselves is work. We have to wrestle with stuff we've been taught to leave to lawyers, politicians, corporate CEOs and experts galore: What is property? Who decides which decisions are public and which are private? What is the relationship between human rights and property interests? Where do freedom and liberty come from? Where do jobs come from? Where does wealth come from? Should a business corporation be regarded by law as a citizen? What freedoms of association should be given to people who work? . . . to capital? What can each generation learn from previous generations about perfecting the nation's plan of governance?

By working together, by promoting discussion and debate in the larger community, we provoke democratic conversations. And with luck, we set in motion the dismantling of minority rule.

# RETHINKING THE CORPORATION

*by Virginia Rasmussen*

CORPORATIONS HAVE MADE themselves the primary defining force on the globe. They shape our cultures and communities, define what is of value and what is not, what news we hear and what we won't, what we trade and what we can't. They define our work, what is produced and consumed, where investments are made, what technologies are developed. They subject the natural world to assault after assault until it can't rise up in the springtime. They craft our laws and policies. They dominate our politicians. Corporations are in charge of our lives.

I think we would agree to describe the reality that flows from this corporate power as anti-democratic, anti-community, anti-worker, anti-person and anti-planet. And who among us believes that, under the current state of affairs, things are about to turn for the better!

Given our relative consensus on this situation, what should we be asking and doing about the corporation? Should we be trying to find out what the varied and endless bad behaviors of corporations are and struggle, like Dianas against Goliaths, to make them a little less harmful? Or should we be trying to find out what corporations are and struggle to make them something different? Don't we need to look at how we are resisting and where it is and is not getting us?

It's critical for all of us to realize that such enormous power belongs to a thing, a legal fiction. In this country, corporations were originally a creation of the people, intended to be subordinate to the people. At that time We the People were propertied white males only, of course, but these morally impaired Founders had one thing right. They knew that if "the people" were to be in charge, they would have to be sovereign over both political and economic life, or they would be sovereign over neither. Corporations were kept on a short and closely watched leash in the 18th and early 19th centuries and their charters revoked by the courts and legislatures if they exceeded their authority or violated the common good. But the corporate form has taken over. Corporate lawyers, their arguments clothed in the garb of freedom, liberty and all manner of property claims, manipulated federal legislators and corruptible judges, bludgeoned opposing voices, and eventually gathered unto the corporation a potent mix of property, political and civil rights.

Indeed, the U.S. Supreme Court in 1886 declared corporations "persons" with regard to the equal protection and due process clauses of the Fourteenth Amendment.[1] We're talking about rights bestowed upon corporations well before most people in this country were considered "persons" under those same laws. Thus, when we add their wealth, influence, privileges, and immunities to this per-

---

This article is provided without copyright. This article is a transcript of a speech delivered at the 1998 "International Congress" of the Women's International League for Peace and Freedom. It was previously published in *Food & Water Journal* (Fall 1998).

sonhood status, corporations become "persons" of most unnatural look, size and power. In truth, the law of real people can no longer direct corporate actions. That is to say, corporations govern. Like Dr. Frankenstein's monster, the creation is now master of the creator.

The global reach of these governing powers grows more evident with each so-called "free trade" agreement, spilling forth in breathtaking numbers. There are already 70 such agreements and more simmering on the front burners. Multinational corporations, not content with eliminating every kind of protective barrier between nations, are now, in the proposed Multinational Agreement on Investment (MAI), going inside the borders. Local, state and national laws passed in the public interest to protect workers, communities, jobs, resources and the natural environment will be prohibited; all impediments, they argue, to the free flow of stuff and money. These free trade agreements are first and foremost multinational corporate rights charters, and they are sweeping clean any remains of democratic control.

How far we have drifted from an opinion given by the New York State Court of Appeals late in the last century when it unanimously revoked a corporate charter for harms done to the general welfare. The court stated that "the life of a corporation is, indeed, less than that of the most humblest citizen."[2]

Those who speak for today's corporations, however, present these corporate bodies as master of all the humble citizens. Consider the following:

- A recent Pfizer Pharmaceutical Corporation advertisement opined that, "With the family and religion, the business corporation is one of the three crucial institutions of civil society."

- On the death last year of Roberto Goizueta, the chairman and chief executive of the Coca-Cola Corporation, his eulogizer, former mayor of Atlanta Andrew Young, stated that "[Goizueta] was marketing more than a product, he was marketing a way of life. We are all better for having come under his influence."

- And how about this vision of the future provided by Robert Bartley, editor of the *Wall Street Journal*: "Yes, [politicians] can presume to decide how much time a new mother should spend in the hospital, rather than wait for wrongs to be redressed by health-care providers seeking market share. Yes, they can still ruin the prospect of a peaceful world by cowardice and duplicity in foreign affairs. In the end, though, the force of history will be more powerful. We will be ruled not so much by the work of politicians as by the logic of markets."

## CONFRONTING CORPORATE TYRANNY

To effectively begin the work of countering what amounts to global corporate tyranny, we'll need to do two kinds of defining: what we wish to see in the future, and what we are seeing in the present.

It is true that we will never take ourselves to a place we can't imagine. But it is equally true that since the journey begins where we are, we must know our reality, critically and deeply, or we'll not remove obstructions in the way; obstructions that will end our travel before we've packed our bags. There are corporate roadblocks out there with the power to keep us running in place— as consumers, workers, taxpayers, even soldiers. But as people subordinate to corporations we cannot be citizens, and we will have no power to chart and take this journey. That clever Frenchman, Alexis de Tocqueville, put it well nearly 170 years ago when he said, "Without power and independence, a town may contain good subjects, but it can contain no citizens."[3]

And let's not fool ourselves. We'll never move these corporate behemoths out of our way with the poking sticks and thin willow reeds available to us through regulatory action. Corporations are too much in control of regulatory law and agencies to get more than a scratch or bump from all our citizen activism around rules and regulations. Nor will we gain their everlasting mercy with pleas for social responsibility or requests to sign a corporate "code of conduct," or the pitiful pleading for side agreements on free-trade pacts. Such agreements are quickly disregarded when the fortunes of corporations are threatened in any way. The corporate "person" cannot be humanized, it cannot care, it cannot be responsible.

So what else is possible?

Since we have grown up in a subordinate relationship to corporations, we have trouble even imagining how a citizenry in charge would see and analyze its reality, what language we would use, how we would act to bring change. Our colonized minds make it difficult to cut through our experience and envision real democracy. We've got a "cop in our head," and the cop comes from corporate headquarters.

How would we bring a polluting, subordinate corporation to its knees! What would a campaign against a free-trade agreement or the MAI sound like or look like in the hands of people consciously working to be dominant over corporations? Or in the hands of

people who knew such proposals for the deregulation of commerce in money and goods were outrageous invasions of people's sovereignty?

This is how we must imagine and think and choose our language and frame our campaigns against respective corporate deeds and proposals. To do less is to choose subservience. It is to accept the corporate terms of our relationship to them, terms that confer domination as a *right* of theirs, and submission as a *duty* of ours. To do less is to guarantee that nothing will really be solved in the course of activist labors, leaving us to wage the same battle over and over again, one trade agreement at a time, one toxic chemical at a time, one waste dump at a time.

What must be done?

When those of us who believe in an empowered citizenship see corporations spewing excrement and oppression with ever greater reach, we need to ask, "By what authority can corporations do that? They have no authority to do that. We never gave them authority." And we must work strategically to challenge their claims to authority as we organize against the waste dump, the cancer-causing herbicide, or the polluting corporation in our town. Excrement and oppression, you see, are not merely evidences of corporate "bad behavior," they reflect the very nature of corporations. Corporations are legally empowered and designed to carry out their mission of ever more growth, production and profit, pursued in the mandated spirit of competition, aggression, amorality and hierarchy.

When we see people increasingly powerless to protect themselves, their communities and countries, from this excrement and oppression, we need to ask, "Why do people have so little authority?" We must work strategically to engage others in that question, and to augment citizen authority with the goal of reversing our legally subordinate relationship to corporations. Remember, a corporation is a thing; it has no more inherent rights than a stepladder or a sewing machine. Laws must change.

When we see nations increasingly doing the corporation's bidding, becoming fellow degraders and oppressors, we must ask, "How it is that our governments protect breathing human beings less and less, while protecting corporations more and more? By what authority does our government trade away to corporations the powers and responsibilities of citizens?" And we must work strategically to shift government protections from the corporations to the people.

Currently there is an increasing number of municipalities in the U.S. drawing up resolutions and referenda vowing refusal of entry to the invading corporate hordes. Will that turn them back? No. But it could serve to awaken and inform the public mind, and pave the way for an organized, mobilized popular movement. I know of no other way to create the demand that will force power to concede (to paraphrase Frederick Douglas). Also, in the United States, no undertaking would be more humane, more just, more globally far-reaching than to work to reverse the 1886 Supreme Court opinion that gave corporations rights of personhood. No campaign would bring more light and hope to our corporatized politics than one to reverse the 1976 Supreme Court decision that equated speech with money, and gave corporations the loudest, wealthiest, most undemocratic voice in the electoral process. 4

But we can't effectively challenge corporate authority at its roots until enough of us de-colonize our minds and stop thinking corporate.

This suggests a second kind of work to be about: reading the news more shrewdly in corporate times. We need to be critiquing, uncovering the context and assumptions of corporate and trade organization talk. It just happens to be the slickest, weightiest propaganda on the scene and it can pack a real mind-colonizing punch.

I came upon a speech by Renato Ruggeiro, Director General of the World Trade Organization (WTO), given in Washington in March 1998. The subject? Celebrating the 50th "birthday" of the General Agreement on Tarriffs and Trade (GATT). It contains, in very direct words, the sweeping agenda for the global future as corporations would have it: a bald expression of private corporate goals parading as public interest. We can see how minds can turn to slush when words and views like these fill the media and national dialogue as though there were no alternative visions. Enormous numbers of people are quieted and co-opted by its sweeping grandeur, false history, and fake wisdom. For example, according to Ruggeiro:

> "The logic of regionalism makes less economic sense in an era of globalization [since it] leads to fragmentation, different rules and discrimination."

> "Over the past 50 years trade has been a powerful engine for growth."

> "The world's prosperity—and that of the United States—rests on maintaining an open international economy based on commonly-agreed rules."

If we want to redefine our local and global lives, it is this context and these assumptions that we need to drag into the light. We must insist that the role of corporations be discussed and challenged in democratic forums. Because it is only through such exposure and engagement that we can liberate ourselves sufficiently to contest corporations' illegitimate authority to distort our language, define our priorities, and design our future.

So, you want to tear the system down and replace it with a culture of peace? It will only be possible when the authority to govern is in the hands of natural persons and not in the boardrooms of corporate entities. ■

---

## Notes

[1] *Santa Clara v. Southern Pacific Railroad Co.*

[2] *People v. North River Sugar Refining Co.*

[3] Tocqueville *et al.* 1966.

[4] *Buckley v. Valeo.* See "Speaking Truth to Power About Campaign Reform" in this volume. —*Ed.*

# Letter To Jerome Groopman

## Harvard Medical School

*by Richard L. Grossman*

---

22 March 2000

Professor Jerome Groopman, M.D.
Harvard Medical School

Dear Dr. Groopman:

I heard you interviewed recently on radio. I am writing to say how refreshing it was indeed to hear a physician talk with passion against the "corporatization"—the literal factorization—of disease care and health care.

But it's only logical, no? The rest of our society has been/is being transformed into assembly lines—of work, of art, of the mind and of the soul.

Listening to you, I thought of Martin Niemöller, the German Protestant pastor who told how he sat by when the Nazis came for people by category. Because, he said, he and so many had done so little to stand up for these "other" categories, the Nazis were able to come for him with no opposition.

Well, most members of the medical profession have not stood up for the millions upon millions of "others" placed in the grip of assembly lines and factories . . . and subjected to the totalitarianism and carnage intrinsic to such abominable constructions so rationalized among educated people as "competitive" and "efficient."

It's not that no one knew, or no one was objecting. For example, the Knights of Labor in the 1880s called for all knowledge and access to information ("transportation of information" was their phrase) to be public. They denounced factories and the wage system as incompatible with the flowering of democracy and self-governance.

But the corporate assembly lines came for the workers, and the doctors were silent. Then the corporate assembly lines came for the farmers, and the doctors were silent. They came for public transport, for public money, for the military budget, and the doctors were out of sight. They came for the educators, and then the legislators, and the judges, and the mayors—and the doctors could not be heard. The corporate assembly lines came for the free press, they came

---

for our elections . . . Now, they're coming for our genes, for food, for the basic biological building blocks of life . . . and where are the doctors?

It's all been of a piece. The corporate assembly lines have come for and gone away with our Constitution, our liberty, our Declaration of Independence. So who should be surprised that *now* they've come for you? Why should anyone care?

But the fact is, *plenty* of people care . . . all the people across generations and vocations who have been resisting the corporate assembly-lining of life and death and work and thought and of the natural world.

So it's not too late for you, for your colleagues, for your students, for your patients, for your spleens and livers. It's not too late to sew the histories together; to make solidarity connections. To speak out. To resist. To join with others. To design new designs.

But it simply will not do to whine about the sad fate of the medical profession, or to salvage some healthcare for some. The few are coming for the many . . . in the name of efficiency, of natural law. The few are coming for the many. As in Nazi Germany, they target people category by category—in the process making each category of people a little less human. They are coming with the protection of the law—of the police, of our learned judges—with the assistance of our own government.

It's a pisser, Jerry, isn't it? ■

# WE THE PEOPLE

## BUILDING A TRULY DEMOCRATIC SOCIETY

*by Ward Morehouse*

MY TASK TODAY is an ambitious one: to persuade you in the brief time we have together to launch a "democratic insurgency" as a first step toward building a truly democratic society. In Daniel Quinn's extraordinary book, *Ishmael: A Novel*, which every person concerned about the human predicament should read, the narrator of the story answers an unusual ad:

> Teacher seeks pupil. Must have an earnest desire to save the world. Apply in person.

To the narrator's surprise, his teacher turns out to be a gorilla named Ishmael. Then ensues an extended dialogue filled with insights about the human condition that only a non-human could have.

In a memorable exchange, Ishmael observes of the young people who were in the vanguard of the struggles of the 60s: "they made an ingenuous and disorganized effort to escape from captivity but ultimately failed because they were unable to find the bars of their cage."

So it is for us today. The bars to our cage are our colonized minds that have led us to surrender our sovereignty to giant corporations which increasingly dominate our society, not to mention the rest of the world.

The principle that We the People are in charge is clearly stated in the preamble to the Constitution:

We the People of the United States, in order to form a more perfect Union, establish justice, ensure domestic tranquility, provide for the common defense, promote the general welfare, and secure the blessings of liberty to ourselves and our posterity, do ordain and establish this Constitution for the United States of America.

But over the intervening decades we have abandoned that principle in practice if not in theory. "American society is disproportionately shaped by the outlooks, interests, and aims of the business community—especially that of big business," observed Cornel West, the social critic and Harvard Professor, "The sheer power of corporate capital is extraordinary. This power makes it difficult even to imagine what a free and democratic society would look like . . ."[1]

What, indeed, should a "free and democratic society" look like? Let us begin by considering the dictionary definition. Democracy, according to Webster's, has two major components: government in which the supreme power is retained by the people; and the less widely recognized belief in and practice of social equality. It is clear that we have strayed a long way from the ideals expressed so eloquently in our Declaration of

---

Independence and the Preamble to the Constitution.

What went wrong? Why do we find ourselves in a plutocracy with such gross inequality? I think there are at least three critical factors growing out of our past. The first is that the foundation for our republic was deeply flawed by design. The political rights set forth in the Constitution were essentially restricted to white property-owning males. A continuing thread in our national history since then has been the struggle by all those excluded from Constitutional "personhood"—women, African-Americans, poor whites, indigenous people—to gain that personhood and the equally determined resistance of those empowered by the Constitution to prevent them from achieving that goal.

Second is the huge internal contradiction in the Constitution between its Preamble and the rest of the Constitution which seeks above all else to protect and give sanctity to property rights over human rights.

Third has been the usurpation of the peoples' authority by corporations, especially during the last 100 years. Although this process did not begin there, it stands exposed by the infamous 1886 decision by the U.S. Supreme Court in *Santa Clara v. Southern Pacific Railroad Co*, which asserted that corporations were like natural persons before the law. From this fundamental determination corporations worked assiduously through the decades to claim more and more constitutional rights of natural persons, including those protected by the First, Fourth, and Fifth Amendments to the Constitution. How ironic it is that corporations achieved their constitutional "personhood" before all of the other natural persons I have just mentioned. And how absurd it is that today corporations have more rights than mortals like you and me.

Closely aligned to this process was defining "liberty" to mean the right of the individual to do whatever he or she wanted to do with his or her property regardless of the social or environmental consequences. The expansion of property rights, carefully and methodically orchestrated by major corporations, has been inexorable. It now includes intangible rights such as managerial prerogative and the business judgment rule which effectively place much of what corporations do beyond democratic control.

The failure of our democracy has been tragically evident in the growing inequality of income and wealth, particularly in the last decade. During the 1980s the net worth of the 400 richest persons in America increased by 522%. During that same decade the bottom 99% lost over 5% of their share of personal income, while the top 1% almost doubled its share from 8 to 14%.

This growing inequality has achieved greatest visibility in the ratio of compensation paid to CEOs of Fortune 500 companies and their lowest paid workers. That ratio now stands at 160 to 1.[2] By contrast, in Europe it is only 20 to 1, and in Japan merely 15 to 1.

In 1993 Michael Eisner, the CEO of Walt Disney Corporation, received $203 million in total compensation. That works out to $84,000 an hour—nice work if you can get it.

Even the much heralded expansion of participation in the closest thing we have to a national lottery—namely, the Stock Exchange—remains highly unequal and largely limited to upper income brackets. The richest 1% have 39% of the stock owned by individuals. The richest 10% own 81%.

This state of affairs leads to the fundamental question: How can we have a democracy when so much power and wealth is concentrated in so few hands? If we are to be true to the ideals of the Declaration of Independence and the Preamble to the Constitution, and to reassert our sovereignty as "We the People," then we must work toward replacing anti-democratic institutions that consolidate wealth and power with democratic institutions which disperse wealth and power.

But in the view of those who have pondered more deeply the meaning of democracy, we must look beyond building institutions. Douglas Lummis, in his seminal book *Radical Democracy*, argues that democracy is more than a set of institutions or a "system." It is rather a state of being.

He observes that many of the experiences most precious to human life can not be institutionalized.

> Laughter cannot be institutionalized—which does not mean that we should abolish institutions such as comic theater. Love cannot be institutionalized—which does not mean that institutions of courtship and marriage are useless. Wisdom cannot be institutionalized—which does not mean that educational institutions are a waste . . . [3]

We design institutions, Lummis states, hoping that they will bring about or preserve a certain kind and state of being. Sometimes they do and sometimes they do not. And sometimes that state of being may appear without the support of any institutions. The same uncertainty of cause and effect is certainly true of democracy. All of the institutions asserted to achieve democracy may be created, and yet still not achieve it. It is also true that all of the institutions designed to suppress it may be established, and democracy may break out before our very eyes.

The essence of democracy is politics—the art of the possible. Democracy is a performance art like music, dance, and theater. We can construct theaters, and assemble troupes of dancers and musicians but the art exists only while it is being performed. So it is with democracy.

But if democracy can not be institutionalized, it none the less tends to take on certain typical forms when it does appear. Again in the words of Lummis:

> People develop a desire to act together, and to talk with one another about their common life. They tend to gather in groups small enough to make this talk possible in what have been called committees of correspondence, councils, soviets, affinity groups, sectoral groups, and so on. These become a form of 'civil society.'

That "civil society" has long been considered one of the distinctive characteristics of these United States, as Alexis de Tocqueville observed many decades ago regarding the propensity of Americans to join associations of all diverse kinds. But from the beginning of our history as an independent country, democratic values and process have been under severe stress.

No one has been more eloquent in advocacy of the task of building a truly democratic society than William Greider in *Who Will Tell the People*. His book is in my view the most important critique of U.S. society since Gunnar Myrdal's study of race relations in North America more than a half-century ago, *An American Dilemma*.

Building such a society, Greider insists, will require citizens to devote themselves to challenging the *status quo*, disrupting the existing contours of power and opening the way for renewal. Just how do we open the way for renewal? Ishmael's pupil was puzzled by the same question.

"What do I do if I earnestly desire to save the world?" he asked Ishmael.

Ishmael frowned at him through the bars of his cage for a long moment. "You want a program?" he asked.

"Of course I want a program" replied his pupil.

"Then here is a program: the story of Genesis must be reversed. First Cain must stop murdering Abel. This is essential if you're to survive . . . And then, of course, you must spit out the fruit of that forbidden tree. You must absolutely and forever relinquish the idea you know who should live and who should die on this planet."

"Yes, I see all that," responded Ishmael's pupil, "but that's a program for mankind, that is not a program for me. What do I do?'

"What you do is to teach a hundred what I've taught you, and inspire each of them to teach a hundred. That's how it's always done."

So that is our program—where we must begin. And we have just started, here today—with this "democratic conversation" in Greider's choice phrase.

"Strange as it may seem to an era governed by mass-market politics, democracy begins in human conversation," Greider insists. "The simplest least threatening investment any citizen may make in democratic renewal is to begin talking with other people about these questions, as though the answers matter to them. Harmless talk around a kitchen table or in a church basement will not affect anyone but themselves, unless they decide that it ought to. When the circle is enlarged to include others, they will be embarking on the fertile terrain of politics that now seems so barren."

It is important to understand that a democratic conversation does not need elaborate rules and procedures or idealistic notions of perfect consensus. What it must have is a spirit of mutual respect—that is, people talking among themselves critically, in an atmosphere of honesty and shared purpose. That respect must even extend to one's adversaries, since the objective of these conversations is not to destroy them but to reach eventual understanding. The very heart of democracy is as simple as that—a society based on mutual respect.

Ishmael's pupil was less than satisfied with Ishmael's definition of the "program."
"Yes, but" he asks Ishmael, "is it enough?"

Ishmael frowned. "Of course it's not enough but if you begin anywhere else there's no hope at all . . . You can't change these things with laws. You must change people's minds first. And you can't just root out a harmful complex of ideas and leave a void behind; you have to give people something that is as meaningful as what they've lost—something that makes better sense."

So, too, will many of you ask: Is a "program" of "democratic conversations," of raising levels of consciousness about the myth of democracy in which we live, and of the possibilities and implementation of a democracy which rises to our highest ideals of self-governance, enough?

Of course it is not enough. But we must start there, for many of the same reasons

Ishmael gives to his pupil. However, we all want to do something, not just sit around talking about the problem. And there are things we can do, but they should grow out of a deeper understanding of democracy, and they should yield real solutions, not cosmetic ones.

Take election campaign finance reform.[4] Persons of genuine commitment to democratic values are rallying around the McCain-Feingold-Thompson Campaign Finance Reform Bill, not because they are oblivious to its limitations but because it seems to be the only game in town.

But the great difficulty with that bill is that, assuming it is passed more or less in its present form, many of those supporting it will conclude that we have solved the problem, making it that much more difficult in the next round of struggle to get at the real causes of corruption of democratic values in our society.

Real campaign reform must address and work toward reversing the Supreme Court's decision in *Buckley v. Valeo* equating money with speech and asserting that, as a form of speech, spending money in election campaigns cannot be limited because it would violate the First Amendment protection of free speech.

For those who say that Supreme Court doctrines cannot be overturned, I respond by pointing to the long struggle for racial equality in the United States. A group of young black lawyers gathered together in 1930 and formulated a plan to overturn the Supreme Court doctrine of "separate but equal" which had been the law of the land since *Plessy v. Ferguson* in 1896. It took them almost a quarter of a century, but led by Thurgood Marshall, they achieved their goal in 1954 with the Supreme Court decision in *Brown v. Board of Education*.

In addition to working toward the overturn of the doctrine that money equates with speech, real campaign finance reform must also:

- Prohibit all paid political ads on radio and television.

- Require all radio and television corporations to provide free air time. (After all, they are using the people's airwaves).

- Mandate only signatures on petitions, not money contributed to a candidate, to qualify for public financing. (Paying money is just what Blacks in the South had to do in order to vote when there was a poll tax.)

- Distinguish between natural persons and corporations, and prohibit profit-making corporations from making any kind of political contribution.

Those who think these are unattainable goals need to be reminded of a Wisconsin Law from 1905 to 1973:

> No corporation doing business in this state shall pay or contribute, or offer, consent or agree to pay or contribute, directly or indirectly, any money, property, free service of its officers or employees, or thing of value to any political party, organization, committee or individual for any political purpose whatsoever or for the purpose of influencing legislation of any kind or to promote or defeat the candidacy of any person for nomination, appointment or election to any political office.[5]

Establishing our democracy must begin with citizens prepared to devote themselves to challenging the *status quo*, and to disrupting the contours of power. But the ultimate task, William Greider reminds us, is much more difficult—creating something that does not now exist—the basis for politics as a shared enterprise. "The search for democratic meaning is necessarily a path of hard conflict," Greider writes, "but the distant horizon is reconciliation. Americans coming to terms with themselves, that is the high purpose politics was meant to serve."

My modest hope for the time we are together is, as I suggested at the outset, to persuade you to launch what Greider calls a "democratic insurgency," individually and collectively.

This insurgency will not begin with abstract ideas or charismatic political leaders. Its origins will lie among ordinary people who have the will to engage themselves with their surrounding reality and to act on the conflict between what they are told and what they experience—thus disrupting existing structures of power and opening up paths for renewal. ∎

## Notes

[1] West 1982, pp. 468-469.

[2] Today it is over 200 to 1. See "The Rising Costs of Inequality in the U.S." in this volume.  —Ed.

[3] Lummis 1996, p. 159.

[4] See "Speaking Truth to Power About Campaign Reform" in this volume.  —Ed.

[5] Wis. Laws, Section 4479a. (Sec. 1, ch 492, 1905).

# LETTER TO AKHIL REED AMAR

## YALE LAW SCHOOL

*by Richard L. Grossman*

---

30 December 1998

Professor Akhil Reed Amar
Yale Law School

Dear Professor Amar:

I have read your intriguing and stimulating *Bill Of Rights*.[1] I have a few questions. First, I would like to reacquaint you with some of your own words:

> In the tradition of the Virginia and Kentucky Resolutions, representatives of the various New England states met in the Hartford convention of 1814-15 to denounce as unconstitutional any national attempt to "subject the militia . . . to forcible drafts, conscriptions, or impressments." The eventual republican triumph on this issue—none of the proposed draft bills passed—should be as central a precedent for our Second Amendment[2] as the 1800 triumph over the Sedition Act[3] is for our First. (p. 58)

> Nor should we ignore the Fourth Amendment's[4] image of federalism. The reasonableness requirement limited all federal officers, and the warrant clause imposed special restrictions on federal judges and magistrates, but vindication of these restrictions would largely come from state bodies. State statutes and state common law, after all, would typically define and protect ordinary individuals' property rights to their "persons, houses, papers, and effects." Thus state law would initially create the trespass cause of action that would enable ordinary men and women to challenge unconstitutional intrusions by federal officials . . . Here, as elsewhere, localism would protect Liberty. (p. 76)

> The framers crafted a system of republican governments, state and federal—governments of, by, and for the people. Here, the people would rule—not day to day, but ultimately, in the long run. All governmental policy and governmental policymakers could, in time, be lawfully replaced by the sovereign people via constitutional conventions and ordinary elections. The ultimate right of the public to change policy and policy makers called for strong presumption that the courts would be open. (p. 112)

---

I'm impressed with your claims about the founders' and the rabbles' intentions to keep power and authority local. But let's jump to today, and consider fundamental decision-making of giant corporations about money, production and governance. This decision-making[5] shapes our lives, communities, politics, work, appetites, aspirations—our nation and the world. Monsanto Corporation creates terminator seeds via genetic engineering; Maxxam Corporation alters the ecology, climate, biology and humanity of vast ecosystems by clear-cutting ancient redwood forests; Exxon Corporation promotes and advantages the burning of fossil fuels while inhibiting transitions to solar energy systems; General Motors Corporation destroys interurban trolley systems and replaces them with corporate buses, trucks and tires and a billion dollar annual propaganda budget, *ad nauseam*.

Such corporate decision-making is treated by law and culture as the domain of private property and private law, the province of the self-regulating market.

Oh, maybe government can intervene to lessen some harmful impacts of these decisions, if enough people spend years educating themselves and raising money via cake and cookie sales, and mobilizing. But I haven't seen acknowledgment (not to mention leadership) within the legal community that We the People have constitutional authority—and obligation—to replace these governing corporate leaders or seriously reconfigure these governing corporations. It's hard enough for shareholders (the human ones, at least) to affect their corporations' leadership.

The courts bestowed civil and political rights of persons upon our giant corporations. So giant corporations quite logically invade and destroy basic self-governance (elections, law-making, jurisprudence and education). They quite logically (and relatively anonymously) take life, liberty and property. Is it likely that flesh and blood people will be able to "lawfully replace" elected officials and appointed judges who (the "rule of law" and "federalism" and "republicanism" and "abuse of authority" notwithstanding) see no alternative to giant business corporations for jobs, progress, liberty, and the American way?

For such remedies, the people's courts today are not open.

On the contrary: the courts are where *corporations* reflexively turn to deny We the People our fundamental rights. The courts are the branch of our republican government which have usurped from localities and states the authority and power to define the political nature of giant corporate entities.

The Ice Cream Manufacturers Association corporation runs to federal court to get a Vermont rBST labeling law declared unconstitutional, and wins.[6] The National Foreign Trade Council corporation runs to federal court to get a Massachusetts don't-buy-from-corporations-doing-business-with-Burma law declared unconstitutional, and wins.[7] The Omnipoint Corporation runs to federal court—citing the 1964 Civil Rights Act no less—to order a municipality to get out of the way and permit the corporation to construct a microwave tower, and wins.[8] Banking corporations run to the Supreme Court to invalidate a Massachusetts law banning corporate contributions to referenda campaigns, and the Supreme Court obliges (overruling not only the legislature and executive branches but also the Commonwealth's unanimous Supreme Judicial Court).[9] Resource extraction corporations get a federal court to throw out a similar Montana law enacted via a people's referendum.[10]

For over a century federal courts have been granting to corporate creations of our states more and more privileges and immunities. With these gifts, artificial entities called corporations have declared themselves independent of their creators . . . beyond the sovereignty of local and state jurisdictions, and essentially answerable to no branch/level of We the People's federal structure.

The *real* lawmakers of this nation have been the minority who own the majority of property and wealth. Behind the government-bestowed authority of the constantly transforming corporation, they have bastardized the idea (and ideal) of self-governance by writing our laws, electing our legislators, shaping our education, defining our work, poisoning our land, infecting our culture.

Our nation's judges, legislators, law school professors, corporate press titans, and university boards of trustees reveal little or no interest in even talking about this reality.

I found your book informative, provocative and even encouraging at times. You have a roving, creative mind. Here are my questions:

1. How did you write this whole book without mentioning the business corporation's transformation of the Fourteenth Amendment—and the Bill of Rights, and the Commerce clause etc.—into organized capital's weapon against not only organized labor but also We the People? Without referring to what Justice Black called the granting of "new and revolutionary rights to corporations"?[11]

2. Where shall the people turn for a republican form of government? How can the people invoke what you call our "ultimate right" to change policy and policymakers? ∎

---

## NOTES

[1] Amar 1998.

[2] The Second Amendment states: "A well regulated Militia, being necessary to the security of a free State, the right of the people to keep and bear Arms, shall not be infringed." —*Ed.*

[3] The Sedition Act of 1798 made it a federal crime for a person to "write, print, utter, or publish, or shall cause or procure to be written, printed, uttered or published, or shall knowingly and willingly assist or aid in writing, printing, uttering or publishing any false, scandalous and malicious writing or writings against the government of the United States . . . with intent to defame the said government . . . or to bring them into contempt or disrepute . . ." —*Ed.*

[4] The Fourth Amendment states: "The right of the people to be secure in their persons, houses, papers, and effects, against unreasonable searches and seizures, shall not be violated, and no Warrants shall issue, but upon probable cause, supported by Oath or affirmation, and particularly describing the place to be searched, and the persons or things to be seized." —*Ed.*

[5] I use the word "decisions" here to encompass not only the corporation's investment, research, technological, production, work and education/propaganda spending decisions, but also its investments to influence government in every nook and cranny of its federalist structure to bend governance to its will—all regarded by law and culture as a corporation's constitutional right.

It's one thing for corporate entities to so invest; it's another thing altogether for such investment to be blessed by educated and honored judges in black robes, reinforced by police and army. See *Re: Debs.*

Those who design strategic implementation of a corporation's financial muscle understand precisely what they do. In contrast to liberal reformers, they deceive not themselves that a little transparency or regulatory reforms or ethical codes will thwart them in the slightest.

Charles Francis Adams observed back almost In The Beginning: "He who owns the thing knows that he must also own the legislature which regulates the thing . . . The man who owns will possess himself of the man who regulates." (Dorfman 1946) Corporations today do not merely own our legislatures. As your book makes clear by its silence on the subject, they own our Constitution.

[6] *International Dairy Foods Assn. v. Amestoy*

[7] *Crosby, Secretary of Administration and Finance of Massachusetts, et al. v. National Foreign Trade Council*

[8] *Omnipoint Communications Enterprises L.P. v. Zoning Hearing Board of Chadds Ford Township*

[9] *First National Bank of Boston v. Bellotti*

[10] *Montana Chamber of Commerce v. Argenbright*

[11] *Connecticut General Life Insurance Company v. Johnson, Treasurer of California*

# LETTER TO THE
# ALLIANCE FOR DEMOCRACY

*by Mike Ferner & POCLAD*

---

24 March 1997

Wade Hudson
Alliance for Democracy

Dear Wade,

I'm writing you this letter on behalf of the Program on Corporations, Law, and Democracy. We hope this will begin an ongoing discussion about corporations and their proper place in a democratic society—something that is important to all of us. What prompts this letter is the November 27, 1996, memo you wrote at the Alliance for Democracy founding convention, reporting on activities at that historic gathering near San Antonio.

Your memo articulated some questions and differences you had with statements made at the Alliance convention by Peter Kellman and Jane Anne Morris. I was at the convention also, but played a minor role. Your memo is valuable because it contains questions we hear as we meet with people around the country. It offers us an opportunity to engage you and other Alliance members who may feel similarly in a discussion that will help make all of our work more successful.

Before addressing individual points of your memo, it's important to summarize the context or the framework within which we labor: As the Preamble to the U.S. Constitution affirms, "We the People" are sovereign in our society. Since these terms are used so frequently these days, we should define their meaning precisely. We mean that "the people" are in charge of fashioning the government, and through it, the economy—particularly the corporate form that was so at issue during the Colonial period and provided significant motivation for the Revolution itself.

Obviously, much easier said than done—and for many reasons. Corporations have had 100+ years to politically, legally, and culturally consolidate gains won in the last century. We've lived all our lives in a corporate culture dominated by corporations, making it hard to think that it's ever *not* been like this. Today's *status quo*, thick with corporate values, surrounds us like the air we breathe. An understanding of history is not valued, since consuming new stuff keeps us busy and profits corporations more.

Thus, it's crucial that we learn precisely how it wasn't always this way; how in fact it got like this; how others attempted to break the bonds; and how we can engage others in a journey of exploration so that together we can begin constructing a way out to a better world.

I've seen this effort illustrated in the book, *Ishmael: A Novel*. Early on the teacher explains to the pupil how young people in the sixties "made an ingenuous and disorganized effort to escape from captivity but ultimately failed, because they were unable to find the bars of the cage . . . If you can't discover what's keeping you in, the will to get out soon becomes confused and ineffectual . . . The world is not going to survive very much longer as humanity's captive . . . yet I think there are many among you who would be glad to release the world from captivity." But, the teacher concludes, they're prevented from doing so because "they're unable to find the bars of the cage."

Those bars are not just the visible harms corporations do, great as those may be. The bars are also in our own minds, reinforced daily in myriad ways by corporations, until we believe there is no alternative. I hope this gives you a sense of our approach.

With that lengthy bit of introduction, on to eight of the points in your memo.

# 1. PURPOSE OF THE AMERICAN REVOLUTION

Was the point to (a) get a new king or (b) replace the monarchy with a republic and create the "myth" of a democracy? Peter Kellman (at the convention) argued it was the latter "because they didn't want corporations ruling them," adding that a similar approach is needed today because there are limits to growth.

Being somewhat of a history nut myself, and retaining perhaps too much of a burnished image of the Revolution taught by grade school nuns, I get a little "ouchy" when people refer to creating the myth of democracy, but I *am* beginning to understand what they mean. This "myth" concept engenders considerable discussion within POCLAD. A

sampling of that discussion: True, the founding fathers left out the majority of human inhabitants in their "We the People." This is not to say, however, that they didn't believe their own rhetoric in the Declaration, Constitution Preamble, and so forth.

But because they defined most of the humans in the 13 colonies as property or non-persons, whole classes of people had to struggle for centuries to overcome this atrocious, immoral, structural mess—that is, to define themselves and not let anyone else define them. The myth of democracy though can be something beyond that grossly incomplete inclusion; something on which we draw in order to proceed. One could argue that America's mythical democracy has inspired many people—here and abroad—to undertake amazing things.

Here at home, as more people realize the inequities, political corruption, etc., one could also argue that the myth is losing its power to glue us together. One of the challenges of creating a real democratic process is grappling with the meaning and details of our myths.

One myth is that of unlimited economic growth. In the interest of getting this to you prior to the arrival of the millennium, let's just say for now that producing more "stuff" in an attempt to lift all boats doesn't seem to have much to recommend it—at least as traditionally described. We could discuss why so many positive aspects of human activity are left out of the Gross Domestic Product; whether "sustainable" economic growth will work where "strength through exhaustion" hasn't, and so forth. The essential debate needs to be about "by whose authority?", or who is in charge and who will set the values—not about "how much." But I say we put this one in committee for the time being.

## 2. To What Extent did Fear of Corporations Motivate the Revolutionists

You opined that "it distorts history to exaggerate the degree to which the Founding Fathers were concerned about corporate power per se . . . since there were so few corporations of any sort, that issue was not of central concern to those who favored independence."

POCLAD needs to understand better to what degree corporate power was of concern. We are discovering, however, that corporate power was not a small concern. By 1776, many colonists knew first hand, or from contemporary culture, about the global corporations of their day . . . and understood that they were unconstitutionalized centers of governing power which they did not want to see arise in the U.S. These corporations were "chips off the old block of sovereignty," as Thomas Hobbes said. They exercised the powers of sovereignty: they governed, tried, convicted, punished, impressed people into the military, built armadas, concluded treaties, and the like.

A few examples of pre-Revolutionary British corporations and their purposes:

- The Africa Company (1553): chartered to participate in the slave trade.

- The Russia Company (1553): chartered to secure trade concessions with Russia.

- The Spanish Company (1577): chartered to secure trade concessions with Spain.

- The Levant Company (1581): chartered to secure trade concessions with Turkey.

- The East India Company (1608): chartered in perpetuity by King James I, dissolved in 1858, with all its dominions becoming part of the British Empire.

Their common mission: get monopoly routes and concessions, control decision-making, conquer other peoples in order to buy cheap and sell dear, destroy local cultures and memories of cultures, and, finally, to create dependence.

- In *Taking Care of Business*, Grossman and Adams cite pamphleteer Thomas Earle: "Chartered privileges are a burthen, under which the people of Britain, and other European nations groan in misery."

- The East India Company was saved from bankruptcy with a bailout of tax dollars from Parliament. That the fortunes of the rich and powerful, including members of Parliament, were saved by that bailout, and that it was the East India Co.'s tea thrown into Boston Harbor, were not lost on the colonists.

- Again, from *Taking Care of Business*, "[The colonists] knew that English kings chartered the East India Co., the Hudson's Bay Co., and many American colonies in order to control property and commerce. Kings appointed governors and judges, dispatched soldiers, dictated taxes, investments, production, labor and markets. The royal charter creating Maryland, for example, required the colony's exports be shipped to or through England."

- Leaders of the Revolution, many of whom were in the planter class like Washington and Jefferson, were burdened by these conditions as were common colonists. Though one could argue that some of them were against these Crown corporations only because they themselves did not own them.

Because of these kinds of experiences, post-revolutionary elected legislatures in the states were given the power to charter and uncharter corporations, with this power used to keep corporations on a very short leash. They were created for very specific purposes (build a road, construct and operate a textile mill); were limited in their capitalization; were prevented from owning another corporation or from owning land not directly needed for the chartered purpose; they were created for a specific length of time; and it was made clear that if they abused the public interest or over-reached their chartered purpose, they would be called before the elected representatives of the people and required to prove "by what authority" (*quo warranto*) they had acted. If found to have violated their purpose, they were declared "beyond the law" (*ultra vires*) and had their charters revoked.

## 3. SIMPLIFYING HISTORY

You commented that "To simplify history and suggest that we merely need to return to some pre-corporate, democratic Golden Age, as POCLAD often suggests, is not a responsible way to build a political movement."

Nobody in POCLAD believes we ever had such a "pre-corporate democratic Golden Age." Romanticizing history is always a dangerous undertaking. That is not our intent. It trivializes what we can learn from people who were defeated and whose history was expunged. It trivializes their struggles.

We do, however, have a legal and constitutional historical record placing corporations subordinate to the people, and making it clear that popular movements consciously intended to keep it that way. These creations of the people were to be defined by and for the people. This was intended to be a democratic arrangement, with people clearly the sovereigns, as the kings had been prior to the Revolution.

We can and should use this history to our advantage. It should be seen as the funda-

mental and originally intended approach to keeping corporations in their appropriate place in a democracy, not as a passing, quaint bit of early Americana. Just as the Founders defined a very incomplete democracy, to be completed only through generations of struggle, so too is the goal of a democratically-controlled economy left up to generations of struggle.

The last time a movement seriously tried to achieve this goal was during the Populist era, about which Alliance members are certainly familiar. We see our common work as rekindling that spirit of populism and democratic control of the economy appropriate for our time.

We do ourselves and the public a disservice if we don't have an understanding of the past upon which to build a better life today. Those who would change the future need to know from whence we came.

## 4. DEFINING VS. REGULATING

Further on, you wrote "The supposed dichotomy between 'redefining' and 'regulating' corporations is not convincing . . . the issue is not either/or. Unless we're talking about abolishing corporations, redefining them will itself constitute a form of regulation."

I can address part of your concern, but none of us should labor under the false impression that somewhere out there exists a 10-point plan to create a democratic economy. We have got to take responsibility for determining how to make corporations serve a public need and no more; how to return our political system to its rightful creators; how to create a democratic culture which will guard against corporations ever again getting off their leashes. How we do these things is clearly the work we have before us.

What POCLAD brings to the task is an

understanding that we must address the fundamental problem that corporations are not subservient to their masters (who created them). We believe it is this lack of democratic control which is at the root—not that we've somehow failed to get the right people on the National Labor Relations Board, or that we've lost the fight to keep the EPA inspection division fully staffed.

Again, some background. Part of the reason it is so difficult to even converse in these terms is that it's been a long time since we viewed ourselves as the source of power in this country. And it's hard to believe we could become that source.

We describe ourselves or let others describe us as "consumers," "taxpayers," "stakeholders," "customers," "employees," instead of as sovereign people; as the "We the People" that ratified the Constitution, from whom all legal power in this nation flows. No wonder then that the proper language has atrophied. Like with an unused limb, working it makes it more powerful. Answering concerns like the ones you raise is therefore a valuable exercise. Here are some recent efforts:

- "Defining" speaks to the nature of the corporation: What shall be its purpose? Shall it exist in perpetuity? May it own other corporations? Shall it have the right to participate in our political systems? Shall it have the right of free speech?

- "Regulating" concedes that corporations and/or their agents will define themselves while we try to keep its harms within limits, concede important rights, scrutinize only its behaviors. Section 5, below, shows the difference from today, when corporations are chartered "for any lawful purpose," forever, with no limits on real estate or capital.

- If we define corporations as not having political rights, not having free speech, not being able to propagandize in our schools, then we don't have to write rules for reporting lunches with lobbyists, limiting/reporting campaign contributions, determining how many minutes of news vs. commercials will be on Channel One in schools.

- The difference between "defining" and "regulating" comes down to two central questions "Who is in charge?" and "How is that power exercised?" We are clear on the "who" (i.e., We the People), and history gives us clues on the "how" (i.e., controlled granting of charters, *quo warranto* hearings, and the like).

What goes into a corporate charter, like the following historic example from Maine, can be simple:

Sect. 1. Lyman Nichols, Benjamin Bates, and William Wood, their associates, successors, and assigns, are constituted and made a body politic and corporate by the name of Nichols Mills, with all the powers and privileges and subject to all the duties and liabilities provided by the laws of this state concerning manufacturing corporations.

Sect. 2. Said corporation is authorized to manufacture cotton, wool, and flax, in the city of Lewiston, to purchase and hold real and personal estate not exceeding twenty-five hundred thousand dollars in value, to build and erect such buildings and machinery as the convenience may require, and make all necessary rules and regulations for the prosecution of the same, consistent with the laws of the state.

Sect. 3. This act shall take effect when approved.

These definitions allow the corporation to provide a public good or service; they do not allow it to exercise the kinds of powers we don't want to see corporations exercising in a democratic society. Granted, what goes into the general corporation laws of a state are more specific, but we're still focusing on the same general principle here: will We the People define what the large institutions of our society will do, or will we allow a few individuals—controlling huge pools of wealth and the branches of our government—to define our lives and our society for us?

## 5. It's Not What Corporations Do Wrong, It's What They Do

By now, perhaps you can begin to see that this statement Kellman and Morris used at the Alliance convention is not "absolutist" as you described it. Here are some of the ways we elaborate.

First, corporations aren't good or bad. They are institutions we can use to further our society or let them enslave us. Love is good. Hate is bad. Corporations just are.[1]

Second, it's not just the most obvious harmful behavior that is at issue, it is the role of corporations in society—their power to rule—that needs changing.

Third, corporations existed for the better part of a century under a system more nearly approaching the "defining" one that we discussed above—much different from the one we've settled for in this century. We don't say corporations shouldn't exist, we are saying they shouldn't exist outside the sovereignty of the people. Rather than designating corporations as "good" or "bad" ones, there are only those corporations as defined by the people or those which are not.

And fourth, the phrase "good corporation" is an irrelevance. It should be that the only corporations we allow to exist and operate are the ones which are subservient, which obey, which do not rebel. If a corporation rebels and acts beyond its authority, it undermines the ability of the people to govern themselves; if *we* are responsible, we treat that corporation like a cancer and cut it out.

## 6. Corporate Responsibility

You write that rejecting this concept "carries with it a similar ambiguity and absolute thinking . . . impl[ies] a rejection of all corporations."

We are responsible for each corporation's existence. Our creation must perform as we have charged it. If it doesn't, it is our responsibility to take appropriate action or suffer the consequences. "Corporate responsibility" can have no other meaning.

In the face of all we know about corporations, why are so many people obedient? Why do we hang on to the absurd hope that corporations can be made socially responsible? A principal purpose of corporations is to protect the managers and directors from responsibility. Only people can be responsible by exercising our authority over all the institutions we create. We are not accountable when we create monster robots which run rampant in our communities, sallying forth across the world to wreak havoc upon other places and upon other people's self-governance. We are not being socially responsible or civically accountable when we permit our agents in government to bestow our sovereignty upon machines. "Corporate responsibility" implies self-defining by corporate boards, CEO's etc., not by We the People.

## 7. Corporate Personhood

To answer your statement that "no simple constitutional amendment will erase corporate personhood," we would say the following.

We don't suggest that any "silver bullet" exists. Constitutional amendment(s) may in fact be a necessary component of our generation's efforts to create a more complete democracy, but there's no such thing as a "simple" constitutional amendment. To amend the constitution for this purpose would require a tremendous change in public consciousness. This can happen only after a historic effort is made to organize and educate the public. That kind of effort is what we intend to create with the help of patriots like yourself.

We're working to engage the nation in debate and action about the proper nature and role of corporations in a democracy. What political and civil rights should it have? Free speech? Should it be allowed to lobby? Should Mobil Oil Corporation be allowed to influence energy policy? Should General Motors Corporation teach us about transportation, or be allowed to buy up trolley systems around the U.S. (as it did), shut them down and replace them with buses?[2]

When millions of Americans are asking these questions and demanding answers, amending the Constitution will seem like a logical next step.

## 8. INCREMENTAL CHANGE

You write: ". . . we can build momentum by winning specific victories that protect the environment and improve people's lives, while at the same time increasing awareness of more fundamental issues and laying the groundwork for systemic change. I am not convinced by arguments that it must be all or nothing and that in the meantime, all we can do is educate."

There are several related points here. Let me start with the last. Education is indeed work. In fact, if done in a well-organized, methodical fashion, it can be a lot of work.

Having attended more meetings than a sane person ever should, I can recall wishing that we would just go out and *do* something. To hell with all the talk. That sentiment is understandable but can lead to activity that, in the long run, does not really produce any positive change. A favorite saw of mine goes: "The wheel that's stuck in the mud spins the fastest."

No one says positive change can't also be incremental. But what's the nature of the change? Sometimes a finger in the dike is needed and may even save lives. But can't we do that and *also* strategically identify how to accomplish a fundamental shift in power, or at least point out what would be different if we could?

You and I and POCLAD and Alliance members have all organized in a dozen different movements. We've observed first-hand the importance of the day-to-day work done in incremental steps, and should never condescend to tell someone that they're just wasting their time if they don't work on some "big picture" as we define it.

What we're doing now is talking with people about the things which I've just written to you; listening to their responses in the context of the work they're doing to stop various corporate harms; and then seeing how together we can stop the harms in ways which take away corporate rights and powers, take away corporate power over our minds, and transfer these rights and powers to people and communities and nature. Along the way we may indeed be engaged in what some may call incremental change, but the nature of it will be transformative.

We are for the incremental shifting of power, but where is that taking place within labor and environmental law over the past 25 years? Aren't corporations stronger and wealthier and more protected by our government today than then?

All of us have laid a good foundation all these years, going after single issue after single issue, corporate symptom after corporate symptom, corporate behavior after corporate behavior. What we've done, what our comrades in arms have done, what we've learned, and the critical nature of the times, all tell us we must start changing the rules of the game and stop playing with that damned stacked deck. Many folks are ready for a big leap. Come with us, Wade. ∎

## Notes

[1] Corporations are proper objects of our authority, not of our emotions. It is said that "guns don't kill people, people kill people." But how guns are used—and to many their very purpose—evokes emotion. Corporations, like guns, are tools, objects. We should exercise our authority over these objects, not have an emotional relationship with them. —Ed.

[2] See "Disappearing Railroad Blues?" in this volume. —Ed.

# Letter to the John D. and Catherine T. MacArthur Foundation

*by Richard L. Grossman & Ward Morehouse*

19 January 2000

Dr. Melanie Beth Oliviero
John D. and Catherine T. MacArthur
Foundation

Dear Dr. Oliviero:

We appreciate your note and your candor.

Here's the thing: for us, "no fit" is the norm. We find this is so with most local elected officials, journalists, academics, potential individual donors, and foundations. That's why we and our colleagues created POCLAD.

To put it another way: we and our partners and supporters working to get corporations out of democracy's way have to create our own "fits." We do this by persistent and labor-intensive engagements with people who are willing to engage.

Foundation money in general perpetuates the idea that dominion over corporate decisions is not the public's business, indeed, is well beyond the public's constitutional authority. With few exceptions, the foundations which demonstrate interest in giant corporations:

1. give money in small dollops to many small citizen groups resisting specific corporate assaults ... one at a time, *ad infinitum;*

2. give larger dollops to trustworthy cultural icons to promote voluntary corporate codes of conduct and encourage "cooperation" between powerful artificial corporate persons and weak natural persons; and

3. give gobs to stagnant think tanks and law professors to explore corporate internal decision-making, efficiency, and transparency, without even lip service to this nation's ideal that in a democracy, it is civil society's responsibility to define all institutions.

So rather than looking for foundation "fits" that do not exist, we seek foundation staff, directors, advisers and donors who are open to talking about the ideals of the American Revolution (such as self-governance and consent of the governed) vs. the Constitution and today's realities; about civil society activism that has extended democracy, in contrast to civil society activism which has legitimated *corporate dominion under law.* We explore histories

---

This article is provided without copyright. It is a response to a very brief rejection notice to POCLAD's sincere and significant investment of time in the foundation's funding process. The rejection notice stated simply that there was "no fit" between the work of POCLAD and the kind of work funded by the Foundation.

of political and social movements; public vs. private; previous generations' critiques of the Constitution; the exclusion of African Americans, women, workers, immigrants, and the natural world from the Constitution and Bill of Rights, and the legal restraints upon the rights and powers of civil society which have resulted.

We have made the assumption that many staff, directors, advisers and donors are serious, dedicated people who want their grants to help society identify genuine problems and nurture appropriate solutions; that they wish to provoke societal changes which solve problems by strengthening democratic institutions and practices. We assume they are interested in challenging themselves to think, and in broadening their perspectives.

Perhaps we are projecting, because this is the work of POCLAD: internally, involving the twelve of us and our close allies; externally, engaging multiple constituency groups, students, scholars and public officials, along with those who might help fund our—and allies'—efforts.

Our work is having an impact. During and after the Seattle anti-WTO protests, for example, we heard from folks that their engagements with us over the past several years helped them understand why in Seattle's streets they were not protected by the First Amendment; why for activists in the U.S. and many other nations where giant corporations *already* use law and the police (that is, the power of government) to prevent communities and states from defining corporate nature and action, too much activist focus on the WTO could be a tactical diversion.

People have been investing precious time and resources in rethinking their organizations' goals and strategies. They've been delving into forgotten histories. Ralph Nader tells us that in his travels he hears new discussions about history, law, the Constitution and people's movements, which he attributes to POCLAD. A few communities have begun to pass laws defining the nature of corporations within their jurisdictions. They are acting in the tradition of this country's great social movements for freedom and self-governance by asserting constitutional rights withheld by the nation's propertied founders, and denied again and again by the nation's appointed judges.

We have concluded that for workers, and for people in general, to gain long-denied human rights vis-a-vis multinational corporations (in developing and developed countries, and *especially in the U.S.*), people and communities must claim all *their* constitutional rights. And people and communities must challenge past corporate seizures of constitutional and human rights.

There could be maximum transparency in corporate boardrooms, in the WTO and in global financial institutions; plus labor, environmental and human rights side agreements to the end of time. But without the majority of people possessing the legal authority and the political levers to govern ourselves—without "consent of the governed" transformed from myth into reality; without corporations ordered out of conversations and debate over what to do with this nation's labor and productive capacity—a handful will continue wielding their special privileges to shape people's work, dictate to communities, frame social and political thought, manufacture history, define elections, absorb legislatures, and pick over the Earth.

Without corporate entities constitutionally and legally subordinated to democratically-organized communities and nations, corporate assaults upon human rights—and self-governance—will continue apace.

What are the MacArthur Foundation's views on these matters? On corporate claims to Bill of Rights powers? On withholding Bill of Rights inside corporate gates? On denying communities the authority to interfere with the so-called "private law" of corporations? Is the corporate charter a "private contract," or "a public law"? What are the foundation's views on the latest thesis of Amory and Hunter Lovins and Paul Hawken (described in their book *Natural Capitalism*), that giant corporations can lead the way to ecologically-sound production, wealth equality, labor rights and democracy?

In 1993, shortly after the publication of *Taking Care Of Business; Citizenship & the Charter of Incorporation*, Richard submitted a proposal to MacArthur's Program on Peace and International Cooperation for a research and writing grant. The project was modest: "Legitimizing Public Debate on the Corporation." The project essay contained this summary paragraph:

> Most theories of the corporation and most public policy discussions about corporations are narrow and divorced from reality. They exclude serious consideration of citizen participation in corporate decision-making. Public reconsideration of the constitutional rights and powers corporate managers and corporate-friendly scholars claim today is regarded as heresy.

The proposal survived the first cut. Though ultimately rejected, it was encouraging to receive a request for reapplication. Richard submitted a rewritten essay, which was rejected in standard "foundationese," without comment as to content. Similar experiences with other foundations have piqued our curiosity: did those application essays about neglected

aspects of American history, about limited public discourse on the dominant institution of our era, provoke thought or discussion? Did they have any impact upon foundations' analyses, goals and grant giving?

We are concerned that internal deliberative processes of American philanthropic institutions—as with government, educational, media and civic groups—do not reflect experiences and histories of the majority of people here and abroad, and so are recklessly limited. We wonder: How *does* a philanthropic institution frame perspectives and fashion its mission? What have foundations learned from the work of their grantees? How many grantees of how many foundations now believe that foundation-supported human rights, labor and environment strategies have *strengthened* the corporate grip on law, history, civil society organizing, culture and governance?

Our work is to marry short-term community resistance against particular corporate assaults with long-term struggles for democratic self-governance. We assist constituency groups to provoke different conversations about history, governance and public policy… and to craft different solutions and strategies. The time-frame for such work is not years, but decades. This calls for finding people who believe that fundamental changes are achievable and worth working for. It also requires sparking healthy ferment within major institutions—including foundations.

All to say, we are interested in more than whether our aspirations and our work "match" MacArthur's. Is the MacArthur Foundation interested in assisting graduates of single issue community struggles now challenging manufactured history, the corporate language of production and consumption without end, and corporate claims to constitutional authority? Exploring constitutional distinctions between natural persons and artificial entities, between public and private? Nurturing consent of the governed? Figuring out why, after decades and decades of labor, consumer, environmental and human rights mobilizations to educate and pass laws, so many corporations can effortlessly assault people, small businesses, democracy and the Earth; why governments can subsidize these assaults; and why these assaults are treated by the nation's dominant intellectual, cultural and policing institutions as legal and unavoidable?

If so, perhaps we can lend a hand. ∎

# LETTER TO FRIENDS

*by Richard L. Grossman & Ward Morehouse*

## INTRODUCTION

I N JULY 1994 the leaders of 15 major environmental groups sent a joint letter to all their members saying:

> You have never received a letter like this before. This is the FIRST TIME the combined leadership of the nation's leading environmental groups have sent a single call to action to our combined memberships. Even during the Reagan/Watt/Gorsuch years, we have never faced such a serious threat to our environmental laws in Congress. Polluters have blocked virtually all of our efforts to strengthen environmental laws, but still they are not satisfied. Now, they are mounting an all-out effort to WEAKEN our most important environmental laws.

The letter was signed by the leaders of the American Oceans Campaign, the Center for Marine Conservation, Defenders of Wildlife, Environmental Action Foundation, Friends of the Earth, Greenpeace USA, League of Conservation Voters, National Audubon Society, National Parks and Conservation Association, National Wildlife Federation, Natural Resources Defense Council, Sierra Club, Sierra Club Legal Defense Fund, The Wilderness Society, and Zero Population Growth.

This week 173 citizens responded to the leaders of the "Big 15" with a letter of their own.

We are responding to your "Dear Environmentalist" letter of mid-July, which you sent to the combined membership of your groups.

We would like very much to meet with you about the problems you raised. We want to talk about something your letter did not mention: the source of these problems.

Some of us are associated with national environmental organizations, while others are actively engaged in community struggles for environmental justice and democracy. We are of diverse colors and backgrounds, live in different regions, and include trade union, religious and electoral activists, as well as survivors of industrial disasters and shareholder rights advocates.

In your letter, you wrote:

> . . . we have never faced such a serious threat to our environmental laws in Congress. Polluters have blocked virtually all of our efforts to strengthen environmental laws . . . [and] they are mounting an all-out effort to weaken our most important environmental laws.

We know this is true. We also know that while such assaults are under way in Congress, people in neighborhoods across the country are suffering injuries to health and life—from

This article is provided without copyright. Previously published in *Rachel's Environmental Weekly* (no. 407, September 15, 1994).

chemicals, radiation, incinerators, power plants, clear-cutting, highway building, disinvestment, and so forth. We also know that dignified jobs doing socially-useful work at fair pay are scarce and getting scarcer; that wages are declining; that democracy is too often a delusion at local, state and federal levels. And we know that nature is under attack, that many species, ecosystems and wilderness areas have been ravaged.

What prompts us to send this letter to you is our conviction that you have not identified those subverting Congress as our *real* adversaries in the struggle to save our communities and the natural world: the leaders of today's giant corporations, and the powerful corporations they direct.

We believe the Earth has never before faced such large-scale devastation as is being inflicted by handfuls of executives running the largest 1000 or so industrial, financial, health, information, agricultural and other corporations. And not since slavery was legal have the laws of the land been used so shamelessly to violate the democratic principles we hold dear.

This was not supposed to happen. It is true that the grand ideals of the American Revolution have not yet been fulfilled, and that many people are still struggling to gain the legal rights and constitutional protection for which so many fought against a tyrannical English monarchy. But for several generations after the nation's founding, the role of corporations in both government and society was strictly limited by law and custom. A corporate charter was considered a public trust. Corporations had no rights at all except what the people chose to give them.

Ironically, however, corporations have achieved a level of constitutional protection which many citizens do not enjoy. The leaders of giant corporations govern as monarchs

of old who claimed legitimacy under divine right theory. Yet your letter never once refers to multi-billion dollar corporations such as Exxon, Philip Morris, General Electric, Union Carbide, Weyerhaueser, or WMX Technologies (formerly Waste Management) corporations.

You write of lobbies, special interests, polluters and radical property rights advocates. But the work of these lobbies, polluters and radical advocates—in Congress and in our communities—is the work of corporations that manipulate assets beyond our imaginations while hiding behind limited liability, perpetual existence, and our Bill of Rights.

To a large extent, corporations have been given these legal rights and privileges not by our elected representatives, but by appointed judges. This did not happen by accident. Corporate leaders funded scores of research, propaganda, and lobbying organizations (using pre-tax dollars, which means that corporate lobbying and propagandizing are subsidized by us). You know the list: the U.S. and state chambers of commerce, the National Association of Manufacturers, the Chemical Manufacturers Association, and the Competitive Enterprise Institute. With "wise use" groups, and the help of foundations such as Olin, Scaife, Bradley and Smith Richardson, along with legal think tanks, corporate executives violate elections, buy and sell our legislators, and intimidate citizens.[1]

We believe that it is too late to counter corporate power by working environmental law by environmental law, or regulatory struggle by regulatory struggle. We don't have sufficient time or resources to organize chemical by chemical, forest by forest, river by river, permit by permit, technology by technology, product by product, corporate disaster by corporate disaster.

But if we curb or cut off corporate power at its source, all our work will become easier.

One major source of corporate power goes back to 1886 when the U.S. Supreme Court decreed that corporations are persons under the law.[2] This legal doctrine of corporate personhood guarantees constitutional free speech and other protection to corporations, thereby preventing our elected legislatures from limiting corporation interference in elections and law-making, in our courts, and in policy debates.[3] Other court-made legal doctrines give corporate leaders legal authority to make private decisions on very public issues: energy, chemical and transportation investments, product choices, forest and mineral use, technology development, etc.

How would restricting corporations' constitutional protections enable us to stop corporate-led environmental destruction? Look at takings, for example.[4]

When government wants to use an individual's property for a park, or for a sewage treatment plant, that individual has every right to petition for redress, for "due process of law." But corporate leaders claim this constitutional right of redress for their corporations, arguing that laws and regulations to protect public health and the environment, to protect workers' rights, are takings "without due process."

They can do this so effectively because a century ago corporate leaders convinced courts to transform our laws. Ever since, wielding property rights through laws backed by our government has been an effective, reliable strategy to build and sustain corporate mastery.

So it is understandable that many people today believe we have no choice but to concede property (such as takings), free speech and other rights to corporations, and to continue addressing corporate harms one-by-one.

We disagree: we believe we have a social

and political responsibility to reject concocted constitutional doctrines which enable undemocratic corporate dominion.

We support without reservation people's rights for redress against government takings, and people's protection against tyranny as provided in our Bill of Rights. But we do not believe corporations share such rights with flesh-and-blood people.

We have no illusions that reclaiming people's rights from the fictions which are corporations will be easy: as Supreme Court Justice Felix Frankfurter observed: the history of constitutional law is "the history of the impact of the modern corporation upon the American scene."[5]

But what's our alternative? The *real* takings going on today are corporate takings—of our lives, liberties and pursuits of happiness, and of other species—without due process of law.

The *real* takings today are planned and executed by corporate executives who are protected by the legal shields which are giant corporations, and who are showered with honors by our corporate-controlled culture.

Corporate tactics such as takings, risk assessment, unfunded mandates—at a time of escalating grassroots opposition to the North American Free Trade Agreement (NAFTA), the General Agreement on Tariffs and Trade (GATT), and to corporate investments around the globe—provide opportunities for your organizations to go on the offensive. You can educate your members that the authority to define corporations still rests with the people.

You can help us change the legal doctrines and laws which give corporations overwhelming advantage over people, communities and nature. Together, we can get the giant corporation out of our elections, out of our legislatures, out of our judges' chambers, out of our communities, and off our backs.

But if you do not write and talk about today's large corporation; if you do not educate and mobilize your members, as you know how to do; then our legislatures will face crisis after crisis like the one you described in your letter. Corporate leaders will strengthen their grip on the law and escalate their takings across the Earth.

Together, we can end the nation's long silence about corporate power and manipulation. We can work together to save our democracy in order to save our communities and our natural environment.

Won't you meet with us to discuss this essential work? ■

---

# NOTES

[1] See "Justice for Sale" in this volume.  —*Ed*

[2] *Santa Clara v. Southern Pacific Railroad Co.*

[3] See "Speaking Truth to Power About Campaign Reform" in this volume.

[4] The Fifth Amendment prohibits the government from the taking of private property for public use without just compensation. These prohibited acts are called "takings."  —*Ed.*

[5] Felix Frankfurter quoted in Miller 1967, p. 1.

# BREAK THE RULES

We the People have the responsibility to contest corporate claims to constitutional powers, to challenge judges who enable corporations to annihilate people's fundamental rights including the right to self-governance, to defy legislators and mayors and governors and presidents complicit in corporate rule. Other species and other peoples around the world are waiting for us to do more than resist one corporate assault at a time, or regulate the planet's destruction.

We can assume the authority to govern. We can act in the spirit of the democratic colonial revolutionaries, along with Abolitionists, Populists, Suffragists, Wobblies, civil rights and environmental workers, gender and gay liberation activists, Native Peoples, ambassadors of other species and countless others in every generation who believed that all political power must rest in the hands of self-governing people, who struggled for "consent of the governed," who refused to submit to the values, cultures and laws dictated by the propertied few.

# STRATEGIES TO
# END CORPORATE RULE

*by Ward Morehouse*

T HE TIME HAS come to devise strategies of resistance commensurate with the crisis confronting us. The growing dominance of the global political economy by the 500 largest corporations has been accompanied by increasing inequality and rampant poverty. Even the World Bank, one of the principal agents of corporate domination of the globe, acknowledges "that around 800 million people go hungry daily and their number is expected to soar." If current trends persist, 1.3 billion people are expected to survive on less than a dollar a day by the year 2000, 200 million more than in 1990.[1]

Thus hundreds of millions of persons are being denied not only their human rights but indeed that most essential of all rights, the "right to be human."[2] Denial of the right to be human on such a vast scale is surely a "crime against humanity," certainly as it is defined in Canadian law C-71, which was passed by the Canadian Parliament on August 28, 1987. This act defines a "crime against humanity" as meaning:

> . . . murder, extermination, enslavement, deportation, persecution or any other inhumane act or omission that is committed against any civilian population or any identifiable persons, whether or not it constitutes a contravention of the law

enforced at the time and in the place of its commission, and that, at the time and in that place, constitutes a contravention of customary international law or conventional international law or is criminal according to the general principals of law recognized by the Community of Nations.[3]

I have chosen Canadian Law C-71 to apply to the Global 500 because Canada is a member of the "Group of Seven" or "G-7,"[4] i.e., the major industrialized countries. Most of the 500 largest corporations in the world are headquartered in the G-7 countries, and the G-7 governments have an obligation to protect internationally recognized human rights, certainly when they involve violations as serious as crimes against humanity. The doctrine of crimes against humanity is solidly embedded in international law. The definition quoted above is drawn from the Charter of the International Military Tribunal at Nuremberg, as subsequently reaffirmed and extended to acts committed at any time (not just wartime) by the United Nations General Assembly.[5]

The International Law Commission, furthermore, has been elaborating on the definition given above, making it even more applicable to the actions of giant global corporations. It makes explicit what is implicit in the

Nuremberg Charter—namely, that inhumane acts become crimes against humanity when they are "committed in a systematic way or on a large scale and instigated or directed by a Government or by any organization or group." The reference to "any organization or group" clearly includes non-state actors such as global corporations bigger than most nation-states.[6]

Under the Canadian definition, the Nuremberg Charter (as reaffirmed by the UN General Assembly) and the work of the International Law Commission, the Global 500 corporations are indictable for crimes against humanity. To make this charge credible we need a deliberative process guided by basic principles of due process in gathering evidence and presenting it to appropriate judicial bodies. The first step will be systematic collection of evidence of human rights violations by the Global 500 through citizen-created and citizen-led "Truth Commissions" and other appropriate means.

The "Permanent Peoples' Tribunal on Global Corporations and Human Wrongs" provides a forum for framing indictments of the Global 500 based on evidence accumulated through the preparatory process leading up to the Tribunal.[7] What then should follow is the trial of each of the Global 500 in appropriate forums around the world, whether they be established courts of law or people's tribunals. The results of these trials should then be aggregated into one comprehensive verdict on the Global 500.

The next task will be to devise sentences appropriate to the severity of the crimes committed by these giant corporations. Under the Canadian Law cited above, the principal sanction applied against those indicted for "crimes against humanity" is expulsion. Dismantling the Global 500 would be an appropriate analogous penalty. ∎

---

## Notes

[1] World Bank, *Strategy for Reducing Poverty and Hunger* (Washington, 1995) and *World Development Report: Workers in an Integrating World* (Washington, 1995) as cited in Clairmont 1997, p. 339. This discussion of global corporations and crimes against humanity is drawn from Morehouse 1997, "Multinational Corporations and Crimes Against Humanity."

[2] Baxi 1989.

[3] "An Act to Amend the Criminal Code, the Immigration Act, 1976, and the Citizenship Act, C-71," in *Parliament, Government of Canada* (1987).

[4] Now the "G-8" including Russia.

[5] Charter of the Nuremberg Tribunal, as given in Friedman 1972. Crimes against humanity as defined in the Nuremberg Charter were reaffirmed by the

UN General Assembly in *Resolution 3(I)* of 13 February 1946 and *Resolution 95(I)* of 11 December 1946. It should be noted that crimes against humanity are qualified as crimes even if such acts do not constitute a violation of the domestic law of the country in which they were committed.

[6] United Nations International Law Commission 1996.

[7] This session of the tribunal was held at the University of Warwick Law School in the United Kingdom on March 22-25, 2000. The discussion is available from the Tribunal secretariat at the Lelio Basso International Foundation, Via della Dogana Vecchia 5, 00186 Rome, Italy (tel. 39-06-68801468; fax 39-06-6877774; filb@iol.it; www.grisnet.it/bilb).

# Turning the Tables on Pennsylvania Agri-Corporations

## An Interview with Thomas Linzey

*by Thomas Linzey & POCLAD*

---

*By What Authority:* Tell us about these township ordinances banning corporate hog farms.

*Thomas Linzey:* Agribusiness corporations are invading Pennsylvania, intent on undermining family farms by creating factory farms across the landscape. Part of their systematic efforts to industrialize food production and land use is to join the Pennsylvania Farm Bureau in pressuring state legislators to prohibit citizens from using their local governments to control what these corporate farms do.

Following the corporations' success in using state law to keep local residents from passing ordinances to deal with various corporate impacts, the CELDF was swamped with calls from voters and elected township officials. Municipal officials were really being squeezed. Residents wanted them to control these absentee-owned animal factories while the Farm Bureau and agribusiness operatives said it was beyond their authority as public officials to take action.

We saw an opening to raise the broader issues of local democratic control and the "corporatization" of agriculture through conversations about manure, lagoons, odor, and flies. We decided to invest half our time and resources to this work. Then we drafted model ordinances which could be adopted by municipal governments—not on manure disposal or hogs per acre, but on the core issue of the people's authority to ban non-family owned corporate farms in Pennsylvania.

Luckily, we didn't have to reinvent the wheel. Nine states—most recently South Dakota and Nebraska—had adopted referenda prohibiting non-family owned corporations from engaging in farming of any kind. Drafting the ordinances was easy, since we built on the work of people before us.

Then came the challenge of gaining the trust of local groups and elected officials, to help them understand how a handful of corporations could make fundamental decisions about how our food was produced and our communities run. It has been educational and exciting to work with POCLAD in looking at the history about how wealthy investors got politicians and judges to give power and legal privilege to corporations, and how people's vision of self-governance took democratic ideals seriously.

To date, five municipal governments in Pennsylvania have adopted ordinances mirroring the laws adopted in those nine states. We are serving as special counsel to ten other local

©2001 by POCLAD. This interview was published in *By What Authority* (vol. 3, no. 2, Spring 2001), a publication of POCLAD. Thomas Linzey founded the Community Environmental Legal Defense Fund (CELDF) in 1995. *By What Authority* interviewed him about his work with Pennsylvania communities.

governments in south-central Pennsylvania which want to enact identical ordinances.

*BWA:* How are corporate operatives reacting?

*TL:* In the beginning, corporations and their nonprofit "shill" groups like the Farm Bureau and the Chamber of Commerce mostly ignored us. Then we were asked by the Chesapeake Bay Foundation to present our ordinances to a statewide local government association conference attended by over 2000 elected officials. After that, things abruptly changed. A ranking Republican state senator demanded that CELDF be banned from such panels. The Farm Bureau actively interfered in one local government's effort to pass the ordinance. And factory farm operatives began attending local government meetings.

The Pennsylvania Chamber of Commerce also became more active, doing what the Chamber was designed to do—painting people like me and public officials who believe in democracy as rabble-driven advocates of no growth and no jobs. The Chamber also labeled as "anti-agriculture" residents who supported our ordinance.

Our work made the cover of the Chamber's monthly *Advocate for Pennsylvania Business*, with an article titled "There's No Business Like No-Bizness in Wayne Township" and a graphic of the township surrounded by barbed wire.

*BWA:* What is your strategy when corporate farms and their allies take you to court?

*TL:* Our basic work with local ordinances is to transform the discussion about factory farms into one about corporate domination of Pennsylvania communities. We are talking about historical precedents, providing discussion groups with reading materials, making presentations to citizens and government officials, writing opinion pieces in local newspapers. In January we brought in attorney David Cobb, who works with POCLAD, to speak at a mass meeting of township officials and residents about generations of community efforts to assert democratic control over agribusiness and other corporations. Folks were so energized that some continued talking long after the event was officially over.

Such efforts help popular support grow strong enough to confront corporate intimidation and lawsuits designed to throw out the township laws and punish elected officials. A legal victory in the courts, powered by the network of residents and officials that we're building, will give us momentum to take our work into county and municipal governments across the state. However, win or lose in the courts, widespread public participation in the suits will help create the public education and organization we need to pass state legislation closing Pennsylvania to corporate farms.

As this struggle spreads around the state and more people compare notes about the corporate domination of our daily lives, I wouldn't be surprised to find more conversations about stripping corporations of privileges like freedom of speech and equal protection of the law. CELDF's job is to provide innovative legal tools to stimulate this discussion about claiming our rightful power.

*BWA:* What will happen if the state courts declare these township ordinances unconstitutional, or if state legislators pass a law banning townships from making the rules for corporate farming within their borders?

*TL:* Given history and the clout that property, contract and constitutional law gives corporations, we expect a "crisis of jurisdiction" between local and state government, which has a corporate-driven interest in enabling corporate agriculture to flourish. State legislators have already begun stripping control from municipalities on things like "manure management." Over the past two years Pennsylvania legislators have also prohibited citizens from using local government to control the spreading of toxic sewage sludge, from using zoning laws to separate industrial farms from traditional farms, and from establishing conservation zones free of timber harvesting.

Such prohibitions are producing a reaction from the local governments themselves. Fifteen of them have formed the "Coalition to Save Local Governments" to contest the authority of state legislators to strip municipalities of their rights and powers and to challenge corporate authority to dictate public policy.

We see CELDF using this crisis to continue raising the issue of self-governance and how corporate assaults like manure, monopoly and giant chain stores destroying local businesses take basic decisions about our health and security out of our hands. We see a growing understanding in Pennsylvania about the incompatibility of corporate governance with people's ability to create sustainable democratic communities.

*BWA:* How will we feed ourselves without these giant industrial corporations?

*TL:* Over the last thirty years we've lost over 300,000 farm families in this country. Over the last two years pork prices were driven by corporate mass production to their lowest levels ever. A 250 pound hog, which sold in 1996 for $51, sold in 1998 for $31. With the cost of production for family farmers $38 for that same hog, most of the family farm hog producers went bankrupt or became employees—wage slaves, really—of the agribusiness corporations.

Farmland preservation has also been a giant local issue. Over 4000 acres of farmland are lost annually in a single county in south-central Pennsylvania. Growing numbers of people around here believe the best way to save farmland is to make our family farms profitable again. Yet state policy paving the way for a corporate factory farm invasion guarantees that family farmers, who take best care of the land, will continue to be wiped out or corporatized.

If absentee corporate owners are allowed to dictate the rules to elected officials, they will continue building monopoly control and driving prices higher, while destroying ground water, property values and quality of life. Even a cursory look at the growing corporate concentration of farm ownership reveals that this transformation is in the 8th inning. Four corporations now control 82% of the beef cattle market, five major packing corporations control 55% of the hog industry. Small family farms—over 94% of all U.S. farms—receive only 41% of all farm income. Suicides have replaced equipment-related deaths as the number one cause of farmer deaths.

We can address this tragedy by substituting the corporate factory farm market with alternatives which support both family farmers and public demand for fresh, safe, organic produce and meats, and for soil and water protection. This means asserting our authority to make the rules over how food is produced in our communities. It means challenging corporate dominance over state legislators, elections, public debate and culture. And of course this involves contesting the crazy notions that corporations should have the constitutional rights of persons and that corporate decisions shaping our communities are private.

CELDF has been active in efforts here to nurture Community Supported Agriculture (CSA). People are able to support local, family-owned farms by buying "shares" of farm production before the growing season begins. In return they receive fresh produce, meat, eggs and cheese weekly from the family farm. We are also hosting several farmers markets, providing farm products directly to the public.

On January 20 and February 3 of 2001 we showcased these components of food production in gatherings of elected officials, citizens, farmers, and activists in Fulton and Cumberland Counties. Discussion focused on building sustainable farming communities through local self-governance. With crises of jurisdiction looming as people educate themselves and organize in rural townships, it's increasingly clear that the real issue is who, in a democracy, is supposed to make the basic decisions about community values, food production and public health.

On the icy, snowy days of a rural Pennsylvania winter, we've taken crucial steps with local communities, who have begun to understand this and now sound the alarm. ∎

# ASSERTING DEMOCRATIC CONTROL OVER CORPORATIONS

## A CALL TO LAWYERS

### by Richard L. Grossman & Ward Morehouse

The judgment sought against the defendant is one of corporate death . . . The life of a corporation is, indeed, less than that of the humblest citizen . . . Corporations may, and often do, exceed their authority only where private rights are affected. When these are adjusted, all mischief ends and all harm is averted. But where the transgression has a wider scope, and threatens the welfare of the people, they may summon the offender to answer for the abuse of its franchise or the violation of its corporate duty. The [North River Sugar Refining] corporation has violated its charter, and failed in the performance of its corporate duties, and that in respects so material and important to justify a judgment of dissolution . . . All concur.[1]

- Justice Finch, for a unanimous Court of Appeals of New York State, 1890

## A CORPORATE COUNTERREVOLUTION

AFTER THE CIVIL WAR bitter struggles erupted between states and corporations, with corporations using the federal courts (along with President Hayes and other elected officials) as their agents. Insurance, banking, railroad, grain and other burgeoning corporations hired the most experienced lawyers they could—including former senators, along with state and U.S. Supreme Court justices.

As Charles McCurdy has described, the Supreme Court first had to be apprised by skillful counsel of the growth-eroding potential of state laws, and to be persuaded that new juridical principles must be forged to pre-serve free trade among the states. Second, the legitimacy of protectionist state legislation had to be challenged by litigants with sufficient resources to finance scores of lawsuits in order both to secure initial favorable decisions and to combat the tendency of state governments to mobilize "counter thrusts" against the Supreme Court's nationalistic doctrines.[2]

When the briefs had settled, corporate leaders and their lawyers, among other accomplishments, had gotten the federal courts:

- to take substantial jurisdiction over corporations from state courts;

- to concoct the "liberty of contract" and other doctrines, and reinterpret the Commerce clause, severely undermining state authority over corporations;

- to apply the Fourteenth Amendment's due process and equal protection clauses to corporations;

- to transfer the authority to set railroad corporation and utility corporation rates from elected state legislators and state commissions to federal judges;

- to broaden the definition of property to encompass economic and political power (making "Cain's motto 'Am I my brother's keeper?' the supreme law of industry," as one legal philosopher has commented);[3]

- to mid-wife the judicial injunction, which corporate lawyers used to cripple the rights of workers and communities resisting corporations' exercise of their new property rights;

- to focus corporate law on the obligation of corporation directors and managers to maximize profits. (With the doctrines of "loyalty" and "care," and the "business judgment rule," federal judges bestowed upon corporate directors great latitude, declaring outside the pale of corporate law—and therefore beyond the reach of the sovereign people—what corporations actually *do*: decide upon investment practices, production, the technologies, industrial processes, and the organization of work.)

Corporations and their lawyers had also:

- shaped law school philosophy and curriculum;

- rewritten legal history; and

- diverted citizen protest by creating federal regulatory agencies—starting with the Interstate Commerce Commission in 1887—to serve as barriers between the sovereign people and corporate fictions, and to co-opt movement leaders and institutions.[4]

Today the wish lists of the nineteenth century's lawyers-for-hire have become America's sacred legal doctrines.

## A CHALLENGE FOR PROGRESSIVE LAWYERS

As the twentieth century winds down, growing numbers of people are no longer willing to grant sweeping powers and privileges to corporations, to their directors, managers and stockholders. The Program On Corporations, Law & Democracy has been bringing such people together in "Rethinking The Corporation, Rethinking Democracy" meetings over the past two years to talk about what is to be done. We have been listening.

What has become clear is that accepting corporate law as it has been created by corporate lawyers and judges, and taught by law schools, means conceding to giant corporations dominance over our nation's elections, laws, money, work, manufacturing, resources, health, education, culture and ecosystems—not to mention over the rest of the world.

Tactically, it means limiting ourselves to resisting harms one corporate site at a time, one corporate chemical or biotechnology product at a time; to correcting imperfections of the market; to working for yet more permitting and disclosure laws; to initiating procedural lawsuits and attempts to win compensation after massive corporate harm has been done; to battling regulatory and administrative agencies; to begging leaders of global corporations to please cause a little less harm.

Frustrated, angry, and in search of new goals and strategies, people have begun examining the nature and history of the modern giant corporation. Looking into their state and the federal constitutions, corporate law and popular resistance to corporate rule, people have been uncovering rich lodes of constitutional provisions and case law (such as *People v. North*

*River Sugar Refining Co.*, quoted above) Even at this early stage of such investigations, Justice Felix Frankfurter's observation that the history of constitutional law is "the history of the impact of the modern corporation upon the American scene"[5] has been amply confirmed.

## A NEW PEOPLE'S MOVEMENT

Uncovering this hidden history is providing precedent—and inspiration—for a new people's movement to disempower the corporation as an institution, revoke the charters of human-rights-denying corporations, and fundamentally redefine the legal relationships between the sovereign people and our enterprises.

Such a movement will require taking the offensive against a century of corporate usurpation and the corporate colonization of our minds. It will require building upon the work of valiant people of past generations, and making new history based on principles as expressed in the Massachusetts Constitution since 1780 (and found in diverse forms in other state constitutions as well):

> No man, nor corporation, or association
> of men, have any other title to obtain
> advantages, or particular and exclusive priv-
> ileges, distinct from those of the commu-
> nity, than what arises from the considera-
> tion of services rendered to the public . . .[6]

The progressive wing of the legal profession has vital roles to play in a people's movement for corporate disempowerment. People's lawyers will need to join organizers as educators, theoreticians, strategists and litigators in community, state, national and international arenas. They will be essential for protecting and expanding human beings' free speech, free assembly and other rights needed for redress of grievances, for protest and education, and for research and writing new law.

## TEN SUGGESTIONS TO STIMULATE THE LEGAL PROFESSION

1. End the virtual monopoly of corporate lawyers by nurturing a new breed of progressive lawyers knowledgeable about constitutional history and corporate law, and committed to helping citizens exert popular authority over corporate fictions.

2. Help plan—and where appropriate litigate—revocation of corporate charters under state laws; investigate potential for "rechartering" corporations with limited powers, explicitly subordinate to the sovereign people; investigate past citizen tactics which used criminal conspiracy as the basis for involuntary corporate dissolution; explore the use of quo warranto and ultra vires, and the removal of liability protections.

3. Help craft amendments to state corporation codes; produce a model "Citizens' State Corporation Code" as an alternative to the American Bar Association's fifty-year effort to help states give away public authority to corporations.

4. Help provoke debate—within the legal community and among the general public—questioning legal doctrines which disempower people, places and the natural world, and empower corporations; work with organizers in the various states to draft ballot initiatives and legislation which confront legal doctrines granting corporations special privileges and immunities.

5. Help document illegal and harmful (but treated as legal) acts of corporations; help uncover and reinterpret judicial precedents, laws and constitutional provisions which people can use in the several states to bring giant corporations and corporate leaders to justice.

6. In daily law practice, question all the rights and powers which corporate lawyers claim for their clients; help people resist clear and present corporate harms in ways which reveal modern giant corporations as unconstitutionalized governments; encourage clients to choose tactics which not only seek justice but also weaken corporate privilege.

7. Help devise theories and strategies which towns, cities and states can use to prohibit all corporate involvement in elections, law-making and the selection of judges—from banning financial contributions, to prohibiting advertising on matters of public policy.

8. Provoke debate from the grassroots up about human rights vs. property rights; explore and expand work on the "reliance interest"[7] and related efforts to establish property rights of workers, communities, other species and places.

9. Defend people and organizations from SLAPP[8] and similar lawsuits, as well as from government, university, shopping mall/real estate corporation efforts to deny speech, assembly, and related rights essential for citizen redress of grievances, education, protest and organizing.

10. Become skilled in the creation and operation of alternative institutions of enterprise, such as those under municipal and worker ownership and control, and cooperatives.

## A HIDDEN HISTORY

Giant corporations, often global in reach, are the dominant governing institutions on our planet today. They function as governments.

The largest U.S. corporations have sales greater than the gross domestic product of many countries. General Motors Corporation, for example, outstrips Denmark, as well as Norway, Hong Kong, Israel, Ireland, New Zealand and Hungary.[9] The world's largest corporations "account for about three-quarters of the world's commodity trade, and fourth-fifths of the trade in technology and managerial skills of [market] economies."[10] The largest 50 corporations obtain over half their revenues from outside their country of origin.[11]

The 500 largest U.S. industrial corporations control 35% of all non-financial corporate assets.[12] From 1980-1992, these corporations more than doubled their assets, from $1.8 trillion to 2.57 trillion.[13] The *Wall Street Journal* proclaimed that the first quarter of 1995 brought "the highest level of corporate profitability in the postwar era, and probably since the latter stages of the Bronze Age."[14]

By corporate decree, poverty is up, wages are down, and millions are literally working their way into poverty.[15] Corporate leaders and their shills order Congress, state legislatures and local officials to fire teachers and public health workers; close schools, libraries, hospitals and parks; gut health and environmental laws; withhold legal aid and other services to young people, the poor, the sick and elderly. And our politicians hop to, as a *New York Times* headline sums it up: "As City and State Budgets are Cut, Millions in Tax Breaks Go to Companies."[16]

Withdrawing constitutional protections from corporate legal fictions and replacing global corporations with politically subordinate institutions of enterprise are the self-evident challenges of our era. Yet we see conference after conference for justice taking place where corporations are barely on the agenda. People work hard to enact election and lobbying reforms which leave corporate claims to free speech unchallenged, permit corporate lobbyists to roam the halls of government and fill our elected officials' pockets with money. Citizen groups hire lawyers to sue regulatory agencies over and over again, but justice is continually mocked by court-sanctioned corporate claims to property rights. Appointed judges keep violating the expressed intentions of laws passed by a century of citizen organizing. And people invest years of time and effort to get corporate leaders to sign codes of conduct which are purely voluntary, and to gain standing in national and international councils only to find that corporations have written all the rules.

It's not "corporate responsibility," or "corporate accountability," or "good corporate citizenship" that sovereign people must seek. Those phrases are all contradictions in terms, and diversions from the public's central task to become unified enough *to exert citizen authority over the creation, structure, and functioning* of all business enterprises.

## This is Not as Crazy as it May Appear

In the United States after the American Revolution, both law and tradition defined corporations as creatures of the state, subordinate to the sovereign people.[17] The people who came—or were forcibly brought—to these shores, knew first-hand that unconstitutionalized business extensions of the state—such as the East India Company, the Hudson's Bay Company, the Royal Africa Company, and the crown corporations which ran colonies in Carolina, Virginia, Pennsylvania and elsewhere—were tyrannical and dictatorial by design. For example, the Royal Africa Company played a major role in the transatlantic slave trade.[18] The directors of the crown corporations in North America exercised total authority over the colonists—conscripting them into corporate militia, instructing them on what to

grow, what work to do, where to buy goods, where to market their products, what to think.

The need to be wary of corporations was expressed by pamphleteering revolutionaries such as Thomas Earle: "Chartered privileges are a burthen, under which the people of Britain, and other European nations, groan in misery."[19] Thomas Jefferson spoke about the need "to crush in its birth the aristocracy of our moneyed corporations, which dare already to challenge our government to a trial of strength, and bid defiance to the laws of our country."[20] Artisans and mechanics made known their concerns as well, that absentee corporate owners would turn them into "a commodity, being as much an article of commerce as woolen, cotton or yarn."[21]

To be sure, great gaps always existed between the ideals and achievements of the American Revolution. The Constitution and laws have served as tools for legalized oppression as well as for inspiration and liberation. But for several generations, incorporation was regarded both by law and by custom as a *privilege*, and all corporations were obligated to serve the public trust. Charters were issued sparingly, and expired after twenty or thirty years. State legislators spelled out rules for each corporation in its charter, and then in state corporation codes. Among the detailed requirements, directors and managers were held liable for corporate harms, capitalization and land holdings were restricted, and the rights of minority shareholders were carefully protected. (For example, unanimous shareholder approval for major corporate decisions was common.)

And legislatures reserved the right to amend and revoke corporate charters at will. Faced with the onslaught of corporate power, they eventually retreated from exercising that right. But the powers, though latent, are still there waiting to be used.

## LATENT STATE POWERS

For example, in Wisconsin during the past hundred years, a corporation could not own another corporation; corporate landholdings and capitalization were limited; corporate officers and directors were liable for all corporate harms; the state reserved the right to amend and revoke corporate charters, as the attorney general once put it, "for no reason at all." Until 1973 corporations were forbidden from contributing money to election campaigns.[22] And until 1953 violating this law constituted a felony.

A federal bankruptcy court construing Florida law in 1984 declared that:

> [It was a] well-settled principle that the legislature cannot bargain away the police power of the sovereign or its power to take appropriate measures to protect the health, safety and morals of its citizens . . . It cannot be gainsaid that corporations are creatures of the state legislature and owe their existence to a grant of the charter by the state. To enforce and control their functions falls, without doubt, within the regulatory power of the state . . . From all this follows that the State of Florida is not prevented to take measures to assure that the corporate charter granted by the State is not misused or that the corporation is not used for purposes that are illegal or expressly prohibited by the charter. Neither is the State powerless to revoke the charter . . .[23]

Article 83 of the New Hampshire Constitution reads:

> The size and function of all corporations should be so limited and regulated as to prohibit fictitious capitalization and provision should be made for the supervision and government thereof. Therefore, all just power

possessed by the state is hereby granted to the general court to enact laws to prevent the operations within the state of all persons and associations, and all trusts and corporations, foreign or domestic, and the officers thereof, who endeavor to raise the price of any article of commerce or to destroy free and fair competition in the trades and industries through combination, conspiracy, monopoly, or any other unfair means.

According to Section 1101 of the New York State Business Corporation Law, the attorney general "may bring an action for the dissolution of a corporation upon one or more of the following grounds . . . That the corporation has exceeded the authority conferred upon it by law, or has violated any provision of law whereby it has forfeited its charter, or carried on, conducted, or transacted its business in a persistently fraudulent or illegal manner, or by the abuse of its powers contrary to the public policy of the state has become liable to be dissolved." That state's constitution, in article XIV, section 4, defines "the public policy of the state":

> The public policy of the state shall be to conserve and protect its natural resources and scenic beauty and encourage the development and improvement of its agricultural lands for the production of food and other agricultural products.

In Washington State:

> Every corporation, whether foreign or domestic, which shall violate any provision of RCW 9A.28.040 [criminal conspiracy], shall forfeit every right and franchise to do business in this state. The attorney general shall begin and conduct all actions and proceedings necessary to enforce the provisions of this subsection.[24]

Forty nine state corporation codes outline grounds for charter revocation. Professor David Millon has observed that:

> . . . state general incorporation laws routinely include provisions reserving the right of amendment and announcing their potentially retroactive force . . . state legislatures define the content of these property rights. By redefining them, the legislatures are simply exercising a prerogative that has always been theirs . . . The manner in which shareholder property rights are defined is a manifestation of the states' general power to specify the content of property rights in order to promote justice or utility. So-called private property rights always exist in order to give expression to public values; the survival of a given property law regime depends ultimately on its social utility.[25]

## LOOKING TO THE FUTURE

In response to accelerating corporate oppression and destruction, an intensification of citizen resistance and opposition is now under way. At some fifteen "Rethinking the Corporation" meetings we have organized in ten states, we find people moving increasingly quickly through discussions about their limited goals, narrow tactics and false victories of recent years, and about the anti-democratic nature of giant corporations.

More and more people are inspired by the legal and corporate histories of their states, which they are discovering for themselves in preparing for these meetings. They are eager to begin the deep educating and organizing work they know is essential for the long haul. This work has begun in Maine, Wisconsin and Oregon, where groups have formed to pursue corporate disempowerment agendas.

Compared with just two years ago, when suggesting that people should organize to get their states to dissolve the most abusive corpo-

rations evoked nervous laughter and advice to "get real," growing numbers of people now see this work as essential for achieving justice and protecting human rights. But they also recognize the difficulties of such undertakings.

For example, how do people avoid ending up in the courts before even a significant minority of the bench and bar has been acquainted with the history of citizen sovereignty over corporations, or before a movement exists to restrain unsavory political, legal and political counterattack by corporate leaders? How do people prepare for—even pre-empt—threats of freezing, starving, joblessness in the dark from corporations, their front groups, politicians and academics? What about the "divide and conquer" efforts that can be anticipated, including what Noam Chomsky has labeled "feigned dissents"[26] intended to divert debate and derail a citizen's movement ... or comparable diversion and derailing by well-meaning people willing to go along with corporate rule because they do not believe there are alternatives to giant corporations?

## IDEOLOGICAL PACIFICATION

There is no avoiding the formidable task of overcoming the colonization of our minds, of uprooting what Edward Said has called the "ideological pacification" that has been taking place for decades because large corporations have dominated so many aspects of our lives and communities.[27] As Cornel West has observed:

> The sheer power of corporate capital . . . makes it difficult even to imagine what a free and democratic society would look like (or how it would operate) if there were publicly accountable mechanisms that alleviated the vast disparities in resources, wealth, and income owing in part to the vast influence of big business on the U.S. government and its legal institutions.[28]

This colonization is at the heart of the TINA (There Is No Alternative) phenomenon, which pervades all aspects of American life. But once people convince each other that there are real alternatives to the present domination by large corporations, then redefining the relationship between the people and our enterprises—based on the principles of citizen sovereignty and self-governance—will no longer seem like an impossible dream. And the adoption of model state corporation codes based on these principles, reinforced by a body of legal doctrines, will appear to be logical, and achievable.

But We the People—and our lawyers—will have to shift our thinking and our strategizing. We can start by figuring out how to resist corporate harm-doing in ways which begin to weaken all corporations, and by seizing the offensive to define the conditions under which corporations may exist and function.

## RECLAIMING SOVEREIGNTY

And as the American people begin reclaiming citizen sovereignty from corporate fictions, there must be deliberate efforts to extend the benefits of sovereignty to those who have historically been excluded from constitutional "personhood"—notably women, people of color, Native Americans, other species, future generations, and the Earth itself.

None of this will be easy or quick. But the only other choice is giving up and living under corporate rule. And failure even to try will abandon our children to the terrifying question posed by the philosopher Morris Raphael Cohen more than a half-century ago:

> Never before have those absorbed in the producing of material things had so much power in the governance of human life . . . But their ultimate criterion is the very simple one of monetary profit. Can the ultimate interest of human life be safely left to be governed by that simple consideration?[29] ∎

## NOTES

[1] *People v. North River Sugar Refining Co..*

[2] McCurdy 1978, pp. 631, 648.

[3] Cohen "Property and Sovereignty" 1933, pp. 41, 44.

[4] See "Sheep in Wolf's Clothing" in this volume —*Ed.*

[5] Felix Frankfurter "The Commerce Clause Under Marshall, Taney and Waite," quoted in Miller 1967.

[6] Mass. Constitution of 1780, p. I, Art. VI.

[7] Singer 1988, p. 614.

[8] SLAPP is an acronym for a "strategic lawsuit against public participation." *Black's Law Dictionary* (seventh ed.) defines it as "a suit brought by a developer, corporate executive, or elected official to stifle those who protest against some type of high-dollar initiative or who take an adverse position on a public-interest issue (often involving the environment)." —*Ed.*

[9] Martin and Tritto 1993, pp. 184-185; The World Bank World Development Report (1994).

[10] United States 1993, p. 38.

[11] *Ibid.*

[12] United States 1994, Tables 839, 870.

[13] *Ibid.*, Table 870.

[14] Lowenstein 1995.

[15] Dembo and Morehouse 1995, pp. 17-32.

[16] Lucck 1995.

[17] Grossman and Adams 1993. See "Taking Care of Business: Citizenship and the Charter of Incorporation" in this volume.

[18] Du Bois 1947, p. 54.

[19] Earle 1823.

[20] People's Bicentennial Commission 1975, p. 154.

[21] Mechanics Free Press, Sept. 20, 1828, quoted in Hartz 1948, p. 197.

[22] Morris 1995. Also see "Speaking Truth to Power About Campaign Reform" in this volume.

[23] *Re: Jesus Loves You, Inc.*

[24] Wash. Rev. Code 9A.08.030(5) (1995) (emphasis added).

[25] Millon 1991, pp. 223, 272-273.

[26] Chomsky and Otero 1988, p. 376.

[27] Said 1993.

[28] West 1982, pp. 468-469.

[29] Grossman 1928, p. 81.

# NATIONAL LAWYERS GUILD RESOLUTION

*by the National Lawyers Guild*

---

## WHEREAS:

A. Giant corporations increasingly govern our lives and communities and define our work and our culture, eroding democratic values and pillaging the environment;

B. Even the Michigan Supreme Court has declared in *Richardson v. Buhl*, 77 Mich. 632, 658 (1889), that "it is doubtful if free government can long exist in a country where such enormous amounts of money are allowed to be accumulated in the vaults of corporations, to be used at discretion in controlling the property and business of the country against the interest of the public";

C. These corporations and their counterparts in other countries aspire to rule the world through the World Trade Organization, NAFTA, and other treaties, conventions, and agreements such as the proposed Multilateral Agreement on Investment which would grant corporations the juridical status of nation-states;

D. The National Lawyers Guild, from its founding in 1937 to the present, has a radical heritage of organizing and providing legal support to virtually every struggle in the United States for economic, social, and political justice;

E. It is important for the National Lawyers Guild to support the work of its members and the movements they support related to the theme of the 1998 National Convention, *Fighting Corporate Power*; and

F. There exists a growing mass people's movement that contests the authority of corporations to govern and works toward restoring sovereignty in the hands of the people, to put human beings back in charge as they should be in a democratic polity.

Therefore be it resolved that the National Lawyers Guild:

I. Adhere to the principle that only natural persons are vested with constitutional rights. Thus, the Guild is opposed to recognizing the personhood of for-profit corporations under the Fourteenth Amendment, and will give priority to working toward challenging and reversing that judicial doctrine;

---

2. Develop long-term strategies to strip for-profit corporations of the constitutional rights of natural persons, including but not limited to First, Fifth, and Fourteenth Amendment rights, and work toward the implementation of these strategies in collaboration with like-minded persons, groups, and movements;

3. The National Executive Committee send information on chartering and charter revocation to each chapter and urge the chapters to work with grassroots groups in their communities to explore the history and precedents for chartering and charter revocation in their states, and undertake together the public education and political organizing essential for effective action;

4. National Lawyers Guild chapters begin to monitor, in collaboration when possible with like-minded persons and groups, proposed changes in state Corporation codes, especially those being promoted by corporations and the American Bar Association, that insulate corporations even further from meaningful democratic control;

5. The Guild call on state attorneys general, legislators, and the judiciary to do their duty by upholding the rule of law and revoking corporate charters when corporations usurp the rights of sovereign people;

6. Guild lawyers are encouraged to explore with their clients ways in which, as they represent their clients' interests, the illegitimate authority of corporations can be challenged;

7. The Guild fight the denial of Bill of Rights protections to workers in the workplace;

8. The Guild invest resources and time in reconsidering the wisdom and appropriateness of granting business corporations limited liability;

9. Guild members, chapters, and committees are encouraged to undertake actions that will end corporate domination of our educational institutions. Actions include, but are not limited to, law student support of the *Democracy Teach-in* movement; the development of relevant course materials for law professors; law review and other scholarly articles, and educational events and dialogues among members, for example, the "Rethinking the Corporation, Rethinking Democracy" seminars;

10. The Guild recognizes the importance of communicating to the widest possible audience the story of the usurpation of the people's sovereignty by corporations and encourages development of written and audio-visual resources toward that end;

11. The Guild encourages its Committee on Corporations, the Constitution and Human Rights and other concerned members to provoke and sustain ferment with progressive teachers of corporate law;

12. Collaboration between, and support of, the diverse Guild efforts at fighting corporate power, such as the Sugar Law Center and HEED, is vital to an effective long-term strategy for fighting corporate power;

13. The Guild will be alert to the efforts of other individuals, groups, and peoples' movements to contest corporate power and will, whenever possible, encourage, support, and defend such efforts; and

14. The Guild recognizes that the ultimate enemy is the concentration of ownership and control of capital, and that the predatory class will continue to be motivated by its lust for wealth and power even as democratic control of corporations becomes more effective. ■

# STATEMENT TO THE DISTRICT OF COLUMBIA SUPERIOR COURT

*by Ward Morehouse*

---

ORTY YEARS AGO I began my professional life working in India. There I came to appreciate the enormous power of non-violent civil disobedience to advance constructive social change through the work of Mohandas Gandhi, one of the leaders of the Indian Freedom Movement.

In the early decades of the twentieth century, in the north of India in a celebrated case, Gandhi sought to help landless peasants claim their rights under British and Indian law. The local magistrate accused Gandhi of disturbing the peace and, therefore, violating the law. In explaining his actions to the courts, he issued a statement that concluded:

> I venture to make this statement not in any way in extenuation of the penalty to be awarded against me, but to show that I have disregarded the order served upon me not for want of respect for local authority, but in obedience to the higher law of our being—the voice of conscience.

So it was in this spirit, your Honor, that I disregarded the orders of the Capitol Police to cease political demonstrating in the Rotunda of the Capitol. For my conscience called on me to demand that all Americans have the right to universal health care, and that corporate money and all other forms of corporate influence be eliminated from the political process as it was in my home state of Wisconsin for a half-century until 1953. Until these happen, the democratic society we all desire for our country will remain an impossible dream. Therefore, your honor, I plead guilty in the service of democracy. ∎

---

# WORKERS' RIGHTS, CORPORATE PRIVILEGES

*by Peter Kellman*

---

I T IS TIME for labor to go beyond signing contracts with corporations. We need to start challenging the very concept of corporate privilege and rule.

The people of this country need to act on the understanding that We the People create corporations through our state legislatures. As the Pennsylvania Legislature declared in 1834: "A corporation in law is just what the incorporation act makes it. It is the creature of the law and may be molded to any shape or for the purpose the Legislature may deem most conducive for the common good."[1] If we don't mold corporations, they will continue to mold us. They will mold us at the expense of our rights, our health, our democracy, our communities, our environment, and most importantly our souls.

For almost 80 years labor's message has been primarily limited to protecting the interests of organized workers. But workers' rights don't exist in a vacuum. A fundamental law of physics can also be applied to politics—two things cannot occupy the same place at the same time. Workers' rights in this country have been relegated to a little space under a chair in the corner of a large room occupied by corporate "rights"— in quotes because only people can have rights, and corporations are not people.

People have *rights*, inalienable rights. Corporations have only the *privileges* We the People give them, because corporations are created by people. Corporations are not mentioned in the United States Constitution. Their privileges stem from Supreme Court cases, judge-made law. These federal judges are lawyers, appointed for life. In *Santa Clara County v. the Southern Pacific Railroad Co.* (1886), the Supreme Court of the United States declared that ". . . equal protection of the laws, applies to these corporations." The meaning of the Court was clear: corporations are persons under the law, deserving "equal protection."

Equal protection is a term used in the Fourteenth Amendment to bring African-Americans under constitutional protection. The activist Court of 1886 bestowed "equal protection" on the corporation. This transference of people's rights to corporate privilege has done much to create the present situation. The price of each expansion of corporate privilege has been a decrease in workers' rights.

Every day union people are confronted with this erosion of their rights in arenas such as union organizing, internal governance, political rights and authority over pension funds. One example is the court's role in diminishing the power of the Occupational Safety and Health Administration (OSHA) to the detriment of workers' rights.

OSHA was put in place by Congress in 1970. When you called up OSHA, it would send an investigator to your place of work. Corporate managers objected and went to court. They argued that the corporation should be afforded the same protection that flesh and blood people have under the Fourth Amendment against unreasonable searches of their property. They said OSHA inspectors needed a search warrant to inspect corporate property!

In 1978, with *Marshall v. Barlow*, the Supreme Court of the United States agreed. So the right of individual people to be protected from the government arbitrarily entering a person's home was extended to corporations. The Court ruled that corporations have the privilege to require OSHA inspectors to get a search warrant before entering corporate property to investigate the complaints of a worker regarding her health and welfare. In essence, the Court interpreted the obligation of the government to "promote the general Welfare" of workers to be secondary to the liberty of a corporation to prevent entry of a government inspector. In this case, while the OSHA inspector is getting a warrant from a judge, the corporation can clean up its act and avoid being found in violation of the law.

The OSHA case is but one example of how the granting of privileges to corporations diminishes the rights of workers. Another is the way corporate employers injected "employer free speech rights" into the process by which workers exercise their "right to associate" in choosing a union to represent them in the workplace.

Under the National Labor Relations Act of 1935 the National Labor Relations Board

(NLRB) required employer neutrality when it came to the self-organization of workers. That is, if an employer interfered in any way with a union organizing drive it was considered a violation of the Act. "The right of employees to choose their representatives when and as they wish is normally no more the affair of the employer than the right of the stockholders to choose directors is the affair of employees,"[2] stated the Board. However, with the 1947 passage of the Taft-Hartley Act (termed "the slave labor act" by labor), corporate privilege was inserted into labor rights and corporations were granted "free speech" in the union certification process.

The concept of "corporate free speech" in the union certification process may sound benign to the casual observer. However, if you are involved in a union organizing drive, the brutality of the corporate employer's use of "free speech" to usurp the workers' right to "freedom of association" becomes apparent in many ways. One example is called the "captive audience meeting" where the employer assembles workers together during working hours and harangues them on the negative effects of unionization. The corporate spokesperson will inject the notion that if the workers choose a union the company might take that as a sign that their facility might not be a good one in which to invest. The company spokesperson will point out that many union shops have been closed over the past couple of decades and the work moved to non-union areas of the country or offshore. The company uses "corporate free speech" to send a clear message: voting for a union means you are voting to close the facility. So much for a workers' right to "freely associate."

The OSHA unreasonable search and the Taft-Hartley corporate free speech cases are examples that illustrate you can't meaningfully assert workers' rights without undermining corporate privilege. But for years most of organized labor's activity has revolved around labor PACs giving money to people running for Congress. The money was followed by union leaders trying to convince union members to vote for endorsed "labor candidates." Then, when the new congress took office, labor lobbyists encourage politicians to support labor issues. The record isn't very good because the focus has been on the money being given to politicians instead of rank-and-file organizing which confronts corporate privilege. Labor will never outspend corporate interests. But we do have more members.

If labor abandoned its PACs and focused its energy on getting members involved in the process, think of the results. First, labor would develop an organization that would put resources into involving the membership in the political process rather than trying to influence politicians with money for their campaigns. Secondly, think of the message that labor would be sending by voluntarily giving up that corrupting influence on our body politic, the Political Action Committee.

The bottom line is that historically managers and large stockholders of corporations have a leg up on the rest of us. This process has gone on now for over 100 years and unlike the union people of a century ago, we no longer understand the origins of corporate privilege. So it is time to take another look. And out of that look needs to come an agenda created by working people that promotes workers' rights and challenges the roots of corporate privilege.

So what is labor to do? Labor should take a sabbatical for a year and use the time to analyze what we have been doing over the past century. Then, with history as a guide and real democratic participation of the membership, labor could put together a new agenda that promotes workers' rights and attacks corporate privileges. ∎

---

# Notes

[1] Goodrich 1967, p. 84.

[2] Brody 1998, p. 132.

# NINE SEMINARS

## AT THE 1996 PUBLIC INTEREST
## ENVIRONMENTAL LAW CONFERENCE

*by POCLAD*

---

## NINE SEMINARS ON CORPORATIONS,
## LAWYERS, DEMOCRACY, JUSTICE & THE LAW

The legal system of any country has a definite history which helps us to understand its provisions and shows how it changes according to varying social conditions, and even according to the will of certain powerful individuals.

- Professor Morris Raphael Cohen

## SEMINAR 1:
## STUDENT ORGANIZING INSIDE
## COLLEGE AND UNIVERSITY CORPORATIONS

The natures and roles of educational institutions (non-profit corporations) in a democracy; the role of students within colleges and universities, and in national political and social movements.

Spurred on by corporations, universities encourage professors to abandon class rooms for research centers and laboratories.[1]
- Lawrence C. Soley

[I]nsofar as a society is dominated by the attitudes of competitive business enterprise, freedom in its proper American meaning cannot be known, and hence, cannot be taught. That is the basic reason why the schools and colleges, which are, presumably, commissioned to study and promote the ways of freedom are so weak, so confused, so ineffectual.
- Alexander Meiklejohn

---

This article is published without copyright. POCLAD organized and facilitated nine seminars at the 1996 "Public Interest Environmental Law Conference" at the University of Oregon Law School, in Eugene (March 1996) which POCLAD co-convened and staffed. See "Revoking the Corporation" in this volume.

## SEMINAR 2:
## CORPORATE VIOLENCE AND LAWLESSNESS AGAINST WORKERS, POLITICAL ACTIVISTS AND THE ENVIRONMENT

> Force could be used when crisis demanded it, and the half-decade ending in 1920 certainly proved that employers would call upon any means at their disposal when their class position was in jeopardy.[2]
> - Richard Edwards

> The laws of the land are supported by the use of violence: that is, the use of physical force to make people obey the law.[3]
> - Myles Horton

## SEMINAR 3:
## CORPORATE LAWYERS AND JUDGES TRANSFORMING THE LAW

The various theories of the corporations; concocted legal doctrines and corporate law—the Commerce clause, personhood, loyalty, care, the business judgment rule; citizen sovereignty, federalism and states' rights; the disempowerment of stockholders.

## SEMINAR 4:
## GIANT CORPORATIONS ACTING AS POLITICAL BODIES

What large corporations are, what they do; the extent of corporate control over elections, law-making, jurisprudential thought, law, work, money, ideas, data, community, production, resources, education.

## SEMINAR 5:
## CITIZEN STRUGGLES AGAINST
## CORPORATE POWER IN THE 20TH CENTURY

How political and social movements have struggled against and conferred legitimacy upon the giant corporation; successes and failures, from anti-trust to environmental legislation, to worker and community uprisings; "feigned dissent" and false victories; the growth and diversion of popular movements; lessons to be learned.

## SEMINAR 6:
## ALTERNATIVES TO GIANT CORPORATIONS

Forging institutional, legal and cultural transitions; redirecting money and resources.

# SEMINAR 7:
## RETHINKING PROPERTY, REGULATORY
## AND ADMINISTRATIVE LAW AS CORPORATE SHIELDS

Intangible corporate "rights" as property; diverse ownership/use perspectives on real property; the reliance interest; liability; the impact of property doctrines upon regulatory and administrative law; regulatory and administrative agencies as barriers between the sovereign people and corporate fictions.


# SEMINAR 8:
## PEOPLE'S LAWYERS IN POPULAR OFFENSIVES
## AGAINST CORPORATE RULE:  WITHDRAWING CONSTITUTIONAL
## PROTECTIONS FROM CORPORATIONS

Legal strategizing and political organizing as part of citizen movements for justice; crafting new constitutional theory, arguments and law; revoking corporate charters; withdrawing personhood and other privileges and immunities from corporations; creative lawyering for defense and offense.

> . . . the lawyer is in reality an activist, shaping the ideas and concepts of bodies in existing law to serve the needs of the forces that the lawyer represents . . . If skilled lawyers for the corporation and for the government understand this fact and function this way in the interest of their establishment clients, why cannot lawyers for the people also fashion legal concepts into weapons of struggle to meet the needs of their clients?[4]
> - Arthur Kinoy


# SEMINAR 9:
## BUILDING A PLANETARY CORPORATE DISEMPOWERMENT AND
## DISMANTLING MOVEMENT

Where do we go from here?  Next steps.  ■

---

# NOTES

[1] Soley 1995.

[2] Edwards 1979.

[3] Horton, Kohl, *et al.*  1990.

[4] Kinoy 1983.

# CREATING A
# MODEL CORPORATION CODE
## ANOTHER AVENUE FOR ACTION

*by Ward Morehouse*

UNDER THE FEDERAL system of governance in the U.S. the states have authority to create corporations. The body of law setting forth the procedures for establishing a corporation and its objectives and powers is known as a "state corporate code." Each state has one.

For several decades the American Bar Association, through its committee on corporate law, has been helping state legislatures to "modernize" their corporation codes by making the codes more "business friendly." The result is that state corporation codes have become major obstacles in the struggle to build a truly democratic society based on the principle of self-governance.

Towards this end, an effort is underway to draft a model state corporation code that will make possible effective democratic control of corporations in a self-governing society. In its present form, this draft code is based on work done and ideas generated by Bennett Zurosky, Esq., Ward Morehouse, Eric Palmer, Thomas Linzey, Esq. of the Community Environmental Legal Defense Fund, and with comments from Jane Anne Morris.

Many of the provisions of this model code were found in corporate charters issued by various states in the early decades of national independence of the United States: time limited charters (30 years or less), incorporation for a specific public purpose, charter revocation if that purpose was not being fulfilled, and prohibition of one corporation owning other corporations.

Other provisions grapple with current assaults on constitutional rights of natural persons, rights which have been appropriated by present-day corporations, including due process, equal protection, personhood, free speech, and privacy (all acquired through a series of judicial decisions).

Still other provisions stipulate that corporations not engage in any activity which raises threats to human health and the environment, including common property such as air, water, and wildlife, and that they observe the precautionary principle of proving a product or process as "safe" before making or using it. In a similar manner, the model corporation code prohibits corporations from abridging the privileges or immunities of their employees under the U.S. Constitution or the constitution of the state issuing the charter, including First Amendment rights of free speech and association. It also establishes that the leading

---

This article is provided without copyright. See "Revolutionizing Corporate Law," "Corporations for the Seventh Generation," and "Wrong Turn in Ohio," "The Corporate Crunch in Vermont," and "A Quick Look at What Happened in New Mexico" for more information on corporation codes.

officials and major investors in a corporation be held liable for certain types of debts.

The drafters of this model corporation code are under no illusions that it will be easily adopted or will solve the problem of corporate rule in the United States or elsewhere in the world. The political culture will need to change in such a way that corporations will be compelled to accept democratic control. But corporation codes based on the principle of self-governance by the people are one element in an unfolding strategy of creating a truly democratic society.

The latest draft of this code is available at www.cipa-apex.org. This draft code is very much a work in progress. Comments and suggestions may be sent to Ward Morehouse at P.O. Box 337, Croton-on-Hudson, NY 10520 (email cipany@igc.org). ■

# STRIP CORPORATIONS OF THEIR CLOAKING DEVICE

*by Jane Anne Morris*

There is looming up a new and dark power . . . the enterprises of the country are aggregating vast corporate combinations of unexampled capital, boldly marching, not for economical conquest only, but for political power. It is unscrupulous, arrogant, and overbearing . . . The question will arise and arise in your day . . . which will rule—wealth or man [sic]; which shall lead—money or intellect; who shall fill public stations—educated and patriotic freemen, or the feudal serfs of corporate capital?

- Chief Justice Ryan of the Wisconsin Supreme Court addressing the UW Law Class of 1873.

WHO SPENDS THE most time in federal courts complaining that their "due process" and "equal protection under the law" rights have been violated? Pushy women? Uppity Blacks? Gray Panthers? Illegal Mexicans? The Sandhill Crane Militia? HIV-positive Navy gunners? You really don't know, do you?

None of the above.

Plaintiffs in such cases are most often large corporations.

That's because before women gained the right to vote, long before Blacks could eat lunch at a drugstore counter, corporations were granted the rights of "natural persons" under the Fourteenth Amendment.

The Fourteenth Amendment (1868) to the U.S. Constitution reads in part:

[No state shall] deprive any person of life, liberty or property, without due process of law; nor deny to any person within its jurisdiction the equal protection of the laws.

The Fourteenth Amendment was passed in 1868 to guarantee to Blacks, especially former slaves, the full protection of the U.S. Constitution and Bill of Rights.

Thanks to an 1886 Supreme Court decision (*Santa Clara v. Southern Pacific Railroad Co.*), since questioned but not yet struck down, corporations are now able to use the Fourteenth Amendment to fight against the government that created them and the people who try to control them.

Corporation lawyers wrapped the fictive corporations they represented in the mantle of personhood and then made their pilgrimage to the highest court in the land. There in 1886 the Supreme Court sanctified the corporate cloaking device that would enable them to elude and evade the will of the people who created them.

What does "personhood" do for corporations?

• It gives them grounds to question in court any government action.

- Along with other legal doctrines, it makes it easier for them to gain a forum in federal courts and thereby escape the state courts, which are usually more reflective of the will of the sovereign people.

- It expands the power of appointed-for-life federal judges to essentially make law.

Think of it this way: Before 1886, people tried to *define* corporations to serve the public interest. This is appropriate for entities that were created for just that purpose. But after 1886, corporations had the rights of constitutional persons, and so the government was reduced to trying futilely to *regulate* them instead.

The constitutional scholar Walton H. Hamilton described the effect of the Fourteenth Amendment in this way:

> A constitutional doctrine contrived to protect the natural rights of men [sic] against corporate monopoly was little by little commuted into a formula for safeguarding the domain of business against the regulatory power of the state.

As countless court cases have affirmed, the purpose of corporations is to serve the public interest. Corporations are created by the sovereign people acting through state legislatures. As legal fictions existing to serve the people, they have no rights or even existence outside of the people's will.

This is not the same thing as saying that corporations should have no rights of any kind. The people, acting through legislatures, may decide that corporations of a certain kind should have the right to sue and be sued; or, the right to be treated similarly to other corporations in the same class. The people may declare that corporations and their officers are subject to criminal prosecution. They may decide that small, local, independent businesses should have rights not extended to huge multinational chains.

But such rights, if appropriate, should be granted singly and consciously, and not as part of a vague judge-made package deal that starts out by giving corporations the rights of "natural persons."

No referendum was ever held on whether corporations should have the natural rights of human persons. No legislature ever passed a bill giving corporations such rights.

We agree with Justice William O. Douglas, who stated in a famous 1948 Supreme Court dissent of *Wheeling Steel Corp. v. Glander*:

> If they [the people] want corporations to be treated as humans are treated, if they want to grant corporations this large degree of emancipation from state regulation, they should say so. The Constitution provides a method by which they may do so. We should not do it for them through the guise of interpretation.

At Democracy Unlimited we concur with Justice Douglas when he said, "I can only conclude that the *Santa Clara* case was wrong and should be overruled." Why wait around?

Democracy Unlimited of Wisconsin is circulating a petition in support of a Wisconsin constitutional amendment that states that in Wisconsin, corporations are not persons with the constitutional rights of persons.

If such an amendment were passed, it would immediately be challenged and could even reach the U.S. Supreme Court. It will not be the first time that our fair state places itself at the forefront to insure that government of the people and by the people does not perish from this Earth.

Let's remove this obscene cloaking device that gives corporations more rights than you. ∎

# LABOR PARTY RESOLUTION

*by the Labor Party*

---

## WHEREAS:

- The Bill of Rights of the United States Constitution does not protect us against the denial of our rights by private concentrations of power and wealth; and

- Whereas, we have wrongly come to accept that *at work* we are not entitled to the rights and privileges we normally enjoy as citizens; and

- Whereas, private wealth has made sure to convince the Supreme Court that although a corporation is not a living person it is afforded the protections and rights of the Bill of Rights, while living persons at work are denied these same protections; and

- Whereas, we therefore find that the corporations and Congress through current law have turned democracy exactly *backward*:

  At work, we are guilty unless proven innocent;
  At work, we obey orders upon penalty of discharge;
  At work, our most fundamental right, that of free speech, does not apply;
  At work, we cannot freely associate with others to protect our interests;
  At work, we have to qualify for rights, forced to take extraordinary efforts to win representation elections, gain government certification, and bargain for employer recognition of even minimal rights.   On the other hand, the corporations are assumed to possess civil rights, do not have to gain such rights, and consequently have more rights under the law than do people, including their "right" to free speech, hold captive meetings of their employees, and express political opinions; and

- Whereas, working peoples' efforts to organize unions and bargain collectively is now made, because of the very imbalance in civil rights and economic power, to be extremely difficult in all workplaces and almost impossible in some sectors of the economy; and

- Whereas, our usual political remedies calls for labor law "reform" and more efficient regulatory agencies miss the main point which is that any legislation or agency that seeks to restrict a corporate "person's" freedom will be rejected, and such efforts have in fact failed miserably under both Democratic and Republican Party administrations; and

- Whereas, in Japan, Canada and throughout Europe, the very countries who are our trading partners, competitors and national peers, there already exists long-standing methods that recognize civil rights at work, including those for forming unions, bargaining collectively, and

---

This article is provided without copyright.  It is a resolution passed at the "First Constitutional Convention of the Labor Party" (November 1998).   See related article "Toward a New Labor Law" in this volume.

otherwise dealing with the employers; and finally

- Whereas, million of U.S. workers are *at this moment* anxious and willing to form unions and bargain with their employers over matters of concern, and are ready to add their huge numbers to our union ranks. In other countries comparable to the United States, these workers would be free to speak, associate, organize unions and bargain with their employees.

## THEREFORE BE IT RESOLVED THAT:

1. The Labor Party rejects the *status quo* of today's workplace where workers are forced to abandon their Constitutional Rights in order to earn their living, and are as a consequence subject to the tyranny of the corporation.

2. The Labor Party demands that workers have the actual right to concerted activity, free from employer involvement or interference, and that *any number of interested workers in a workplace* must have the right to form a union and bargain with their employer.

3. The Labor Party insists that all workers must have the ability to exercise their rights to concerted activity irrespective of job titles and responsibilities, citizenship status, method of payment, or sector of the economy in which employed.

4. The Labor Party holds that workers, including workfare, contingent, part-time, temporary, and contract workers, must have the right to bargain over the terms and conditions of their labor with the employer(s) who controls or influences their work environment irrespective of ownership title.

5. The Labor Party insists upon the restoration of all rights to free association including the voluntary joining together to redress grievances by strikes, economic boycotts, sympathy actions, "hot cargo" agreements, and common situs picketing.

6. The Labor Party rejects limits on subjects upon which employees and unions may bargain with employers.

7. In order for this Campaign to be advanced, the Labor Party commits itself to:

   a. Popularize this Campaign through Labor Party communications and with unions affiliated to the Labor Party;

   b. Select a state in which to develop a state-based campaign to reform state labor relations laws and statutes in accordance with the above principles;

   c. Select a state which presently does not permit collective bargaining rights for public employees in which to develop a state-based campaign for rights in accordance with the above principles;

   d. Select a city or other location in which to popularize, build support around, and in other ways make real the Labor Party's campaign to bring the Bill of Rights into the workplace;

   e. Conduct educational work within the trade union movement helping all of us to rethink what we mean by workplace rights, to learn what is the practice in other countries similar to the United States, and how the current imbalance between corporations and individual rights has evolved in our own country, and how the Labor Party proposes to change this; and

   f. Support the formation of committees of fired workers wherever possible to organize and support their fight for workers' rights. ■

# POINT ARENA
# CITY COUNCIL RESOLUTION

*by Alis Valencia & Jan Edwards*

O N APRIL 25, 2000, the City
Council of Point Arena,
California, passed by a vote of
four to one, a non-binding resolution that
challenges the concept of corporate personhood. Why this is significant:

• This is the first such action taken in the
United States.

• It represents a new strategy designed to
define corporate power. Rather than use
incentives and regulations to guide corporate behavior—practices that at best
result in incremental gains in the public
interest—the citizens of Point Arena
have asserted their democratic right to
challenge a fundamental aspect of corporate existence. They have taken a step to
assert sovereignty over corporations.

• Communities and groups across the United
States and Canada are pursuing comple-
mentary tactics designed to define what
corporations can and cannot do.

• These activities are manifestations of a
new movement supporting the spread of
political and economic democracy.

## BACKGROUND

The Supreme Court first gave corporations, a legal creation, personhood (for

purposes of the Fourteenth Amendment)
in an 1886 decision.[1] Corporations have
used this court-assigned status since the
late nineteenth century to advocate successfully for having the protections and rights
granted to people by the U.S. Constitution
and Bill of Rights—with the complicity of
the courts and legislature. As a consequence, corporations have been able to
limit governmental efforts at regulation,
constrain the workings of democracy, and
subordinate the rights of people.

Members of the Redwood Coast Chapter
of the Alliance for Democracy were inspired
to challenge corporate personhood by the
work of the Program on Corporations, Law
and Democracy (POCLAD), an organization devoted to "instigating democratic conversations and actions that contest the
authority of corporations to govern."
Alliance members engaged members of the
community of Point Arena in learning about
corporate personhood, its history and consequences, and the consequences of revoking
it. They then placed a Resolution on
Corporate Personhood before the City
Council. Following sessions of public
debate and revisions of the original document, the City Council adopted the following resolution.

## Resolution on Corporate Personhood in the City of Point Arena

- Whereas, the Citizens of the City of Point Arena hope to nurture and expand democracy in our community and our nation; and

- Whereas, democracy means governance by the people and only natural persons should be able to participate in the democratic process; and

- Whereas, interference in the democratic process by corporations frequently usurps the rights of citizens to govern; and

- Whereas, corporations are artificial entities separate and apart from natural persons, are not naturally endowed with conscious-

ness or the rights of natural persons, are creations of law and are only permitted to do what is authorized under law; and

- Whereas, rejecting the concept of corporate personhood will advance meaningful campaign finance reform.

- Now, therefore, be it resolved that: the City Council of the City of Point Arena agrees with Supreme Court Justice Hugo Black in a 1938 opinion in which he stated, "I do not believe the word 'person' in the Fourteenth Amendment includes corporations;"[2] and

Be it further resolved that the City of Point Arena shall encourage public discussion on the role of corporations in public life and urge other cities to foster similar public discussion. ∎

---

## Notes

[1] *Santa Clara v. Southern Pacific Railroad Co.*

[2] *Connecticut General Life Insurance Company v. Johnson, Treasurer of California*, p. 82.

# CERTIFICATE OF DISSOLUTION: WEYERHAEUSER CORPORATION

*by Asante Riverwind & Paloma Galindo*

---

THE WEYERHAEUSER COMPANY is guilty of gross felony criminal conduct. Weyerhaeuser is licensed in the name of the citizens of Washington. The company is mandated to operate within the bounds of law, and for the long term interests and well-being of the people and communities of the state. Instead they have repeatedly violated state, local, and federal law; irreparably degraded the environment of the Northwest, Canada, Asia, and other areas worldwide; are one of the major causes in the irretrievable and impending extinction of numerous salmon runs; are responsible for repeated releases of carcinogens and toxic pollutants; have violated Native sovereignty claims, treaty rights, and destroyed numerous Native sacred sites; illegally obtained much of their lands through fraudulent railroad land grant schemes; have played a dominant role in the corporate control and corruption of Congress and the American political system through corporate financing/buying politicians; have consistently deceived the public (re: "the tree growing company") to hide the fact that they have clear-cut over 4 million acres and continue to profit from the exportation of the ecological heritage of the Northwest while mills and communities suffer the economic consequences; and are one of the responsible parties for the continuing decline and imperilment of the spotted owl, marbled murrelet, goshawk, pine marten, fisher, bull trout, rainbow trout, steelhead, salmon, and numerous other wildlife and aquatic species.

The Weyerhaeuser corporation is in violation of Washington criminal codes 9A.08.030 and 9A.28.040. The requirements of these laws and the decrees of Washington State laws 23B.14.300, 24.03.265, 24.03.250, 23B14.330 provide for the involuntary dissolution and the seizure of its assets. These assets are to be used to provide for the restoration of the degraded lands (providing employment for generations), the economic well being of affected dependent communities, restitution to Native peoples including the return of Native lands, and compensation to peoples of other countries for irreparable damages caused by the company in their illegal, destructive quest for profits.

The people of the U.S. retain the unalterable right to revoke the charter of corporations which violate the common good. Originally, after the American Revolution, charters were rarely grant-

---

ed, and often revoked—with their assets distributed to compensate for damages and the corporate owners held accountable for their criminal acts. Today we are re-invoking this right. In addition, the inalienable rights of the existence of numerous species of life upon this Earth demand this revocation. Therefore be it ordained, by the powers of the laws of Washington State and the higher laws of Nature, that the corporate charter of Weyerhaeuser be revoked and the said company dissolved.

Dated this 16th of April, 1995.

## THE WEYERHAEUSER CORPORATION: ON THE RECORD

• By its own estimate, since 1900 Weyerhaeuser has clear-cut four million acres; of that 600,000 acres have not been replanted.

• Weyerhaeuser has or has had subsidiaries in the Philippines, Indonesia, and Malaysia. Weyerhaeuser's Pacific Hardwoods is the fourth-largest saw timber and fifth-largest plywood exporter from Malaysia. The tally in Asia: two million acres clear-cut.

• Raw exports, speeding deforestation while sending jobs overseas, low pulp prices and high chip prices resulted in the following mill closures: Snoqualmie, WA mill in 1989; Longview, WA B mill in 1991; Springfield, OR mill in 1991; Klamath Falls, WA mill in 1992. Other mills reduced or ceased production to avoid the expenditure of $40 million in air and water pollution control investments, though the corporation had received tax breaks to do so (worth $19 million in 1992).

• The Washington State Assistant Attorney General called the company's salvage logging by the Toutle River "the largest and most blatant violation of the State Shoreline Act."

• Court order for monopolistic dissolution in 1906.

• Indicted in 1940 with Boise Cascade and Potlatch for anti-trust violations. Potlatch and Boise Cascade incorporated by and remain linked to Weyerhaeuser.

• Convicted and fined for price fixing in 1978 (along with Boise Cascade and Potlatch). Fined $54 million.

• Potentially responsible party at 13 Superfund sites, ranks fourth-worst in the industry.

- From 1985 to 1991, the Washington Department of Ecology recorded 137 pollution notices, orders and/or penalties against Weyerhaeuser.

- De Queen, Arkansas, wood treating plant leaked pentachlorophenol & other chemicals into groundwater.

- Cosmopolis/Aberdeen Washington, violated the Clean Water Act, for paint waste and wash-water dumped into Shannon Slough for nine years.

- For their activities in Longview, Washington, they paid the largest penalty assessed for dangerous waste violations: unlabeled tanks and drums, and pentachlorophenol "spilling onto the ground" with "a potential for the material to get into the Columbia River."

- Aberdeen, Washington, lawsuits over health effects of pulp mill waste ponds; 241 residents sought damages in individual suits, with nose bleeds, sore throats, lung disease, and cancer caused by hydrogen sulfide, sulfuric acid, and chloroform.

- Operations in 44 states and 19 countries, ranking number 7 out of 20 timber companies in raw toxic releases.

- Dioxin cancer risk noted in four plants in 1988 EPA study and 1990 EPA listing.

- Ranked third of all companies for occupational safety and health violations.

- Political connections: Weyerhaeuser heir Booth Gardner was Governor of Washington, during the 1980's and the U.S. ambassador to GATT in 1993. W. Ruckleshaus, company director since 1976, was administrator of the EPA. R. Ingersoll, another company director, was U.S. ambassador to Japan and Deputy Secretary of State. Political contributions ranked 51 out of 100 companies (1992).

- Profited from numerous public taxpayer subsidized buy-backs of logged land originally acquired as federal government railroad land grants at little or no cost to the company.

- Public subsidized dredging to allow export vessels to reach the company docks on the Chehalis river ($43.6 million) and the Coos Bay channel to facilitate exporting of raw lumber. ∎

# Point of Departure

Let's take it from here. We're in good company.

# REACHING BACK, DIGGING DEEP
## STRATEGIES IN CONTEXT

*by Virginia Rasmussen*

A S ACTIVISTS WHO struggle to put people and not corporations in charge of our lives and governance, who seek real and sustainable victories toward that goal, it is vital that we link our dissent, our strategies and our vision to their roots.

Alexander Mieklejohn, a thoughtful student and teacher on matters of the Constitution and the First Amendment, was right when he suggested that "we underestimate . . . the task of using our minds [and I would add 'our hearts'], to which we are summoned by our plan of government." Indeed, for activists, understandings and undertakings that do not reach deep, that are insufficiently informed by the history and worldview that brought us our present, will greatly exhaust our energies and weakly reward our hopes. In the critical work of ending corporate dominance and building real democracy, we must always be on guard against the threat of deradicalism.

I'd like to introduce three realms of our work where these roots must play a critiquing and clarifying role if we are to celebrate true rather than false victories.

The *first realm* is associated with *how we take things in*: how we listen, our habits of noticing, our care in reading and commenting. We can learn and we can teach only that for which our receptors are tuned. If we tune our minds and our hearts rigorously and radically, we will have a chance of bringing just and democratic betterment. But if we are tuned imprecisely, the hard work of learning, teaching, planning, organizing, mobilizing too often ends in the mere shuffling of things rather than genuine change.

The *second realm* to which roots and rigor must be brought to bear is in the *kind of strategies* we design into our campaigns against corporate power. These strategies need to reflect an understanding of the current "rule of law" that puts We the People subordinate to the propertied few organized in their corporate forms, and they must reflect our commitment to reversing that law. In addition, our strategies and actions must make the case for redefining what corporations *are* and what they *do*, rather than merely reducing the damage from what they do *wrong*.

The *third realm* to which we must bring critically fundamental thought and feeling relates to our vision of what is possible. For us to propose that people have the capacity for true, inclusive, democratic self-governance is to place ourselves within a worldview and set of assumptions wholly contradictory to the patriarchal worldview that brought us our present earthly and human predicament. We

This article is published without a copyright. It is a transcript of Virginia Rasmussen's keynote speech at the "End Corporate Dominance" conference held in Portland, Oregon (May 2000).

must, therefore, incorporate into our learning and our political work at every level this larger kind of contextual understanding. Without the opportunity to effectively engage this conversation, people will flounder, will be highly skeptical that anything better is possible from us human beings.

## THE FIRST REALM

Let's examine more closely the first realm, that of awakening and tuning our receptors so that we hear, read and speak *with a radical precision.* We know that our activist and public mind suffers from "mush syndrome" as a consequence of our corporate grooming, from those subtle and not so subtle messages, biases and MISinformation that rain down on us relentlessly. They leave us with minds congealed, self-governing impulses dulled, our demands for the removal of myriad of corporate abuses shrunken to pleadings for a little less harm.

And these mind-numbing messages don't always originate in corporate boardrooms, or willful, mind-shaping advertisements or government bodies speaking in support of corporate privilege. We activists contribute to it, as well. When our words and language lack precision, when our work or proposals are without thoughtful analysis, our cause suffers because our words are received by those who trust us, who want to believe us, who may even wish to join us.

There is, for example, no historical "golden age" that will provide "the answer" to the worsening corporate destruction of life, communities, law, government and culture. The Program on Corporations, Law and Democracy set forth, more directly than others, the history of the nineteenth century's state chartering approach to allowable corporate activity. And yes, charters were revoked, accompanied by some brilliant judicial language reflecting the sovereignty of humble citizens and all that. But we are in one hell of a mess today. So that "chartering thing" might hold a piece of the answer, but we know it is not so simple as this single measure in isolation of many others, and we do damage to our work and its possibilities by not interrupting that wrong perception.

We hear calls from the political podium during this 2000 election campaign to revisit the heyday of the "regulatory seventies," to find therein appropriate responses to the corporate abominations of this new century. And what a heyday that was. I remember it well: the National Environmental Policy Act, Clean Air Act, Federal Water Pollution Control Act, Toxic Substances Control Act, Resource Conservation and Recovery Act, the Endangered Species Act, the Occupational Safety and Health Act, the Consumer Product Safety Act ... It leaves one breathless!

I was teaching environmental studies at the time and thought I had died and gone to ecological heaven. But we're in a hell of a mess today. So perhaps in the guts and gusto of that era there rests a piece of the answer. But given that the OSHA prosecuted only 14 cases of industrial negligence in 20 years, with only 10 convictions and no jail time, our confidence should be shaken. Knowing that in the 20 years after the passage of the Clean Air Act not a single toxic pollutant from industrial sources was yet being regulated by the EPA should give us great pause. When we learn that it took the FDA 25 years to restrict the use of cancer-causing red dyes in food while it endured 28 corporate-pressured delays, we get more than a clue about the power corporate boardrooms wield over those laws and agencies.[1]

Singing the praises of the regulatory era of the seventies will not forward our goal to end corporate governance and build democracy. We must meet such praise with a critique that opens the way for learning the whole, sorry regulatory story[2] and its meaning for our work.

We often hear from activists that our work must be about insisting on corporate "social responsibility," about "taming" or "reining in" the monster in our midst, about making it "behave" better, sign a conduct code, be a better "neighbor." But such requests deny the current nature and mandate of this creation of ours that's driving economic life. This corporate form is a thing, it's *not* a person; it does not possess the capacity for responsibility, for neighborliness. And when the chips are down, when competition is tough, when consumption isn't up to last year's maximum, "responsible" isn't part of the mandate, "neighborliness" gets snipped right off the corporate agenda. People and organizations that champion corporate responsibility in the struggle against corporate afflictions hand corporations opportunities for public relations maneuvers that stunt public understanding of what we're really up against.

Jane Anne Morris, in a recent article in POCLAD's publication *By What Authority*, put it this way:

> The notions of corporate trusteeship, the civic duty of a corporation, corporate citizenship, corporate social responsibility and the corporate social audit—all originated in the desire of corporate managers to thwart unionization, forestall revolt, avoid government action, and, above all, retain control by shaping public debate.[3]

Building democracy in which *people* govern means putting *all* creations of We the People subordinate to us. That is, *we* are responsible for designing processes and institutions that *define* corporate bodies, and when the need arises, in order to heal damage they might inflict on any aspect of our human and planetary life, any aspect of the body politic, *we* REdefine those creations. That's what sovereignty and democracy mean. We may seek information from people associated with a corporation. But we seek and accept from them no advice, we brook no interference, we abide no threats or promises, no lies or distortions, no pressuring, delays or dilutions. The marketplace of corporate entities—whether they be for the conduct of business or health care or education or entertainment or communication—should be subservient to the people. To bring others to a movement on behalf of real democracy means to bring others to that rigorous attitude about the relationship between people and their corporations.

How do we engender a culture of care and clarity about our sovereign status? We take time, we take notice, we practice and we engage others in practicing precision. In the Women's International League for Peace and Freedom, we have set up study groups within a campaign titled "Challenging Corporate Power, Asserting the People's Rights." The study groups will apply their learning to a campaign around a local corporation that has usurped the rights and powers that belong to citizens. During this work we have people critique news items, e-mail pieces, columns, public or corporate utterances. It allows easy conversation, wide participation. Sadly, there's juicy material everywhere around us.

As an example, the following message came through the e-mail to our office a few weeks ago from the national field office of a major social justice organization. It registers enthusiasm for recent developments around the gun control issue in the U.S. Here is the heart of their statement:

Smith and Wesson, the nation's largest gun manufacturer, agreed last week to change the way it designs, distributes and markets guns. In exchange, the Clinton administration agreed to drop a threatened lawsuit against the company. The agreement marks the first big concession by industry to the mounting public and political pressure for stronger gun controls.

Note the word "corporation" is never used. This is typical of so much reporting and even activist language. We see in place of the word "corporation," references such as "industry," or "manufacturer," or "big business," or "big tobacco," or "business enterprise." Yet it's the "corporation" that is the legal actor and it's the corporation identifier that *must* be used again and again and again if the public is to make the appropriate connection between assault and assaulter.

Note that the corporation is acknowledged as autonomous and in charge. It "agreed to" take such an action; that the people of this country are taken to be subordinate, the mere beneficiaries of this corporation's decision; that the people's government is simply a negotiator with the corporation; and notice the perception of "victory" as a concession brought about by public pressure, rather than a policy change as a result of citizen instruction!

Being tuned to the verbal signals all around us and within our own activist world, talking together about their significance in shaping thought, attitude and behavior can help us as a people begin to define the public interest for ourselves, to yank it from the corporate grip and agenda, and thus make change toward a democratic reality possible. Is this not a critical piece of our daily work?

So how have these corporations we've created acquired this advanced stage of INsubordination? Must we not know this story before we can change this story? If we

are oblivious to it, is not much of our labor for change a labor of pretense? This brings us to the second realm in which our dissent, made real through the strategies and actions we devise, must be connected to its roots if it is to help us take the journey we hope to take.

## THE SECOND REALM

We know that corporate dominance arises out of legal designations and powers corporations possess, designations and powers that are simply absurd. The key ones being:

- The absurdity that corporations—despite their creation by the people to serve the people—were held by the courts to be *private institutions*, off bounds to public definition and control. What a dangerous master stroke of judicial politics! Ah yes, the courts in 1937 allowed regulatory laws,[4] but these laws, standards and enforcement patterns are in the clutches of corporate rule-making, not people's rule-making. Why do giant business corporations continue to make the rules? Because while regulatory laws were okayed, the economy was not placed subservient to the people. Maximum production of absolutely everything and maximum competition remained the goals of the corporate capitalist economy, goals that had become the protected private property of so-called "private" corporations. Any interference with those goals was therefore unlawful, and the might of the nation could be arrayed in full against any who would threaten those corporate liberties declared "property" by the courts.

- The absurdity that corporations have "rights" granted them by courts and legislatures over the years. Surely it is only people who have rights. Our creations merely have privileges which we give them and which we can withdraw as we see fit.

- The absurdity that corporations are "persons" under the law with Bill of Rights protections and the protections of due process of law over their "life," liberty and property. This absurdity put a high wall between us and our creations, provides them cover against *our* defining what they do, how they do it, the contracts they may or may not make, the rights and protections they give to workers, communities, the Earth, the people. Decisions over all those things are their private property, said the courts. The people and their legislatures were left out in the cold, cold consequences of these very political-judicial decisions.

Indeed, Lawrence Friedman, in his book *A History of American Law*, writes that the "courts turned corporate practice into law. The general trend was for law to allow corporations to do whatever they wished, to exercise any power, to build up the freedom of corporate management." In time there developed a kind of "national free market in laws," and "the corporation escaped the chains fashioned by earlier generations," i.e., the chartering process.

What was the corporate route to such usurpation? What door in our nation's early structure was left ajar, inviting such a corporate takeover? This was a nation that established a way of life and of governing that gave first priority to property, not to people. Nearly all people, as we know, were *not* persons under the law, but were either non-persons or property. All the inevitable crap that would eventually reveal itself from such an ordering of trust and value is now hitting the fan. Here we have a governmental set up that makes its first priority the protection of private property, and grants to its courts (not to the people through their political arenas) the power to define "property" and extend to it "rights" in excess of those it extends to people. Should

we be surprised that such an arrangement of importance, over time, has private property governing natural persons?

The colonists, at the outset, had no intention of granting to corporations property's associative form, such overwhelming power. They sought to keep it in check through the chartering and revocation process. Their goal was to put economic life under the control of the people through their legislatures. But such "chains" were not strong enough to contain the growing might of corporate capitalism's nineteenth century rise, and its ruthlessness in getting the courts, legislatures and the law to serve their propertied interests. Friedman mentions that "corporations confronted law at every point. In all the great cases on rate-making, labor relations, and social welfare, corporations were litigants, bystanders, protagonists or devils." Indeed, from the beginning the courts were authorized to define property and to protect it from the threat of democracy. And in those courts the corporation was property's business and political vehicle for concentrating wealth and power.

This history of the corporation's road to power, with the help of public officials, legislatures and courts that handed over the rights and responsibilities of citizens all along the way, brought us today's frightening and oppressive realities. These corporations, with a mission to produce absolutely everything at the cost of absolutely anything, are now positioned to *define it all*: values, work, production, investment, politics, law, trade, the environment, education, entertainment, sport, culture, crops, soil, genes.

It's this history that brought forth the World Trade Organization (WTO). Corporate powers to govern and define, gained by giant corporations in this country, are now being written into the laws of other countries and into international trade agreements and corporate trade bodies all around the world. As we know, the WTO is an instrument of law-making and enforcing by giant corporations that run roughshod over democracy. Yet, the WTO is a creation of governments, the most powerful of which are so-called democracies! So getting the WTO off the scene will not, in itself, take with it the pathological sources from which its anti-democratic, anti-labor, anti-community, anti-Earth policies spring. Our primary focus needs to be in this country, pulling out the pathological tap root of virulent, illegitimate corporate law and power along with the government complicity that made it possible.

As an example, it's this history that now bears down on the Commonwealth of Massachusetts, as its law of 1996, imposing restrictions on state purchases from corporations doing business with Burma, stands before the nine great robed ones in the Supreme Court. The people of the Commonwealth knew that to do business with Burma is to do business with the Burmese military junta, is to collude with massive assaults upon human beings, democracy and the natural world in that country. So the people asserted their sovereign authority to define state expenditures, their collective resources, in relation to chosen standards.

But we soon discover yet again that our governmental bodies and courts of law are far readier to protect the sweeping, illegitimate rights of corporate property and corporate commerce than they are to protect and defend democracy, not only in Burma or any other foreign country, but also within the Commonwealth of Massachusetts or any other state.

Hot on the heels of the Massachusetts statute came a suit against the state by the National Foreign Trade Council (NFTC), one of those non-profit shills for the corporations. Its nearly 600 members consist of manufacturing and financial corporations, 34 of which are listed in the Massachusetts "Restricted Burma Purchase List." There's a lot of oil and gas and timber in what is now called the Union of Myanmar. The NFTC sued on the basis that selective purchase law encroaches on U.S. foreign policy, reserved for the federal government under the supremacy clause, and that the Constitution prohibits states and localities from regulation or taxation if such measures burden interstate or foreign commerce (can't interfere with all those goods moving around no matter the reason, can we?).

Alas, in 1998 Boston's Federal District Court, in a decision later upheld by a Federal Court of Appeals, affirmed the corporations' Trade Council complaint on the grounds that this purchasing limitation was an interference with the U.S. government's ability to manage foreign affairs and that the free flow of commerce was, indeed, burdened.

Just seven weeks ago the Massachusetts Attorney General's office, with support from 78 congressional representatives, including the entire Massachusetts delegation, and 22 state attorneys general, took this matter before the United States Supreme Court. What argument did the Attorney General wage in defending the right of the people of the Commonwealth to pass such legislation?

- Is there reflected in the legal strategy a claim to the right of natural persons, allegedly the source of political authority in the U.S., to require legislators to serve the popular will?

- Is there anything in their strategy about this law being the voice of the sovereign people with authority to act against our corporate creations that do business with an oppressive regime, a business in stuff that ultimately enslaves and kills?

- Is justification made for the right of a Commonwealth to apply *any* standard in the spending of its collective money, and certainly not to be hassled by its creations, those "private" business corporations, that go whining and crying to the federal courts to protect their autonomy and wealth?

- Is there any question raised about whether these corporations, hiding behind their corporate shill, the NFTC, are exceeding their authority in this country of presumably self-governing people?

All of the above were either absent or peripheral in the arguments before the court. Instead, the case is being defended primarily out of a state position wholly subordinate to property and to corporate power, that this is about *consumer* rights and power. Sadly, there is no argument made that this legal and judicial matter is most *fundamentally about democracy and citizen power in Massachusetts* and only then is it about democracy in Burma.

"Oh no," says the Massachusetts Attorney General, "we're not interfering with the Commerce clause, why we're just consumers, exercising our purchasing power, just participating in the marketplace, not regulating it, not trying to be in charge of it! We're just doing a little politics while we're shopping, like any 'private actor' (hear 'corporation') would enjoy as a matter of contract and property rights." No talk of sovereignty in that thinking. Notice the state, clamoring, pleading really, to have equal power with its own creation, the now "private" corporation.

Massachusetts is also standing before that big Supreme Court and saying the equivalent of "Hey, if private corporations can stop doing business with Burma (and many have, by the way), then why can't we? If they can do it, so can a state; gee whiz, it's only fair." Again, pleading for rights equal to that of the "private" business corporation we should be sovereign over. Truly, this is the language, behavior and strategy of blubbering supplicants!

We are witness here to a strategy of capitulation. By playing for a chance to win, we lose no matter the outcome.[5] The story of the Massachusetts Burma Law in the courts could have been more than a ripple against the strong, destructive current of corporate rule. It could have been intended and designed very differently—in its language and arguments, its urgency, its vision and context, in the way our state's political leaders might have brought it forth as a public issue, raising holy hell around it. It could have put wind in the sails of democracy, of sovereignty, of citizens taking charge of their corporate bodies. But that's not to be. Yet this largely pitiful defense of the Burma law reminds us activists that if our own strategies are carefully, thoughtfully designed within the rigorous framework of our self-governing rights, if we fully stretch ourselves in the direction we wish to move, then democratic movement is inevitable despite immediate wins or losses.

## THE THIRD REALM

And briefly, the third realm in which our work must link to its roots relates to the mindset and assumptions that brought us where we are, and which cry out for radical change. We must work toward a spiritual and philosophical worldview that says entirely different things about who we are as human beings on the Earth; about what our true nature is in relationship to one another and the planet; about what we really need, to be nourished, valued and successful. Those of you at this conference know of what I speak. In the absence of this larger context our political work will likely come to naught.

The country the founders set on course was forged out of the harsh, hierarchical, dominating, conquering, divorced-from-nature assumptions, behaviors and realities of patriarchy and its thousands of years of institutions that promoted those assumptions and patterns: the classical empires, the ecclesiastical institutions, the nation-states and the early forms of the corporation. This *exploiting* mindset put trust in the few rather than the many, in the individual rather than the community, in autonomy rather than connection. Their central theme was private rights as opposed to a larger public virtue; they were committed to the understanding of things in their isolated nature, not in their contextual nature; they sought security and stability through property and its protection, not through the capacities and possibilities of all the people.

There were, at the time, people advocating alternative ways of thinking. Other frameworks of assumption and trust were brought to the debate. But they lost. And when the winners got to form a new government, those other possibilities suffered a speedy disappearance.

For those who sought controlling power over masses of people, the assumption that we are incorrigibly selfish and inevitably singular

served well. But to share a view of Anne Scales from her article "The Emergence of a Feminist Jurisprudence":

> It is insane at the end of the twentieth century to adhere to the belief that people are innately horrid and can do no better. Rather we must recognize that our fears— of contingency, of dependency, of unimportance—have put us on a suicidal path.[6]

The corporate culture of today thrives on those same miserable assumptions about who we are. The forces of a corporatized mass society (technologies, corporate work, mobility, suburban design) keep us from engaging one another in matters of common destiny. This culture of isolation creates a loneliness that can render us pathetic and dangerous unto ourselves as we become prey to a thousand varieties of political manipulation.

Our focusing task as we pursue a revaluing of the public quest for the common good and the end of corporate dominance is to build community as we put *property*—in particular property in the corporate form—*in its place*: subordinate to and serving of the people. If we do that work, conscious of rigor and roots, our culture will also shift, toward placing trust in different kinds of things, believing in ourselves, finding security and stability in one another, in our communal being, and in our capacity to create a caring self-governance. ∎

## NOTES

[1] For more information on the failure of the regulatory process, see Greider 1992.

[2] See "Sheep in Wolf's Clothing" in this volume.

[3] See "Corporate Responsibility: Kick the Habit" in this volume.

[4] *National Labor Relations Board v. Jones & Laughlin Steel Corp.*

[5] The Supreme Court nullified the Massachusetts law by a vote of 9-0. Case closed. See *Crosby, Secretary of Administration and Finance of Massachusetts, et al. v. National Foreign Trade Council.* —*Ed.*

[6] Scales 1986, p. 1393.

# DEMANDING HUMAN RIGHTS TO FIGHT CORPORATE POWER

*by Ward Morehouse & Richard L. Grossman*

O N DECEMBER 10, 1998, the 50th birthday of a potent instrument in the fight against corporate power was celebrated around the world. The Universal Declaration of Human Rights (UDHR), adopted by the United Nations General Assembly in 1948, sets forth normative standards in pursuit of universal social justice or "the right to be human."[1]

"A moral document of first importance,"[2] the UDHR asserts that everyone has the right to work at compensation sufficient to live in human dignity with a standard of living adequate for the well-being of himself or herself and his or her family, including food, clothing, housing, and healthcare (Articles 23 and 25). The Declaration also asserts the right to recognition as a "person" before the law (Article 6), equal protection of the law (Article 7), and the right to an effective remedy against acts violating fundamental rights of natural persons (Article 8). Most importantly in the struggle against corporate power, the right to self-governance states that "the will of the people shall be the basis of the authority of government" (Article 21).[3]

For the past half-century people have generally regarded governments as the principal violators of human rights. Hence, struggles have been focused on getting governments to correct harms and to protect people's basic rights. But all too often, when there has been conflict between the rights of capital and the rights of natural persons, governments have given priority to the former.[4]

However, we now have another group of key players to consider: giant global corporations with gross incomes greater than the gross domestic products (GDPs) of most nation states. These players have been growing at an awesome rate. The increase in capital assets by the top 200 corporations, measured as a share of world GDP, is stunning: from 17 percent in the mid-1960s to 24 percent in 1982 to over 32 percent in 1995.[5]

While the massive presence of these giant corporations may be a relatively recent phenomenon, their impact on the world scene is not new. In the seventeenth century colonial trading corporations such as the East India Company and the Africa Company mounted major attacks on the rights of human persons. These corporations systematically used the special privileges and legitimacy bestowed by governments to assault people and place, under cover of law and backed by force and violence of the state.

Then and now, global business corporations govern. But they are much greater in size and in their capacity to overwhelm those who would proclaim the "moral authority" of the Universal Declaration of Human Rights. These corporations, like their predecessors in previous centuries, are creations of governments. But because of their vast aggregations of capital and property rights, they are beyond meaningful control by the very governments that created them.

As a result, most of the assaults by global corporations on life, liberty and property are considered legal, even necessary and essential. They are rarely defined as human rights violations. Yet these corporations have propagated systems of values, thought, and law which favor the rights of property and capital over the rights of humans, including the rights of people to own property, own their own work, and be in charge of their own lives. A century of legal precedent in the United States is now being spread around the world through corporate control of information, penetration of education, and codification of law in international trade and investment agreements such as the World Trade Organization (WTO), North American Free Trade Agreement (NAFTA), and proposed Multilateral Agreement on Investment (MAI).[6]

Fashioning responses to these assaults on human rights requires clear understanding of corporate control over people's governance. When corporations conspire with governments to write rules, to define values, to propagandize people's minds, and use law to prevent self-governance, it is fundamental human rights violations which are occurring.

From such clarity of understanding can flow effective strategies for global mass action to contest corporations' authority to govern. The first task is redefining people's struggles for *human rights* as struggles for *self-governance*. From that critical vantage point, we can define human rights as superior to the rights of capital, define property as subordinate to people, and end special privileges usurped by corporations over the last century—from perpetual existence to limited liability.

It has been said that "the historic mission of 'contemporary' human rights is to give voice to *human suffering*, to make it visible, and to ameliorate it."[7] This mission will be achieved as larger and larger numbers of people, in country after country, mobilize to assert the people's right to self-government. Such work will require a different kind of human rights action, one which exposes and strips corporations of the unconstitutionalized governing functions which they have seized.

This quotation from a corporate U.S. think tank underscores the urgency of the task of not only resisting harmful corporate assaults but also asserting the people's right to govern themselves.

> What is the right to vote compared with the right to start a business, draw wages . . . keep the fruits of our labor safe for the future. These are all components of capitalism, which the Chinese people are discovering is the only system compatible with the first and most important of human rights: the right to own and control what is yours.[8]

The time has come for We the People to take back the language and ideals of human rights from the corporations which have usurped them. ∎

## NOTES

[1] Pereira 1997, p. 6. On "the right to be human" see Baxi 1989, p. 152.

[2] Boutrous-Ghali 1993, p. v.

[3] The text of the Universal Declaration of Human Rights and a brief history of its formulation and adoption is given in the *International Bill of Human Rights, ibid.*

[4] For a biting critique of these perversions of "western" human rights standards, see Pereira 1997. On the philosophical dilemmas posed by conflicts in rights, see Rosemont 1998.

[5] See "The Multilateral Agreement on Investment" in this volume. —*Ed.*

[6] For examination of how the Multilateral Agreement on Investment would infringe upon the rights of natural persons while strengthening corporate governance, see Barlow and Clarke 1998. See also Ad Hoc Working Group on the MAI 1998.

[7] Baxi 1998, p. 127.

[8] Llewellyn Rockwell, Jr., President, Ludwig von Mises Institute in Alabama, as quoted in Rosemont 1998.

# BRIEF IN SUPPORT OF THE MOTION FOR PEREMPTORY JUDGEMENT

*by Thomas Linzey & Richard L. Grossman*

## THE ROLE OF THE JUDICIARY IN GRANTING EXPANDED RIGHTS TO CORPORATIONS OVER THE PAST CENTURY INSTILLS A RESPONSIBILITY IN THIS COURT TO REMEDY GRIEVANCES BROUGHT AGAINST CORPORATIONS

THE SUPREME COURT of Colorado, in *People v. Curtice*, 117 P. 357 (Colo. 1911), dealt with a constitutional provision passed by the people that altered corporate obligations to the state. In ruling on the challenge (p. 358) the Court declared that:

> [w]hen the whole people speak through a fundamental law, or by amendment thereto, not in conflict with the federal Constitution, all should hear and heed, more especially the courts, whose function is to interpret, and where possible uphold and enforce, not nullify, overthrow and destroy the law.

Many bestowals of rights and privileges upon corporations occurred several generations ago and have been absorbed into legal lore and accepted, their origins forgotten or simply neglected. These bestowals, and their diverse impacts on ensuing generations, do not appear to be the subjects of sustained, intense debate within the legal community. From this lack of debate, it may appear to this Court that such matters relating to the rights and privileges of the modern corporation are not the subject of sustained, intense debate among the people of this Commonwealth and this country.

It is the Plaintiffs' contention that, in fact, the citizens of this country during this century have been engaged in passionate and sustained debate about the rights and powers of corporations, on the proper nature of corporations in a democracy, on what should be the relationship between the sovereign people of each state and the fiction which is the modern giant corporation. This debate has not been expressed in such terms; rather, it has been expressed in the self-education about corporations and the long list of specific problems confronted by communities stemming largely from corporate decision-making.

This debate is perhaps better known in the form of citizen resistance to corporate decisions to produce and use toxic chemicals in great quantities, to favor particular forms of energy production over others, to invest in chemical and energy intensive agriculture, to

This article is provided without copyright. In 1996 the Community Environmental Legal Defense Fund (CELDF) brought suit to compel the State Attorney General to revoke the Certificates of Authority to Do Business which had been granted by the Commonwealth of Pennsylvania to WMX Technologies Corporation (formerly Waste Management, Inc.), and its wholly owned subsidiaries. (Docket: Civ. no. 1074 M.D. 1996) This is an except from that brief.

favor the internal combustion engine and individual motor vehicles over mass transit, to pursue destructive forest practices both on public land and land owned by paper corporations, to create the savings and loan debacle, and to site toxic factories or dumps. In addition, this public debate has focused on the proper role of the corporation in elections, law-making, a free press, and education.

The Plaintiffs in this instance, like their fellow citizens around the country, are deeply engaged in this debate, as manifested by their active engagement in issues surrounding landfills and in their active participation in the local governmental process. They have done so to protect their homes, communities, and democracy. In the process, they have confronted an exceedingly large, wealthy, and global corporation.

Justice Rehnquist, in *First National Bank of Boston v. Bellotti*, expressed these concerns over this growing political and economic power of the corporation and the Court's acquiescence in its growth. He asserted that the "[s]tates might reasonably fear that the corporation would use its economic power to obtain further benefits beyond those already bestowed." In line with this contention, he urged the Court to grant "considerable deference" to state legislatures which "have concluded that restrictions upon the political activity of business corporations are both politically desirable and constitutionally permissible."

Precisely because the judiciary has played such a major role in the design and development of legal doctrines that helped to create the contemporary modern, large corporation with its broad array of rights, privileges, and powers, the Plaintiffs believe that the court has a special responsibility when petitioned by citizens of this Commonwealth for redress for injuries caused by the corporation. The Plaintiffs also ask this court to recognize that, although within the legal community these doctrines of property and personhood rights appear to be long accepted, within the body politic there continues to be active questioning and resistance to these doctrines in practice. In short, it is logical to posit that when individuals and organizations petition the courts for redress of injuries caused by this century-long extension of rights to the corporation, that the courts have a duty, in equity, to remedy their injuries. This proposition seems to hold especially true when faced with the instant situation, in which both private and public injuries have been caused by a corporation.

Over the past century, the courts have narrowed the spectrum of available legal remedies against the corporation and the injuries that it causes. To now further narrow that avenue and declare that the power of the Attorney General, when presented with a factual petition that addresses a history of lawbreaking, is completely discretionary, is to relieve citizens of one of their last control mechanisms over the artificial creature called the corporation. ∎

# TOWARD A NEW LABOR LAW

*by James Pope, Ed Bruno & Peter Kellman*

## THE PROBLEM

A S UNIONISTS KNOW from bitter experience, the National Labor Relations Act (NLRA) gives employers plenty of ways to prevent workers from exercising freedom of association. For just one example, the Act's guarantee of the right to organize is so poorly enforced that employers fire about 3-5 workers for every 100 who have the nerve to vote union in a secret ballot election.[1] With these odds, would you speak up for a union if you worked in a non-union workplace? Thanks to this kind of employer opposition, union organizing efforts can't keep pace with the loss of union jobs to outsourcing, automation, and job export.

So if the law is so bad, why not change it? For more than a half-century the labor movement has thrown energy and money into a series of unsuccessful campaigns for labor law reform. In 1949 labor's crusade to repeal the Taft-Hartley Act went down to defeat despite Democratic majorities in both houses of Congress and President Truman in the White House. And in 1978 a modest reform bill fell to a filibuster, again with Democrats holding both houses of Congress and the Presidency.

This record of failure will not be reversed with more money, better lobbying, or stronger electioneering. The fact is that—absent very extraordinary circumstances—business interests hold a veto power over labor rights legislation in this country. This is not because business outspends labor 15-1 on political campaigns, although it does. It is because business occupies what political scientist Charles Lindblom calls a "privileged position" in our political system. Public officials need cooperation from business, and they cannot take it for granted.[2] While corporations can and do threaten to withhold cooperation or to move away if government does not meet their demands, workers and unions almost never do likewise. (When was the last time you heard of any private-sector workers threatening to strike if government didn't meet their demands?) In short, government leaders can usually afford to stiff unions, but they must do what it takes to obtain the cooperation of business.[3]

## A SOLUTION

In November 1998 the delegates to the first constitutional convention of the Labor Party declared that "we have wrongly come to accept that at work we are not entitled to the rights and privileges we normally enjoy as citizens." The convention then proceeded to resolve that the "Labor Party rejects the *status quo* of today's workplace where workers are forced to abandon their Constitutional Rights in order to earn their living, and are as a consequence subject to the tyranny of the corporation."

Maybe, instead of beating our heads against the wall of labor law reform, we should go back to constitutional fundamentals. Imagine that in place of our half-century-old labor law—with its government-determined bargaining units and government-certified bargaining representatives, we had a labor law based on the constitutional rights of free speech, assembly, and labor freedom.

After more than a half-century of treating labor rights as the end of a free flow of commerce, what would happen if we were to get back on the track of treating labor rights as fundamental human rights that are valuable in and of themselves?

## THE LABOR PARTY PROPOSES

We start from the proposition that workers must enjoy effective freedom of speech, effective freedom of association, and effective freedom of labor. These three freedoms are already guaranteed, in theory, by the First and Thirteenth Amendments to the U.S. Constitution. In addition, they have been embodied in the Norris-LaGuardia Act and in section 7 of the National Labor Relations Act. In practice, however, the law does not permit the effective exercise of these freedoms. By "effective," we do not mean that workers must win all of their protests. We mean that in actual practice:

1.  Workers must be able to communicate with one another and with the broader public free from government and employer censorship.

2.  Workers must be able to associate together in forms chosen by themselves and not by government or employers.

3.  Workers must be able to exercise control over their personal labor power.

If all of these conditions are fulfilled, workers may or may not succeed in a particular protest. For example, even if a group of

employees manages to shut down an employer completely, they have only equalized the contest. Now, each side can veto production—instead of just the employer. With this in mind, here are the minimum rights necessary to make possible effective freedom of speech, effective freedom of association, and effective freedom of labor.

## FREEDOM OF SPEECH

Up to now courts have privileged employers' property rights over the workers' free speech rights. If workers are to enjoy effective freedom of speech and expression, this must change in at least three ways:

1.  Workers must enjoy freedom of speech on as well as off the employer's property. Under current law we have freedom of speech on public property. On private property the owners of the property generally determine who can speak and who cannot. Workers surrender their First Amendment rights when they enter the workplace. Unfortunately for us, the privately-owned work site is increasingly the only place where it is possible to speak with workers as a group. Gone are the days when most workers lived near their work sites and could be reached off the employer's property. But union representatives and co-workers from other enterprises cannot speak with workers at their work sites because the Supreme Court has determined that the employer's property rights trump the workers' right of self-organization. According to the Court, the NLRA permits the employer to exclude anyone it wants even if there is no legitimate business reason for doing so. Meanwhile, we supposedly have the "reasonable" alternative of trying to track down individual workers by their license

plate numbers, or of buying advertisements in general-circulation newspapers. This ridiculous "alternative" only demonstrates the Court's contempt for our rights. It does not take any leap of imagination to recognize that when an employer has the power to effectively determine who will—and who will not—speak to "its" workers, the employer is acting as a master and it is putting the workers in the position of dependent slaves.

2. Workers must be free from employer as well as government censorship except where job performance is at stake. The NLRA does prohibit an employer from interfering with communication among its employees about "mutual aid or protection," but the Supreme Court has created an exception for "disloyal" speech, which may include anything from impolite criticism of the employer, to commentary on issues that courts think are for management alone (like product selection or quality). For example, judges have held that a worker who participates in a march protesting the employer's labor policies can be fired for disloyalty merely because some marchers were urging a boycott of the employer. But isn't a peaceful boycott exactly the kind of "concerted activity for mutual aid or protection" that the NLRA was intended to protect? When an employer censors a worker's speech for reasons unrelated to job performance, it is acting as a master and putting the worker in the position of a slave.

3. The people—including workers—must be free to express themselves by withholding patronage and requesting others to withhold patronage. In theory, working people can express solidarity by withholding patronage from employers who are unfair to labor. Unfortunately, many employers do not sell their own products directly to consumers. Often, the only way for people to cast effective "consumer votes" is to request retailers to remove the offending employer's products from the shelves, and then boycott the retailer if it refuses. But the NLRA prohibits unions from peacefully picketing such retailers on the ground that the retailer is a "neutral" in the dispute between the union and the offending employer.[4] In other words, the NLRA seeks to protect the "neutral" by preventing the union from informing the public that the "neutral" is serving as a retail outlet for the unfair employer. If consumers don't know about the connection, then they cannot express their disapproval, and the "neutral" can continue to profit from its sale of the unfair employer's products. When workers are prohibited from effectively communicating truthful information about employers, then they are treated more like slaves than like citizens.

## FREEDOM OF ASSOCIATION

Under the NLRA, the government decides what groups of workers may assemble together for collective action and bargaining. If workers are to enjoy effective freedom of association, this must change in at least two ways:

1. Any size group of workers can form an association (such as a union) and present and resolve grievances and make agreements with the employer. According to the NLRB, the NLRA does not fully protect the rights of a union that has not established majority support in a govern-

ment- or employer-approved bargaining unit. When an individual worker is forced to face the collective power of a corporate employer without the support of his or her union, she is placed in the position of a helpless slave dealing with a powerful master.

2. Workers, not the government or the employer, must determine the scope of their own associations for purposes of collective action and bargaining. When we think about freedom of association, this point seems obvious. After all, what is collective bargaining other than a group of workers getting together to bargain with the employer? But the NLRA is not based on freedom of association. Instead of protecting the right of workers to join together and deal with the employer, the Act establishes a system of government-approved "bargaining units." The Board and the courts decide which workers will be in which units, and they give the desires of the employer at least as much weight as those of the workers. When workers cannot determine who they will associate with for mutual aid and protection, they are denied a basic right of citizenship.

## FREEDOM OF LABOR

Under current law, the workers' freedom of labor is subordinated to employer property rights. For workers to enjoy effective freedom of labor, this must change in at least four ways:

1. The right to strike must include the right not to lose permanently one's job to a strikebreaker. Under current law, workers may not be fired for striking, but they may be "permanently replaced" by strikebreakers even if the employer has no need to offer permanent employment in order

to obtain sufficient strikebreakers to operate. The employer's property right "to protect and continue his business" trumps the workers' right to strike.[5] In practice, then, an employer can permanently replace strikers as a way of punishing them for exercising their "right" to strike. When an employer has the power to punish workers for exercising their fundamental rights, the employer is acting as a master and the employee is a slave whose rights mean nothing.

2. The freedom of labor must include the right to refuse to contribute personal labor to enterprises that assist unfair employers by, for example, supplying them with parts, distributing their products, or financing their operations. Under the NLRA, companies that deal with unfair employers are considered to be innocent "neutrals" that should be insulated against worker protest. Workers who refuse to handle the products of an unfair employer are seeking, as Samuel Gompers put it: "to exercise control of their own labor power, . . . to control their own movements, the expending of their own efforts, the giving of that service which constitutes their voluntary contribution to the welfare of society."[6] Even if a worker is not personally involved in handling the unfair employer's product, he or she is helping her "neutral" employer to continue "business as usual" with the unfair employer. When a "neutral" employer can compel a worker to contribute his or her personal labor to assist another employer in violating the human rights of its employees, the employer is placed in the position of a master and the worker in that of a slave with no control over his or her personal labor.

3.  The freedom of labor must include the right to bargain with, and to strike and boycott against, the company that actually controls terms and conditions of employment. Under the NLRA, companies can insulate themselves against worker protest by subcontracting work and creating artificial corporate boundaries. For example, when employees of the Hearst Corporation's Baltimore radio station picketed at the Hearst Corporation's Baltimore newspaper, they discovered that they were guilty of engaging in a secondary boycott against the "neutral" newspaper. Why? Because the radio station and the newspaper were—on paper—separate corporations; it just happened that both were wholly owned by Hearst. Of course, in the real world the Hearst Corporation can spread the costs of the radio strike over all of its operations; the strike does not exert serious pressure unless Hearst is feeling its effects. When employers can use corporate formalities to render workers' rights meaningless, the employer is acting like a master and the employee is reduced to slavery.

4.  The freedom of labor must include the right to withhold personal labor in solidarity with workers in other countries. With corporations organized on a multinational basis, effective labor freedom necessarily requires the right to combine across borders. But many efforts at international solidarity run up against the secondary boycott prohibition. When American longshoremen joined other dock workers around the world in refusing to unload cargo from the Neptune Jade, they were hit with secondary boycott charges. When corporations are permitted to organize multinationally, while workers are limited to local protests because of artificial corporate boundaries, then corporations become arrogant masters while workers are reduced to dependent slavery.

## FROM HERE TO THERE

Suppose we did decide that we wanted to get on the fundamental rights track. What then? Obviously, we are talking about long-term change. No Congress is likely to enact protections for fundamental labor rights in the near future. Nevertheless, we would not be limited entirely to the standard programs for long term change (like education and modest, local campaigns). Where opportunities arose, we could begin to exercise our fundamental rights then and there. Because these rights derive from the Constitution, they trump any statutory or judge-made law to the contrary. The reason why we have a written Constitution is so that the people—not just lawyers and judges—can read it and enforce it against the rulers of the land.

Before the NLRA, the labor movement understood the importance of exercising labor's fundamental rights even when courts and legislatures repudiated them. The delegates to the 1919 convention of the American Federation of Labor resolved unanimously to "stand firmly and conscientiously on our rights as free men and treat all injunctive decrees that invade our personal liberties as . . . illegal[,] as being in violation of our constitutional safeguards, and accept whatever consequences may follow."[7]

A half-century ago, with the labor movement at a crossroads, John L. Lewis thundered his support for this policy. The big issue at the annual convention of the American Federation of Labor was whether to engage in constitutional resistance against what union-ists were calling the Taft-Hartley "Slave Labor Act." After an initial outburst of saber-rat-tling, the AFL's top leadership had lost enthu-siasm for the struggle. John L. Lewis turned his oratorical skills to reviving the spirit of resistance:

> This Act was passed to oppress labor, to make difficult its current enterprises for collective bargaining, to make more diffi-cult the securing of new members for this labor movement, without which our move-ment will become so possessed of inertia that there is no action and no growth, and in a labor movement where there is no growth there is no security for its existence, because deterioration sets in and unions, like men, retrograde. I wonder what built up the labor movement in this country? Was it protesting laws and statutes that protected the organizers of our movement when they went out to the meetings? Oh, no? The founders of our Federation had no such protection. They had to fight for the right to be heard. They had to fight for the right to hold a meeting, and men had to sacrifice and sometimes die for the right to join a union . . . And what you are doing today [by complying with Taft-Hartley]—you are repealing the 1919 injunction policy . . . and you are humbling yourselves in abasement before the return of government by injunction.[8]

AFL Secretary-Treasurer George Meany deliv-ered the administration's response. It was a complete negation of the very idea that labor could develop and live by an independent interpretation of the constitution. Despite his public position that Taft-Hartley was unconstitutional, Meany claimed that it was "the law of the land":

> Whether you like it or not, whether the National Association of Manufacturers and the representatives of the reactionary employers bought the Republican party or not, as someone seems to think, the fact remains that they counted the votes in Washington, and the Taft-Hartley Law is on the statute books. No one asked for a recount. Our representatives were there when the votes were cast, and no matter what the reason, whether it is the sinister reason attributed here today or not, the fact remains that they did pass this law. It is now the law of the land.[9]

With the Cold War in full swing, and the labor movement singled out as a hotbed of communism, constitutional resistance seemed un-American to Meany. "We know it is a bad law," he continued, "but it was placed on the statute books by our representatives under the American democratic system, and the only way it is going to be changed is by our repre-sentatives under that system."[10] Teamster President Daniel Tobin agreed that this "is a law that we will resent, but there is a certain legal procedure to change the law, and it isn't by revolution."[11] Meany's speech was greeted with thunderous applause, and his position prevailed by a wide margin.

For the next half-century the movement dutifully lobbied and electioneered for labor law reform. The Thirteenth Amendment the-ory of labor liberty lay dormant as union lawyers paid it no more than lip service, the Supreme Court dodged the issue, and labor leaders gradually forgot about it as they became increasingly dependent on government protection.

Now, at the turn of the millennium, many labor activists and leaders have come to share Lewis' view that Taft-Hartley is indeed caus-ing the movement to languish and decline. In the meantime, the chilling pressure of the Cold War has lifted. And, last but not least, the recent change in leadership at the AFL-CIO makes it possible to look back on the most famous lines of Lewis' 1947 speech with more optimism than would previously have been possible. The Mine Workers' President had threatened to resign from the Federation's Executive Council if it failed to defy Taft-Hartley. In regard to that threat, he declared:

> Perhaps . . . you will say "John L. Lewis is trying to hold a gun to the head of the convention." That is not true. I don't think anyone can hold a gun to the head of this convention . . . As far as that is concerned, on this particular issue, I don't think that the Federation has a head. I think its neck has just grown up and haired over.[12]

Where an employer has flagrantly violated labor rights, and where the law prohibits the victims from effectively protesting, we might do well to recall Samuel Gompers' words:

> History honors none above those who, in the past, have set themselves against unjust laws, even unto the point of rebellion. The Republic of the United States is founded upon defiance of unjust law . . . The American Federation of Labor and its president have declared that manifestly unjust decisions of courts must be defied, and there is no disposition to recant.[13] ∎

---

# NOTES

[1] See Weiler 1983. He estimates that one in 20 pro-union voters in representation elections had been discharged in retaliation for union activity. Also see LaLonde and Meltzer 1991. They put that estimate at one in 36. Also see Weiler 1983. In that article Weiler argues that any estimate based on official determinations of retaliatory discharge is likely to understate the actual number because only a fraction of such discharges are litigated to a conclusion.

[2] Lindblom 1977, p. 175.

[3] *Ibid.*, p. 176.

[4] Unions do have a First Amendment right to leaflet with this message but, according to the U.S. Supreme Court, that is only because leafleting is "much less effective than labor picketing." *Edward J. De Bartolo Corp. v. Florida Gulf Coast Bldg. & Constr. Trades Council* quoting *NLRB v. Retail Store Employees Union, etc.*

[5] *NLRB v. Mackay Radio & Tel. Co.*

[6] Gompers 1921, p. 222.

[7] American Federation of Labor 1919, pp. 361-362.

[8] American Federation of Labor 1947, pp. 487, 490, 492.

[9] *Ibid.*, p. 495.

[10] *Ibid.*

[11] *Ibid.*, p. 493.

[12] *Ibid.*, p. 492.

[13] Gompers 1921, p. 222.

# SOME LESSONS LEARNED

*by POCLAD*

---

POCLAD'S SUSTAINED ENGAGEMENT with diverse people around the country and the world has been stimulating reexamination of our goals, our analyses, our context, and our language. Here are several of our conclusions.

I.  People cannot challenge the illegitimacy of corporate governance without contesting the corporate culture of endless expansion and its astounding estrangement from the natural world.

The iron law of the corporate culture is simple: every nation requires constantly-expanding production and consumption of everything. Eternally increasing sales, accompanied by larger and larger profits (and fewer and fewer employees) are proof of efficiency and successful management.

Corporations instruct us that constant expansion of production, consumption and profits is the source of jobs, paychecks, progress, survival and freedom. We are told that to avoid freezing and starving in the dark, people, communities, states and nations must compete against one another to create the best climates for global corporations. All the Earth and outer space must be made available for corporate use, at bargain prices and without acknowledging the reality of the Earth's natural systems and natural economy.

The tasks ahead call upon people to reflect and act as participants in human, biological and constitutional communities, as people who are practicing self-governance to honor life and to preserve the integral economy of planet Earth.

The widespread public debate—*ferment*, really—necessary to delegitimate corporate authority over people and the planet must grapple with the purpose of life, with humans' place in the natural world, along with the assumed goals of work, technology, production and great national wealth.

2.  Discussions about corporations must address the authority and responsibility of a sovereign people, "We the People" of our Constitution's Preamble.

When we bring people together for discussions about corporations, they start off, predictably, talking about the especially harmful acts of corporations (primarily industrial and financial, but also service, educational and charitable). It does not take long, however, for democracy to become a central topic. We then encourage explorations of self-governance and the purpose of governments by examining the Preamble to the U.S. Constitution.

We ask: What are our rights and responsibilities as sovereign people? Why were so many classes of people excluded from We the People in Revolutionary times? How have

---

©1997 by POCLAD. This article is an except from a 1997 document titled *The POCLAD Story: Lessons Learned, Future Directions*, written for the benefit of potential grant and funding organizations, as well as for POCLAD and its allies. This excerpted section concerns the lessons learned.

activists in every generation redefined the meaning of "We the People"? What work remains to be done?

Why have We the People empowered corporate bodies to commit sustained violence against people, species, the Earth and democratic processes?

The 53-word Preamble does not bestow property, political or human rights upon corporations. It does not prescribe competition or maximum production as the nation's basic values. Rather, it proclaims:

> We the people of the United States, in order to form a more perfect union, establish justice, insure domestic tranquility, provide for the common defense, promote the general welfare and secure the blessings of liberty to ourselves and our posterity do ordain and establish this Constitution for the United States of America.

The challenge becomes clear: to contrast and invoke the Preamble against jurisprudence and legislation limiting the authority of a sovereign people over all our own institutional creations, corporate *and* government.

3.  Organizing to define "personhood" has been an essential part of every generation's struggle for democratic self-governance. Activists need to make moral, political and strategic distinctions between corporate entities and human persons.

Despite the nation's persistent rhetoric of equality, a minority of the people in the 13 colonies were powerful enough to define the majority of people—Africans, Native peoples, women, men without property, debtors—as property, or as non-persons, without legal standing. They also defined the Earth and its creatures as having no legal rights, no standing.

Whole classes of human beings, therefore, have had to organize to define themselves as "persons" so they too could govern themselves, fulfill their humanity, defend their communities, other species and the Earth. This has not been easy work.

As corporations amassed wealth and power from government spending and great land/resource grabs during the Civil War, corporate leaders set out to change legal theory and the law. The Supreme Court and legislative bodies began to grant business corporations political and civil rights originally held by the young nation's property-owning white male founders.

By 1886 just about a century after the Constitution was written, the corporate fiction had achieved *de facto* the civil, political and property rights of enfranchised natural persons. This was *well before* the majority of human beings in this country gained *their* civil rights.

By the early twentieth century legislatures and the courts had also declared decision-making about investment, production and work to be corporations' private property. Federal courts in particular had asserted their authority to limit the ability of states and municipal governments to define and instruct the corporation within their jurisdictions.

Corporations have had over a century to prevent people from using our state and municipal governments to spell out corporate nature.

Corporate leaders also created their story, and made it the nation's ("What's good for General Motors…"[1]). Corporations' success in manufacturing and spreading their version of this country's history, while they *sell* or *rent* us our own resources, is a major reason why so many people today believe that the way things are is the way they have always been, were meant to be . . . that there can be no alternatives. Corporations have planted the notion deep in people's consciousness that corporate decisions about investment, production and the organization of work are beyond the authority of the American people; and that it is proper for corporations to shape not only economic decisions, but also a supposedly sovereign people's education, public policy debates, elections, lawmaking, and jurisprudence.

Activist organizing must broaden the inclusiveness of We the People, and strip giant corporations of their claim to political rights of natural persons.

4.  Efforts to revoke corporate charters, change legal doctrines and challenge our corporate culture make sense only in the context of sustained, democratic, political and social movements.

As POCLAD explored the nature and history of giant global corporations—whether the East India Company or the Virginia Company of the eighteenth century, the Africa Company of the nineteenth century, or the WMX Technologies[2] and Union Carbide Corporation of the late twentieth century— we realized that they all were designed to destroy or limit competition, buy cheap and sell dear, destroy local cultures and historical memories, control dispute resolution, define what's public and what's private and who is a person before the law, shape public policy debate and law, commit legalized violence, spread their values. In other words, *they were designed to govern.*

But in the U.S. system of constitutional self-governance, the authority to shape our society and define our culture is supposed to be solely in the hands of the people. The power to create and define government or business institutions to "promote the general welfare" is the people's.

During the twentieth century, and certainly over the past decades, activist groups have been resisting corporate harms, and properly so. But few of these organizations have paid much attention to the corporate form itself, to the rights and powers corporations seized from the people, to the judicial origins of corporations' constitutional protections, or to the responsibility of a sovereign people to keep all our corporate bodies in check.

In other words, activists have not been looking at the relationship between persons and corporate fictions. Indeed, We the People have been conceding authority and power to great corporate bodies, and not even talking about it. We have allowed our *institutional servants* to become our *masters.*

While this is the reality which groups, formed to resist corporate harms one by one, confront today, countless activist struggles have laid the groundwork for creative, sustained and escalating challenges to the authority of *all* giant corporate bodies.

5.  Public debate on property rights, sovereignty and liberty is long overdue.

Starting in the nineteenth century, corporate leaders aped the nation's founders by couching their demands for property rights in the language of liberty for natural persons. Ever since, they have contended that any decrease in a corporation's property rights constitutes an assault upon the freedom and liberty of all people in this nation.

A property right is the right to exclude others. As Professor Morris R. Cohen wrote several generations ago, property rights "compelling service and obedience" confer a certain sovereign power upon concentrations of wealth, land and power.[3]

As another commentator has noted, ownership rights have always been "legal creations

. . . Economic value does not predate law; it is created by law."[4]

The American Revolution wrested sovereignty from the English Monarchy and vested it not in state or federal governments but in the people. Many who fought in the Revolution, along with later generations of Africans, Native peoples, women, urban artisans and mechanics like the Loco Focos, Jacksonians, Knights of Labor, Populists, Anarchists and Wobblies, among others, understood that to a truly sovereign people, no categories of information or arenas of decision-making could properly be declared off-limits, beyond their authority.

They understood that concentrations of property assaulted individual persons, self-governing institutions and the Earth. So they resisted the concept that property rights were irreversibly defined by monarchs or by the wealthy. Indeed, activists in every generation insisted that the task of defining property relationships in these United States were political questions, which must be settled through democratic processes in which only human persons could participate.

They were not willing to concede political rights and sovereign-like powers to agglomerations of property called "corporations."

Leaders and organizations of the so-called "Progressive Era," along with twentieth century liberals, however, *were* willing. For example, they accepted federal courts' decrees that a corporation's investment, production and work decisions were property rights sheltered by the U.S. Constitution, and that workers did not enjoy Bill of Rights protections from their corporate employers. In so doing, they contributed to today's great inequalities as well as to confusions about public and private decision-making, about public and private property.

Waves of distorted corporate stories about property and political liberty have resulted in an over-powering culture that legitimates corporate rule. Revealing and debunking today's corporate story by weaving diverse people's and the planet's stories, and by contesting corporate authority, are essential for the decolonizing of our minds.

This is akin to what Tom Paine's *Common Sense*—and the ferment leading up to the American Revolution—accomplished: the exposure of the British monarchy, with all its laws and pomp and histories and legal violence, as merely the *concoctions of ordinary human beings*.

It was this ferment which nurtured the widespread belief that the monarchy could be uprooted and replaced with a revolutionary idea—self governance.

6. People's struggles against corporate rule need to take the offensive, reflect the histories and circumstances of their particular countries, and act in solidarity with one another.

At the height of its power in India during the late eighteenth and early nineteenth centuries, the East India Company still sought charters and licenses from the various principalities and provinces of the subcontinent. Then, as now, business leaders wanted their corporations to govern "legally." They wanted *governments* to do the heavy lifting needed to keep people in line.

As they did in the U.S. a century ago, corporations are now reconfiguring laws, legal doctrines, histories and cultures of other nations. And they are obscuring their handiwork by ascribing the rise of global corporations to natural, inevitable market mechanisms, which they label "globalization." All the while, they are fashioning cultural environments that encourage people to embrace the idea that today's global corporations have the same inherent, inalienable rights, freedoms and mobility as natural persons.

POCLAD is engaging activists in the U.S. and other countries in examining globalization as only the *latest manifestation of global "corporatization."* Our strategy sessions with activist groups include discussions of how the corporate power grab required deliberate planning and sustained effort over several generations, involving:

- cloaking their demands in the language of individual human liberty and property rights;

- bribery, intimidation and violence;

- manipulating local, state and federal governments to weaken vigorous popular movements;

- counter-revolution in the courts to undermine the authority of municipalities and states to define corporations;

- the corporate crafting of regulatory and administrative law "reforms," accompanied by the obscuring of this corporate triumph behind the labels (and mythologies) of "efficient," "progressive" and "liberal";

- perfecting the corporate story of history and culture—including the "inevitability" and "irreplaceability" of giant corporations; and

- ongoing efforts all through the twentieth century: (1) to direct activist movements *toward* campaigns over corporate behaviors, one at a time, in stacked-deck regulatory and administrative arenas; and (2) to divert activist movements for justice *away* from struggles over who is in charge—corporations or We the People.

POCLAD regards repealing North American Free Trade Agreement (NAFTA) and General Agreement on Tariffs and Trade (GATT), and resisting the forthcoming trade agreements of the Americas, and the Multilateral Agreement on Investment (MAI), as tasks ideally suited for instigating debates—on every continent— about property rights and democratic values, and the nature of giant corporations today. We will continue to challenge popular notions about these struggles.

For example, while we applaud the November 1997 defeat of "fast track" legislation in the U.S. Congress, we vigorously dispute the observation of *The Nation* magazine's editors that "it surely tolls the passing of the era of untrammeled corporate globalization."[5] Such hyperbole, passing as analysis, is a grave disservice to activists grappling to understand and contest corporate rule today.

7.  Resisting corporate assaults in regulatory and administrative agencies, and appealing to corporate leaders to act responsibly via voluntary "codes of conduct," leave the structures of corporate power essentially intact, and fail to move public discourse forward.

Through most of the nineteenth century, the mechanisms people used to define corporations were:

- actively debating and redefining the society's values and principles; writing, issuing and enforcing corporate charters;

- writing, amending and enforcing state corporation codes and state constitutions; and

- convening *quo warranto* ("by what authority") hearings to dissolve corporations which had become cancers upon the body politic.

By World War I corporations had replaced these mechanisms of sovereignty with regulatory and administrative statutes they helped write—statutes which conceded fundamental civil and property rights to corporations.[6] Historian Gabriel Kolko, a leader in rethinking the "Progressive Era," has noted:

> There were any number of options involving government and economics abstractly available to national political leaders during the period 1900-1916, and in virtually every case they chose those solutions to problems advocated by the representatives of concerned business and financial interests.[7]

We the People's authority *to define the nature of our corporate bodies* was replaced with rules which sought instead *to regulate corporations' behavior*, one harm at a time, and usually after the fact. All through the twentieth century, corporations have worked hard to divert movements for justice from taking their struggles into political arenas of authority, of sovereignty. ■

---

# Notes

[1] Charlie Wilson of General Motors Corporation made this statement in testimony before the U.S. Congress in 1953. –*Ed.*

[2] Waste Management, Inc.

[3] Cohen "Property and Sovereignty", 1933.

[4] Sunstein 1993, p. 51.

[5] The Nation 1997.

[6] Indeed, this is the logic of the Waste Management Corporation brief in Thomas Linzey's Pennsylvania case—that environmental, health, labor, securities, consumer, and other "regulation" had supplanted the "arcane" defining mechanisms of common law, charters and corporations codes. Thus, in the view of this corporation's attorneys, the fact that Waste Management Corporation had been found guilty of hundreds of regulatory violations, year after year, and had paid its (tax deductible) fines, simply "proved" that the regulatory system "worked." It is not much of a leap from here to a corporation such as Smithfield Foods, Inc., which a U.S. District Court judge ruled on August 8, 1997, had committed nearly 7,000 violations of the Clean Water Act since 1991. The more a corporation violates state and federal regulations, the more people can rest easy because the regulatory system works.

[7] Kolko 1963.

# REVOLUTIONIZING CORPORATE LAW

*by Richard L. Grossman*

THE TITLE OF this session is "Revolutionizing Corporate Law." But I believe that rather than revolutionizing corporate law, we must revolutionize the Constitution. Let me explain.

Corporations have successfully claimed an enormous array of human rights, of people's constitutional rights—such as freedom of speech, due process, equal protection. And law and culture treat corporations as private entities.

There are two consequences: first, corporate managers wield our Bill of Rights—which means they use the Constitution to turn the coercive force of our local, state and federal governments against us. Second, *defining the corporation* is removed beyond the authority of the American people—outside the reach of public, democratic processes.

What IS the corporation which governs us today? The corporation is not a market mechanism, but a political force. Its purpose is to concentrate wealth and power, in order to define work; to dictate investment; to choose technologies, to design whole systems for production and delivery of people's basic needs (for example, energy, health care, transportation, and food); to fashion the nation's relations with other countries, the nation's role around the world.

In other words, corporations define this society and, increasingly, the Earth. Giant corporations govern.

That's what they DO. Their managers and directors make private decisions which in an authentic democracy would be made by the people through democratic processes not dominated by a wealthy, propertied few. Corporations which usurp the rights of persons and function as private governments are, by definition, denying people's basic rights, including the right to govern ourselves. This is what giant corporations are designed to do, and they do it well.

So asking corporate leaders to be less oppressive does not undo what corporations are designed for. Investing years in regulatory struggles to set "acceptable" levels of corporate poisoning does not undo what corporations are designed for. Regulating corporate buying of elected officials or union activity, or establishing voluntary "codes of corporate conduct" or "patients' bills of rights," does not undo what corporations are designed for. In fact, all such efforts keep more people from seeing that property rules, not people.

What should we NOT do?

If we focus on one harmful corporate behavior at a time we miss seeing that such behavior is not an isolated thing, but part of the broad corporate invasion into our self-governance, enabled and validated by our culture. For example, when corporations inject great sums of money into our elections and law-making, when they make sure a policy debate has been framed long before it comes before the public, they are using the tools of corporate rule that are protected by law.

What we should do is be intentional about understanding the essence and purpose of corporations, and craft goals and strategies accordingly.

Let me describe two examples.

The Abolitionists did not spring from out of the blue in the 1820s with a clear understanding of how to frame their work. They could, after all, have ended up demanding a slavery protection agency—you know, the equivalent of today's Environmental Protection Agency—to make slaves' conditions a little less bad. They could have persuaded their supporters to back a slave owners' voluntary "codes of conduct." They could have sought authority for defenders of slaves to bring lawsuits on slaves' behalf.

Over the course of two generations, from 1820 to 1860, the many people who considered themselves Abolitionists engaged in an extraordinary, vigorous process towards defining their goal. They invested time and energy defining the problem and then fashioning appropriate remedies. And here's how they ended up.

- They defined slavery as a fundamental denial of basic human rights.

- They accused the United States Government and public officials of complicity in this denial of rights.

- They denounced the Constitution, and openly violated federal and state laws by aiding runaway slaves.

- Slaves themselves revolted and escaped. Judges and juries openly supported the growing Abolitionists' defilement of the

law of the land.

In other words, their ideas of "remedy" centered around changing how the nation understood slavery so that popular organizing could challenge not only slave owners but also the makers and enforcers of law, and change the Constitution.

By the time the bloody Civil War offered the opportunity, they had built a political movement skilled at and characterized by defiance, and with the clout to get their three constitutional amendments enacted.

A generation later saw the flowering of the Populist movement. Farmers had organized around the reality that they were beholden to the merchants who sold them seeds and who bought their crops, and to the banks that loaned them money. So they started off forming cooperatives, pooling their resources to borrow money, buy supplies and market their products. As they gained power, the banks refused to lend them money. Realizing that they did not understand money, they undertook to study it.

What they came up with were not lending regulations which banks and merchants had to obey; not voluntary or compulsory codes of conduct, but something else. Their investigations and discussions revealed that their government printed money and gave it to the banks, which then sold it to the people. Their solution was to eliminate the banks, so that people could, for example, go down to the post office and get loans at pretty much no interest. They said: it's our government, it's our money. Why can't we decide what to do with our money?

Provoked by the oppression they were experiencing in their communities which they had traced back to banking and other corporations, they set out to challenge the corporate state which had been making the rules of property,

contracts, commerce and money. They realized that they wanted to define the system, and
no longer let the system define them.

For this purpose, they built what historian
Lawrence Goodwyn called "the largest democratic mass movement in U.S. history."

My purpose in offering these two examples is
to indicate that there have been occasions
when people came together to analyze their
common problems, and came up with solutions designed not to just make their conditions a little less bad, which did not just ask
their oppressors to be a little less oppressive.

Instead, people mobilized to eliminate the
*source* of their problems and their oppression.

Let's return to the title of this panel:
"Revolutionizing        Corporate        Law."
Corporate law, as far as I can tell, refers to
internal corporate governance.    So when
lawyers and politicians talk about corporate
law they are not talking about the relationship between corporations and the sovereign
people in a democracy.  They are talking
about the relations among corporate directors, managers and shareholders.  And maybe
sometimes with the suppliers also.    Not
about the workers, because workers are basically a cost, a liability, and anyway, workers
have no constitutional rights a corporate
employer is bound to respect.  Not about the
broader community, for the same reason.

Just pick up some corporate law books.
One of my favorites is Easterbrook and
Fischel's *The Economic Structure of Corporate Law.*
They are pretty clear:

> . . . a corporation is a complex set of
> explicit and implicit contracts.  Corporate
> law enables the participants to select the

optimum arrangement for the many different set of risks and opportunities that are
available in a large economy.

Here is another quote from the same book:

> The corporate code in almost every state is
> an "enabling" statute.  An enabling statute
> allows managers and investors to write
> their own tickets, to establish systems of
> governance without substantive scrutiny
> from a regulator.  The handiwork of man-
> agers is final in all but exceptional or trivial
> instances.  Courts apply the "business
> judgment rule," a hands-off approach that
> judges would not dream of applying to the
> decisions of administrative agencies.

Elected legislators write these enabling
statutes,[1] like they write labor, environmental,
tax, health and other laws.  They live in this
corporate culture, so they are shaped and driv-
en by the culture's underlying assumptions and
values about how things must work.  And they
are instructed by the rule of law; by judicial
interpretations of the Constitution regarding
property and personhood, contracts and commerce.  These interpretations have turned the
corporation into a private entity, defined
"decision-making" as a corporation's private
property; and enabled corporations to deny
the rest of us our most fundamental rights.

Elected officials—along with newspaper
publishers and other pillars of our communities—have been taught that the people who
run corporations have the constitutional
authority to direct "their" resources, to dictate
"their" investments, to choose "their" technologies, to order "their" workers, to fix elections, to write laws—to do pretty much what
they want, however they want it.  That's what
this "enabling" stuff means.  That's "the
handiwork of managers" which judges are not
to trample upon.

So the work of people today yearning to be free and self-governing is to challenge the basic nonsense and distortions masquerading as eternal truths—as slaves and Abolitionists did with slavery, as Populists did with money and banks. Today we must challenge the nonsense that the corporation is private, that the corporation legitimately wields any rights, much less We the People's constitutional rights.

We need to see that if an artificial entity—a mere creation of law—is empowered with the constitutional rights of human persons, then we human persons will simply not be able to govern ourselves. That when corporations are empowered with the constitutional rights of human persons, there can be no consent of the governed. No democracy.

And we need to see that our public officials are complicit in this generations-old usurpation by men of property and their corporations.

If we define our problem as men of property using the Constitution, and therefore public officials, the courts, police and armed forces, to deny us our fundamental rights, then the solution is clear. We the People must defy the illegitimate authority of corporations to govern. We must contest and replace public officials who enable corporations to compel our obedience.

Where can we look for help? Well, the courts have played a major role in denying human rights, worker rights, self-governing rights, and in bestowing power and authority on property and wielders of property. Our state and national legislators have also been denying or giving away the people's authority since 1787. A powerful corporate culture and a rule of law have been miseducating people, misdirecting the nation's labor and wealth, colonizing people abroad and destroying the Earth's natural systems.

So our collective task is to create a lively ferment throughout our culture characterized by defiance to unjust laws. Our task is to educate and organize ourselves to such an extent that people can force legislators and judges, mayors and presidents, to change the law of the land. The way to do this is not by legitimating regulatory law by pretending it can solve our problems; not by asking more corporate leaders to please cause a little less harm; not by tinkering around the margins of corporate behaviors.

We need to launch escalating challenges to illegitimate corporate authority and to the public officials complicit in corporate usurpations.

As Guild lawyers, you represent individuals, unions and other organizations in disputes with corporations and with governments. You can help your institutional and individual clients contest corporate claims to rights; and challenge public officials' complicit in the corporate-plus-government denial of your clients' rights.

You can work with many different people and organizations to nurture a political movement to strip property of its power to deny fundamental human rights, and to elect public servants trained by this movement to understand that in a democracy, the people—not property organized in the corporate form—must govern. ∎

## NOTES

[1] See "Corporations for the Seventh Generation," "Wrong Turn in Ohio," "The Corporate Crunch in Vermont," and "A Quick Look at What Happened in New Mexico" for more information on corporation codes.

# A GOAL, A FRAMEWORK, A MYTH

*by Peter Kellman*

GROSSMAN AND ADAMS wrote a booklet a few years ago and they said, "It's the corporations, stupid!"[1] Which all makes a lot of sense. But what to do? As we have begun to apply this new knowledge we have gotten some answers... and more questions.

Our initial response to the question "What to do?" was "Let's launch a movement to revoke charters and knock off the worst 1000 corporations." But, as we thought about charter revocation we came to the conclusion that there was more to the problem of corporate harms than meets the eye. We discovered that what is most wrong with corporations is not what they do wrong, but what they *do*.

If what corporations do is poison and kill, then knocking off 1000 or even one big bad one might help solve the problem. But, we discovered what is really wrong with corporations is that they control, define and direct our lives and culture. These institutions consolidate wealth and power in the hands of the few. The rub is, they not only consolidate power in the hands of a few, these institutions also make it possible for the few to exercise that power. And that is the basis of our next question. Can we have a democracy when a few people have so much power?

So what we learned in the process was that *we need to define corporations* and not let them define us. This of course led us to look at

U.S. history a little differently. We came to the conclusion that the Populist movement was the last American movement that challenged the very essence of corporate rule, and that the Progressives took a leap backwards when they gave up on defining corporations and went with trying to regulate them.

The problem for us is we were brought up in a struggle primarily confined to the regulatory process. We don't know about defining corporate institutions. We only know about trying to make them act responsibly by punishing them a little when they commit obvious harms, punishing them through a regulatory process that they define and control.

So our task is to come to grips with how to start a movement that has lain dormant in our culture for 100 years. No wonder some of us feel a little lost.

## GOAL

Let's begin our discussion with the assumption that our final goal is to replace corporate, anti-democratic institutions that consolidate wealth and power in the hands of a few with democratic institutions that disperse power and wealth in the hands of the many. If we can agree on that, what is the first major task that will put us on the road to this new world?

The first step in solving a problem is realizing you have one. Today there is much debate over the problems that a pro-corporate

---

world ideology is creating for the majority of people. The stock market goes up as unemployment goes up, and down as unemployment goes down. The rich are getting richer as every one else gets poorer. Some of the impacts, especially economic, on average people are discussed, but the fundamental role of the corporation is not questioned. So our first goal is *to create, in the body politic, a discussion which questions the authority and legitimacy of corporations to rule our society...* just as the American Revolutionaries of old questioned not just the authority of a particular king to rule, they also challenged the concept of monarchy. And so they not only trashed a king, they also threw out the concepts that underpinned the authority and legitimacy of monarchy.

If we can agree on this first objective—*to create a debate*—then we can develop a strategy and the tactics to achieve it.

## FRAMEWORK AND MYTH

In order to sustain a debate we need a framework of ideas to fall back on, and a myth to sustain us.[2] The framework we have been using seems to me in pretty good shape.

Basically it encompasses *Taking Care of Business* and a few new concepts not included, like the need to define corporations. But our work in the short term needs to include fleshing out the framework to include every field of endeavor, from semantics to anthropology. Toward this end, a data base of original source material and current writings needs to be developed and made available.

Finally, as we launch our debate and finish up the framework, we need consciously to use these activities to create our own myth. A myth that can sustain and give direction to the struggles of people to create societies where all the institutions are founded on democratic principles, where power is shared and competition is replaced with cooperation. We need to consciously create the myth of the democratic culture and begin to weave it into the debate and, finally, into our own vision. A vision that challenges Milton Friedman, Steve Forbes, Ross Perot, Horatio Alger, Ayn Rand and John Wayne. A vision that cuts the lifeline to the idea that property is endowed with human rights. ■

## NOTES

[1] Grossman and Adams 1993. See "Taking Care of Business: Citizenship and the Charter of Incorporation" in this volume.

[2] My concept of "myth" is taken from *Ishmael: A Novel*, (Quinn 1992). Myths are stories, passed from generation to generation, that attempt to explain basic truths and values. Ishmael is a gorilla who teaches a man that we can use our myths to both explain the past and *to create our vision of the future.*

# APPENDICES

# BIOGRAPHIES OF POCLAD PRINCIPALS

## BILL BACHLE
## LONDON, UK

Communications strategist for non-profit groups. Consultant to the Secretary General's Office at the United Nations on global communications campaigns, and for UNICEF, UNIFEM, UNDP and the Office of the Special Representative for War-Affected Children. Formerly, Peace Corps volunteer in El Salvador; writer for Robert Kennedy and George McGovern; fundraiser for the Committee for Nuclear Disarmament, UK.

## GREG COLERIDGE
## AKRON, OHIO

Director of the Economic Justice & Empowerment Program of the Northeast Ohio American Friends Service Committee (AFSC). A founder of the Ohio Committee on Corporations, Law and Democracy; co-author of *Citizens over Corporations: A Brief History of Corporations and Democracy in Ohio*. Member of the National Governing Board, Common Cause. Greg's work includes grassroots leadership development; educating and organizing on budget priorities, economic conversion, the arms race, housing, local currencies and campaign finance reform.

## KAREN COULTER
## FOSSIL, OREGON

Co-director of the Blue Mountains Biodiversity Project in eastern Oregon. Karen has been a grass-roots activist on environmental, anti-nuclear and social justice issues since 1980 and part of the Earth First! movement since 1984. She worked for the AFSC against the MX missile and for Greenpeace International as Acid Rain Campaigner and international lobbyist on ozone depletion. Helped create the Alliance for Sustainable Jobs and the Environment. Graduate of Reed College.

## MIKE FERNER
## TOLEDO, OHIO

Served two terms as an independent member of Toledo City Council, 1989-93; independent candidate for mayor in 1993. Formerly, union organizer for the American Federation of State, County and Municipal Employees (AFSCME); communications director for the Farm Labor Organizing Committee (FLOC) AFL-CIO. Co-founder of the Toledo Coalition for Safe Energy. US Navy Hospital Corps 1969-73. Member, Veterans for Peace, Labor Party, ACLU .

## RICHARD GROSSMAN
## MILTON MILLS, NEW HAMPSHIRE

POCLAD co-founder and co-director. Formerly, Peace Corps volunteer in the Philippines; director of Environmentalists For Full Employment; organizer of the Labor Committee For Safe Energy & Full Employment; · co-founder of the Highlander Center's STP (Stop the Poisoning) Schools. Author of books and articles on labor, environment, job blackmail, energy and economics.

## DAVE HENSON
## OCCIDENTAL, CALIFORNIA

Director of the Occidental Arts and Ecology Center (OAEC). OAEC, an 80-acre organic farm, ecology education center and intentional community in Northern California, works for local democracy through programs in ecological literacy, food crop and wild land biodiversity, food systems, watershed ecology and land reform. Formerly, Dave trained community-based environmental, social justice and farm groups in non-violent direct action and strategic campaign planning.

## PETER KELLMAN
## NORTH BERWICK, MAINE

Author of articles on labor, on the Dartmouth College case and the POCLAD booklet, *Building Unions: Past, Present and Future*. Edited *Pain on Their Faces*, a book of workers' reflections on the 1987-88 Paperworkers' strike in Jay, ME, and served as a strategist during that strike. Formerly, organizer with the Student Non-Violent Coordinating Committee (SNCC) in Alabama; helped start the anti-draft phase of Vietnam War resistance; president of Shoe Workers Local 82; helped lead Clamshell Alliance anti-nuclear resistance in Seabrook, NH.

## WARD MOREHOUSE
## CROTON-ON-HUDSON, NEW YORK

POCLAD co-founder and co-director; president of the Council on International and Public Affairs (CIPA); founder of the International Coalition for Justice in Bhopal, India. Human rights activist and author or editor of 20 books. Ward has taught at New York University, the University of Lund in Sweden and the Administrative Staff College of India in Hyderabad and consulted with various United Nations agencies, including UNESCO, UNIDO, UNCTAD, and the Centre on Transnational Corporations.

## JANE ANNE MORRIS
## MADISON, WISCONSIN

Corporate anthropologist. Formerly active in anti-war, women's and environmental struggles since the 1970s. Jane Anne's work on energy issues in Texas during the 1980s was the basis for her 1999 book *Not In My Backyard: The Handbook*. Has taught GED in prison, ESL to migrant workers and anthropology to undergraduates.

## JIM PRICE
## BIRMINGHAM, ALABAMA

Staff director, Sierra Club Southeast Office. Program director, Sierra Club National Environmental Justice Grassroots Organizing Program; staff liaison, Sierra Club Corporate Accountability Committee; member of the advisory committee, Center for Popular Economics, Amherst, Massachusetts. Jim holds Master of Public Administration and Master of City Planning degrees and worked for the Birmingham Regional Planning Commission and the Northwest Alabama Council of Local Governments. Served on the National Council, Alliance for Democracy.

VIRGINIA RASMUSSEN
S. YARMOUTH, MASSACHUSETTS

Co-chair of the Women's International League for Peace and Freedom (WILPF) campaign, "Challenge Corporate Power, Assert the People's Rights." Formerly, director of the Environmental Studies Program, Alfred University, and mayor of Alfred Village, NY; education director at the New Alchemy Institute on Cape Cod; director of the Cape Cod Campaign for Civil Rights. Virginia has a Ph.D. in inorganic chemistry from Syracuse University.

MARY ZEPERNICK
S. YARMOUTH, MASSACHUSETTS

Editor of POCLAD's *By What Authority* (BWA) and POCLAD office coordinator. Co-chairs WILPF's "Challenge Corporate Power" campaign; author of a biweekly opinion column for the *Cape Cod Times*. A long-time teacher and trainer, Mary conducts workshops on the democratic arts and is a past president of U.S. WILPF.

# WORKS CITED

Ad Hoc Working Group on the MAI. *The MAI: Democracy for Sale?* New York, N.Y.: The Apex Press, 1998.

Adams, Nathaniel. *Reports of Cases Argued and Determined in the Superior Court of Judicature for the State of New Hampshire, from September 1816 to February 1819.* Exeter, N.H.: J.J. Williams, 1819.

Alfange, Dean. *The Supreme Court and the National Will.* Garden City, N.Y.: Doubleday Doran, 1937.

Altman, Andrew. *Arguing About Law: An Introduction to Legal Philosophy.* 2nd ed. Belmont, Calif.: Wadsworth Publishing Company, 2001.

Amar, Akhil Reed. *The Bill of Rights: Creation and Reconstruction.* New Haven, Conn.: Yale University Press, 1998.

American Federation of Labor. "Report of the Proceedings of the Sixty-Seventh Annual Convention." 1947.

American Federation of Labor. "Report of the Proceedings of the Thirty-Ninth Annual Convention." 1919.

Andersen, Alfred F. "Where Western Civilization Went Wrong and What To Do About It." *Deep Democracy,* Spring 1998.

Anshen, Melvin. *Managing the Socially Responsible Corporation.* New York, N.Y.: Macmillan, 1974.

Arendt, Hannah. *Eichmann in Jerusalem: A Report on the Banality of Evil.* New York, N.Y.: Viking Press, 1963.

Associated Press News Service "Court Allows Keating Ruling To Stay." *Associated Press News Service,* 2 October 2000.

Barlow, Maude, and Tony Clarke. *MAI: The Multilateral Agreement on Investment and the Threat to American Freedom.* New York, N.Y.: Stoddart, 1998.

Barnet, Richard J., and John Cavanagh. *Global Dreams: Imperial Corporations and the New World Order.* New York, N.Y.: Simon & Schuster, 1994.

Batt Ph.D., William. "How Our Towns Got That Way." N.p., n.d.

Baxandall, Rosalyn Fraad, Linda Gordon, and Susan Reverby. *America's Working Women: A Documentary History, 1600 to the Present.* New York, N.Y.: Vintage Books, 1976.

Baxi, Upendra. "From Human Rights to the Right to be Human: Some Heresies." In *Rethinking Human Rights: Challenges for Theory and Action,* edited by Smitu Kothari and Harsh Sethi, 187. New York, N.Y.: New Horizons Press; Delhi, India: Lokayan, 1989.

Baxi, Upendra. "Voices of Suffering and the Future of Human Rights." *Transnational Law and Contemporary Problems* 8, no. 113 (1998).

Beard, Charles Austin. *An Economic Interpretation of the Constitution of the United States.* New York, N.Y.: Free Press; London, U.K.: Collier Macmillan, 1986.

Beard, Charles Austin. *The Republic: Conversations on Fundamentals.* New York, N.Y.: The Viking Press, 1943.

Beard, Charles Austin, and Mary Ritter Beard. *The Rise of American Civilization.* 4 vols. Vol. I. New York, N.Y.: The Macmillan Company, 1927.

Beitzinger, Alfons J. *Edward G. Ryan: Lion of the Law.* Madison, Wis.: The State Historical Society of Wisconsin, 1960.

Benson, Robert. "The Seventh Generation Act: A Model Law Allowing Law Suits for Damage to Natural Resources Needed to Sustain Future Generations." *International Law Center for Human Economic and Environmental Defense,* Summer (1997).

Berle, Adolf A., Jr. *Handwritten Research Notes of 1929-1930*: Special Collections of Columbia University Law Library.

Berle, Adolf A., Jr. "Historical Inheritance of American Corporations." In *Social Meaning of Legal Concepts*, edited by Edmond N. Cahn, 189-218. New York, N.Y.: New York University, School of Law, 1950.

Berle, Adolf A., Jr., and Gardiner C. Means. *The Modern Corporation and Private Property*. New York, N.Y.: The Macmillan Company, 1933.

Berman, Neil, "A Short History of Corporations in Massachusetts" (report). South Yarmouth, Mass.: POCLAD, 1995.

Bernstein, Marver H. *Regulating Business by Independent Commission*. Princeton, N.J.,: Princeton University Press, 1955.

Berzok, Robert M. (Director of Corporate Communications at Union Carbide Corporation). "Letter to the Editor." *The Nation*, 23 January 1995.

Bhopal Group for Information and Action, "Voices from Bhopal" (report). 1990.

Bidwai, P. "Bhopal: A Dismal Balance Sheet." *The Economic Times*, 29 November 1993.

Black, Henry Campbell, and Joseph R. Nolan. *Black's Law Dictionary: Definitions of the Terms and Phrases of American and English Jurisprudence, Ancient and Modern*. 6th ed. St. Paul, Minn.: West Publishing Company, 1990.

Blair, John M. *Economic Concentration, Structure, Behavior and Public Policy*. New York, N.Y.: Harcourt, Brace, Jovanovich, 1972.

Blau, Joseph L. *Social Theories of Jacksonian Democracy: Representative Writings of the Period 1825-1850, The American Heritage*. New York, N.Y.: Hafner Pub. Co., 1947.

Boutrous-Ghali, Boutrous. *International Bill of Human Rights*. New York, N.Y.: United Nations, 1993.

Brody, David. "A Question of Rights." *New Labor Forum*, Fall/Winter 1998.

Byrdsall, Fitzwilliam. *The History of the Loco-Focos, or Equal Rights Party*. Reprinted ed. New York, N.Y.: Burt Franklin, 1967.

Cadman, John William. *The Corporation in New Jersey: Business and Politics, 1791-1875, Studies in Economic History*. Cambridge, Mass.: Harvard University Press, 1949.

Carson, Rachel. *Silent Spring*. Boston, Mass.: Houghton Mifflin, 1962.

Center for Defense of Free Enterprise, "Getting Rich: The Environmental Movement's Income, Salary, Contributor, and Investment Patterns" (report). Bellevue, Wash.: Center for Defense of Free Enterprise, 1994.

Chomsky, Noam, and Carlos Peregrín Otero. *Language and Politics*. Montréal, Canada; Cheektowaga, N.Y.: Black Rose Books, 1988.

Chouhan, T.R., et al. *Bhopal: The Inside Story: Carbide Workers Speak Out on the World's Worst Industrial Disaster*. New York, N.Y.: The Apex Press; Mapusa, Goa: The Other India Press, 1994.

Clairmont, Frederic F. *The Rise and Fall of Economic Liberalism: The Making of the Economic Gulag*. Revised ed. Penang: Southbound Books; Mapusa, Goa: The Other India Press, 1996.

Clairmont, Frederic F. "Transnational Gulag: Reflections on Power Inc." *Economic and Political Weekly*, 1-8 March 1997, 450.

Clarke, Tony, "The Corporate Rule Treaty: A Preliminary Analysis" (report). Ottawa: Canadian Centre for Policy Alternatives, 1997.

Clarke, Tony. "Dismantling Corporate Rule." Paper presented at the International Forum on Globalization, San Francisco, Calif. 1996.

Cleveland, Grover. "Fourth Annual Message to Congress, 3 December 1888." In *Messages and Papers of the Presidents*, edited by James D. Richardson. Washington, D.C.: Government Printing Office, 1989.

Clews, Elsie W. *Education Legislation and Administration of the Colonial Governments.* New York, N.Y.: Macmillan Company, 1899.

Cohen, Morris Raphael. "The Process of Judicial Legislation." In *Law and the Social Order: Essays in Legal Philosophy*, 112-147. New York, N.Y.: Harcourt Brace and Company, 1933.

Cohen, Morris Raphael. "Property and Sovereignty." In *Law and the Social Order: Essays in Legal Philosophy*, 41-68. New York, N.Y.: Harcourt Brace and Company, 1933.

Cohn, Jules. *The Conscience of the Corporations: Business and Urban Affairs, 1967-1970, Policy studies in employment and welfare.* Baltimore, Md.: Johns Hopkins Press, 1971.

Cornwell, Dan. *Social Security: The Case for Pay-As-You-Go.* Madison, Wis.: N.p., 1997.

Dembo, David, and Ward Morehouse. *The Underbelly of the U. S. Economy: Joblessness and the Pauperization of Work in America.* New York, N.Y.: The Apex Press, 1995.

Dodd, E. Merrick. *American Business Corporations Until 1860, With Special Reference to Massachusetts.* Cambridge, Mass.: Harvard University Press, 1954.

Dorfman, Joseph. *The Economic Mind in American Civilization.* 3 vols. Vol. 3. New York, N.Y.: Viking Press, 1946.

Drucker, Peter. *The Concept of the Corporation.* Revised ed. New York, N.Y.: New American Library, 1983.

Du Bois, W. E. B. *The World and Africa: An Inquiry Into the Part Which Africa Has Played in World History.* New York, N.Y.: The Viking Press, 1947.

Earle, Thomas. *The Right of States to Alter and Annul Charters, Considered, and the Decisions of the Supreme Court of the United States Therein Examined.* Philadelphia, Pa.: Carey and Lea, 1823.

Easterbrook, Frank H., and Daniel R. Fischel. *The Economic Structure of Corporate Law.* Cambridge, Mass.: Harvard University Press, 1991.

Edwards, Richard. *Contested Terrain: The Transformation of the Workplace in the Twentieth Century.* New York, N.Y.: Basic Books, 1979.

Epstein, Robin. "Toxics Corporations: Ranking the Heavy Emitters." *The Nation*, 5 December 1994, 88-94.

Fairlie, John. "The Municipal Crisis in Ohio." *Michigan Law Review* I (1902-3): 352-363.

Fink, Leon. *In Search of the Working Class: Essays in American Labor History and Political Culture, The Working Class in American History.* Urbana, Ill.: University of Illinois Press, 1994.

Fletcher, William Meade, and Callaghan and Company. *Fletcher Cyclopedia of the Law of Private Corporations.* Permanent ed. Deerfield, Ill.: Callaghan, 1931.

Foley, Conal. "Communities, Land and the Law, Common Law vs. Corporate Law in Massachusetts." *Deep Democracy*, Spring 1998.

Forbath, William E. *Law and the Shaping of the American Labor Movement.* Cambridge, Mass.: Harvard University Press, 1991.

Fresia, Jerry. *Toward an American Revolution: Exposing the Constitution & Other Illusions.* Boston, Mass.: South End Press, 1988.

Friedman, Lawrence Meir. *A History of American Law.* New York, N.Y.: Simon and Schuster, 1973.

Friedman, Leon. "Charter of the Nuremberg Tribunal." In *The Law of War: A Documentary History*, edited by Leon Friedman. New York, N.Y.: Random House, 1972.

Geoghegan, Thomas. *Which Side Are You On?: Trying to be For Labor When it's Flat on its Back.* New York, N.Y.: Farrar Straus Giroux, 1991.

Gillette, King Camp. *World Corporation.* Boston, Mass.: The New England News Company, 1910.

Ginsberg, Eli, and Ivar E. Berg. *Democratic Values and the Rights of Management.* New York, N.Y.: Columbia University Press, 1963.

Gompers, Samuel. "The Courts and Mr. Taft on Labor." *American Federationist* 28 (1921): 220.

Goodrich, Carter. *The Government and the Economy, 1783-1861.* Indianapolis, Ind.: Bobbs-Merril Company, 1967.

Goodwyn, Lawrence. *The Populist Moment: A Short History of the Agrarian Revolt in America.* New York, N.Y.: Oxford University Press, 1978.

Graham, Howard Jay. "Procedure to Substance: Extrajudicial Rise of Due Process, 1830-1860." In *Everyman's Constitution; Historical Essays on the Fourteenth Amendment, the "Conspiracy Theory," and American Constitutionalism,* xiv, 631. Madison, Wis.: State Historical Society of Wisconsin, 1968.

Greenhouse, Steven. "A.F.L.-C.I.O Turns Energy Against Pacts on Free Trade." *New York Times,* 24 September 1997.

Greider, William. *Who Will Tell the People: The Betrayal of American Democracy.* New York, N.Y.: Simon & Schuster, 1992.

Grossman, Max. *A Tribute to Professor Morris Raphael Cohen, Teacher & Philosopher.* New York, N.Y.: City University of New York City College, 1928.

Grossman, Richard L. (letter to Jeff Kaplin), 30 November 1998.

Grossman, Richard L., (manuscript). Milton Mills, N.H.: 29 November 1998.

Grossman, Richard L., (manuscript). Milton Mills, N.H.: 11 January 1999.

Grossman, Richard L., and Frank T. Adams. *Taking Care of Business: Citizenship and the Charter of Incorporation.* N.p.: Charter, Ink, 1993.

Hamilton, Walter. *The Path of Due Process of Law.* N.p., 1937.

Hamilton, Walton. *Encyclopedia of the Social Sciences.* N.p., 1934.

Handlin, Oscar, and Mary F. Handlin. *Commonwealth: A Study of the Role of Government in the American Economy, Massachusetts, 1774-1861.* Cambridge, Mass.: Harvard University Press, 1947.

Hartz, Louis. *Economic Policy and Democratic Thought: Pennsylvania, 1776-1860.* Cambridge, Mass.: Harvard University Press, 1948.

Hawken, Paul. "A Declaration of Sustainability." *Utne Reader,* September/October 1993, 54-61.

Hawken, Paul, Amory Lovins, and L. Hunter Lovins. *Natural Capitalism: Creating the Next Industrial Revolution.* Boston, Mass.: Little, Brown and Co., 1999.

Horton, Myles, Judith Kohl, and Herbert R. Kohl. *The Long Haul: An Autobiography.* New York, N.Y.: Doubleday, 1990.

Horwitz, Morton J. *The Transformation of American Law, 1780-1860, Studies in Legal History.* Cambridge, Mass.: Harvard University Press, 1977.

Horwitz, Morton J. *The Transformation of American Law, 1870-1960: The Crisis of Legal Orthodoxy.* New York, N.Y.: Oxford University Press, 1992.

International Confederation of Free Trade Unions and International Federation of Chemical, Energy, and General Workers' Union. "The Trade Union Report on Bhopal" (report). Geneva and Brussels: International Confederation of Free Trade Unions and International Federation of Chemical, Energy, and General Workers' Union, 1985.

International Federation of Chemical, Energy, Mine and General Workers Unions. *ICEM Info* Issue 4, 1997.

International Federation of Chemical, Energy, Mine and General Workers Unions. *ICEM Info* Issue 1, 1998.

Jones, Mary. *The Autobiography of Mother Jones.* 3rd revised ed. Chicago, Ill.: Charles H. Kerr Publishing Company, 1976.

Kalish, David E. *Wisconsin State Journal,* 6 June 1995.

Kaplin, Jeff, "Whiteness as Property and the Personification of the Corporation" (manuscript). Berkeley, Calif., 1998.

Karliner, Joshua. *The Corporate Planet: Ecology and Politics in the Age of Globalization.* San Francisco, Calif.: Sierra Club Books, 1997.

Kazis, Richard, and Richard L. Grossman. *Fear at Work: Job Blackmail, Labor, and the Environment.* Second ed. Philadelphia, Pa.: New Society Publishers, 1991.

Kinoy, Arthur. *Rights on Trial: The Odyssey of a People's Lawyer.* Cambridge, Mass.: Harvard University Press, 1983.

Kolko, Gabriel. *Railroads and Regulation, 1877-1916.* Princeton, N.J.,: Princeton University Press, 1965.

Kolko, Gabriel. *The Triumph of Conservatism: A Reinterpretation of American History, 1900-1916.* New York, N.Y.: Free Press of Glencoe, 1963.

Korten, David C. *When Corporations Rule the World.* West Hartford, Conn.: Kumarian Press; San Francisco, Calif.: Barrett-Koehler Publishers, 1995.

LaDuke, Winona. "The Common Property Constitutional Amendment." In *Alternative Radio.* Boulder, Colo., 1996.

LaLonde, Robert J., and Bernard D. Meltzer. "Hard Times for Unions: Another Look at the Significance of Employer Illegalities." *University of Chicago Law Review* 58, no. 3 (1991): 953-1014.

Landis, James M., "Report to the President-Elect Regulatory Commissions" (report). 1960.

Lehner, Urban C. "Money Hungry: As Global Competition for Capital Heats Up, the Implications for World-Wide Investors and Borrowers are Enormous." *Wall Street Journal,* September 18 1997.

Lerner, Max. *Minority Rule and the Constitutional Tradition.* N.p., n.d.

Levine, Bruce C., and American Social History Project. *Who Built America?: Working People and the Nation's Economy, Politics, Culture, and Society.* New York, N.Y.: Pantheon Books, 1989.

Lindblom, Charles Edward. *Politics and Markets: The World's Political Economic Systems.* New York, N.Y.: Basic Books, 1977.

Linowes, David F. *The Corporate Conscience.* New York, N.Y.: Hawthorn Books, 1974.

Lloyd, Henry Demarest. *Wealth Against Commonwealth.* New York, N.Y.: Harper & Brothers, 1894.

Lovins, Amory. "Energy Strategy: The Road Not Taken?" *Foreign Affairs* 55, no. 1 (1976): 65-96.

Lowenstein, Roger. "The '20% Club' No Longer Is Exclusive." *Wall Street Journal,* 4 May 1995, C1.

Lucck, Thomas J. "Tax Breaks for Companies Flow Despite Budget Cuts in New York." *New York Times,* 5 July 1995, A1, A18.

Lummis, C. Douglas. *Radical Democracy.* Ithaca, N.Y.: Cornell University Press, 1996.

Lustig, R. Jeffrey. *Corporate Liberalism: The Origins of Modern American Political Theory, 1890-1920.* Berkeley, Calif.: University of California Press, 1982.

Lynd, Robert Staughton. *Knowledge For What? The Place of Social Science in American Culture.* Princeton, N.J.: Princeton University Press, 1939.

Martin, Edwin Winslow. *History of the Grange Movement, or The Farmer's War Against Monopolies.* Philadelphia, Pa.: National Publishing Company, 1873.

Martin, Hans-Peter, and Harald Schumann. *The Global Trap: Globalization and the Assault on Prosperity and Democracy.* New York, N.Y.: Zed Books, 1997.

Martin, Justin, and Lorrain Tritto. "The Fortune 500 Ranked by Sales." *Fortune,* 19 April 1993, 184.

Mayer, Carl J. "Personalizing the Impersonal: Corporations and the Bill of Rights." *The Hastings Law Journal* 41, no. 13 (1990): 577-667.

McCurdy, Charles W. "American Law and the Marketing Structure of the Large Corporation." *Journal of Economic History* 38, no. 3 (1978): 631-549.

McGovney, Dudley O. "A Supreme Court Fiction: Corporations in the Diverse Citizenship Jurisdiction of the Federal Courts." *Harvard Law Review* 56, no. 6 (1943): 853-898.

Meier, August. *Negro Thought in America, 1880-1915.* Ann Arbor, Mich.: University of Michigan Press, 1966.

Meiklejohn, Alexander. *What Does America Mean?* New York, N.Y.: W.W. Norton & Company Inc., 1935.

Meiklejohn, Alexander, Cynthia Stokes Brown, and Meiklejohn Civil Liberties Institute. *Alexander Meiklejohn: Teacher of Freedom.* Berkeley, Calif.: Meiklejohn Civil Liberties Institute, 1981.

Miller, Arthur Selwyn. *The Supreme Court and American Capitalism.* New York, N.Y.: Free Press, 1967.

Millon, David. "Redefining Corporate Law." *Indiana Law Review* 24, no. 2 (1991).

Morehouse, Ward. "And Not to Yield: The Long Struggle Against Union Carbide." *SAMAR (South Asian Magazine for Action and Reflection),* Summer/Fall 1997.

Morehouse, Ward. "The Ethics of Industrial Disasters in a Transnational World: The Elusive Quest for Justice and Accountability in Bhopal." *Alternative* 1993, 475-574.

Morehouse, Ward. "Multinational Corporations and Crimes Against Humanity." In *A World That Works: Building Blocks for a Just and Sustainable Society,* edited by Trent Schroyer. New York, N.Y.: The Bootstrap Press, 1997.

Morehouse, Ward. "Unfinished Business: Bhopal Ten Years After." *The Ecologist,* September/October 1994, 164-168.

Morehouse, Ward, and M. Arun Subramaniam. *The Bhopal Tragedy: What Really Happened and What it Means for the American Workers and Communities at Risk.* New York, N.Y.: Council on International and Public Affairs, 1986.

Morris, Jane Anne, "Is It Live or Is It Corporate?" (manuscript). Madison, Wis.: 1995.

Myrdal, Gunnar, Richard Mauritz Edvard Sterner, and Arnold Marshall Rose. *An American Dilemma: The Negro Problem and Modern Democracy.* New York, N.Y.: Harper & Brothers, 1944.

Nader, Ralph, Mark Green, and Joel Seligman. *Corporate Power in America.* New York, N.Y.: Norton, 1976.

The Nation. "Editorial." *The Nation* Dec. 1, 1997, 4.

National Institute for a New Corporate Vision. "Transforming the SOUL of Business" (conference announcement). Mansfield Center, Conn.: National Institute for a New Corporate Vision.

Nedelsky, Jennifer. *Private Property and the Limits of American Constitutionalism: The Madisonian Framework and its Legacy.* Chicago, Ill.: University of Chicago Press, 1990.

Oneal, James. *The Workers in American History.* Fourth, rev. and enl. ed. New York, N.Y.: The Rand School of Social Science, 1921.

Paine, Thomas. *Common Sense.* New York, N.Y.: Penguin Classics, 1986.

Paluszek, John L. *Will the Corporation Survive?* Reston, Va.: Reston Publishing Company, 1977.

Papanikolas, Zeese. *Buried Unsung: Louis Tikas and the Ludlow Massacre.* Salt Lake City, Utah: University of Utah Press, 1982.

People's Bicentennial Commission. *The Voices of the American Revolution,* 1975.

Pereira, Winin. *Inhuman Rights.* Mapusa, Goa: The Other India Press; Penang: Third World Network; New York, N.Y.: The Apex Press, 1997.

Pramas, Jason. "A Strategy for the Defense and Expansion of the Social Security System." *Social Policy* 29, no. 1 (1998): 8-18.

Quinn, Daniel. *Ishmael: A Novel.* New York, N.Y.: Bantam/Turner Book, 1992.

*Rachel's Environmental Health Weekly.* Nos. 455, 571, 572, 573, 575. These issues are available from www.rachel.org.

Randall, Willard Sterne. *George Washington: A Life.* New York, N.Y.: Henry Holt, 1997.

Read, Conyers, and American Historical Association. *The Constitution Reconsidered.* New York, N.Y.: Columbia University Press, 1938.

Richman, Barry. "New Paths to Corporate Social Responsibility." In *Managing Corporate Social Responsibility,* edited by Archie B. Carroll. Boston, Mass.: Little, Brown and Company, 1977.

Roche, John P. "Entrepreneurial Liberty and the Commerce Power: Expansion, Contraction and Casuistry in the Age of Enterprise." *The Constitution in the Industrial Age,* n.d.

Rosemont, Henry Jr. "Reflections on Human Rights Conflicts: When Individual and Social Rights Clash." *Resist* 7, no. 9 (1998): 1.

Said, Edward W. *Culture and Imperialism.* First ed. New York, N.Y.: Knopf, 1993.

Scales, Ann C. "The Emergence of Feminist Jurisprudence: An Essay." *The Yale Law Journal* 95 (1986): 1373.

Singer, Joseph. "The Reliance Interest in Property." *Stanford Law Review* 40, no. 3 (1988).

Sklar, Martin J. *The Corporate Reconstruction of American Capitalism, 1890-1916: The Market, the Law, and Politics.* Cambridge, New York: Cambridge University Press, 1988.

Smith, Abbot Emerson, and Institute of Early American History and Culture. *Colonists in Bondage: White Servitude and Convict Labor in America, 1607-1776.* Baltimore, Md.: Genealogical Company, 1998.

Smith, Robert Rutherford. "Social Responsibility: A Term We Can Do Without." In *Corporate Social Policy: Selections from Business and Society Review,* edited by Robert L. Heilbroner and Paul A. London. Reading, Mass.: Addison-Wesley Publishing Company, 1975.

Snyder, Gary. *The Practice of the Wild.* San Francisco, Calif.: North Point Press, 1990.

Social Investment Forum. "News, Views and Commentary." *Social Investment Forum Newsletter,* Winter 1995.

Soley, Lawrence C. *Leasing the Ivory Tower: The Corporate Takeover of Academia.* Boston, Mass.: South End Press, 1995.

Starhawk. *Dreaming the Dark: Magic, Sex, & Politics.* Boston, Mass.: Beacon Press, 1982.

Stauber, John C., and Sheldon Rampton. *Toxic Sludge is Good for You: Lies, Damn Lies, and the Public Relations Industry*. Monroe, Maine: Common Courage Press, 1995.

Steffens, Lincoln. "Ohio: A Tale of Two Cities." *McClure's* 1905, 293-311.

Steingraber, Sandra. *Living Downstream: An Ecologist Looks at Cancer and the Environment*. Reading, Mass.: Addison-Wesley Publishing, 1997.

Stone, Christopher D. *Where the Law Ends: The Social Control of Corporate Behavior*. New York, N.Y.: Harper & Row, 1975.

Stone, Geoffrey R., Louis M. Seidman, Cass R. Sunstein, and Mark V. Tushnet. *Constitutional Law*. Third ed. Boston, Mass.: Little Brown & Co., 1996.

Sunstein, Cass R. *The Partial Constitution*. Cambridge, Mass.: Harvard University Press, 1993.

Tocqueville, Alexis de, J. P. Mayer, Max Lerner, and George Lawrence. *Democracy in America*. New York, N.Y.: Harper & Row, 1966.

Turnbull, Shann. "Ownership Transfer Corporations." In *Building Sustainable Communities: Tools and Concepts for Self-Reliant Economic Change*, edited by Ward Morehouse. New York, N.Y.: The Bootstrap Press, 1997.

United for a Fair Economy, "1998 Wage Gap Organizing Kit" (report). Boston, Mass.: UFE, 1998.

United Nations International Law Commission, "Report of the 48th Session" (report). New York, N.Y.: United Nations, 1996.

United States. Bureau of the Census. *Statistical Abstract of the United States*, 1994.

United States. Congressional Office of Technology Assessment. *Multinationals and the National Interest: Playing by Different Rules*. Washington, D.C.: Office of Technology Assessment, U.S. Congress, 1993.

United States, National Commission on Excellence in Education. *A Nation at Risk: The Imperative for Educational Reform: A Report to the Nation and the Secretary of Education, United States Department of Education*. Washington, D.C.: The Commission [Supt. of Docs. U.S. G.P.O. distributor], 1983.

Urofsky, Melvin I. *Louis D. Brandeis and the Progressive Tradition*. Boston, Mass.: Little, Brown & Co., 1981.

Weiler, Paul C. "Hard Times for Unions: Challenging Times for Scholars." *University of Chicago Law Review* 58, no. 3 (1991): 1015-1032.

Weiler, Paul C. "Promises to Keep: Securing Workers' Rights to Self-Organization Under the NLRA." *Harvard Law Review* 96, no. 8 (1983): 1769-1827.

Weinstein, James. *The Corporate Ideal in the Liberal State, 1900-1918*. Boston, Mass.: Beacon Press, 1968.

West, Cornel. "The Role of the Progressive Politics." In *The Politics of Law: A Progressive Critique*, edited by David Kairys. New York, N.Y.: Pantheon Books, 1982.

Williams, William Appleman. *The Contours of American History*. Chicago, Ill.: Quadrangle Books, 1961.

Working Men's Republican Association of the Northern Liberties. "Circular to the Working Men of the City and County of Philadelphia." *Mechanics' Free Press*, 17 April 1830.

World Bank, "The World Bank World Development Report" (report). The World Bank, 1994.

Zadek, Simon, "Trading Ethics: Auditing the Market" (report). Boston, Mass.: Conference of the Association of Evolutionary Economics, 1994.

Zinn, Howard. *Failure to Quit: Reflections of an Optimistic Historian*. Monroe, Maine: Common Courage Press, 1993.

# INDEX OF CASES

Nearly all of the Supreme Court opinions (those with a "U.S." in their citation) can be located on the Internet through such sites as FindLaw (http://supreme.lp.findlaw.com/) or from the web site for the U.S. Supreme Court (www.supremecourtus.gov). Or visit your local law library if there is one in your town.

# INDEX OF SUBJECTS

# OTHER COMMENTS ON POCLAD AND DEFYING CORPORATIONS, DEFINING DEMOCRACY

"We know that when we walk into a migrant labor camp, the law says we have no First Amendment right to talk with farm workers. But we do it anyway. FLOC has beaten stacked-deck labor laws with organizing based on human rights and people power. So we know how important it is that POCLAD is helping organizers get off the defensive to challenge employer privilege and Supreme Court decisions that shackle workers' rights."

Baldemar Velasquez
President of the Farm Labor Organizer Committee (FLOC), AFL-CIO

"As a People's lawyer for over half a century, I am excited to see POCLAD helping activists transform defensive battles into struggles for human rights and self-governance. Don't just read this book. <u>Use it</u> to get corporations out of our Constitution."

Arthur Kinoy
Professor Emeritus, Rutgers University School of Law; Co-president of the Center for Constitutional Rights; author of *Rights on Trial: The Odyssey of a People's Lawyer*

"Because there is a growing recognition among Americans that corporate power is an assault on democracy, this volume of thoughtful essays arrives at just the right time. An ideal handbook on the pernicious role of corporations, it could have a crucial effect in securing power to the people, where power belongs."

Howard Zinn
Professor Emeritus of Political Science, Boston University;
author of *A People's History of the United States* and many other books.

"I, like most of the recent generation of anti-corporate activists, owe POCLAD a huge debt. The impact of POCLAD's work on the latest wave of popular mobilization is difficult to overstate. Their work has influenced thousands of key organizers and leaders and helped build a strong foundation for more systemic anti-corporate and social justice campaigns. POCLAD has inspired us to break out of the shackles that the powerful have historically used to cripple struggles for justice, democracy and ecological sanity. POCLAD has given so many of us the vision, the hope, and some of the tools that we will need.

Patrick Reinsborough
Rainforest Action Network (RAN)

"The work of POCLAD, both theoretical and action-oriented, has been essential to this evolving new direction in WILPF's work. Our national campaign, *Challenge Corporate Power, Assert the People's Rights*, has drawn extensively from POCLAD's research, information and comprehensive analysis of democracy and corporations."
>	Charmaine Sprengelmeyer
>	Women's International League for Peace and Freedom (WILPF)

"Over the past five years, POCLAD has played a crucial role in our development as an organization. Our work with people resisting factory farm corporations in Pennsylvania—which has evolved from regulatory ordinances to local laws establishing community control over food production in South-Central Pennsylvania—has been heavily influenced by POCLAD. Indeed, we believe that POCLAD's assistance has been one of the primary reasons for this work's success."
>	Thomas Linzey
>	President, Community Environmental Legal Defense Fund (CELDF)

"POCLAD has broadened and deepened our work on behalf of self-governance and in its challenge to our corporate culture."
>	Michael McConnell
>	Regional Director, American Friends Service Committee (AFSC)

"POCLAD has helped us adapt concepts like 'corporate personhood' to our summer 2001 production, *1600 Transylvania Avenue*."
>	Ed Holmes
>	San Francisco Mime Troupe

"The delicate balance of interdependencies in our world is severely threatened by the constant intrusions of corporate power, even as we falsely assume that balance is protected by the rule of law. This book is a compelling call to us as citizens to take back the power to shape and protect the ways in which we live together on this planet."
>	Elise Boulding
>	Professor Emerita of Sociology, Dartmouth College

"POCLAD would have us redefine and affirm our rights and identities as sovereign citizens. We cede the very fiber of our Constitution if we fail to take up this challenge."
>	Representative Dennis Kucinich
>	Ohio Congressman

"This collection of POCLAD research and analysis on corporate law, history, and activist strategy is a work of historic importance. It is impossible to read without concluding that the publicly-traded, limited-liability corporation is the mortal enemy of democracy, economic justice and environmental sustainability. An essential resource for all who believe in democracy."
>	David Korten
>	Author of *When Corporations Rule the World*